The Budget and Economic Outlook:
Fiscal Years 2004-2013

January 2003

The Congress of the United States ■ Congressional Budget Office

Notes

Unless otherwise indicated, the years referred to in this report are federal fiscal years, which run from October 1 to September 30.

Numbers in the text and tables may not add up to totals because of rounding.

Some of the figures in Chapter 2 use shaded vertical bars to indicate periods of recession. The bars extend from the peak to the trough of each recession. The end of the most recent recession has not yet been determined by the National Bureau of Economic Research, the organization charged with that duty. CBO has assumed that the recession concluded at the end of calendar year 2001.

Data for real gross domestic product are based on chained 1996 dollars.

Preface

This volume is one of a series of reports on the state of the budget and the economy that the Congressional Budget Office (CBO) issues each year. It satisfies the requirement of section 202(e) of the Congressional Budget Act of 1974 for CBO to submit to the Committees on the Budget periodic reports about fiscal policy and to provide baseline projections of the federal budget. In accordance with CBO's mandate to provide impartial analysis, the report makes no recommendations.

The baseline spending projections were prepared by the staff of CBO's Budget Analysis Division under the supervision of Robert Sunshine, Peter Fontaine, Janet Airis, Thomas Bradley, Kim Cawley, Paul Cullinan, Jeffrey Holland, and Jo Ann Vines. The revenue estimates were prepared by the staff of the Tax Analysis Division under the supervision of Thomas Woodward, Mark Booth, and David Weiner.

The economic outlook presented in Chapter 2 was prepared by the Macroeconomic Analysis Division under the direction of Robert Dennis. John F. Peterson, Robert Arnold, and Brian Mathis carried out the economic forecast and projections. David Brauer, Ufuk Demiroglu, Tracy Foertsch, Douglas Hamilton, Juann Hung, Kim Kowalewski, Mark Lasky, Angelo Mascaro, Shinichi Nishiyama, Benjamin Page, Frank Russek, Robert Shackleton, John Sturrock, and Christopher Williams contributed to the analysis. Tumi Coker, John McMurray, and Brian Mathis provided research assistance.

CBO's Panel of Economic Advisers commented on an early version of the economic forecast underlying this report. Members of the panel are Andrew B. Abel, Michael J. Boskin, Barry P. Bosworth, Robert G. Dederick, William C. Dudley, Martin Feldstein, Robert J. Gordon, Robert E. Hall, N. Gregory Mankiw, Allan Meltzer, William Niskanen, William D. Nordhaus, June E. O'Neill, Rudolph G. Penner, James Poterba, Michael Prell, Robert Reischauer, Alice Rivlin, Joel Slemrod, and Martin B. Zimmerman. Kurt Karl attended the panel's meeting as a guest. Although CBO's outside advisers provided considerable assistance, they are not responsible for the contents of this report.

Jeffrey Holland wrote the summary. Sandy Davis and Felix LoStracco wrote Chapter 1, with assistance from Mark Booth and Jo Ann Vines. David Brauer was the lead author for Chapter 2. Mark Booth and Thomas Woodward wrote Chapter 3. Ellen Hays and Barry Blom wrote Chapter 4. Robert Dennis and Frank Russek wrote Chapter 5, with assistance from Ufuk Demiroglu. Sandy Davis and Felix LoStracco wrote Appendix A. Adaeze Enekwechi wrote Appendixes B, C, and F. Barry Blom wrote Appendix D. Jennifer Smith produced the glossary.

Until he left the agency in early January, former CBO Director Dan L. Crippen directed the analytical work that supports this report.

Christine Bogusz, Leah Mazade, John Skeen, and Christian Spoor edited the report. Marion Curry, Linda Lewis Harris, and Denise Williams assisted in its preparation. Kathryn Winstead prepared the report for publication, with assistance from Sharon Corbin-Jallow, and Annette Kalicki, with help from Martina Wojak-Piotrow, produced the electronic versions for CBO's Web site (www.cbo.gov).

Barry B. Anderson
Acting Director

January 2003

CONTENTS

Summary *xv*

1 The Budget Outlook *1*

Uncertainty and the Projection Horizon *3*

The Return of the Deficit in 2002 *6*

The Concept Behind CBO's Baseline *7*

Changes in CBO's Projections Since August 2002 *7*

The Outlook for Federal Debt *16*

Trust Funds and the Budget *20*

The Expiration of Budget Enforcement Procedures *21*

2 The Economic Outlook *23*

Recent Economic Developments *28*

CBO's Economic Forecast for 2003 and 2004 *40*

The Economic Outlook Beyond 2004 *42*

3 The Revenue Outlook *49*

Recent Revisions to CBO's Revenue Projections *50*

Revenues by Source *53*

The Growing Significance of the AMT in CBO's Projections *68*

The Effects of Expiring Tax Provisions *70*

4 The Spending Outlook *75*

Discretionary Spending *77*

Entitlements and Other Mandatory Spending *79*

Net Interest *91*

5

The Uncertainty of Budget Projections *95*

The Accuracy of CBO's Past Budget Projections *96*

Alternative Economic and Budget Scenarios *101*

Appendix A

The Expiration of Budget Enforcement Procedures: Issues and Options *109*

Appendix B

Budget Resolution Targets and Actual Outcomes *123*

Appendix C

How Changes in Assumptions Can Affect Budget Projections *131*

Appendix D

The Federal Sector of the National Income and Product Accounts *137*

Appendix E

CBO's Economic Projections for 2003 Through 2013 *143*

Appendix F

Historical Budget Data *147*

Appendix G

Contributors to the Revenue and Spending Projections *161*

Glossary *165*

Tables

S-1.	The Budget Outlook Under CBO's Adjusted Baseline	xvi
S-2.	CBO's Economic Forecast for Calendar Years 2003 and 2004	xviii
1-1.	The Budget Outlook	2
1-2.	CBO's Budget Projections Under Its Adjusted Baseline	4
1-3.	Changes in CBO's Projections of the Surplus or Deficit Since August 2002 Under the Adjusted Baseline	12
1-4.	CBO's Projections of Federal Debt Under Its Adjusted Baseline	17
1-5.	CBO's Projections of Trust Fund Surpluses or Deficits	19
2-1.	CBO's Economic Projections for Calendar Years 2003 Through 2013	24
2-2.	CBO's Economic Forecast for 2003 and 2004	40
2-3.	Comparison of *Blue Chip*'s and CBO's Forecast for Calendar Years 2003 and 2004	42
2-4.	CBO's Current and Previous Economic Projections for Calendar Years 2003 Through 2012	43
2-5.	Key Assumptions in CBO's Projection of Potential GDP	45
3-1.	Changes in CBO's Projections of Revenues Since August 2002	51
3-2.	CBO's Projections of Revenues	54
3-3.	CBO's Projections of Individual Income Tax Receipts and the NIPA Tax Base	56
3-4.	Why Did Individual Income Tax Liability Grow Faster Than GDP From 1994 Through 2000?	57
3-5.	Actual and Projected Capital Gains Realizations and Taxes	60

3-6.	CBO's Projections of Social Insurance Tax Receipts and the Social Insurance Tax Base	63
3-7.	CBO's Projections of Social Insurance Tax Receipts, by Source	64
3-8.	CBO's Projections of Corporate Income Tax Receipts and Tax Bases	65
3-9.	CBO's Projections of Excise Tax Receipts, by Source	66
3-10.	CBO's Projections of Other Sources of Revenue	68
3-11.	Effect of Extending Tax Provisions That Will Expire Before 2013	72
4-1.	CBO's Projections of Outlays Under Its Adjusted Baseline	78
4-2.	Average Annual Rate of Growth in Outlays Under CBO's Adjusted Baseline	80
4-3.	Defense and Nondefense Discretionary Outlays	81
4-4.	CBO's Projections of Discretionary Spending Under Alternative Paths	82
4-5.	CBO's Baseline Projections of Mandatory Spending	84
4-6.	Sources of Growth in Mandatory Outlays	88
4-7.	CBO's Baseline Projections of Offsetting Receipts	90
4-8.	Costs for Mandatory Programs That CBO's Baseline Assumes Will Continue Beyond Their Current Expiration Dates	92
4-9.	CBO's Projections of Federal Interest Outlays Under Its Adjusted Baseline	94
5-1.	Average Difference Between CBO's Budget Projections and Actual Outcomes Since 1981, Adjusted for Subsequent Legislation	99
5-2.	Alternative Scenarios for the Economy and the Budget in the Short Term	103

5-3.	Potential Economic and Budgetary Effects of War in Iraq	104
5-4.	Alternative 10-Year Scenarios for the Economy and the Budget	106
A-1.	The Deficit Compared with the Gramm-Rudman-Hollings Targets	111
A-2.	Discretionary Spending Under the Budget Enforcement Act	115
A-3.	Balances Eliminated by Statute from the Pay-As-You-Go-Scorecard	117
B-1.	Comparison of Budget Resolution Targets and Actual Budget Totals for 2002	125
B-2.	Differences Between Budget Resolution Targets and Actual Budget Totals for 2002	126
B-3.	Differences Between Budget Resolution Targets and Actual Budget Totals, 1980-2002	128
C-1.	Estimated Effects of Selected Economic Changes on CBO's Budget Projections	132
C-2.	Estimated Effects on CBO's Baseline of Increasing Discretionary Budget Authority by $10 Billion in 2003	133
C-3.	Estimated Savings in Net Interest from Borrowing $10 Billion Less	134
D-1.	Relationship of the Budget to the Federal Sector of the National Income and Product Accounts	138
D-2.	Projections of Baseline Receipts and Expenditures as Measured by the National Income and Product Accounts	141
E-1.	CBO's Year-by-Year Forecast and Projections for Calendar Years 2003 Through 2013	144
E-2.	CBO's Year-by-Year Forecast and Projections for Fiscal Years 2003 Through 2013	145

F-1.	Revenues, Outlays, Surpluses, Deficits, and Debt Held by the Public, 1962-2002 (In billions of dollars)	148
F-2.	Revenues, Outlays, Surpluses, Deficits, and Debt Held by the Public, 1962-2002 (As a percentage of GDP)	149
F-3.	Revenues by Major Source, 1962-2002 (In billions of dollars)	150
F-4.	Revenues by Major Source, 1962-2002 (As a percentage of GDP)	151
F-5.	Outlays by Major Spending Category, 1962-2002 (In billions of dollars)	152
F-6.	Outlays by Major Spending Category, 1962-2002 (As a percentage of GDP)	153
F-7.	Discretionary Outlays, 1962-2002 (In billions of dollars)	154
F-8.	Discretionary Outlays, 1962-2002 (As a percentage of GDP)	155
F-9.	Outlays for Entitlements and Other Mandatory Spending, 1962-2002 (In billions of dollars)	156
F-10.	Outlays for Entitlements and Other Mandatory Spending, 1962-2002 (As a percentage of GDP)	157
F-11.	Surpluses, Deficits, Debt, and Related Series, 1960-2002	158
F-12.	Standardized-Budget Surplus or Deficit and Related Series, 1960-2002 (In billions of dollars)	159
F-13.	Standardized-Budget Surplus or Deficit and Related Series, 1960-2002 (As a percentage of potential GDP)	160

Figures

S-1.	Total Revenues and Outlays as a Share of GDP, 1962-2013	xvii
S-2.	Uncertainty of CBO's Projections of the Total Budget Surplus Under Current Policies	xix
1-1.	Total Deficits and Surpluses as a Share of GDP, 1967-2013	6
1-2.	Total Debt Subject to Limit, August 2000 Through August 2004	18

CONTENTS

1-3.	Surpluses or Deficits (Excluding Interest) of the Social Security and Medicare Hospital Insurance Trust Funds	21
2-1.	The Economic Forecast and Projections	25
2-2.	The Federal Funds Interest Rate	28
2-3.	An Index of Monetary and Financial Conditions	29
2-4.	Interest Rate Spreads on Corporate Bonds	29
2-5.	Employment in the Private Nonfarm Sector	30
2-6.	Civilian Unemployment Rate	31
2-7.	Growth in Disposable Income	31
2-8.	Household Net Wealth	32
2-9.	Mortgage Delinquency Rates	34
2-10.	Delinquency Rates on Consumer Loans at Banks	34
2-11.	Sales of New Homes	35
2-12.	Mortgage Interest Rates for Existing Homes	35
2-13.	Sales of Cars and Light Trucks	36
2-14.	The Rate of Capacity Utilization in Manufacturing	36
2-15.	Business Investment in Inventory	37
2-16.	The Current-Account Balance	38
2-17.	The Fiscal Positions of State and Local Governments	39
2-18.	Inflation in the Consumer Price Index	40
2-19.	Actual and Potential Total Factor Productivity	46
2-20.	Corporate Profits	47
2-21.	Wages and Salaries	47
3-1.	Total Revenues as a Share of GDP, 1946-2013	49

3-2.	Annual Growth of Federal Revenues and GDP, 1961-2013	50
3-3.	Revenues, by Source, as a Share of GDP, 1960-2013	53
3-4.	Effective Tax Rate on Individual Income, Tax Years 1994-2000	61
3-5.	Capital Gains Realizations as a Share of GDP, Calendar Years 1990-2013	62
3-6.	Projected Effects of the Individual Alternative Minimum Tax	69
4-1.	Major Components of Spending, 1962-2002	77
5-1.	Uncertainty of CBO's Projections of the Total Budget Surplus Under Current Policies	96
5-2.	Misestimates in CBO's Projections Made from 1981 to 1997	97
A-1.	Actual Discretionary Outlays Compared with the Spending Limits as Originally Enacted	110
A-2.	Emergency Budget Authority Under the Budget Enforcement Act	116

Boxes

1-1.	CBO's Adjusted Baseline	3
1-2.	The Expiration of Revenue Provisions	8
1-3.	An Estimate of the Costs of a Potential Conflict with Iraq	10
1-4.	The Budgetary Effects of Freezing Total Discretionary Appropriations at $751 Billion	11
2-1.	The Economic Effects of Expiring Tax Cuts	26
2-2.	The Wealth Effect and Personal Saving	33
3-1.	Tax Bases and Tax Liability	58
4-1.	Categories of Federal Spending	76
5-1.	How CBO Analyzed Its Past Misestimates	98
5-2.	The Costs and Risks of Deflation	102
5-3.	Potential Effect of an Unfavorable Trend in Workers' Level of Education	107
A-1.	Expiring Voting Requirements for a Three-Fifths Majority to Waive Budget Points of Order in the Senate	113
A-2.	Is It Time for a New Budget Concepts Commission?	121

Summary

Each January, the Congressional Budget Office (CBO) issues its outlook for the budget and the economy to help the Congress prepare for the upcoming legislative year. The baseline budget projections that CBO provides are based on the assumption that current laws and policies remain unchanged as well as on various estimates and assumptions about how the economy will behave and government programs will operate. Such projections are always uncertain, but this year, the uncertainty seems to be magnified. As a result, estimates of budgetary outcomes should be interpreted cautiously.

Uncertainty in the Outlook

The uncertainty that surrounds the baseline can be broken down into three main types: economic, geopolitical, and legislative. Many of the possible outcomes encompassed by that uncertainty are more likely to worsen than to improve the budget outlook.

Economic Uncertainty

The economy continues to rebound from the recession of 2001. The future course of the recovery depends in large part on whether consumers will continue to provide the foundation for the economy's growth. Despite the three-year decline in the stock market, the household sector has been a source of strength throughout the recession and into the recovery. The growth of consumer spending is uncertain in the near term, however, because demand is weak in many other sectors of the economy. Spending by the business sector has not yet recovered, as weak corporate profits and excess capacity from overinvestment during the "bubble" years of the late 1990s have inhibited investment. Moreover, uncertainty about the strength of demand, and about the risks arising from terrorism and war, have led businesses to be particularly cautious in hiring. In addition, deteriorating state and local government finances have curtailed spending and may prompt some tax increases.

Nevertheless, some indications point to a brighter outlook for the economy as the year goes forward. Investors and consumers appear to have gained confidence in recent months, and the stock market has moved tentatively upward since its low in October. Spending by businesses on equipment and software, particularly on information technology, strengthened last year, and inventories may be reaching the point at which firms need to restock their shelves. Finally, the drop in the exchange value of the U.S. dollar sets the stage for stronger growth of exports.

Over the longer haul, the question of labor productivity looms large. From 1951 through 1973, the growth of gross domestic product (GDP) per worker—after adjusting for the business cycle—averaged about 2.2 percent a year. However, from 1974 through 1995, the growth of productivity slowed substantially, to a rate that was little more than half as fast. More recently, though, productivity growth picked up again, to about the same rate experienced during the high-growth period.

CBO's economic projections incorporate the assumption that the growth of GDP per worker will average 2 percent per year from 2003 through 2013. Productivity growth could turn out to be lower than that, however, as it was for nearly a quarter-century before the acceleration in the mid-1990s. Lower growth of productivity would reduce economic growth and worsen the budget's bottom line. Alternatively, productivity could rise more quickly than CBO has anticipated, mirroring the period of faster growth in the late 1990s. That outcome would reduce projected deficits or increase projected surpluses.

Summary Table 1.
The Budget Outlook Under CBO's Adjusted Baseline
(In billions of dollars)

	Actual 2002	2003	2004	2005	2006	2007	2008	2009	2010	2011	2012	2013	Total, 2004-2008	Total, 2004-2013
On-Budget	-317	-361	-319	-268	-228	-205	-185	-165	-145	-26	134	177	-1,206	-1,231
Off-Budget[a]	160	162	174	195	212	231	250	268	286	303	317	330	1,063	2,568
Total Surplus or Deficit (-)	**-158**	**-199**	**-145**	**-73**	**-16**	**26**	**65**	**103**	**140**	**277**	**451**	**508**	**-143**	**1,336**
Total Surplus or Deficit (-) as a Percentage of GDP	-1.5	-1.9	-1.3	-0.6	-0.1	0.2	0.5	0.7	0.9	1.7	2.7	2.8	-0.2[b]	0.9[b]
Debt Held by the Public at the End of the Year	3,540	3,766	3,927	4,013	4,045	4,034	3,983	3,894	3,766	3,501	3,062	2,565	n.a.	n.a.
Debt Held by the Public at the End of the Year as a Percentage of GDP	34.3	35.0	34.7	33.6	32.2	30.4	28.5	26.5	24.3	21.5	18.0	14.4	n.a.	n.a.

Source: Congressional Budget Office.

Notes: These projections incorporate the assumption that discretionary budget authority totals $751 billion for 2003 and grows with inflation thereafter.

n.a. = not applicable.

a. Off-budget surpluses comprise surpluses in the Social Security trust funds as well as the net cash flow of the Postal Service.
b. As a percentage of cumulative GDP over the period.

Geopolitical Uncertainty

Instability in the international arena could certainly have implications for the U.S. economy and the budget. War with Iraq, for example, would require increased defense spending for supplies and other near-term needs as well as for the future replenishment of resources used in combat. Substantial resources might also be needed for reconstruction, occupation, and assistance to allies. In addition, such a war could have implications for oil prices (positive ones if the war went quickly and smoothly; negative ones if it took longer than expected and production was disrupted), which would ripple through the economy.

The ongoing threat of terrorism is also likely to have budgetary implications. Shortly after the terrorist attacks of September 11, 2001, the Congress and the President enacted $40 billion in supplemental appropriations; another $25 billion was approved last summer. Concerns about homeland security and the implementation of measures to prevent future attacks will maintain the pressure to increase federal spending. And any additional terrorist attacks could threaten the economy's recovery.

Legislative Uncertainty

CBO's baseline projections are intended to serve as a neutral benchmark against which to measure the effects of possible changes in tax and spending policies—they are not a forecast or prediction of future budgetary outcomes. The projections are constructed according to both rules set forth in law and long-standing practices and are designed to project federal revenues and spending under the assumption that current laws and policies remain unchanged. Thus, legislation enacted by the Congress and the President is likely to alter the bottom line in the baseline.

Pressures to increase spending and reduce taxes could lead to a substantially worsened budgetary picture. For example, final appropriations for fiscal year 2003 could exceed the $751 billion that apparently has been agreed upon by the Republican leadership and the President, especially if supplemental appropriations were enacted later in the year. Other legislative action could also dim the outlook. Measures intended to stimulate the economy, fund military action and subsequent redevelopment in Iraq, extend expiring tax cuts, modify the alternative minimum tax, establish a prescription drug benefit for the elderly, or meet other pressing national needs could substantially increase projected deficits or reduce projected surpluses in the future.

The Budget Outlook

If current policies remained in place, the federal budget deficit would grow from $158 billion in 2002 to $199 billion in 2003, by CBO's projections (*see Summary Table 1*). In nominal dollars, such a deficit would be the largest since 1994; however, at 1.9 percent of GDP, it would be well below the share of the economy that deficits accounted for in the 1980s through the mid-1990s.

Revenues in CBO's outlook are anticipated to resume their upward path in 2003 after falling in both 2001 and 2002. (The decrease in revenues from 2001 to 2002—nearly 7 percent—was the largest annual drop, in percentage terms, since 1946.) Total revenues are projected to grow to $1.9 trillion this year—about $68 billion (or 3.7 percent) above the amount recorded in 2002 but well below the $2.0 trillion that the government collected in the peak year of 2000. Much of that projected growth can be traced to the improved economic prospects that CBO forecasts for 2003. At 17.9 percent of GDP, estimated revenues for this year are roughly at the average for the 1962-2002 period (*see Summary Figure 1*).

Outlays, by CBO's estimates, will grow to over $2.1 trillion this year, a rise of $110 billion (or 5.5 percent) from 2002. Although net interest costs are falling (because of low interest rates), spending for all of the government's other programs and activities is projected to grow by 6.7 percent. That rate of increase is well below the 11 percent growth of noninterest spending in 2002—but still greater than the 3 percent average growth during most of the 1990s.

Fueling the rise in spending are boosts in discretionary outlays and continued growth of entitlements. Both defense discretionary spending (up by $28 billion from 2002) and nondefense discretionary spending (up by $30 billion) are expected to rise by nearly 8 percent this year. Those estimates are based on the assumption that discre-

Summary Figure 1.
Total Revenues and Outlays as a Share of GDP, 1962-2013
(Percentage of GDP)

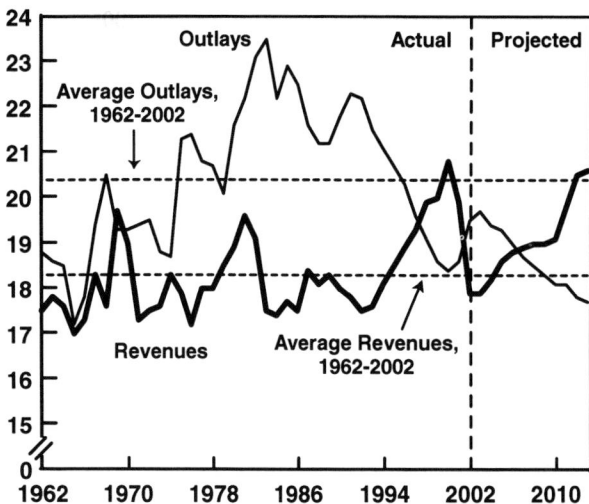

Sources: Congressional Budget Office (projections); Office of Management and Budget (historical budget data).

Note: CBO's projections incorporate the assumption that discretionary budget authority totals $751 billion for 2003 and grows with inflation thereafter.

tionary budget authority for 2003 will total $751 billion.[1] Both kinds of discretionary spending grew even faster in 2002 than the growth projected for 2003: defense outlays rose by 14 percent, and nondefense outlays, by 12.3 percent.

Spending for mandatory programs—which now consumes over half of all federal outlays—is estimated to increase in 2003 by $66 billion over its level in 2002. Social Security, Medicare, and Medicaid account for much of that jump. Total mandatory spending is projected to rise more slowly in 2003, at a rate of 6.0 per-

---

1. Programs funded by 11 of the 13 regular appropriation bills are currently governed by a continuing resolution that, for the most part, provides funding authority at the 2002 level. However, the apparent agreement by the President and the Republican leadership would put total appropriations for 2003 in those 13 bills at about $751 billion. Pending enactment of the regular appropriations, CBO has used that figure as the basis for projecting discretionary spending.

Summary Table 2.
CBO's Economic Forecast for Calendar Years 2003 and 2004

	Estimated 2002	Forecast 2003	Forecast 2004
Nominal GDP (Percentage change)	3.6	4.2	5.4
Real GDP (Percentage change)	2.4	2.5	3.6
Consumer Price Index (Percentage change)[a]	1.6	2.3	2.2
Unemployment Rate (Percent)	5.8	5.9	5.7
Three-Month Treasury Bill Rate (Percent)	1.6	1.4	3.5
Ten-Year Treasury Note Rate (Percent)	4.6	4.4	5.2

Sources: Congressional Budget Office; Department of Commerce, Bureau of Economic Analysis; Department of Labor, Bureau of Labor Statistics; Federal Reserve Board.

a. The consumer price index for all urban consumers.

---

cent, than it did in 2002—when it climbed by 9.6 percent. In particular, the rate of growth of Medicaid outlays is expected to drop from 13.2 percent in 2002 to 6.4 percent in 2003 as a result of slower growth in enrollment, smaller increases in payment rates, and restrictions on certain types of spending.

Declining interest payments will offset some of the increases in discretionary and mandatory outlays, CBO estimates. Despite a rise in debt held by the public, low interest rates in 2003 are projected to reduce net interest payments by $14 billion (or 8.1 percent).

As the 10-year budget period (2004 through 2013) progresses, revenues are estimated to grow more quickly than outlays under baseline assumptions. CBO projects that revenues will grow by an average annual rate of 6.3 percent through 2010—increasing from 17.9 percent of GDP in 2003 to 19.1 percent in 2010. That increase occurs principally because of the tendency of the tax system, as income grows, to increase the proportion of income that it collects in taxes. After 2010, that tendency is exacerbated by the scheduled expiration of the tax cuts enacted in 2001 in the Economic Growth and Tax Relief Reconciliation Act (EGTRRA).

In contrast to the rise in revenues relative to GDP, the growth of total outlays under baseline assumptions does not keep pace with the growth of the economy. Mandatory spending—led by Medicare and Medicaid—is expected to grow slightly faster than the economy (at an average annual rate of 5.4 percent, compared with projected growth in nominal GDP of 5.2 percent). But discretionary spending in CBO's projections rises only by the rate of inflation (as specified in the Balanced Budget and Emergency Deficit Control Act of 1985), or about half as fast as nominal GDP. And interest payments—with debt held by the public growing slowly in the near term and shrinking in later years—are estimated to decline from 1.5 percent of GDP in 2003 to 0.9 percent in 2013.

For the five years from 2004 through 2008, CBO projects that if current policies remained unchanged (and the economy followed the path of CBO's projections), deficits would diminish and surpluses would reappear, leaving the budget roughly balanced. Over the 2004-2008 period, the cumulative deficit would total $143 billion, or 0.2 percent of GDP, by CBO's estimates.

For the 10-year period from 2004 through 2013, the cumulative surplus is projected to total $1.3 trillion. But the last three years of the period are almost entirely responsible for that total. Projected surpluses from 2011 through 2013—the years after EGTRRA is scheduled to expire—account for nearly 93 percent of the 10-year sum. (CBO estimates that if EGTRRA is not extended, revenues will climb to more than 20.5 percent of GDP—a level previously seen only during World War II and in 2000.) Through 2010, the budget is projected to be close to balance; annual deficits and surpluses generally total 1 percent or less of GDP.

Just past the 10-year baseline period, however, loom significant long-term strains on the budget that intensify as the baby-boom generation ages. The number of people of retirement age will surge by about 80 percent over the next 30 years—increasing costs for federal benefit programs—while the number of workers whose taxes help pay for those benefits is expected to grow by only 15 percent. In addition to the demographic situation, the costs per enrollee in federal health care programs are likely to grow much faster than inflation. As a result, the amount that the government spends on its major health and retirement programs (Medicare, Medicaid, and Social Security) is projected to consume a substantial portion of what the government now spends on the entire budget.

The Economic Outlook

CBO expects that the slow economic recovery will continue, with real (inflation-adjusted) GDP growing by 2.5 percent in calendar year 2003 and 3.6 percent in 2004 (see Summary Table 2). That growth is comparable to the pace following the 1990-1991 recession. The unemployment rate is expected to stabilize in 2003 at 5.9 percent and then edge down to 5.7 percent in 2004. As the recovery achieves a firmer footing, CBO assumes that the Federal Reserve will gradually shift monetary policy from its current accommodative stance toward a more neutral one; consequently, both short- and long-term interest rates are expected to rise in late 2003 and during 2004. In CBO's current forecast, inflation in the consumer price index (CPI) remains below 2.5 percent for the next two years.

For the period from 2005 through 2013, CBO estimates that real GDP will grow at an average annual rate of 3.0 percent. CBO's projections for unemployment, interest rates, and inflation during that period are quite similar to the ones it published last August. Thus, CBO projects that the unemployment rate will decline to 5.2 percent (which equals CBO's estimate of the nonaccelerating inflation rate of unemployment); the interest rate on three-month Treasury bills will reach 4.9 percent; the 10-year note rate will average 5.8 percent; and CPI inflation will average 2.5 percent annually.

Uncertainty and Budget Projections

As discussed earlier, significant uncertainty surrounds CBO's baseline projections, some of which is intentionally not factored into the estimates. For example, CBO does not predict future legislative changes—indeed, any attempt to incorporate those actions would undermine the usefulness of the baseline as a benchmark.

Summary Figure 2.

Uncertainty of CBO's Projections of the Total Budget Surplus Under Current Policies

(In trillions of dollars)

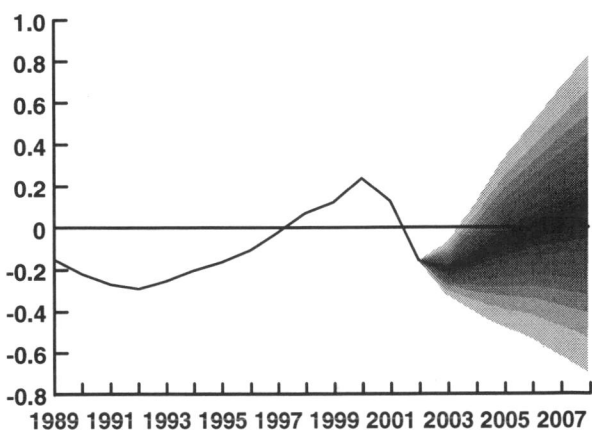

Source: Congressional Budget Office.

Note: Calculated on the basis of CBO's forecasting track record, this figure shows the estimated likelihood of alternative projections of the total budget surplus under current policies. CBO's projections described in Chapter 1 fall in the middle of the darkest area. Under the assumption that tax and spending policies do not change, the probability is 10 percent that actual deficits or surpluses will fall in the darkest area and 90 percent that they will fall within the whole shaded area.

Actual surpluses or deficits will of course be affected by legislation enacted during the next 10 years, including decisions about discretionary spending. The effects of future legislation are not included in this figure.

For an explanation of how CBO calculates the probability distribution, see *Uncertainties in Projecting Budget Surpluses: A Discussion of Data and Methods* (February 2002), available at www.cbo.gov; an update of that publication will appear shortly.

Much uncertainty also stems from the fact, however, that the U.S. economy and the federal budget are highly complex and are affected by many economic and technical factors that are difficult to foresee. CBO's baseline projections represent the midrange of possible outcomes, calculated on the basis of past and current trends and the assumption that current policies do not change. But actual budgetary outcomes will almost certainly differ from CBO's baseline projections.

In view of that sort of uncertainty, the outlook for the budget can best be described as a fan of probabilities surrounding the point estimates presented in this report (*see Summary Figure 2 on page xix*). Not surprisingly, those probabilities widen as the projection period extends. As the fan chart makes clear, outcomes quite different from those in CBO's baseline have a significant likelihood of coming to pass.

CHAPTER

1

The Budget Outlook

The Congressional Budget Office (CBO) projects that if current policies remained unchanged, federal budget deficits—which reemerged in 2002 after four consecutive years of surpluses—would peak in 2003, decline steadily thereafter, and again yield to small but growing surpluses beginning in 2007. That improving outlook, however, is bound to the assumption that no policy will change, and as such should be viewed cautiously. For example, the major provisions of the tax cut enacted in 2001 are due to expire at the end of 2010. If policymakers extended those provisions, or made them permanent, projected surpluses would decrease significantly after 2010. Also, there is likely to be strong pressure in the 108th Congress for new initiatives to increase spending and reduce taxes—and a war in Iraq would necessitate additional outlays. Those changes could boost deficits considerably in the near term and delay or even prevent a return to surpluses over the next 10 years. Beyond that horizon loom budgetary pressures linked to the aging of the baby-boom generation, which could lead to unsustainable levels of deficits and debt over the longer term.

CBO's projections under current tax and spending policies show total budget deficits of $199 billion in 2003 and $145 billion in 2004—or, as a percentage of gross domestic product (GDP), 1.9 percent and 1.3 percent, respectively (*see Table 1-1 on page 2 and Table 1-2 on page 4*).[1] Those projections have been adjusted to incorporate the assumption that budget authority for discretionary appropriations for 2003 will total about $751 billion (*see Box 1-1*). That amount is about $12 billion more than the amount available for the year under the temporary continuing resolution that was in effect when CBO prepared this report.

Under CBO's adjusted baseline, deficits would continue to shrink after 2004, and a small budget surplus of $26 billion would emerge in 2007. Over the 2004-2008 period, by CBO's estimates, the cumulative deficit would total $143 billion, or 0.2 percent of GDP. Over the following five years, surpluses would steadily mount and, for the full 10-year projection period from 2004 to 2013, accumulate to $1.3 trillion. However, over 90 percent of that amount would be recorded in the years 2011 to 2013 —that is, after the 2001 tax cuts are scheduled to expire and when the projections are the most uncertain.

Unlike total surpluses, on-budget surpluses—which exclude the off-budget transactions of Social Security and the Postal Service—would not reappear until 2012 in CBO's adjusted baseline. Although projections of off-budget transactions (which are dominated by Social Security) show net surpluses every year through 2013, the rest of the budget is projected to post deficits of $361 billion in 2003, $319 billion in 2004, and slowly declining amounts through 2011.

CBO developed its latest projections following a period of significant economic and fiscal change. As recently as January 2001, CBO was projecting record levels of surpluses for the 2002-2011 period—totaling $5.6 trillion— under its baseline assumptions. That estimate reflected years of robust economic growth and surging federal revenues—but later proved to be the high-water mark. The recession in 2001 (and a declining stock market) together

---

1. Total budget amounts include the off-budget transactions of the Social Security trust funds and the Postal Service.

Table 1-1.

The Budget Outlook

(In billions of dollars)

	Actual 2002	2003	2004	2005	2006	2007	2008	2009	2010	2011	2012	2013	Total, 2004-2008	Total, 2004-2013
Surplus or Deficit (-) Assuming $751 Billion in Discretionary Appropriations for 2003
On-Budget	-317	-361	-319	-268	-228	-205	-185	-165	-145	-26	134	177	-1,206	-1,231
Off-Budget[a]	160	162	174	195	212	231	250	268	286	303	317	330	1,063	2,568
Total Surplus or Deficit (-)	-158	-199	-145	-73	-16	26	65	103	140	277	451	508	-143	1,336
Total Surplus or Deficit (-) as a Percentage of GDP	-1.5	-1.9	-1.3	-0.6	-0.1	0.2	0.5	0.7	0.9	1.7	2.7	2.8	-0.2[b]	0.9[b]
Surplus or Deficit (-) Assuming $738 Billion in Discretionary Appropriations for 2003
On-Budget	-317	-354	-309	-255	-214	-189	-168	-146	-126	-5	157	202	-1,135	-1,053
Off-Budget[a]	160	162	174	195	212	231	250	268	286	303	317	330	1,063	2,568
Total Surplus or Deficit (-)	-158	-193	-134	-60	-2	42	82	122	160	298	474	532	-72	1,515
Total Surplus or Deficit (-) as a Percentage of GDP	-1.5	-1.8	-1.2	-0.5	*	0.3	0.6	0.8	1.0	1.8	2.8	3.0	-0.1[b]	1.0[b]
Memorandum:
Social Security Surplus	159	160	175	194	212	231	250	268	286	303	317	330	1,062	2,567
Postal Service Outlays[c]	-1	-1	**	-1	1	0	0	0	0	0	0	0	**	**

Source: Congressional Budget Office.

Notes: The 2003 appropriation acts for defense and military construction provide $365 billion in discretionary budget authority for most defense programs. Some defense discretionary programs are funded in other appropriation acts. CBO assumes that those programs are funded at $16 billion, the level provided in the current continuing resolution (Public Law 108-2).

* = between zero and 0.05 percent; ** = between -$500 million and $500 million.

a. Off-budget surpluses comprise surpluses in the Social Security trust funds as well as the net cash flow of the Postal Service.
b. As a percentage of cumulative GDP over the period.
c. Negative numbers denote that the Postal Service's income exceeds its expenses, increasing the off-budget surplus.

---

with the terrorist attacks of September 11—and lawmakers' responses to those events—caused a sharp drop in federal revenues and a spike in spending in 2002, which led to similar changes in CBO's estimates for later years. Major new policies, including the tax cuts enacted in the Economic Growth and Tax Relief Reconciliation Act of 2001 (EGTRRA), a sizable boost in regular appropriations, and other initiatives, contributed to those trends. Now, just two years later, CBO estimates that the projected cumulative surplus for the 2002-2011 period has been all but eliminated.

Despite that dramatic reversal, the budget outlook over the next decade (2004 to 2013) under the assumptions of CBO's adjusted baseline remains relatively bright, by historical standards. Before 1998, the government had recorded deficits in every year since 1969. Moreover, the shortfalls for 2002 and 2003—1.5 percent and 1.9 percent of GDP, respectively—are relatively small when compared with the chronic deficits of the 1980s and early 1990s, which ranged from 3 percent to 6 percent (*see Figure 1-1 on page 6*). Also, the amount of federal debt held by the public, which for the most part reflects government borrowing to finance past deficits, is projected

Box 1-1.
CBO's Adjusted Baseline

In general, the Congressional Budget Office's (CBO's) baseline comprises projections of future levels of spending and revenues under laws that are currently in effect (see the discussion of the baseline concept later in this chapter). Ordinarily, CBO's projections incorporate the assumption that over the 10-year budget horizon, discretionary appropriations grow with inflation from the current year's level. But full-year appropriations for the programs and activities covered by 11 of the 13 regular appropriation bills had not been enacted for 2003 at the time of this writing.

The programs and activities in those 11 bills are being funded temporarily under a continuing resolution (Public Law 108-2), which expires on January 31, 2003. (The two regular appropriation laws for defense and military construction, which fund most defense discretionary programs, were enacted separately and provide discretionary budget authority totaling about $365 billion for 2003.)[1] The current continuing resolution is the latest in a series of temporary funding laws, dating back to last fall, to be enacted pending final agreement on the remaining regular appropriation bills for the year. For the most part, the resolution supports funding at the rate of governmental operations that lawmakers provided in 2002. If that rate was continued for all of 2003, it would yield an estimated $738 billion in total (both defense and nondefense) discretionary budget authority for the year.

However, the President and the Republican leadership in the Congress have apparently agreed that regular appropriations for 2003 should total about $751 billion in budget authority. As this report was being prepared, the 11 nondefense appropriation bills had not yet been enacted. But it seems clear that discretionary budget authority for 2003 is much more likely to total about $751 billion (or an amount close to that figure) than the rate of $738 billion that was estimated for the continuing resolution. Thus, in the absence of enactment of the regular appropriation bills, CBO has used the $751 billion figure as the basis for its adjusted baseline projections in this report. Relative to the continuing resolution, that adjustment increases estimated outlays by almost $7 billion in 2003 and by $11 billion to $15 billion per year over the 2004-2013 period. On balance, it reduces surpluses by $179 billion for the 10-year period (a figure that includes the associated increases in debt-service costs).

---

1. Some defense discretionary programs are funded in the energy and water act and in other appropriation laws. The adjusted baseline incorporates the assumption that those programs are funded at the levels provided in the current continuing resolution (about $16 billion).

---

to decline relative to GDP throughout the 2004-2013 period. (See the discussion of federal debt later in this chapter.) Nevertheless, the return of deficits after a decade of improving federal finances illustrates how quickly the nation's budgetary fortunes can change. It also shows how closely the budget is linked to the uncertain fiscal and economic circumstances that lawmakers now confront.

Uncertainty and the Projection Horizon

Budget projections are always subject to considerable uncertainty. CBO's adjusted baseline shows future spending and revenues under current laws and policies—even though those laws and policies will almost certainly change. Thus, the actual budget totals for the projection period are virtually guaranteed to differ from the estimates in this report, and perhaps substantially. This year, however, the uncertainty that normally accompanies CBO's baseline projections is heightened.

Certain current policies as they are now reflected in the baseline may prove to be unrealistic. The major tax-cutting provisions of EGTRRA are scheduled to expire at the end of December 2010, and if they do, tax rates will rise to their pre-2001 levels. But many people contend that it is unrealistic to assume that lawmakers would

Table 1-2.
CBO's Budget Projections Under Its Adjusted Baseline

	Actual 2002	2003	2004	2005	2006	2007	2008	2009
						In Billions of Dollars		
Revenues								
Individual income taxes	858	899	954	1,031	1,099	1,176	1,259	1,349
Social insurance taxes	701	725	766	811	856	901	944	989
Corporate income taxes	148	156	185	228	249	260	269	276
Other	146	141	150	156	166	169	176	184
Total	**1,853**	**1,922**	**2,054**	**2,225**	**2,370**	**2,505**	**2,648**	**2,798**
On-budget	1,338	1,390	1,496	1,637	1,751	1,853	1,963	2,079
Off-budget	515	532	558	588	619	651	685	719
Outlays								
Discretionary spending	734	792	817	834	848	866	891	915
Mandatory spending[b]	1,106	1,172	1,218	1,270	1,326	1,396	1,475	1,566
Net interest	171	157	165	194	212	217	217	214
Total	**2,011**	**2,121**	**2,199**	**2,298**	**2,387**	**2,479**	**2,583**	**2,695**
On-budget	1,655	1,751	1,816	1,905	1,979	2,058	2,149	2,243
Off-budget	356	370	383	393	407	420	434	451
Surplus or Deficit (-)	**-158**	**-199**	**-145**	**-73**	**-16**	**26**	**65**	**103**
On-budget	-317	-361	-319	-268	-228	-205	-185	-165
Off-budget	160	162	174	195	212	231	250	268
Memorandum:								
Debt Held by the Public at the End of the Year	3,540	3,766	3,927	4,013	4,045	4,034	3,983	3,894
Gross Domestic Product	10,337	10,756	11,309	11,934	12,582	13,263	13,972	14,712
						As a Percentage of GDP		
Revenues								
Individual income taxes	8.3	8.4	8.4	8.6	8.7	8.9	9.0	9.2
Social insurance taxes	6.8	6.7	6.8	6.8	6.8	6.8	6.8	6.7
Corporate income taxes	1.4	1.5	1.6	1.9	2.0	2.0	1.9	1.9
Other	1.4	1.3	1.3	1.3	1.3	1.3	1.3	1.3
Total	**17.9**	**17.9**	**18.2**	**18.6**	**18.8**	**18.9**	**19.0**	**19.0**
On-budget	12.9	12.9	13.2	13.7	13.9	14.0	14.1	14.1
Off-budget	5.0	4.9	4.9	4.9	4.9	4.9	4.9	4.9
Outlays								
Discretionary spending	7.1	7.4	7.2	7.0	6.7	6.5	6.4	6.2
Mandatory spending[b]	10.7	10.9	10.8	10.6	10.5	10.5	10.6	10.6
Net interest	1.7	1.5	1.5	1.6	1.7	1.6	1.6	1.5
Total	**19.5**	**19.7**	**19.4**	**19.3**	**19.0**	**18.7**	**18.5**	**18.3**
On-budget	16.0	16.3	16.1	16.0	15.7	15.5	15.4	15.2
Off-budget	3.4	3.4	3.4	3.3	3.2	3.2	3.1	3.1
Surplus or Deficit (-)	**-1.5**	**-1.9**	**-1.3**	**-0.6**	**-0.1**	**0.2**	**0.5**	**0.7**
On-budget	-3.1	-3.4	-2.8	-2.2	-1.8	-1.5	-1.3	-1.1
Off-budget	1.5	1.5	1.5	1.6	1.7	1.7	1.8	1.8
Memorandum:								
Debt Held by the Public at the End of the Year	34.3	35.0	34.7	33.6	32.2	30.4	28.5	26.5

Source: Congressional Budget Office.

Notes: These projections incorporate the assumption that discretionary budget authority totals $751 billion for 2003 and grows with inflation thereafter.

n.a. = not applicable.

a. Numbers in the bottom half of the column are shown as a percentage of cumulative GDP over this period.
b. Includes offsetting receipts.

	2010	2011	2012	2013	Total, 2004-2008[a]	Total, 2004-2013[a]
	1,447	1,649	1,819	1,939	5,518	13,720
	1,037	1,085	1,134	1,188	4,277	9,709
	285	295	306	316	1,190	2,669
	181	191	221	231	817	1,825
	2,949	**3,220**	**3,480**	**3,674**	**11,802**	**27,923**
	2,193	2,428	2,650	2,805	8,701	20,856
	756	792	830	870	3,101	7,067
	940	969	989	1,020	4,257	9,089
	1,661	1,774	1,856	1,988	6,684	15,529
	208	199	184	159	1,004	1,968
	2,809	**2,943**	**3,029**	**3,167**	**11,945**	**26,587**
	2,339	2,454	2,516	2,627	9,908	22,087
	470	489	512	539	2,038	4,500
	140	**277**	**451**	**508**	**-143**	**1,336**
	-145	-26	134	177	-1,206	-1,231
	286	303	317	330	1,063	2,568
	3,766	3,501	3,062	2,565	n.a.	n.a.
	15,480	16,250	17,013	17,851	n.a.	n.a.
	9.3	10.1	10.7	10.9	8.8	9.5
	6.7	6.7	6.7	6.7	6.8	6.7
	1.8	1.8	1.8	1.8	1.9	1.8
	1.2	1.2	1.3	1.3	1.3	1.3
	19.1	**19.8**	**20.5**	**20.6**	**18.7**	**19.3**
	14.2	14.9	15.6	15.7	13.8	14.4
	4.9	4.9	4.9	4.9	4.9	4.9
	6.1	6.0	5.8	5.7	6.8	6.3
	10.7	10.9	10.9	11.1	10.6	10.8
	1.3	1.2	1.1	0.9	1.6	1.4
	18.1	**18.1**	**17.8**	**17.7**	**18.9**	**18.4**
	15.1	15.1	14.8	14.7	15.7	15.3
	3.0	3.0	3.0	3.0	3.2	3.1
	0.9	**1.7**	**2.7**	**2.8**	**-0.2**	**0.9**
	-0.9	-0.2	0.8	1.0	-1.9	-0.9
	1.8	1.9	1.9	1.9	1.7	1.8
	24.3	21.5	18.0	14.4	n.a.	n.a.

permit that to happen. Allowing those provisions to expire, as current law provides, would significantly boost revenues for 2011 through 2013. And that upswing is the main reason that the baseline shows large surpluses for that period. If those and other expiring tax cuts were made permanent, the total 10-year surplus in CBO's adjusted baseline would be essentially eliminated. (*Box 1-2 on pages 8 and 9* discusses the effects on federal revenues of extending expiring tax provisions.)

Other factors might also create strong budgetary pressures this year and in later years, leading to changes in current spending or revenue policies that could increase deficits or diminish surpluses. For example, the nation continues to fight the war on terrorism, which may lead to additional spending. The possibility of war with Iraq clouds the budgetary picture as well, with its uncertain costs and possible economic effects (*see Box 1-3 on page 10*). Lawmakers are also under pressure to enact new tax and spending legislation to stimulate the sluggish economy. And there is interest in enacting other costly initiatives, such as a prescription drug benefit for Medicare beneficiaries and changes in the alternative minimum tax.

Another source of considerable uncertainty in the budget outlook is the accuracy of the economic and technical assumptions that underlie CBO's adjusted baseline. The economy is recovering slowly from the 2001 recession. CBO's baseline budget projections hinge in part on estimates of the timing and strength of that recovery (see Chapter 5 for more details). And technical factors that influence revenue collections—such as the behavior of the stock market and changes in taxable income—could also determine whether federal revenues bounce back as projected (see Chapter 3).

Uncertainty compounds as the projection horizon lengthens. Even small annual differences in the many key factors that influence CBO's budget projections—factors such as inflation, increases in productivity, economic growth, the distribution of income, and rates of growth for Medicare and Medicaid spending—can add up to substantial differences in budgetary outcomes 10 years from now. For details of how changes in several key assumptions would affect the budget outlook, see Appendix C.

Figure 1-1.
Total Deficits and Surpluses as a Share of GDP, 1967-2013
(Percentage of GDP)

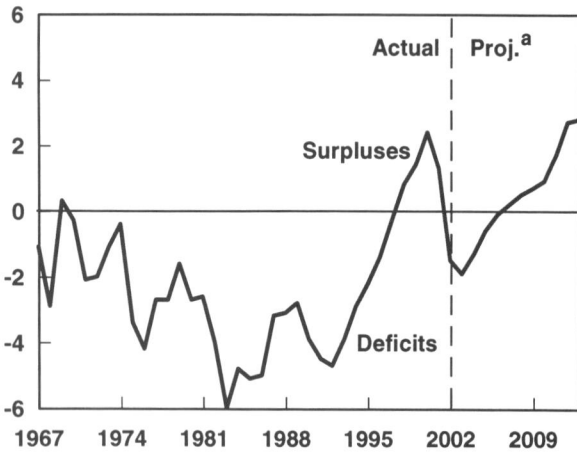

Source: Congressional Budget Office.

a. These projections incorporate the assumption that discretionary budget authority totals $751 billion for 2003 and grows with inflation thereafter.

Given such uncertainty, five-year projections may be more useful than 10-year numbers. As noted earlier, CBO's current 10-year projections of revenues are significantly influenced by the scheduled expiration of EGTRRA at the end of 2010. Also, the budget horizon has now shifted forward one year, which eliminates the year in which the deficit is estimated to peak (2003) and adds a year in which the baseline surplus is projected to be large and perhaps artificially high (2013). To provide a more complete budgetary picture, many of the tables in this report show both five-year (2004 to 2008) and 10-year (2004 to 2013) totals for the adjusted baseline.

Nonetheless, the longer term (beyond the 10-year horizon) is a critical consideration for lawmakers as the baby-boom generation ages. The worsening of the budget outlook since January 2001—along with its heightened uncertainty—exacerbates the budgetary challenges that lurk beyond the 10-year projection period. Toward the end of that span, the baby-boom generation will begin qualifying in large numbers for Social Security and Medicare benefits, putting increased pressure on those programs. And by 2030, the number of workers paying Social Security and Medicare taxes is expected to rise by only about 15 percent while the number of beneficiaries of those programs is projected to balloon by about 80 percent. Growth in the number of beneficiaries, combined with increases in life expectancy, will boost spending for long-term care, about half of which is financed by Medicaid and Medicare.[2] Together, demographic changes and the growth of medical costs are projected to push total federal spending for Medicare, Medicaid, and Social Security as a share of GDP sharply higher over the next few decades.

The Return of the Deficit in 2002

The $158 billion budget deficit in 2002 marked the end of a period of surpluses—four consecutive years—the likes of which had not been seen since the late 1920s. The total shortfall for 2002 was a net reversal of $285 billion from the $127 billion surplus recorded for 2001. The on-budget deficit was $317 billion, and the off-budget surplus was $160 billion.

Revenues fell for the second consecutive year in 2002, following annual increases from 1994 through 2000 that averaged more than 8 percent. The decline in 2002 revenues of nearly 7 percent ($138 billion) was the largest percentage drop since the mid-1940s; it stemmed primarily from the weak economy, fewer realizations of capital gains, and, to a much smaller extent, the tax cuts enacted in the past two years. Declines in the two major sources of revenues were even greater, on a percentage basis, than the overall drop. Revenues from individual income taxes in 2002 were 14 percent lower than in the previous year. (Although the tax cuts enacted in 2001 and 2002 held down the growth of revenues from that source, those revenues would have fallen by approximately 10 percent over the year, by CBO's estimates, even without the cuts.) In recent years, revenues from corporate sources have followed a similar path. After growing at an average annual rate of almost 7 percent from 1994 through 2000, they fell off sharply after corporate profits began declining in 2000.

---

2. See Congressional Budget Office, *Projections of Expenditures for Long-Term Care Services for the Elderly* (March 1999), pp. 1, 5-6.

While revenues dwindled in 2002, outlays grew by $147 billion, topping $2 trillion for the first time. Large increases in appropriations for both defense and nondefense programs, a steep rise in payments for unemployment benefits, and substantial growth of Medicaid outlays led to the largest percentage jump in noninterest spending since 1981—about 11 percent. Defense outlays (including a shift in payment dates) grew by 14 percent in 2002; more than half of that growth was due to initiatives that were in place before the September 11 terrorist attacks, CBO estimates. The rise in nondefense discretionary spending was spread among numerous programs—three areas with the largest increases were health, education, and transportation. The slowdown in the economy caused the unemployment rate to peak at 6.0 percent in late 2002, which resulted in a record amount of spending for unemployment compensation—$51 billion (including $8 billion in extended benefits.) Medicaid spending also grew rapidly, increasing by more than 13 percent over the previous year's level.

The Concept Behind CBO's Baseline

The projections that make up CBO's baseline are not intended to be predictions of future budgetary outcomes but rather CBO's best judgment about how the economy and other factors will affect federal revenues and spending under current laws and policies. CBO constructs its baseline according to rules set forth in law, mainly in the Balanced Budget and Emergency Deficit Control Act of 1985 and the Congressional Budget and Impoundment Control Act of 1974. In general, those laws instruct CBO and the Office of Management and Budget to project federal spending and revenues under current policies. Lawmakers can use the baseline as a neutral benchmark to measure the effects of proposed changes in tax and spending policies.

For revenues and mandatory spending, the Deficit Control Act requires that the baseline be projected under the assumption that current laws continue without change. In most cases, the laws that govern revenues and mandatory spending are permanent. The baseline projections reflect anticipated changes in the economy, demographics, and other relevant factors that affect the implementation of those laws.[3]

The baseline rules are different for discretionary spending, which is governed by annual appropriation acts. The Deficit Control Act states that after the current year, projections of discretionary budget authority should be adjusted to reflect inflation—using specified indexes—as well as other factors (such as the cost of annualizing adjustments to federal pay). That approach to developing baseline projections can be problematic when lawmakers do not complete action on all of the appropriation acts, as is the case this year. Programs that have not yet received full-year funding are operating, as discussed earlier, under a continuing resolution that expires on January 31, 2003. However, the President and the Republican leadership in the Congress have apparently agreed on a total funding level of about $751 billion for all of the regular appropriations for 2003. CBO therefore has adjusted its baseline to incorporate that assumption—pending enactment of the remaining discretionary appropriation bills—and extrapolated that funding level over the next 10 years (adjusting it for projected rates of inflation and other specified factors).

By convention, CBO has prepared another benchmark for discretionary spending. Lawmakers sometimes use a freeze in appropriations—a set amount of budget authority without an adjustment for inflation—to gauge the impact of proposed levels of discretionary spending. The budget outlook under an effective freeze of $751 billion per year is shown in *Box 1-4 on page 11*.

---

3. The Deficit Control Act also specifies that baseline projections incorporate the assumption that expiring spending programs will continue if they have outlays of more than $50 million in the current year and were established on or before the date on which the Balanced Budget Act of 1997 was enacted. Programs established after that date are not automatically continued in the baseline. Another requirement of the act is that expiring excise taxes dedicated to a trust fund be extended at current rates. However, the Deficit Control Act does not provide for the extension of other expiring tax provisions, including those that have been routinely extended in the past.

8 THE BUDGET AND ECONOMIC OUTLOOK: FISCAL YEARS 2004-2013

Box 1-2.
The Expiration of Revenue Provisions

The budget outlook for the next 10 years is strongly affected by the scheduled expiration of various revenue provisions.[1] The Economic Growth and Tax Relief Reconciliation Act of 2001 (EGTRRA) plays a big role: three items are scheduled to end on or before December 31, 2006, and the rest of the law's provisions—which represent the bulk of its budgetary cost—expire on December 31, 2010. Another major impact would come from the economic stimulus law that policymakers enacted in March 2002 (the Job Creation and Worker Assistance Act of 2002). That law established new tax cuts for businesses; in most cases, those cuts end during the next two years. And many other provisions of the tax code that were enacted before EGTRRA are scheduled to expire over the next decade.

By law, the Congressional Budget Office's (CBO's) baseline budget projections incorporate the assumption that almost all expiring tax provisions end as scheduled. (The only exception is for expiring excise taxes dedicated to trust funds.) An alternative measure of the long-term budgetary effects of current policy could incorporate a different assumption: that all of those expirations do not occur as scheduled and instead the provisions are immediately and permanently extended. Under that assumption, as the Joint Committee on Taxation (JCT) and CBO estimate, federal revenues would be $1.2 trillion lower during the 2004-2013 period than the amount projected in CBO's adjusted baseline (*see the table at right*). About two-thirds of that estimated decline ($785 billion) would come from extending EGTRRA. And about 85 percent of that EGTRRA-related drop would occur from 2011 to 2013, immediately after most of the law's provisions are scheduled to expire. Some effects, however, would be felt earlier. For example, extending the changes that the law made to estate and gift taxes could reduce revenues as early as 2003—because if taxpayers knew that those changes would become permanent in 2011, some people might postpone until then making some taxable gifts that they would otherwise have made earlier in the decade.

Under a more limited alternative measure, all expiring tax provisions would be extended except the ones created by the economic stimulus law, which were not intended to be permanent. (Those provisions include allowing businesses to take an additional first-year deduction for depreciation of certain property and targeting tax benefits to the area of New York City that was damaged in the September 11 terrorist attacks.) If all but those expiring provisions were extended, federal revenues would be $960 billion lower during the 2004-2013 period, JCT and CBO project.

---

1. The provisions' expiration can also be expected to affect the economy, but only some of those effects are reflected in the estimates presented here—for example, the estimates do not reflect macroeconomic changes. (For a discussion of those effects, see Box 2-1 on pages 26 and 27.)

Changes in CBO's Projections Since August 2002

CBO's projection of the cumulative surplus for the 2003-2012 period has fallen by $385 billion since last summer (*see Table 1-3 on pages 12 and 13*). By convention, CBO attributes changes in its projections to three factors: recently enacted legislation; modifications to its outlook for the economy; and changes in other conditions that affect the budget (a category labeled technical).[4]

---

4. That categorization of revisions should be interpreted with caution, however. For example, distinguishing between economic and technical reestimates is imprecise. Changes in some factors that are related to the performance of the economy (such as capital gains realizations) are classified as technical reestimates because they are not driven directly by changes in the components of CBO's economic forecast.

Box 1-2.
Continued

Effects on Revenues of Extending Expiring Tax Provisions (In billions of dollars)

	2003	2004	2005	2006	2007	2008	2009	2010	2011	2012	2013	Total, 2004-2008	Total, 2004-2013
Economic Growth and Tax Relief Reconciliation Act of 2001													
Provisions expiring in 2010	*	-1	-1	-1	-1	-2	-2	-2	-131	-230	-240	-5	-610
Provisions expiring before 2010[a]	n.a.	n.a.	-3	-12	-17	-22	-26	-29	-25	-18	-21	-55	-175
Subtotal	*	-1	-4	-13	-19	-24	-28	-32	-156	-249	-260	-60	-785
Job Creation and Worker Assistance Act of 2002[b]	n.a.	*	-28	-42	-40	-35	-30	-26	-22	-20	-19	-145	-262
Other Expiring Tax Provisions[c]	*	1	-3	-8	-12	-15	-17	-20	-23	-27	-30	-36	-152
Estimated Interaction Effects from Enacting All Provisions Simultaneously	0	0	1	1	1	1	1	1	-4	-12	-12	4	-23
Total Effect on Revenues	*	*	-34	-61	-69	-73	-74	-76	-206	-308	-321	-237	-1,222
Memorandum: Total Effect on Revenues Excluding the Job Creation and Worker Assistance Act	*	*	-6	-19	-30	-37	-44	-50	-184	-288	-302	-93	-960

Sources: Congressional Budget Office; Joint Committee on Taxation.

Notes: The estimates incorporate the assumptions that the expiring provisions are extended immediately rather than when they are about to expire and that they are extended at the rates or levels existing at the time of expiration. The estimates do not include effects on debt-service costs.

When this report went to press, JCT's estimates were unavailable for several expiring tax provisions—most significantly, for EGTRRA's major individual income tax provisions that expire in 2010 and for the provisions of the alternative minimum tax (AMT) that expire in earlier years. CBO estimated the effects of extending those provisions and of the interaction from extending all expiring tax provisions simultaneously. As a result, cost estimates by JCT for legislative proposals to extend the EGTRRA and AMT provisions might not match the figures shown here.

n.a. = not applicable; * = between -$500 million and $500 million.

a. Includes the increased exemption amount for the alternative minimum tax (expires in 2004), the deduction for qualified education expenses (expires in 2005), and the credit for individual retirement accounts and 401(k)-type plans (expires in 2006).
b. New provisions in the Job Creation and Worker Assistance Act that are scheduled to expire include special depreciation-expensing allowances for certain property and tax benefits for the area of New York City that was damaged in the September 11 terrorist attacks. The provisions that allowed a special five-year carryback of net operating losses have already expired and are not included in these estimates. The estimates also do not include provisions in the law that had existed and been extended in previous years. The effects of extending those provisions again are included in the line for other expiring tax provisions.
c. Includes numerous items, such as the tax credit for research and experimentation.

Revisions that are technical in nature account for essentially the entire decline in the projected surplus relative to CBO's previous estimates; changes that fall into the other two categories are much smaller and almost completely offset each other. Legislative actions (including the apparent agreement to set the level of total appropriations at $751 billion for 2003) have lowered the projected cumulative surplus by $64 billion for the 2003-2012 period. However, changes stemming from revisions in CBO's economic forecast add $67 billion to the 10-year surplus estimates.

Legislative Changes

Relatively little legislation affecting the budget has been enacted since CBO last published its baseline.[5] Legislative

---
5. Congressional Budget Office, *The Budget and Economic Outlook: An Update* (August 2002).

Box 1-3.
An Estimate of the Costs of a Potential Conflict with Iraq

Recently, the Congressional Budget Office (CBO) was asked to gauge the costs of activities related to possible military operations in Iraq.[1] Estimates of the total cost of a military conflict with Iraq and such a conflict's aftermath are highly uncertain. They depend on many factors that are unknown at this time, including the size of the force that is deployed, the strategy to be used, the duration of the conflict, the number of casualties, the equipment lost, and the need for reconstruction of Iraq's infrastructure.

Of the many force levels that might be used to prosecute such a war, CBO examined two representative examples. Both alternatives were based to some extent on the forces that the Department of Defense (DoD) had previously indicated it would require for a major theater war. The first of CBO's examples emphasized U.S. ground forces. This so-called Heavy Ground option would include about five Army divisions and five Air Force tactical fighter wings. The second option relied more on air power. Termed the Heavy Air option, it would comprise two and one-third Army divisions and 10 Air Force tactical fighter wings. Using those forces, CBO employed various methods to develop its estimates, including the use of data on the cost of prior and current military operations—most notably, those in the Balkans, Afghanistan, and Desert Shield/Desert Storm.

Using those two examples, CBO estimated that the incremental costs of deploying a force to the Persian Gulf (that is, the costs that would be incurred above those budgeted for routine operations) would be between $9 billion and $13 billion. Prosecuting a war would cost between $6 billion and $9 billion a month —although how long such a war might last could not be estimated. After hostilities ended, the costs to return U.S. forces to their home bases would range between $5 billion and $7 billion, CBO estimated. Further, the incremental cost of an occupation following combat operations would vary from about $1 billion to $4 billion a month. CBO had no basis for estimating any costs for reconstruction or for foreign aid that the United States might choose to extend after a conflict had ended.

Many alternative force structures—other than the two options that CBO used in its estimates—could be fielded. And whatever forces were used, multiple unknown factors would characterize any scenario of how a conflict with Iraq might actually unfold. On the one hand, if the Iraqi leadership or selected elements of its military forces quickly capitulated, ground combat could be of short duration, as in Desert Storm. On the other hand, if the leadership and military chose to fight, Iraq's use of chemical or biological weapons (CBW) against regional military or transportation facilities could extend the war, as could the need to engage in protracted urban fighting. Given those uncertainties, CBO's estimates of the monthly costs of operations exclude expenditures for decontaminating areas or equipment affected by CBW attacks.

A war in Iraq could lead to substantial costs in later years that were not included in CBO's estimates, either because their magnitude could not be assessed even roughly or because they depended on highly uncertain decisions about future policy. For example, the United States might leave troops or equipment in Iraq, which could require the construction of new military bases. Sustaining the occupation over time could require either increases in overall active-duty and reserve force levels or major changes in current policies on basing and deployment. The United States might provide Iraq with funds for humanitarian assistance and reconstruction. And substantial aid might be provided in the future to allies and other friendly nations in the region.

---

1. See CBO's letter to Senator Kent Conrad and Congressman John M. Spratt, Jr., on September 30, 2002, *Estimated Costs of a Potential Conflict with Iraq*, which is available at www.cbo.gov.

Box 1-4.
The Budgetary Effects of Freezing Total Discretionary Appropriations at $751 Billion

Some lawmakers view a freeze in discretionary spending as the most logical starting point from which to measure the effects of appropriations—rather than a baseline for such spending based on the assumption that spending would grow with inflation. If total discretionary appropriations were effectively frozen at $751 billion and current policies remained unchanged, by CBO's estimates the budget would return to surplus in 2006. Under that scenario, the total budget surplus would equal 4.5 percent of gross domestic product (GDP) by 2013 (see the table below). At that point, discretionary outlays would be 4.4 percent of GDP, down from the share of 7.4 percent that CBO's adjusted baseline anticipates for 2003. Under the adjusted baseline, discretionary spending would be 5.7 percent of GDP in 2013.

The Budget Outlook Assuming That Discretionary Appropriations Are Frozen at $751 Billion (In billions of dollars)

	Actual 2002	2003	2004	2005	2006	2007	2008	2009	2010	2011	2012	2013	Total, 2004-2008	Total, 2004-2013
On-Budget	-317	-361	-307	-238	-177	-127	-75	-23	30	186	384	470	-925	121
Off-Budget	160	162	175	195	212	232	251	269	287	304	318	332	1,064	2,574
Total Surplus or Deficit (-)	-158	-199	-133	-43	35	104	176	245	316	490	702	802	139	2,695
Memorandum: Total Surplus or Deficit (-) as a Percentage of GDP	-1.5	-1.9	-1.2	-0.4	0.3	0.8	1.3	1.7	2.0	3.0	4.1	4.5	0.2[a]	1.9[a]

Source: Congressional Budget Office.

a. As a percentage of cumulative GDP over the period.

actions have increased CBO's projections of revenues and outlays over the 2003-2012 period by $5 billion and $68 billion, respectively. Included in the projection of outlays is the adjustment to CBO's baseline to account for the level of discretionary spending for 2003—$751 billion— that appears to have been agreed to by the President and the Congress's Republican leadership. As a result, discretionary budget authority for nondefense programs totals $369 billion in CBO's adjusted baseline—or $17 billion below the level that CBO had projected in August by inflating 2002 appropriations. Using the adjusted level as the basis for projections through 2013 results in a cumulative drop in nondefense outlays of $112 billion.

Two of the 13 regular appropriation acts—defense and military construction—have already been enacted, and they provide funding for 2003 that is about $13 billion above August's baseline levels. However, some defense programs are funded in other appropriation acts. Under CBO's adjusted baseline, those programs are funded at the levels in the current continuing resolution, which are marginally lower than the levels projected in the August baseline. Over the next decade, additional appropriations for defense discretionary programs are projected to boost outlays by $137 billion. Combining that addition with the lower level of spending for nondefense programs brings total discretionary outlays in CBO's adjusted baseline for the 2003-2012 period to a cumulative $25 billion above the amounts projected in August.

Other legislative changes have raised CBO's projection of mandatory outlays (excluding debt-service costs) by about $24 billion through 2012. About one-third of that amount will be spent in 2003; it stems from the five-

12 THE BUDGET AND ECONOMIC OUTLOOK: FISCAL YEARS 2004-2013

Table 1-3.
Changes in CBO's Projections of the Surplus or Deficit Since August 2002 Under the Adjusted Baseline
(In billions of dollars)

	2003	2004	2005	2006	2007	2008	2009	2010	2011	2012	Total, 2003-2007	Total, 2003-2012
Total Surplus or Deficit (-) as Projected in August 2002	-145	-111	-39	15	52	88	133	177	323	522	-229	1,015
Changes to Revenue Projections												
Legislative	*	*	*	*	*	1	1	1	1	1	1	5
Economic	-9	-14	-8	-2	-1	-6	-9	-16	-31	-50	-34	-146
Technical	-32	-15	-11	-10	-8	-5	-2	*	7	8	-76	-67
Total Revenue Changes	-41	-29	-19	-11	-9	-10	-11	-15	-23	-41	-109	-208
Changes to Outlay Projections												
Legislative												
Discretionary												
Defense	7	12	14	14	14	15	15	15	16	16	60	137
Nondefense[a]	-1	-4	-8	-11	-13	-14	-15	-15	-15	-16	-37	-112
Subtotal, discretionary	5	8	6	3	1	*	*	1	*	*	23	25
Mandatory												
Unemployment insurance	8	0	0	0	0	0	0	0	0	0	8	8
Terrorism insurance	*	1	2	2	1	1	*	*	*	*	5	6
Debt service	*	1	1	2	2	2	3	3	3	3	6	20
Other	*	1	1	1	1	1	1	1	1	1	5	10
Subtotal, mandatory	8	2	4	5	4	4	4	4	4	4	23	43
Subtotal, legislative	13	10	10	8	5	4	4	4	4	5	47	68
Economic												
Discretionary	*	*	-1	-1	-1	-1	-1	-1	*	1	-3	-5
Mandatory												
Social Security	*	-1	-3	-4	-5	-5	-6	-7	-8	-9	-14	-49
Medicare	*	*	-1	-1	-2	-2	-2	-3	-3	-3	-4	-18
Medicaid	1	*	*	-1	-1	-1	-2	-2	-2	-2	-1	-10
Unemployment insurance	-2	3	2	1	1	*	*	*	-1	-1	4	3
Net interest	-12	-31	-20	-9	-5	-4	-3	-2	-2	-2	-77	-90
Debt service	*	*	-1	-2	-3	-4	-5	-5	-5	-4	-8	-31
Other	-1	-1	-1	-2	-1	-1	-2	-1	-1	-2	-6	-13
Subtotal, mandatory	-14	-31	-25	-19	-17	-19	-19	-20	-22	-23	-105	-208
Subtotal, economic	-14	-31	-25	-20	-18	-20	-20	-21	-22	-22	-108	-213

(Continued)

Table 1-3.
Continued

(In billions of dollars)

	2003	2004	2005	2006	2007	2008	2009	2010	2011	2012	Total, 2003-2007	Total, 2003-2012
Changes to Outlay Projections (Continued)												
Technical												
Discretionary	4	6	2	2	2	3	3	4	3	5	16	34
Mandatory												
Social Security	1	1	2	2	2	2	2	3	3	3	7	21
Veterans' benefits	1	2	3	3	2	2	2	2	2	1	11	19
Medicare	5	9	10	9	8	5	4	4	6	8	41	68
Commodity Credit Corporation	-6	-3	1	2	2	3	4	4	4	4	-5	15
Unemployment insurance	1	1	2	2	2	2	2	2	2	2	7	17
Electromagnetic spectrum transactions	4	4	4	2	*	-2	*	*	*	*	14	12
Net interest	4	3	1	2	2	3	3	3	4	5	14	31
Debt service	*	2	5	7	9	11	13	15	16	18	23	95
Other	*	1	1	2	*	1	2	1	*	1	5	10
Subtotal, mandatory	10	20	28	30	27	27	32	34	37	42	116	287
Subtotal, technical	14	26	30	32	30	29	35	37	40	47	132	321
Total Outlay Changes	13	5	15	20	17	14	19	21	23	29	70	177
Total Impact on the Surplus	-54	-34	-34	-32	-26	-23	-30	-37	-46	-70	-179	-385
Total Surplus or Deficit (-) as Projected in January 2003	-199	-145	-73	-16	26	65	103	140	277	451	-408	629
Memorandum:												
Total Legislative Changes	-13	-10	-10	-7	-5	-4	-3	-4	-4	-4	-45	-64
Total Economic Changes	5	16	18	18	16	14	11	5	-9	-28	74	67
Total Technical Changes	-46	-40	-41	-42	-37	-34	-37	-38	-33	-39	-208	-388

Source: Congressional Budget Office.

Note: * = between -$500 million and $500 million.

a. Reflects the effect on outlays if budget authority for 2003 totals $751 billion rather than the level provided by the continuing resolution ($738 billion).

month extension of certain unemployment benefits enacted in Public Law 108-1.[6] The Terrorism Risk Insurance Act of 2002 (P.L. 107-297), which would provide financial assistance to insurers for certain losses from future terrorist acts, will also increase projected mandatory outlays over the next 10 years by $6 billion. (CBO based that projection on assumptions about various outcomes of terrorist attacks—ranging from no damages to very large effects.) During the 10-year period, approximately half of that cost would be offset by revenues collected from assessments on the insurance industry.

---

6. An Act to provide for a 5-month extension of the Temporary Extended Unemployment Compensation Act of 2002 and for a transition period for individuals receiving compensation when the program under such Act ends.

Another change in projected outlays that CBO has attributed to legislation is the additional interest payments on the government's debt. Because legislative actions since August have decreased projections of the cumulative surplus over the 2003-2012 period, debt-service costs in the adjusted baseline would be $20 billion higher over that decade, CBO estimates.

Economic Changes

Economic revisions to the baseline have added a relatively small amount to the projection of the cumulative surplus. In light of recent developments, CBO has lowered its forecast for short- and long-term interest rates, inflation, wages and salaries, and corporate profits. (For a detailed discussion of CBO's new economic forecast, see Chapter 2.) Those revisions in turn reduce projections of both revenues and outlays, leading to an increase of $67 billion in the projected cumulative surplus over the 2003-2012 period.

Revenues. A dimmer outlook for nominal income has reduced CBO's projections of revenues by $146 billion over the 10-year period. Over half of that drop stems from the assumption, beginning in 2011, of a slightly slower rate of growth of aggregate income than CBO had previously used. Over the 2003-2012 period, lower projections of personal income reduce revenues from both individual income and social insurance taxes by $168 billion. But partially offsetting that decline is an upward reestimate of corporate profits in the near term. That change increases projected revenues from corporate income taxes by $30 billion over the decade.

Outlays. Revisions to CBO's economic forecast reduce its projection of spending over the 2003-2012 period by $213 billion—which more than offsets the change in revenues that was attributed to economic factors. The impact of lower interest rates on net interest payments explains a large part of the decline in projected spending. An additional factor is lower projections of certain measures of inflation, which reduce estimated outlays for Social Security and Medicare.

Compared with its August outlook, CBO has lowered its forecast for interest rates on three-month Treasury bills by nearly 110 basis points for 2003 and 165 basis points for 2004. (A basis point is one-hundredth of a percentage point.) Similarly, CBO has lowered its forecast for rates on 10-year Treasury notes by almost 100 basis points for 2003 and about 70 basis points for 2004. Those lower estimated rates decrease projections of net interest costs by $90 billion over the 2003-2012 period; nearly 70 percent of those savings would accrue through 2005.

Although mandatory spending flows from the provisions of permanent laws, the growth or contraction of many mandatory programs is keyed to the economy. Thus, lower estimated wage growth and cost-of-living adjustments in large part have led CBO to reduce its 10-year projections of spending for Social Security (by $49 billion) and Medicare (by $18 billion). For unemployment compensation, revisions to CBO's economic forecast did not result in a substantial change in projected spending over the decade. In the near term, however, CBO now projects $2 billion less in unemployment compensation for 2003, $3 billion more in such spending for 2004, and $2 billion more for 2005.

Because changes in CBO's economic forecast increase projected surpluses, debt-service costs are projected to decline by $31 billion over the 10-year period, with most of the change occurring over the latter half of the projection horizon.

Technical Changes

Reestimates that cannot be ascribed either to legislative actions or to changes in CBO's economic assumptions have reduced the projected cumulative surplus for the 2003-2012 period by $388 billion. Almost a quarter of that change is the additional debt-service costs that result from all technical revisions.

Revenues. Since August, CBO has cut its projection of revenues for 2003 through 2012 by $67 billion. The largest revision—$140 billion over the 10-year period—flows from the smaller amount of revenues projected for individual and social insurance tax collections. Offsetting $65 billion of the decline, however, are higher projections of revenues from corporate sources.

The reestimate of revenues is based on several factors. First, the weak performance of the stock market in 2002 led CBO to reduce its projection of revenues from capital gains realizations in the near term. (CBO has not changed its assumptions about the long-term relationship of capital gains realizations to GDP.) Second, current revenue collections are running below the amounts that might be expected given the level of economic activity, capital gains, retirement distributions, and other factors that influence the effective tax rate. CBO's projections incorporate the assumption that the shortfall will continue in the near term but diminish in later years. Third, CBO has reduced its projections of revenues from social insurance taxes largely because of new information about the composition of recent receipts.

Higher projections of income taxes paid by corporations partially offset the downward reestimate for revenues. Last summer, CBO recognized that corporate tax receipts were lower than anticipated, given economic conditions, and projected that shortfalls would continue. CBO now believes that some of the weakness will be temporary. Evidence suggests that a portion of the drop-off in corporate revenues occurred because corporations had been receiving larger-than-expected "carryback" refunds, mainly as a result of temporary provisions enacted last year in the Job Creation and Worker Assistance Act of 2002 (P.L. 107-147).[7] That high level of refunds will persist in 2003, CBO expects. However, as provisions in that act expire, refunds are likely to return to more typical levels.

Outlays. Technical reestimates increased projections of spending for both discretionary and mandatory programs by a total of $321 billion over the 2003-2012 period. Of that amount, discretionary outlays account for $34 billion, mostly for nondefense programs. Revisions in the projections for the Section 8 housing program, which derive from higher-than-anticipated costs for rent subsidies, are the largest contributor to the rise in nondefense discretionary spending. For defense discretionary outlays, increases are mainly related to the accrual charge that pays for the health care of future military retirees, their dependents, and surviving spouses. Because the estimated payments for that accrual charge add to other costs for military personnel, CBO has adjusted its projection of the inflators applied to personnel spending to more accurately reflect the charge's future cost.

On the mandatory spending side, technical reestimates have increased projections of outlays for many programs. For example, expectations of faster growth in numbers of participants have contributed to higher projected outlays for both Social Security and veterans' compensation over the 10-year period. CBO also increased its projections of Medicare outlays over the decade by $68 billion, mostly because higher-than-anticipated spending was recorded in 2002 for hospice care, outpatient services furnished by facilities or nonphysician professionals, and ancillary services (such as prosthetics, orthotics, and durable medical equipment; laboratory tests; ambulance services; and outpatient prescription drugs).

Since the summer, CBO has also increased its projection of spending for the Commodity Credit Corporation (CCC), raising it by $15 billion over the 10-year period. (The CCC makes loans and payments to farmers to support farm income and prices.) In the near term, the projection is lower than it was last August because drought has spurred recent increases in crop prices; over the longer term, however, CBO expects that those prices will fall and push CCC outlays higher. In addition, CBO has modified its baseline estimating procedures to account for variations in future commodity prices, which should provide more-accurate projections of agricultural spending over the next decade.

CBO's projections for unemployment insurance and spectrum-related transactions have also risen. Outlays for unemployment insurance are projected to be $17 billion higher during the 2003-2012 period because of an upward adjustment in the estimated average benefit. Contributing to that change were revised estimates of the impact of legislation previously enacted in California, which nearly doubles the state's maximum benefit by 2005. (Unemployment insurance is a joint federal/state program, and federal outlays are tied to the eligibility requirements and benefit levels set by each state.) CBO has lowered its projection of the amounts that are likely to be paid for licenses to use the electromagnetic spectrum; that change results in net federal outlays that are an estimated $12 billion higher over the period. Roughly half of the rise stems from a recent ruling by the Federal

---

7. A carryback refund is a refund of taxes paid by a corporation in a previous year that is based on the corporation's losses in the current year. For more information, see Chapter 3.

Communications Commission that allowed companies to withdraw their offers to pay for certain disputed licenses. Most of the remaining amount derives from recent trends in the price and quantity of spectrum that is likely to be auctioned in the future.

Adjustments that CBO has made to its projections of net interest reflect new data on the stock of outstanding federal debt and revised assumptions about the future composition of debt held by the public. (CBO now assumes that more longer-term debt will be issued than it had estimated in August.) Those changes boost projected net interest outlays over the 10-year period by $31 billion. In addition, debt-service costs attributable to technical changes boost net interest outlays by another $95 billion from 2003 through 2012.

The Outlook for Federal Debt

Federal debt consists of two main components: debt held by the public and debt held by government accounts. Debt held by the public—the most meaningful measure of debt in terms of its relationship to the economy—is issued by the federal government to raise cash. Debt held by government accounts is purely an intragovernmental IOU and involves no cash transactions. It is used as an accounting device to track cash flows relating to specific federal programs (for example, Social Security).

Debt held by the public and debt held by government accounts follow different paths in CBO's projections. The holdings of government accounts have risen steadily for several decades and are expected to continue doing so through the projection period. Debt held by the public, in contrast, fluctuates according to changes in the government's borrowing needs. As a percentage of GDP, publicly held debt had reached 50 percent as recently as 1993. Since 1994, it had been falling, but it rose to about 34 percent of GDP in 2002 (see Table 1-4). If current policies remained the same—that is, discretionary appropriations of $751 billion for 2003 grew with inflation and the tax cuts enacted in EGTRRA expired as scheduled—debt held by the public would fall below 15 percent of GDP by 2013. Indeed, publicly held debt is projected to decline even before EGTRRA is due to expire—dropping to approximately 24 percent of GDP in 2010—because under CBO's projections, the amount of debt would remain roughly stable while the economy grew steadily.

Debt Held by the Public

When revenues are insufficient to cover spending, the Department of the Treasury raises money by selling securities in the capital markets to investors. Debt held by the public represents the accumulation of those sales. For example, between 1969 and 1997, the Treasury sold debt to finance deficits, and debt held by the public climbed each year, peaking at $3.8 trillion in 1997. That trend reversed in 1998 with the onset of budget surpluses. By the end of 2001, debt held by the public had dropped to $3.3 trillion.

Under current tax and spending policies, debt held by the public, as projected by CBO, would grow over the next few years as deficits necessitated additional borrowing. The level of publicly held debt would reach a high of over $4 trillion in 2006, by CBO's estimate, before beginning to decline again. However, after 2003, debt held by the public as a percentage of GDP would begin to fall again because projected deficits in the near term are relatively small.

The Composition of Debt Held by the Public. Over 85 percent of publicly held debt consists of marketable securities, such as Treasury bills, notes, and bonds, and inflation-indexed notes and bonds. The remainder of that debt comprises nonmarketable securities (such as savings bonds and state and local government securities), which are nonnegotiable, nontransferable debt instruments that are issued to specific investors.

The Treasury sells marketable securities in regularly scheduled auctions, although the size of those auctions varies according to fluctuations in the government's cash flow. (It also sells cash management bills periodically to cover shortfalls in cash balances.) For some time, the Treasury has been shifting its borrowing toward shorter-term bills and notes. For example, in 2001, it introduced a four-week bill and eliminated the 30-year bond; as a result, the Treasury securities that are now sold to the public range in maturity from four weeks to 10 years. Those changes may alter the composition of outstanding public debt in the future. However, the trend toward shorter average maturity may be slowed if the Treasury

Table 1-4.
CBO's Projections of Federal Debt Under Its Adjusted Baseline
(In billions of dollars)

	Actual 2002	2003	2004	2005	2006	2007	2008	2009	2010	2011	2012	2013
Debt Held by the Public at the Beginning of the Year	3,320	3,540	3,766	3,927	4,013	4,045	4,034	3,983	3,894	3,766	3,501	3,062
Changes to Debt Held by the Public												
Surplus (-) or deficit	158	199	145	73	16	-26	-65	-103	-140	-277	-451	-508
Other means of financing	63	27	16	13	16	15	14	14	13	12	12	11
Total	220	226	161	86	32	-11	-51	-90	-127	-265	-440	-497
Debt Held by the Public at the End of the Year	3,540	3,766	3,927	4,013	4,045	4,034	3,983	3,894	3,766	3,501	3,062	2,565
Debt Held by Government Accounts												
Social Security	1,329	1,489	1,664	1,858	2,070	2,302	2,552	2,820	3,106	3,409	3,727	4,057
Other government accounts[a]	1,329	1,364	1,447	1,546	1,660	1,780	1,907	2,038	2,174	2,315	2,463	2,615
Total	2,658	2,854	3,112	3,404	3,730	4,082	4,459	4,858	5,280	5,724	6,190	6,671
Gross Federal Debt	6,198	6,620	7,039	7,417	7,776	8,116	8,442	8,752	9,046	9,225	9,251	9,236
Debt Subject to Limit[b]	6,161	6,598	7,017	7,395	7,753	8,094	8,419	8,729	9,023	9,201	9,227	9,212
Memorandum:												
Debt Held by the Public at the End of the Year as a Percentage of GDP	34.3	35.0	34.7	33.6	32.2	30.4	28.5	26.5	24.3	21.5	18.0	14.4

Source: Congressional Budget Office.

Note: These projections incorporate the assumption that discretionary budget authority totals $751 billion for 2003 and grows with inflation thereafter.

a. Mainly the Civil Service Retirement, Military Retirement, Medicare, Unemployment Insurance, and Airport and Airway Trust Funds.
b. Differs from gross federal debt primarily because it excludes most debt issued by agencies other than the Treasury. The current debt limit is $6,400 billion.

curtails its program to buy back bonds before they reach maturity.

Why Changes in Debt Held by the Public Do Not Equal the Size of Surpluses and Deficits. In most years, the amount that the Treasury borrows or redeems approximates the total surplus or deficit. However, a number of factors broadly labeled "other means of financing" also affect the government's need to borrow money from the public. Over the 2004-2013 period, CBO projects that public debt will increase by more than the amount of deficits and decrease by less than the amount of surpluses as other means of financing increase the Treasury's borrowing needs.

In most years, the largest component of those other means of financing is the capitalization of financing accounts used for federal credit programs. Direct student loans, rural housing programs, loans by the Small Business Administration, and other credit programs require the government to disburse money in anticipation of repayment at a later date. Those initial outlays are not counted in the budget, which reflects only the estimated subsidy costs of such programs. For the 10 years of CBO's current baseline, the amount of the loans being disbursed will typically exceed the repayments and interest. Thus, the government's annual borrowing needs will be $9 billion to $16 billion greater than the annual budget surplus or deficit would indicate.

Figure 1-2.
Total Debt Subject to Limit, August 2000 Through August 2004
(In trillions of dollars)

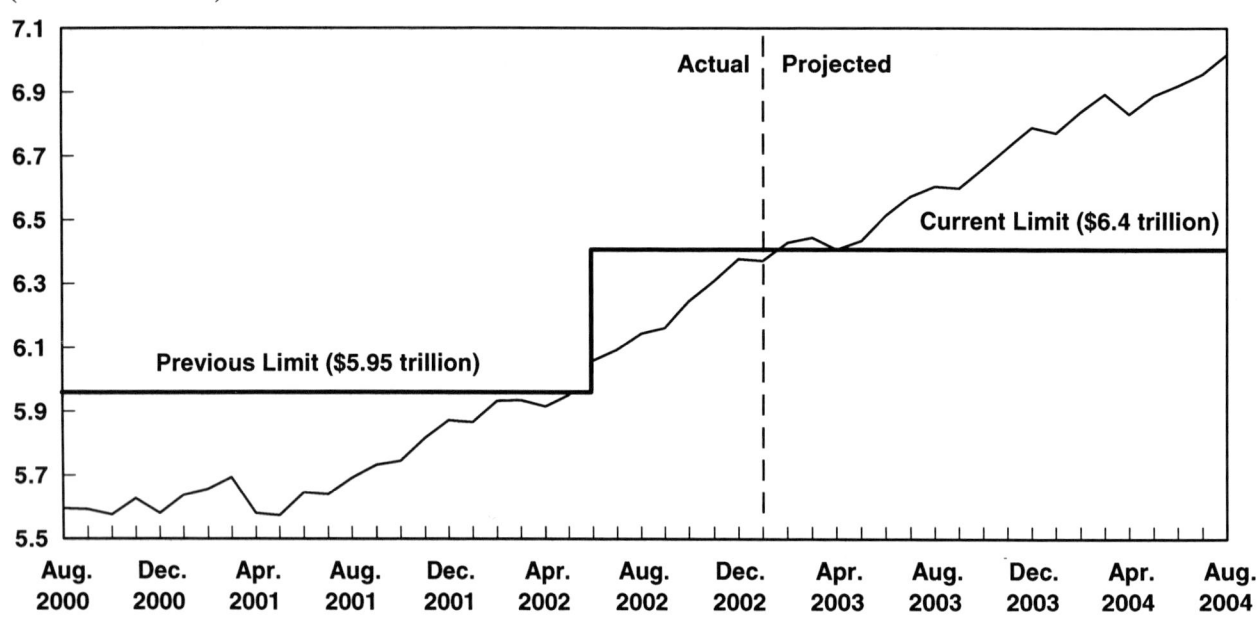

Source: Congressional Budget Office.

Note: These projections incorporate the assumption that discretionary budget authority totals $751 billion for 2003 and grows with inflation thereafter.

In 2002, other means of financing led to a net rise of $63 billion in the government's borrowing—an abnormally large amount. About one-quarter of that total reflected capitalization of financing accounts for credit programs. The remaining $47 billion reflected higher-than-average increases in a host of financing activities, including cash held by the Treasury, cash balances held in commercial banks as compensation for financial services, and premiums paid in the Treasury's bond buyback program.

In CBO's projection of other means of financing for 2003, borrowing rises by $27 billion, or about $10 billion to $15 billion more than in the other years of the projection period. Two factors account for most of that net difference. Purchases of private securities and Treasury debt by the National Railroad Retirement Investment Trust are expected to total about $18 billion; such purchases are counted as a means of financing in the budget. That amount will be partially offset by a decline in the Treasury's cash balance. (CBO assumed that the Treasury would decrease its cash balance by nearly $11 billion over the course of the year to reach its desired year-end target of about $50 billion.) The rest of the difference between the amount estimated for 2003 and the amounts projected for future years is largely attributable to lower projections of the cash flows into financing accounts for credit programs.

Debt Held by Government Accounts
In addition to the securities it sells to the public, the Treasury has issued almost $2.7 trillion in securities to various federal government accounts. All of the major trust funds and many other government funds invest in special, nonmarketable Treasury securities known as the government account series. In practical terms, those securities represent credits to the various government accounts and are redeemed when funds are needed to pay benefits and other expenses. In the meantime, the government pays interest to itself on that debt (that is, it credits interest earnings to the funds holding those securities).

Debt issued to government accounts is handled within the Treasury and does not flow through the credit markets. Because those transactions and the interest accrued

Table 1-5.
CBO's Projections of Trust Fund Surpluses or Deficits

(In billions of dollars)

Trust Funds	Actual 2002	2003	2004	2005	2006	2007	2008	2009	2010	2011	2012	2013
Social Security	159	160	175	194	212	231	250	268	286	303	317	330
Medicare												
Hospital Insurance (Part A)	32	26	28	29	34	34	36	37	38	37	39	36
Supplementary Medical Insurance (Part B)	-3	-7	1	2	2	2	3	3	4	5	5	6
Subtotal	29	19	29	31	36	37	39	40	42	42	45	42
Military Retirement	9	8	9	9	10	10	11	11	12	13	14	15
Civilian Retirement[a]	32	34	34	35	35	36	37	37	38	39	39	40
Unemployment Insurance	-20	-22	-7	3	8	10	10	8	8	7	7	7
Highway and Mass Transit	-5	-7	-6	-4	-3	-2	-2	-1	-1	-1	*	*
Airport and Airway	-3	-2	-2	-2	-2	-2	-1	-1	-1	-1	*	*
Other[b]	3	4	4	3	3	2	2	2	2	2	2	2
Total Trust Fund Surpluses	202	193	236	269	299	322	345	365	385	404	422	435
Intragovernmental Transfers to Trust Funds[c]	343	352	371	396	421	452	486	523	564	612	657	707
Net Budgetary Impact of Trust Fund Programs	-141	-158	-135	-128	-122	-130	-141	-158	-179	-209	-235	-273

Source: Congressional Budget Office.

Note: * = between -$500 million and zero.

a. Includes the Civil Service Retirement, Foreign Service Retirement, and several smaller retirement trust funds.
b. Primarily the trust funds for Railroad Retirement (both Treasury and non-Treasury holdings), federal employees' health and life insurance, and Superfund, and various veterans' insurance trust funds. Beginning in 2003, it also reflects the Department of Defense's Medicare-Eligible Retiree Health Care Fund.
c. Includes interest paid to trust funds, payments from the general fund to the Supplementary Medical Insurance program, the employer's share of employee retirement, lump-sum payments to the Civil Service and Military Retirement Trust Funds, taxes on Social Security benefits, and smaller miscellaneous payments.

on them are intragovernmental, they have no direct effect on the economy and no net effect on the budget. The largest balances of such debt are in the Social Security trust funds (more than $1.3 trillion at the end of 2002) and the retirement funds for federal civilian employees ($574 billion). If current policies remained unchanged, the balance of the Social Security trust funds would rise to $4.1 trillion by 2013, CBO estimates, and the balance of all government accounts would climb to $6.7 trillion.

Gross Federal Debt and Debt Subject to Limit

Gross federal debt and its companion measure, debt subject to limit, comprise debt issued to government accounts as well as debt held by the public. The future path of gross federal debt will be determined by the interaction of those two components. In CBO's projections, gross debt increases every year through 2012 as the growth of debt held by government accounts outpaces the future redemption of debt held by the public. In 2013, the last year of the projection period, slightly more debt could be redeemed (by using the projected surplus) than would be issued to government accounts. However, in developing that estimate, CBO assumed that all provisions of EGTRRA would expire at the end of 2010.

The Treasury's authority to issue debt is restricted by a statutory limit set by the Congress. (The debt subject to limit is nearly identical to gross federal debt, except that it excludes securities issued by agencies other than the Treasury, such as the Tennessee Valley Authority.) The current debt ceiling, which was enacted in June 2002, is $6.4 trillion (*see Figure 1-2*). By CBO's estimates, debt would exceed that limit sometime this year—possibly as early as the end of February—if current laws remained in place.

Trust Funds and the Budget

The federal government has more than 200 trust funds, although fewer than a dozen account for the bulk of trust fund dollars. Among the largest are the two Social Security trust funds (the Old-Age and Survivors Insurance Trust Fund and the Disability Insurance Trust Fund) and those dedicated to Civil Service Retirement, Hospital Insurance (Part A of Medicare), and Military Retirement (*see Table 1-5 on page 19*). Trust funds have no particular economic significance; they do not hold separate cash balances and function primarily as accounting mechanisms to track receipts and spending for programs that have specific taxes or other revenues earmarked for their use.

When a trust fund receives payroll taxes or other income that is not currently needed to pay benefits, the excess is loaned to the Treasury. As a result, the government borrows less from the public, collects less in taxes, or spends more on other programs or activities than it would in the absence of those excess funds. The process is reversed when revenues for a trust fund program fall short of its expenses. In that case, the government raises the necessary cash by borrowing more, collecting more in taxes, or spending less on other programs or activities than it otherwise would.

Including the cash receipts and expenditures of trust funds in the budget totals with other federal programs is necessary to assess how federal activities affect the economy and capital markets. CBO, the Office of Management and Budget, and other fiscal analysts therefore focus on the total surplus or deficit.

In CBO's current baseline, trust funds as a whole are projected to run a surplus of $193 billion in 2003. That balance is somewhat misleading, however, because trust funds receive much of their income in the form of transfers from other parts of the budget. Such intragovernmental transfers reallocate costs from one part of the budget to another; they do not change the total surplus or the government's borrowing needs. Consequently, they have no effect on the economy or on the government's future ability to sustain spending at the levels indicated by current policies. For 2003, those intragovernmental transfers are estimated to total $352 billion. The largest of them involve interest credited to trust funds on their government securities ($156 billion in CBO's projections); transfers of federal funds to Medicare for Hospital Insurance, or Part A ($9 billion), and Supplementary Medical Insurance, or Part B ($83 billion); and contributions by government agencies to retirement funds for their current and former employees ($41 billion). When intragovernmental transfers are excluded and only income from sources outside the government is counted, the trust funds as a whole are projected to run deficits every year in the projection period; those shortfalls grow from $158 billion in 2003 to $273 billion in 2013.

Although the budgetary impact of the baby-boom generation's aging will not be completely realized during the 2003-2013 period, CBO's current projections provide initial indications of the coming budgetary pressures. Charting the differences between projected receipts and outlays for the Social Security and Medicare Hospital Insurance trust funds (excluding intragovernmental interest payments) illustrates that point (*see Figure 1-3*). Under current policies, receipts would exceed expenditures throughout the period, but after reaching nearly $130 billion between 2008 and 2011, the excess of revenues over outlays would fall to about $110 billion in 2013. At that point, outlays would be increasing by almost 7 percent per year, but annual growth of noninterest receipts would be only slightly higher than 5 percent. Thus, in CBO's projections, the capacity of the Social Security and Medicare Hospital Insurance trust funds to offset some of the net deficit in the rest of the budget—as they currently do—will begin to dwindle during the coming decade. Shortly thereafter, those programs are projected to begin adding to deficits or reducing surpluses.

Figure 1-3.
Surpluses or Deficits (Excluding Interest) of the Social Security and Medicare Hospital Insurance Trust Funds

(In billions of dollars)

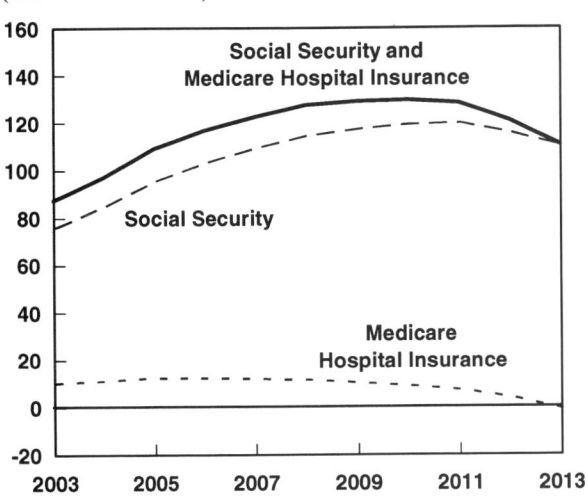

Source: Congressional Budget Office.

Note: Hospital Insurance surpluses are calculated with adjustments for shifts in the timing of payments to Medicare+Choice plans in 2005, 2006, 2011, and 2012.

The Expiration of Budget Enforcement Procedures

The rules that formed the basic framework for budgetary decisionmaking for more than a decade—the annual limits on discretionary appropriations and the pay-as-you-go requirement for new mandatory spending or revenue laws—expired on September 30, 2002. That framework was established by the Budget Enforcement Act of 1990 (and later extensions) to enforce a series of multiyear budget agreements aimed at reducing and eliminating budget deficits. In general, the procedures were meant to ensure that the net budgetary effects of new laws would not increase projected deficits (or lower projected surpluses).

Although the effectiveness of the Budget Enforcement Act was mixed, lawmakers are facing the issue of whether that framework should be revived or something similar to it instituted. CBO's adjusted baseline shows the return of deficits as short-lived. However, the uncertainty of those estimates and the near and long-term budgetary pressures that confront lawmakers may necessitate some type of statutory framework of constraints. (For details on the expiration of budget enforcement procedures, see Appendix A.)

CHAPTER 2

The Economic Outlook

The economy continues to suffer from some aftereffects of the bursting of the "bubble economy" of the late 1990s. Although consumer spending is expanding moderately, business investment remains weak, and financial markets are uncertain about the durability of the current recovery. Nevertheless, the Congressional Budget Office believes that the stage is set for stronger economic activity this year—an opinion shared by many private-sector economists, as represented by the *Blue Chip* consensus forecast.

Much of the boom of the late 1990s was based on persistently faster growth in productivity. However, the tremendous surges in the stock market and in investment spending that occurred at that time were partly based on expectations for corporate profits that are now understood to have been unreasonable. That "bubble" part of the boom burst in early 2000, and the following year the economy entered a relatively shallow recession (as measured by the drop in output). The economy recovered in 2002, but it was buffeted by revelations that a small number of notable corporations had engaged in accounting irregularities during the bubble years. Those revelations shook the confidence of investors, consumers, and businesses. The stock market fell sharply again, and private-sector employment declined in the second half of the year.

The strength of the economy in 2003 depends in large part on whether consumer spending will continue to provide the economy's foundation. Throughout the 2001 recession and the early recovery, the household sector has been a source of strength. Expansionary fiscal and monetary policies are partly responsible for that strength: the lowest mortgage interest rates since the 1960s have triggered a wave of refinancing and contributed to a boom in housing, zero percent financing has spurred sales of cars and light trucks, and tax cuts have bolstered disposable income. Those factors have largely offset the drag on consumer spending caused by declines in the stock market. In the future, however, they will play a smaller role in supporting spending. Thus, the growth of consumer spending will depend primarily on the growth of personal income.

The prospects for personal income in the short run are uncertain, however, because demand is anemic in many other parts of the economy. Spending by the business sector remains weak, as low corporate profits and excess capacity from overinvestment during the bubble years have inhibited investment. Uncertainty about the strength of demand and about the risks arising from terrorism and war have led businesses to be particularly cautious in hiring. In addition, state and local governments have had their spending weakened by deteriorating finances.

Nevertheless, some indicators point to a brighter outlook for the economy this year. Investors and consumers appear to have gained a bit more confidence about the economy in recent months. The stock market has tentatively moved upward since its low in October. The spread between interest rates on corporate bonds and Treasury notes narrowed slightly toward the end of 2002, suggesting that credit markets are somewhat less worried about corporate finances than they were earlier in the year. Consumer sentiment and expectations also appear to have stabilized late last year. Business spending on equipment and software, particularly on information technology, appears to have strengthened in 2002, and inventories may be reaching the point at which businesses need to restock their shelves. Finally, a drop in the exchange value of the U.S. dollar is conducive to stronger growth of exports.

CBO's economic forecast expects the recovery to continue, with real (inflation-adjusted) gross domestic product growing by 2.5 percent in calendar year 2003 and 3.6 percent in 2004 (see Table 2-1). That growth is slower than in most past recoveries but is comparable to the pace after the 1990-1991 recession (see Figure 2-1). The growth of housing investment is expected to slow substantially, while real spending for personal consumption should continue to increase by about 3 percent a year. Investment in producers' durable equipment is expected to recover, but investment in structures will remain weak for some time. In CBO's forecast, the unemployment rate is stable in 2003, averaging 5.9 percent, and then edges down only to an average rate of 5.7 percent in 2004. As the recovery achieves a firmer footing, the Federal Reserve is assumed to shift monetary policy gradually from its current accommodative stance toward a more neutral one; consequently, both short-term and long-term interest rates are expected to rise in late 2003 and during 2004. In this near-term forecast, inflation—as measured by the consumer price index for all urban consumers (CPI-U)—remains below 2.5 percent a year.

CBO's forecast assumes that there will be no significant repercussions for the U.S. economy from any war with Iraq and no shocks to the economy from major acts of terrorism. However, uncertainty about war and terrorism may continue to weigh on consumers and businesses, either directly or through its impact on stock prices. The forecast assumes that such uncertainty is not fully re-

Table 2-1.

CBO's Economic Projections for Calendar Years 2003 Through 2013

	Estimated 2002	Forecast 2003	Forecast 2004	Projected Annual Average 2005-2008	Projected Annual Average 2009-2013
Nominal GDP (Billions of dollars)	10,443	10,880	11,465	14,154[a]	18,066[b]
Nominal GDP (Percentage change)	3.6	4.2	5.4	5.4	5.0
Real GDP (Percentage change)	2.4	2.5	3.6	3.2	2.7
GDP Price Index (Percentage change)	1.1	1.6	1.7	2.1	2.2
Consumer Price Index[c] (Percentage change)	1.6	2.3	2.2	2.5	2.5
Unemployment Rate (Percent)	5.8	5.9	5.7	5.3	5.2
Three-Month Treasury Bill Rate (Percent)	1.6	1.4	3.5	4.9	4.9
Ten-Year Treasury Note Rate (Percent)	4.6	4.4	5.2	5.8	5.8
Tax Bases (Percentage of GDP)					
Corporate book profits	6.2	6.8	7.3	9.2	8.4
Wages and salaries	48.1	48.1	48.1	48.0	47.8
Tax Bases (Billions of dollars)					
Corporate book profits	653	739	842	1,267[a]	1,474[b]
Wages and salaries	5,025	5,237	5,518	6,782[a]	8,635[b]

Sources: Congressional Budget Office; Department of Commerce, Bureau of Economic Analysis; Department of Labor, Bureau of Labor Statistics; Federal Reserve Board.

Notes: Percentage changes are year over year.

Year-by-year economic projections for calendar and fiscal years 2003 through 2013 appear in Appendix E.

a. Level in 2008.
b. Level in 2013.
c. The consumer price index for all urban consumers.

CHAPTER TWO THE ECONOMIC OUTLOOK 25

Figure 2-1.

The Economic Forecast and Projections

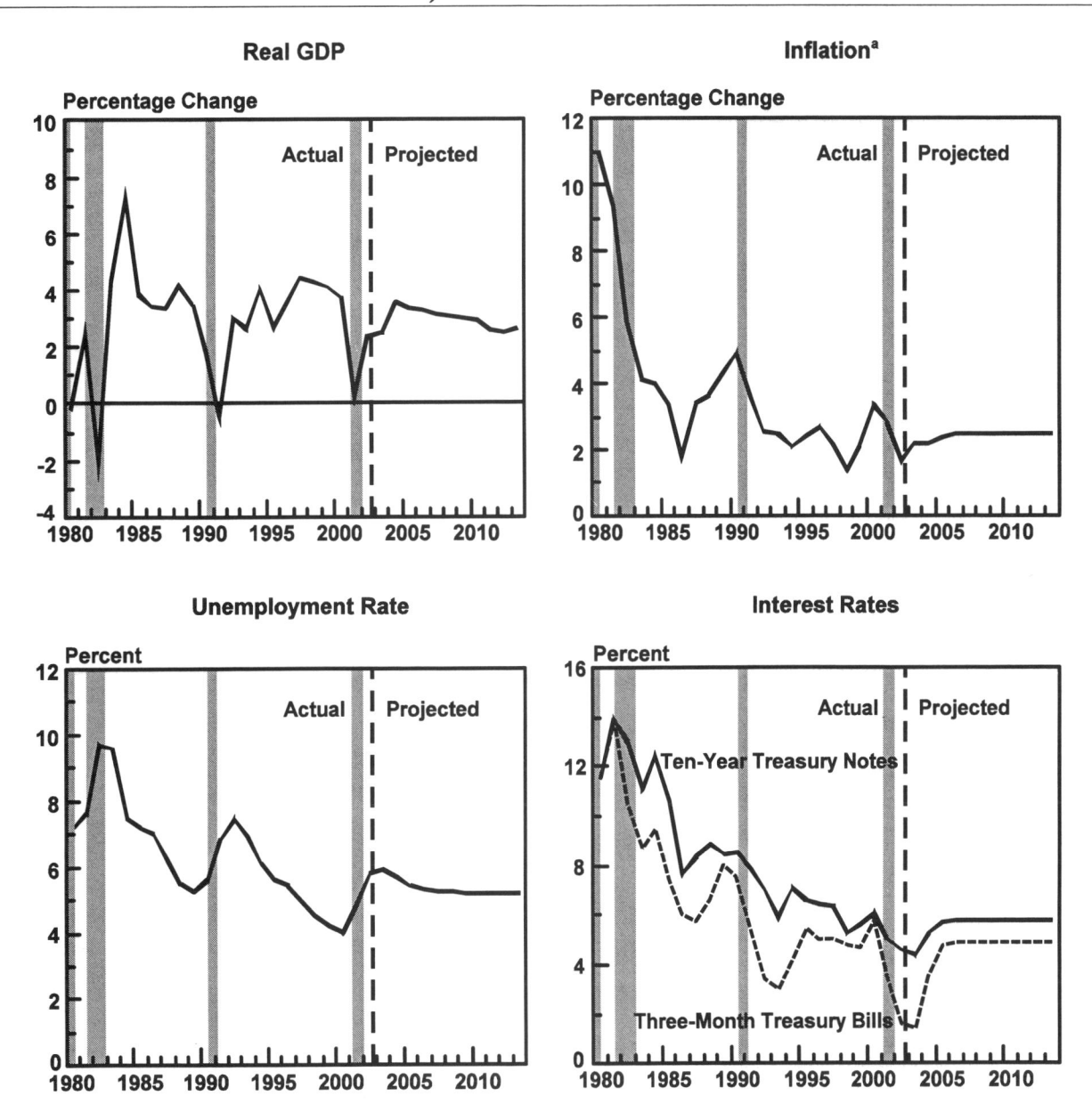

Real GDP
Percentage Change
Actual | Projected

Inflation[a]
Percentage Change
Actual | Projected

Unemployment Rate
Percent
Actual | Projected

Interest Rates
Percent
Actual | Projected
Ten-Year Treasury Notes
Three-Month Treasury Bills

Sources: Congressional Budget Office; Department of Commerce, Bureau of Economic Analysis; Department of Labor, Bureau of Labor Statistics; Federal Reserve Board.

Note: All data are annual values; percentage changes are year over year.

a. The change in the consumer price index for all urban consumers, applying the current methodology to historical price data (CPI-U-RS).

Box 2-1.
The Economic Effects of Expiring Tax Cuts

The Economic Growth and Tax Relief Reconciliation Act of 2001 (EGTRRA) is scheduled to expire in 2010. As a result, under current law, marginal income tax rates will rise in 2011, provisions for child credits and marriage-penalty relief will cease to apply, and estate and gift taxes will be reinstated. That expiration (often called a sunset) will also affect provisions in the tax code for pensions, individual retirement accounts, education, and miscellaneous items. (Those effects are described in detail in Chapter 3.)

The sunset of the 2001 tax law will have a complicated impact on the economy. The expiration of some provisions (such as those affecting marginal tax rates) will reduce gross domestic product, whereas the sunset of other provisions (such as the child credits) will increase it. On net, CBO estimates, the expiration of EGTRRA will lower GDP by about half a percent by 2013. That estimate is very uncertain, however, and CBO may revise that figure as it continues to analyze the issue.[1]

The major economic effect of the sunset stems from the rise in marginal tax rates. Those rates influence people's incentives to work and save because they determine how much additional income taxpayers can keep when they decide to work an extra hour or save an extra dollar. The sunset will also decrease the proportion of total income that is subject to taxation—as marginal tax rates rise, more people may seek to shelter more of their income by taking it in nontaxable rather than taxable forms.[2]

CBO estimates that in 2011, the first year after EGTRRA expires, the effective marginal tax rate on labor will rise by about 1.8 percentage points, while the effective tax rate on capital will increase by 0.6 percentage points (*see the table*). Those changes in effective tax rates are smaller than the changes in statutory income tax rates that will occur, because some income is not taxed.

Effective Marginal Income Tax Rates, 2001-2013
(In percent)

	Tax Rate on Labor	Tax Rate on Capital
2001	20.7	15.5
2002	20.5	15.5
2003	20.7	15.5
2004	20.3	15.4
2005	20.3	15.4
2006	19.9	15.1
2007	20.1	15.1
2008	20.3	15.1
2009	20.5	15.1
2010	20.7	15.1
2011	22.5	15.7
2012	22.8	15.7
2013	22.9	15.7

Source: Congressional Budget Office.

Note: Includes federal individual and corporate income taxes; excludes payroll taxes.

In the three years between the end of 2010 and the end of CBO's current projection period, the largest economic effects of the higher tax rates are likely to involve labor supply, which may shrink by between 0.4 percent and 1.2 percent from what it would have otherwise been. National saving, by contrast, is likely to rise.[3] But in a period as short as three years, changes in saving—and consequent increases in the capital stock—will probably not be large enough to offset the impact of a reduction in labor supply on the nation's productive capacity.

Economic outcomes could also be affected by the extent to which people anticipate the 2011 tax increase ahead of time. Workers who know that taxes will rise in a few years

---

1. The effect of taxes on the economy remains an unsettled area of economics. Some models suggest that GDP could decline by more than half a percent from the sunset of EGTRRA; other models suggest that GDP might increase.

2. Estimates of the increase in the extent of tax sheltering are normally the responsibility of the Joint Committee on Taxation. Preliminary CBO estimates are reflected in the Box 1-2 table in Chapter 1 and in Table 3-11 in Chapter 3.

3. National saving includes both government saving and private saving. Although private saving will probably decline because of the increase in marginal tax rates, government saving will rise (under current law) from the additional tax revenues. Simulations with several models suggest that, on net, national saving is likely to increase.

Box 2-1.
Continued

may tend to adjust their work so as to concentrate their income in the years before taxes go up. For instance, people close to retirement may work overtime in the lower-tax years and then retire somewhat earlier when taxes increase. Second earners in married-couple households may choose to work and earn income when taxes are relatively low and then leave the labor force when taxes are high. Thus, anticipation of the tax increase might increase GDP before 2011. However, people have different opinions about when and whether the tax law will expire—and also have widely varying opportunities to shift their income from one year to another—so making projections about those anticipatory responses is difficult. CBO assumed that, on average, anticipation of the tax increase would boost the annual level of GDP by less than 0.05 percent between now and 2011.

The economic effects of the sunset during CBO's projection period will also depend on people's expectations about what policymakers will do in later years (after 2013). Logically, there are several alternatives. CBO's budget baseline assumes that tax rates will be higher from 2011 to 2013, but because that baseline extends only through 2013, CBO is not required to make any specific assumption for subsequent years. One possibility is that the additional revenues and lower debt will allow taxes to be lower at some point after 2013 than they would be otherwise. If so, some people may choose to work less than they otherwise would when tax rates are high (such as between 2011 and 2013) but work more later when tax rates are low. Alternatively, people may assume that taxes will remain relatively high and that the additional revenues will lead to higher levels of spending. In that case, people will not change their labor supply as much as in the previous example. In any event, it is unclear when—or even if—people expect any of those changes to take place.

Simulations from economic models suggest that assumptions about future policy can significantly influence the long-term impact of a tax increase. If people expect that paying more taxes now means that tax rates can be lower in the future, GDP is generally higher in the long run. But if people think higher tax rates now mean that government consumption can be higher in the future (rather than taxes lower), then GDP is likely to be lower in the long run. However, those uncertainties affect the period after 2013 much more than the years from 2011 to 2013. CBO's simulations suggest that regardless of the policy choices made after the projection period, the sunset of EGTRRA will decrease GDP in the last three years of that period, although the amount of the decrease varies according to what is assumed about future policy. CBO was unable to determine what assumption about future policy was most appropriate. Thus, in constructing its baseline, CBO simply chose to use an average from a number of different assumptions and different models of the economy.

The estimated budgetary implications of those scenarios are strikingly small compared with the overall uncertainty of 10-year budget projections. (That uncertainty is detailed in Chapter 5.) The economic weakening caused by even so large a tax increase as the one that will occur when EGTRRA expires could reduce revenues by about $40 billion: $6 billion in 2011, $15 billion in 2012, and $18 billion in 2013. (The tax increase itself is expected to raise annual revenues by a total of about $600 billion over those three years). To the extent that people anticipate the tax increase and boost their taxable income in the lower-tax years before the sunset, revenues could be increased in those years. As a result, the economic repercussions of the sunset are likely to reduce revenues by less than that $40 billion over the entire 10-year period. By contrast, the difference between reasonably optimistic and pessimistic budget projections could amount to more than $6 trillion over those 10 years (see Chapter 5)—more than 100 times the difference caused by the tax increase. Clearly, even large percentage errors in calculating the economic impact of the sunset would play little role in the overall uncertainty of long-term budget projections.

A sudden tax increase such as that caused by the expiration of EGTRRA after 2010 might also risk creating a short-term economic slowdown. CBO does not attempt to forecast the cyclical movement of the economy more than two years ahead, so its baseline does not contain a recession in 2010. In the case of EGTRRA, moreover, it may not be reasonable to expect that the sunset would cause much of a slowdown. To the extent that disruptions would predictably affect the unemployment rate and inflation, the Federal Reserve could anticipate and offset those disruptions. Its task might be more difficult, however, if tax policy remained unclear in the years before the sunset.

solved in the near term. (For a discussion of how war might affect the U.S. economy under several alternative military scenarios, see Chapter 5.)

Beyond 2004, CBO projects that growth of real GDP will average 3.2 percent a year from 2005 through 2008 and then slow to 2.7 percent a year from 2009 through 2013. That downward trend in economic growth over the next decade primarily reflects slower growth in the labor force as the oldest members of the baby-boom generation begin to retire. The unemployment rate is expected to average 5.2 percent after 2008.

CBO's baseline projections reflect current law, which includes the expiration of the tax-cutting Economic Growth and Tax Relief Reconciliation Act of 2001 at the end of 2010. Thus, in CBO's baseline, tax rates will return to their pre-2001 levels in 2011. The expiration of that law will have complicated effects on the economy, although those effects are small relative to the overall uncertainty of the economic forecast (*see Box 2-1 on pages 26 and 27*). The most noticeable impact is that the growth of real GDP is reduced in 2011 and 2012.

Recent Economic Developments

The slow recovery from the 2001 recession continues. Consumer spending is still rising—helped by moderate growth in wages and salaries, the contribution of lower income tax rates to disposable income, and proceeds from the refinancing of home mortgages, but hindered by a decline in stock market wealth. The housing market, fueled by low interest rates, has been a consistent source of strength. Investment in business equipment has begun to revive, as some of the excess capacity built up in the late 1990s has been worked off. But that investment remains weak because of subdued demand.

Financial Market Conditions

The Federal Reserve has eased monetary policy aggressively since the beginning of 2001, including cutting the federal funds rate by 0.5 percentage points in November 2002 (*see Figure 2-2*). Nevertheless, overall conditions in financial markets have not been conducive to economic growth. The plunge in stock values last year has substantially reduced household wealth and at the same time has raised businesses' cost of capital. Meanwhile, overall interest rates on corporate bonds have not fallen in tandem with rates on long-term Treasury securities because investors continue to perceive businesses as having a high risk of default. That perception has also caused banks to keep loan standards tight for many corporate borrowers. Those standards, along with weak demand for loans, have contributed to a relatively large drop in bank loans to businesses, even though the banking system is in good shape.

One way to assess the impact on the economy of overall conditions in financial markets is to use an index—such as the one calculated by Macroeconomic Advisers (MA), a private forecasting firm—that combines the stance of monetary policy with a quantitative assessment of the channels through which that policy operates. MA's index draws on statistical relationships between GDP and financial variables such as interest rates, exchange rates, and measures of the stock market. It suggests that despite the Federal Reserve's policies, financial market conditions deteriorated sharply in 2002 (*see Figure 2-3*). The stimulative effect of the decline in short-term interest rates has been more than counteracted by the drop in the stock

Figure 2-2.

The Federal Funds Interest Rate

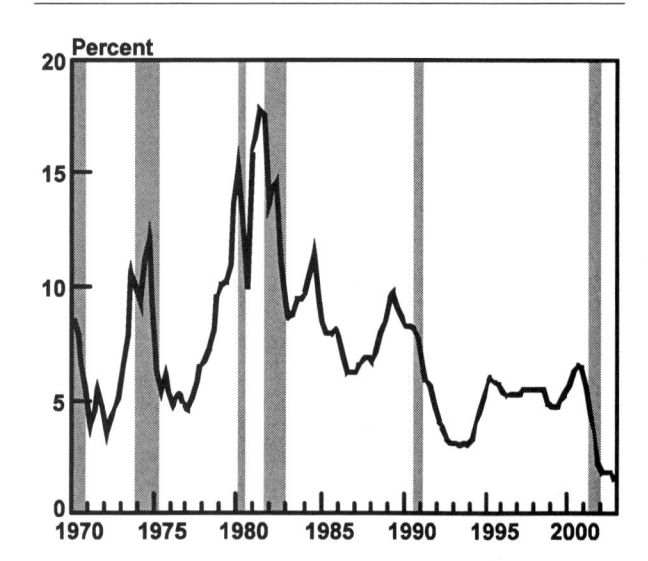

Sources: Congressional Budget Office; Federal Reserve Board.

Note: The federal funds rate is the interest rate that banks charge for overnight loans.

Figure 2-3.
An Index of Monetary and Financial Conditions

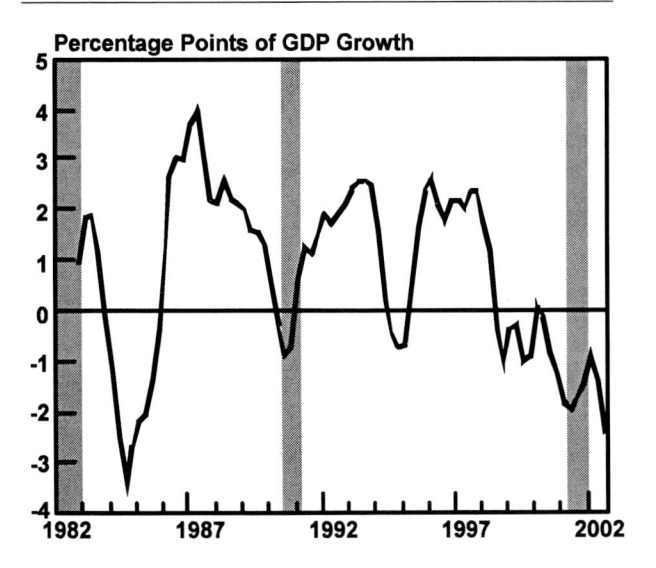

Sources: Congressional Budget Office; Macroeconomic Advisers, LLC.

Note: The index measures how financial variables such as interest rates, exchange rates, and the stock market affect the growth rate of real (inflation-adjusted) GDP.

market and the still-elevated interest rates on corporate bonds, especially for riskier companies.

Although the Federal Reserve acted quickly and aggressively to bolster the economy in 2001—before the recession was generally acknowledged—by early in 2002 its rate-cutting cycle appeared to have ended. The March 2002 statement of the Federal Open Market Committee (FOMC) noted that with a recovery under way, risks to its twin goals of price stability and sustainable economic growth had become balanced. By the committee's August meeting, however, the recovery seemed to be in danger of stalling, and the FOMC shifted back toward the view that risks were more heavily weighted toward economic weakness than toward inflation. That shift was followed by a cut in the target federal funds rate (to 1.25 percent) in early November, when the FOMC cited "greater uncertainty, in part attributable to heightened geopolitical risks, . . . currently inhibiting spending, production, and employment." The FOMC suggested that after the November cut, risks were once again in balance; as of mid-January, financial markets believe that further rate reductions are unlikely.

The stimulative effect of that monetary policy has been partly offset by a moribund stock market. The market typically rises at the beginning of a recovery, but the broad-based Standard & Poor's 500 index fell by 23 percent last year—the third consecutive year of decline. Analysts believe that decline was caused not only by uncertainty about the viability of the recovery but also by new concerns about corporate governance and the integrity of corporate earnings reports.

The corporate bond market has also counterbalanced some of the stimulative impact of monetary policy, as rates on corporate bonds have fallen less than interest rates on Treasury bonds of comparable maturity. In fact, the spread between interest rates on Treasury bonds and rates on corporate bonds—including those of investment grade—has increased to levels not seen since the early to mid-1980s (*see Figure 2-4*). The bond market is still plagued by the lingering effects of the late 1990s boom and its aftermath, when a number of once-high-flying firms (such as Enron and WorldCom) wound up defaulting. Through the end of 2002, credit-rating firms continued to issue more downgrades than upgrades. That

Figure 2-4.
Interest Rate Spreads on Corporate Bonds

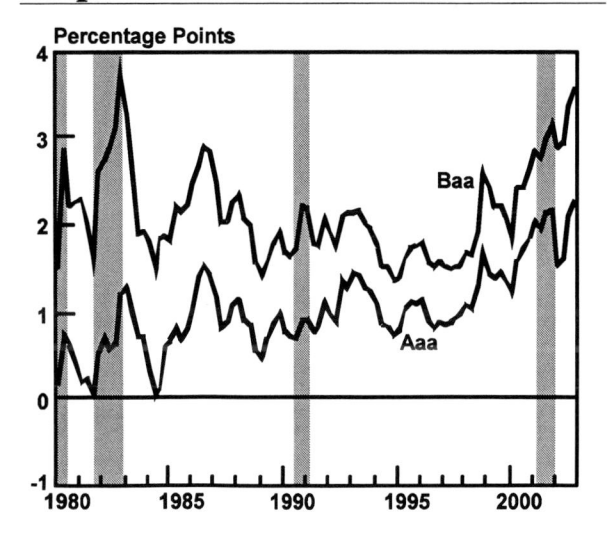

Sources: Congressional Budget Office; Federal Reserve Board.

Note: These spreads measure the difference between interest rates on corporate bonds with an Aaa or Baa rating and interest rates on 10-year Treasury notes. The higher the spread, the riskier that investors believe corporate bonds to be.

situation, along with the perception that default risks are still high, is keeping the spread between interest rates wide, in contrast to the marked narrowing that typically occurs during the early stages of a recovery. Although conditions in the bond market appear to be stabilizing, any improvement in that market remains tentative, hampered by uncertainty about the durability of the recovery.

Even so, less risky industrial and financial borrowers can still raise funds in credit markets, albeit subject to those wide spreads. The level of net new issues in the domestic bond market (although down by 26 percent from its high in 2001) amounted to nearly $500 billion during the first three quarters of 2002. New debt backed by collateral amounted to another $360 billion, up by 12 percent from a year earlier. Insurance companies and mutual funds have been significant buyers of corporate bonds, and foreigners remain substantial purchasers.

The banking system as a whole is healthy, although lending standards are still tight. Unlike in the early 1990s, few banks face difficulties from inadequate capitalization. In fact, bank capitalization has improved since the start of the recession. Nevertheless, banks have tightened their standards and terms of lending in the face of heightened uncertainty about the economy. Consequently, overall bank lending has grown at a tepid pace—one that is characteristic of recessions and early recoveries rather than expansions.

The Household Sector

Spending by households held up well last year despite the continued drop in the stock market. Real personal consumption expenditures rose at an average annual rate of 3 percent during the first three quarters of 2002, only about half a percentage point less than the average growth rate during the post-World War II period. (Those expenditures rose at a slightly higher rate, 3.1 percent, excluding spending on motor vehicles and parts.) In the fourth quarter of 2002, nominal retail and food-service sales grew by only 1.2 percent overall—but by a stronger 4.4 percent excluding motor vehicles and parts.[1] Both new and existing home sales reached record highs in 2002.

---

1. Data on real personal consumption expenditures for the fourth quarter of 2002 were not available when this report went to press.

Figure 2-5.
Employment in the Private Nonfarm Sector

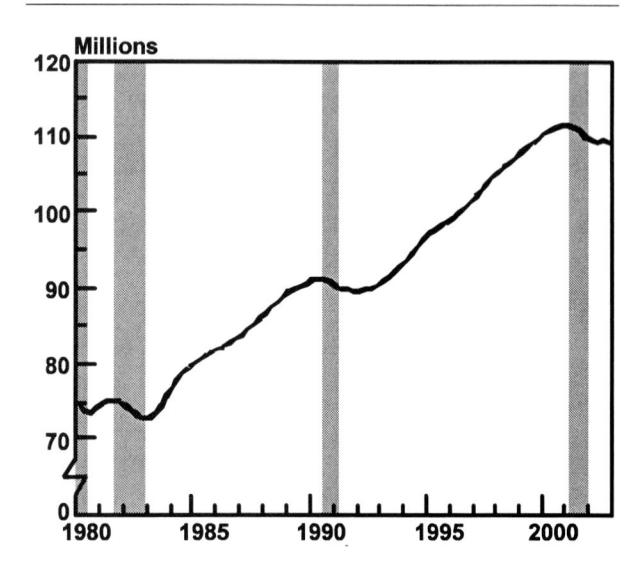

Sources: Congressional Budget Office; Department of Labor, Bureau of Labor Statistics.

Household spending last year was bolstered by strong gains in disposable income, rising home values, near-record-low mortgage rates, and sales incentives for motor vehicles. Moderate growth in wages and salaries supported the growth of disposable income, which received a sharp boost from lower income tax payments. The continued rise in home values in many areas, combined with low mortgage interest rates, encouraged homeowners to refinance their mortgages to reduce their interest costs. Many homeowners also took out some equity from their homes when they refinanced so they could spend more on consumer goods and home improvements or repay other debts. Particularly attractive sales incentives boosted automobile purchases at the end of 2002. Strong growth in household borrowing, despite the opportunity to reduce debt-service burdens through refinancing, led to a slight deterioration in the financial health of households last year.

Employment and Income. A slight decline in employment was the reason that wages and salaries grew only moderately last year. Private nonfarm payroll employment decreased by 0.4 percent (or 438,000) between December 2001 and December 2002, despite the growth in real output (*see Figure 2-5*). Although employment appeared to stabilize during the middle of 2002, it began declining again, with a net 189,000 jobs lost in November and December. The manufacturing sector, which accounted for much of the total employment loss, continued to shed jobs at the end of last year, albeit at a slower pace than during the recession. Manufacturing employment looked poised for recovery in the spring of 2002, as the average workweek rose from its low of late 2001 and the pace of job loss slowed. After that, however, the gains in average weekly manufacturing hours disappeared, and the rate of job loss quickened. The temporary-help industry exhibited modest increases throughout the spring and summer of 2002, but they mostly evaporated late in the year. Employment in services (excluding temporary help) has resumed growing, but at a pace that is slower than typically occurs during a robust recovery.

Despite a choppy monthly pattern, the broad movement in the unemployment rate reflects the weak employment picture. That rate reached a cyclical high of 6.0 percent in April 2002, up from an average of just 4.0 percent in 2000 (*see Figure 2-6*). The unemployment rate subsequently declined to 5.6 percent before climbing back to 6.0 percent at the end of 2002.

Figure 2-6.
Civilian Unemployment Rate

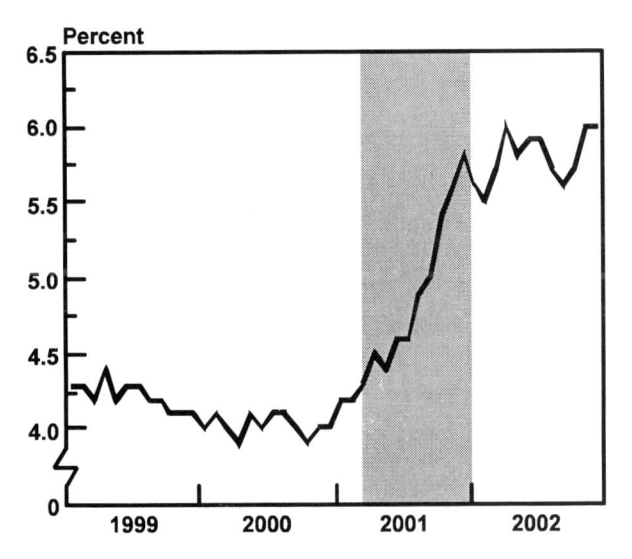

Sources: Congressional Budget Office; Department of Labor, Bureau of Labor Statistics.

Figure 2-7.
Growth in Disposable Income

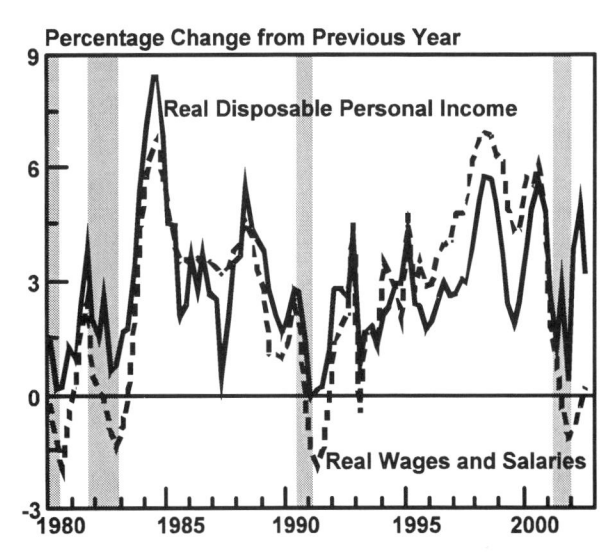

Sources: Congressional Budget Office; Department of Commerce, Bureau of Economic Analysis.

In spite of the decline in employment, real wage and salary income has begun increasing, offering modest support for household spending (*see Figure 2-7*). Wages and salaries in the private sector rose at an annual rate of 3.1 percent in the second quarter of 2002 and 3.7 percent in the third quarter; they appear to have risen at a 3 percent to 4 percent rate in the fourth quarter. Because productivity is growing rapidly, employers have been able to increase workers' real hourly wages without hampering profits. That wage growth has outstripped price increases (consumer price inflation is running in the 2 percent to 2.5 percent range), which has allowed for a modest recovery in households' purchasing power.

In addition to higher wages and salaries, lower tax payments substantially augmented the growth of disposable income and supported consumer spending in late 2001 and 2002. Most households received tax rebates in the third quarter of 2001 (up to $600 for joint tax returns). At the same time, a decline of 1 percentage point in tax rates for people in the 28 percent and higher brackets went into effect. Beginning in January 2002, rates of withholding from paychecks were adjusted to take into account the new 10 percent bracket. Those various tax cuts reduced tax payments by about $67 billion in calendar year 2002. The amount of taxes owed by households fell significantly more than that, however, because of the weak economy, reduced realizations of stock options and capital gains, and fewer people in the highest tax brackets.

In all, real disposable personal income rose at an annual rate of 7.0 percent between the fourth quarter of 2001 and the third quarter of 2002—a stronger pace than in most past recoveries. More than half of that growth resulted from lower tax payments rather than higher pretax income. Unless lawmakers reach agreement on current proposals for additional fiscal stimulus, tax cuts will not provide further stimulus this year. In that case, additional increases in disposable income will have to come mainly from improved labor market conditions and wage gains.

Household Net Wealth. The continued drop in the stock market further eroded the net wealth of households last year (*see Figure 2-8*). Between the end of 2001 and the third quarter of 2002 (the latest data available), net household wealth dropped by $2.8 trillion because of the decline in stock prices. That decline probably reduced nominal consumer spending by around $100 billion, or slightly less than 1½ percent. Given the small rise in the stock market at the end of 2002, it seems likely that net wealth did not deteriorate further in the fourth quarter.

Thus far, the personal saving rate has not responded noticeably to last year's drop in net wealth, and the possibility exists of a sharp rise in the saving rate (and a concomitant decrease in consumer spending), which would reduce economic growth. That risk is not included in CBO's forecast (*see Box 2-2*).

The effect of falling stock prices on household wealth has been counteracted, to a limited degree, by rising housing prices. In the third quarter of 2002, prices of single-family homes were 6.2 percent higher than in the same quarter a year earlier, according to the Office of Federal Housing Enterprise Oversight. Those high housing prices have combined with low interest rates to trigger a boom in mortgage refinancing. Refinancing activity last year surpassed the record pace of 2001 by 37 percent. When homeowners refinance mortgages, many of them convert some of their accumulated housing equity into cash. Survey data indicate that roughly half of those proceeds are typically used for either consumer spending or home improvements. Thus, the refinancing boom probably con-

tributed a few tenths of a percentage point to last year's growth in personal consumption spending.

The Financial Health of the Household Sector. Consumers' financial health has eroded slightly, and households are more indebted than they were before the 2001 recession. As a result, the household sector is vulnerable to financial problems should the growth of income falter.

Real household debt has risen much faster than is normally seen during a recession and early recovery. The growth of real mortgage debt continued to accelerate in 2002, to its fastest pace since 1990, and consumer credit grew a bit more slowly than disposable personal income. Because interest rates have stayed low, the rapid rise in debt has not increased households' debt-service burden markedly. But that burden has not fallen, as it typically does during and immediately after a recession.

The rate of delinquencies on conventional mortgages has increased in the past few years (although it is lower than in the 1981-1982 recession and about the same as during the 1990-1991 recession). The delinquency rate is especially large on higher-risk FHA loans (*see Figure 2-9*).

Figure 2-8.
Household Net Wealth

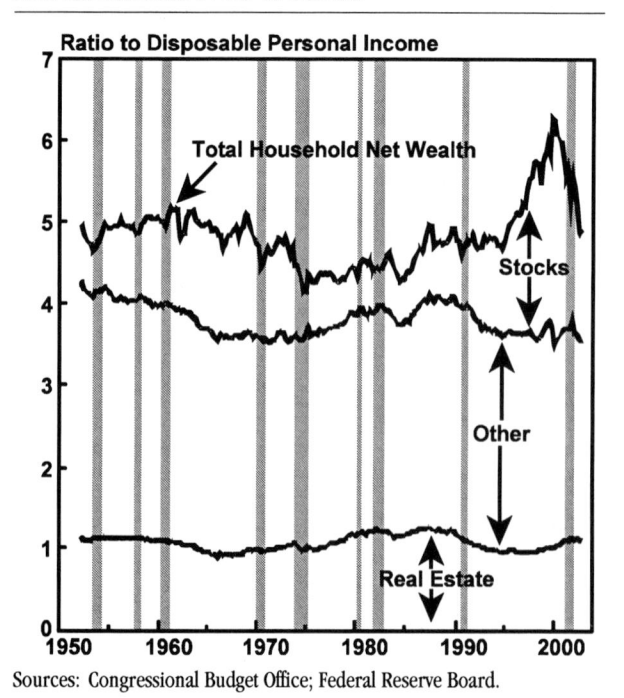

Ratio to Disposable Personal Income

Sources: Congressional Budget Office; Federal Reserve Board.

Box 2-2.
The Wealth Effect and Personal Saving

The unusually low rate of personal saving in recent years prompts concern about the strength of consumer spending in 2003. Between 1994 and 1999, the personal saving rate (personal saving as a percentage of disposable income) averaged only 4.7 percent, considerably below the average of 8.7 percent before 1994. Economists believe that a key reason for that low rate was a tremendous increase in stock prices and thus in consumers' net wealth. Between 1993 and 1999, consumers' net wealth rose by an astounding $18.3 trillion, and the ratio of net wealth to disposable personal income grew from 4.9 to 6.4—the highest level since at least 1952. That sharp rise in wealth allowed consumers to increase their spending faster than their income rose, causing the personal saving rate to plummet—from 7.1 percent in 1993 to 2.6 percent in 1999. Since 1999, by contrast, consumer net wealth has fallen markedly, and the ratio of net wealth to income has declined nearly to its value in 1993. But the personal saving rate has not risen to anywhere near its 1993 level. If consumers curtail their spending in an attempt to raise their saving rate to levels typically seen before the 1990s, they could undermine the economic recovery.

Current data, however, suggest that the personal saving rate may not return to the levels that prevailed before the 1990s. The reason is that the relationship between the personal saving rate and the ratio of consumers' net wealth to disposable income seems to have undergone a fundamental shift. That change is visible in the figure at right. The higher group of data points shows the relationship between the saving rate and the wealth-to-income ratio from 1952 to 1993; the lower set of points shows that relationship from 1994 to 2002. Trend lines drawn through the two groups of data points illustrate the shift. Although the wealth-to-income ratio in the third quarter of 2002 (4.9, the latest figure available) is within the 1952-1993 range of values, the personal saving rate in that quarter (3.8 percent) is below even the post-1993 trend.

Why the relationship shifted in 1994 is unclear. One possibility is that the change is a statistical artifact that will disappear in future data revisions. In recent years, the Department of Commerce's Bureau of Economic Analysis has frequently revised the saving rate upward on the basis of more complete data and other changes when it annually revises the national income and product accounts.

Personal Saving Rate Versus Net Wealth

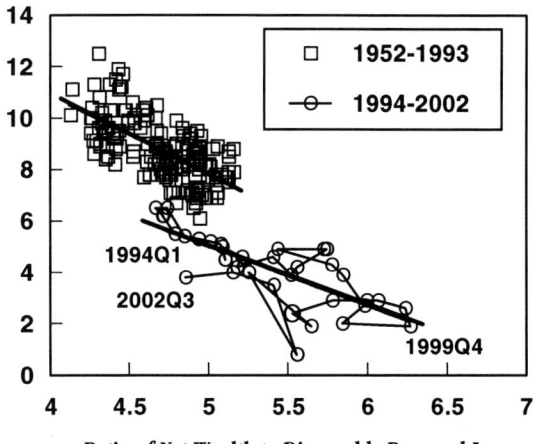

Sources: Department of Commerce, Bureau of Economic Analysis; Federal Reserve Board.

Another possibility is that changes in the markets for consumer credit and mortgage loans have made it easier and cheaper for consumers to borrow. As a consequence, consumers do not need to save as much in advance for purchases and for down payments on homes.

The shift does not appear to depend on the definition of the personal saving rate. The saving rate used in the figure is the measure from the national income and product accounts. It considers saving to be all income from current production that is not spent on consumer goods and services, interest paid by persons, and personal transfer payments to the rest of the world. A different measure comes from the flow-of-funds accounts maintained by the Federal Reserve Board.[1] That measure defines personal saving as the household sector's net acquisition of financial assets plus the net investment in tangible assets minus the net increase in liabilities. A shift is apparent using that measure. Other measures of personal saving do not appear to explain the shift either.[2]

---

1. Board of Governors of the Federal Reserve System, *Flow of Funds Accounts of the United States* (December 5, 2002).

2. Examples of other measures are described in Maria G. Perozek and Marshall B. Reinsdorf, "Alternative Measures of Personal Saving," *Survey of Current Business* (April 2002), pp. 13-24.

Figure 2-9.
Mortgage Delinquency Rates

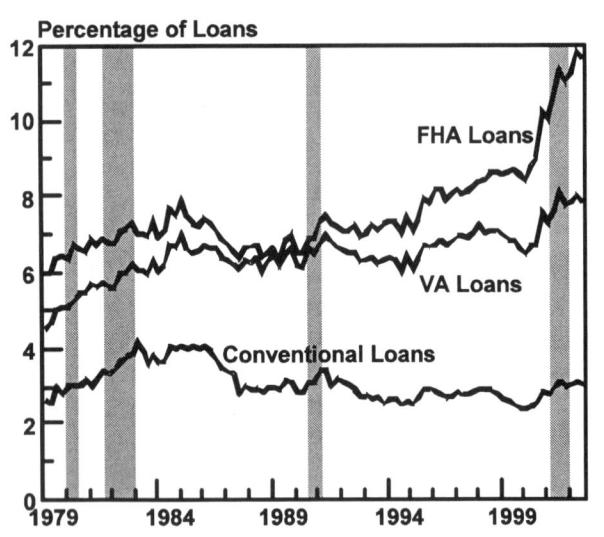

Sources: Congressional Budget Office; Mortgage Bankers Association.

Notes: FHA = Federal Housing Administration; VA = Department of Veterans Affairs.

However, mortgage delinquencies and foreclosures appear to be lagging indicators, so they may peak soon if the economy continues to recover. Indeed, mortgage delinquency rates edged down in the third quarter of 2002.

The delinquency rate on a broad range of consumer loans at commercial banks, by contrast, is lower than it was at the start of the 2001 recession. That relatively better rate may reflect the fact that households used some of the proceeds from refinancing mortgages to pay down consumer loans. In addition, banks have kept a tight rein on standards and terms of such loans, helping to minimize delinquencies. Nevertheless, the delinquency rate on credit cards surged in 2001 and remained at a very high level in 2002, suggesting credit problems among some borrowers (see Figure 2-10).

The Housing Market. The market for housing has been a source of strength in this recovery. Real residential investment surged to all-time highs in each of the first three quarters of 2002, and housing starts for the year as a whole were at their highest level since 1986. Moreover, sales of both new and existing single-family homes reached record levels in 2002 (see Figure 2-11). Those sales have been fueled by the lowest mortgage rates since the 1960s (see Figure 2-12). According to Freddie Mac, late in 2002, interest rates were just above 6 percent for 30-year fixed-rate mortgages, around 5.5 percent for 15-year fixed-rate mortgages, and between 4 percent and 4.25 percent for one-year adjustable-rate mortgages. All of those rates were about a percentage point lower than they were early in 2002.

Several indicators suggest, however, that the housing market may decelerate soon. Nationally, the increase in housing prices has slowed, suggesting lower growth in demand, and prices in some areas have begun to decline. Some analysts suggest that housing prices may have risen by more than the underlying conditions of supply and demand warrant, at least in some metropolitan areas, which means that prices in those areas could fall. In addition, the rise in delinquencies among high-risk borrowers could cause mortgage lenders to tighten credit terms and standards for such borrowers.

Motor Vehicles. Purchases of cars and light trucks have been another important element bolstering consumer spending over the past year. After the terrorist attacks of September 11, 2001, automakers feared that consumers would stop buying major items such as cars. To prevent

Figure 2-10.
Delinquency Rates on Consumer Loans at Banks

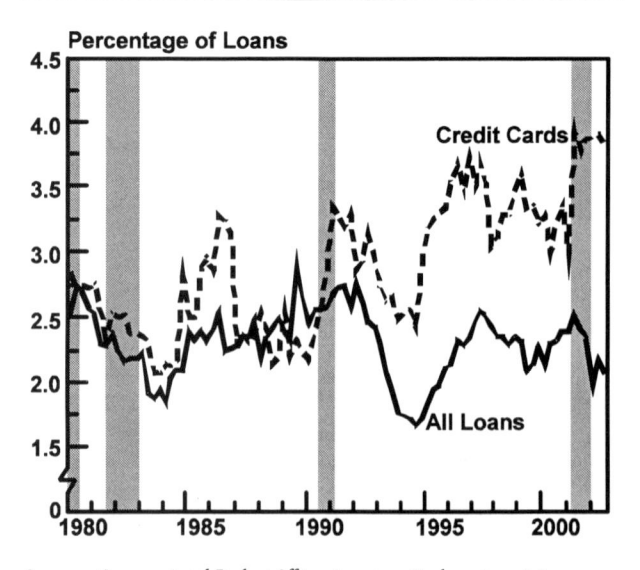

Sources: Congressional Budget Office; American Bankers Association.

Figure 2-11.
Sales of New Homes

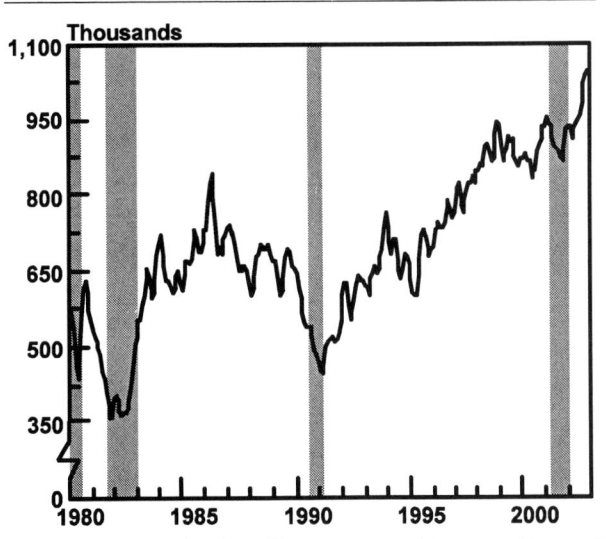

Sources: Congressional Budget Office; Department of Commerce, Bureau of Census.

Note: Data are three-month moving averages.

that from happening, General Motors offered its customers zero-interest financing beginning in October 2001; Ford and the Chrysler unit of Daimler-Chrysler quickly matched that offer. As a result, sales of cars and light trucks reached a near-record level that month—an annual rate of 21.1 million vehicles—and remained at high levels throughout most of 2002 (*see Figure 2-13*). Some industry observers fear that those incentives may soon lose much of their impact, but vehicle sales remained strong at the end of 2002.

The Corporate Sector

Whereas spending by the household sector has helped the economy recover, weakness in the corporate sector restrained growth last year. Excess capacity, weak corporate profits, the high cost of raising funds for investment in either the stock or bond market, sluggish growth of final sales, and pervasive uncertainty have all inhibited companies from making new investments in plant and equipment, rebuilding inventories, and restoring the growth of employment.

Corporate investment has been on a roller-coaster ride in recent years. It grew explosively during the late 1990s, fueled by rising stock prices, strong growth in demand, and excessive investment in information technology (computers, software, and telecommunications equipment). Real investment in producers' durable equipment and software surged at a rate of 11.6 percent a year, on average, between 1994 and 2000. Although much of that growth came from purchases of computers and software (prompted in part by rapid declines in quality-adjusted computer prices), other investment in producers' durable equipment rose at a healthy pace.

In late 2000, however, investment growth slowed sharply as stock prices fell and businesses began to pull back from investing in information technology. In 2001, investment in overall producers' durable equipment and software declined by 6.4 percent. Investment in nonresidential structures (which had stayed strong through the summer of 2000 before declining in early 2001) plummeted at an annual rate of 30 percent in the fourth quarter of 2001 and continued to fall at double-digit rates throughout 2002. Today, equipment investment appears to be recovering modestly, mainly because businesses have eliminated much of the overhang of excess investment in information technology built up during the boom years. Nonetheless, business fixed investment is unlikely to return to the high

Figure 2-12.
Mortgage Interest Rates for Existing Homes

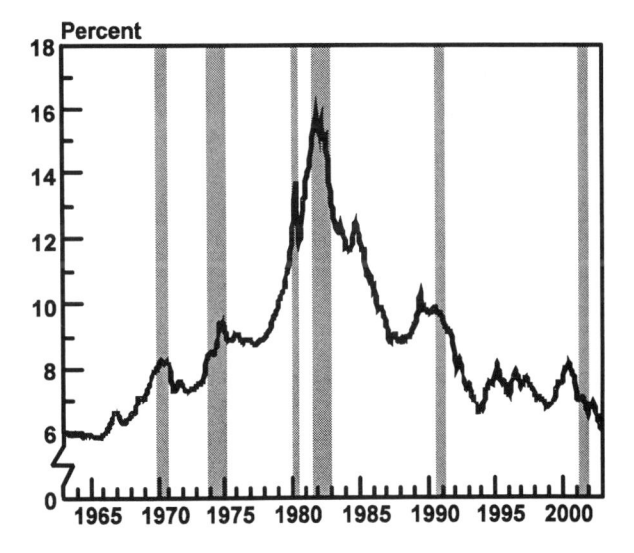

Sources: Congressional Budget Office; Federal Housing Finance Board.

Figure 2-13.
Sales of Cars and Light Trucks

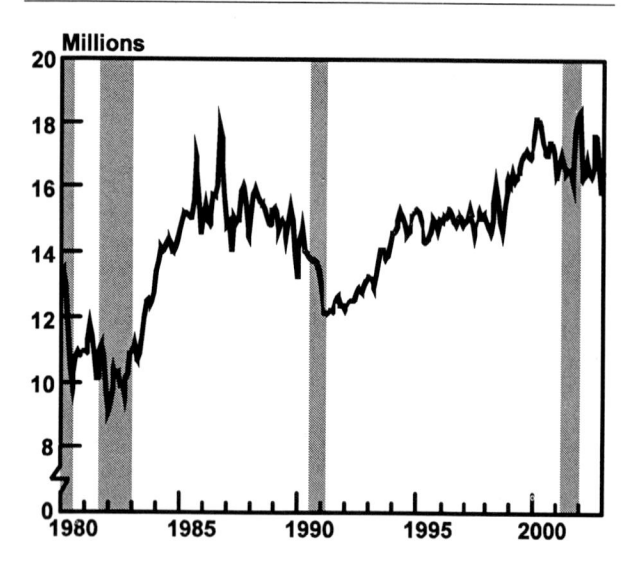

Sources: Congressional Budget Office; Department of Commerce, Bureau of Economic Analysis.

Note: Data are three-month moving averages of annual rates.

share of GDP that it constituted in the late 1990s, because the factors that caused that share are not expected to recur on a sustained basis.

An important factor inhibiting a revival of investment so far is excess capacity. The rate of capacity utilization in manufacturing plunged from 82.2 percent in the first half of 2000 to 73.4 percent in the fourth quarter of 2001, driven by a decline in demand for goods (see Figure 2-14). That drop left the capacity utilization rate considerably lower than during the 1990-1991 recession (when it fell only to around 78 percent), though not as low as during the 1973-1975 and 1981-1982 recessions.

Confronted with so much excess capacity, businesses not only delayed expanding their capacity but did not fully replace existing capacity as it depreciated. Robust growth of productivity during late 2001 and early 2002 further reduced the need to replace depreciating capacity. During 2002, modest growth in demand encouraged businesses to replace a bit more of their depreciating capacity, exemplified by the rebound in computer purchases. However, any investment aimed at expansion awaits further improvement in demand. Investment in structures is likely to be the last part of corporate investment to recover, given elevated vacancy rates for offices.

Corporate profits have begun growing again, but weakly. Their performance so far in this recovery sharply contrasts with the strong rebound in profits typical of most recoveries. The current weakness reflects a slow recovery and declining output prices in much of the nonfinancial corporate sector. If that subpar recovery continues, the growth of profits is likely to stay unusually slow for several quarters, and corporate profits as a share of GDP will remain low until the middle of this year or later.

Despite the Federal Reserve's accommodative monetary policy, businesses' cost of capital has actually risen. That rise stems mainly from declines in stock prices, which make it more difficult and costly to pay for investment by issuing stock. In addition, increasing spreads between interest rates on most newly issued corporate bonds and rates on Treasury bonds of similar maturities have offset some of the impact of the Federal Reserve's actions on the cost of debt (see Figure 2-4 on page 29). With many "dot-com" firms defaulting after the technology boom faded, more-speculative ventures now have trouble getting funded.

Figure 2-14.
The Rate of Capacity Utilization in Manufacturing

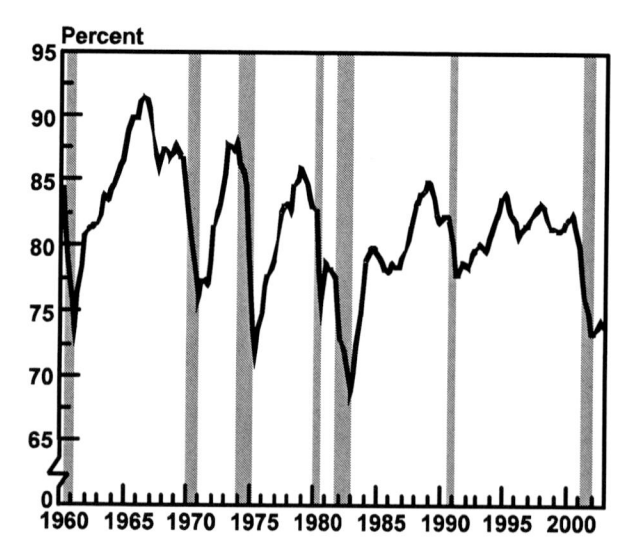

Sources: Congressional Budget Office; Federal Reserve Board.

Figure 2-15.
Business Investment in Inventory

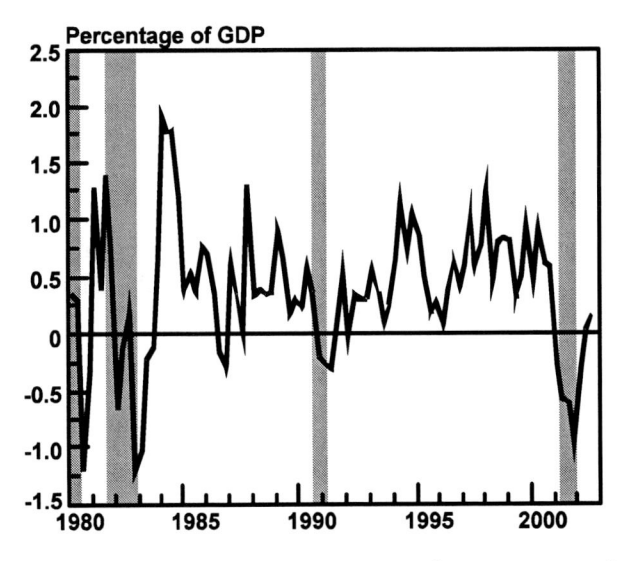

Sources: Congressional Budget Office; Department of Commerce, Bureau of Economic Analysis.

A provision of the March 2002 economic stimulus law has temporarily reduced the cost of capital but has not offset the impact of declining stock prices. That provision allows firms to partially expense some of their new investment for tax purposes (thus augmenting the tax benefits from existing rules, which already allow tax depreciation that is usually much more favorable than the estimated value of true economic depreciation). The new provision was made retroactive to September 11, 2001, and is scheduled to expire in September 2004. CBO estimates that it will add 1 percentage point to the growth of business fixed investment, on average, in 2002 and 2003. The effect could be much greater in 2004 as firms speed up planned investment projects to take advantage of the accelerated depreciation allowance before it expires.

After drawing down inventories rapidly in 2001, businesses have now cautiously begun to rebuild them (see Figure 2-15). The average ratio of inventories to sales has fallen over the past 20 years as manufacturers and retailers have adopted better inventory-management techniques. Those ratios typically rise shortly before and during a recession (as falling demand leaves producers with more inventory than they had planned) and decline when the economy begins to recover. The ratio rose only slightly in 2000, however, and then fell sharply in late 2001 and early 2002. Even allowing for the historical trend and for continuing improvements in inventory management, inventories currently appear to be lower than most firms desire. Consequently, CBO expects inventory rebuilding to at least keep pace with any upturn in sales.

The International Situation

Although foreign economies will grow faster this year than in 2002, on average, the outlook for growth overseas has dimmed since last summer, when CBO's previous economic forecast was published. The near-term outlook points toward only weak recoveries in Japan and Germany, and many South American economies continue to battle the fallout from financial crises. Just a handful of the United States' major trading partners—namely, Canada, South Korea, and China—have economies that are growing at healthy rates.

Because of weaker foreign growth last year and the relatively high exchange value of the dollar at the beginning of that year, the U.S. current-account balance fell sharply in 2002 (see Figure 2-16).[2] The dollar also trended downward, falling from a high of 1.16 euros to the dollar to about 0.98 in December 2002. According to the Federal Reserve, the dollar fell by 7 percent in 2002 against a trade-weighted basket of major currencies.

Global Economic Conditions. Economic recoveries around the world have largely stalled since last summer. Growth in the euro countries has been slow, and that weakness is generally expected to continue. As unemployment in those nations edges higher, consumers are reining in spending. Investment there is hampered by low domestic demand, excess capacity, stock market weakness, and heightened global uncertainties. The growth of exports is likely to be curtailed by the euro's rise against the dollar late in 2002. The euro countries with the two largest

---

2. The current-account balance is the net revenues that arise from a country's international sales and purchases of goods and services plus its net international transfers (public or private gifts or donations) and net factor income (primarily capital income from foreign property owned by residents of that country minus capital income from domestic property owned by nonresidents). The current-account balance differs from net exports in that it includes international transfers and net factor income.

Figure 2-16.
The Current-Account Balance

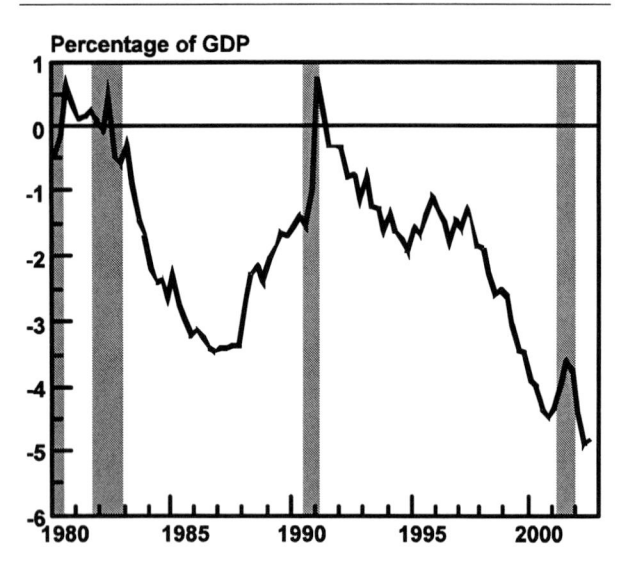

(Percentage of GDP)

Sources: Congressional Budget Office; Department of Commerce, Bureau of the Census.

---

economies—Germany and France—have budget deficits that are already near or above the limit (3 percent of GDP) set by the European Union's growth and stability pact; thus, they have little room for fiscal stimulus. In December, the European Central Bank cut its interest rate target by 0.5 percentage points after keeping that target at 3.25 percent throughout 2002. Although the cut will help bolster the region's economy to some extent, it will not be enough by itself to produce a significant acceleration in growth.

The Japanese economy had staged a rebound since the first quarter of 2002 but is again showing signs of weakening. It continues to be depressed by low demand for investment, ballooning government debt, massive nonperforming bank loans, and entrenched deflation. The plight of the economy has apparently prompted the Japanese government to renew its efforts to tackle the deepening banking crisis, but whether those efforts will be sufficient to revive economic growth is unclear.

Conditions in the rest of the world are mixed. The economic turmoil in South America has recently stabilized, but the region remains vulnerable to shocks. Argentina's economy has been in recession for more than four years and is still having difficulty gaining access to external credit. Brazil continues to face an uphill battle to tame inflation, control its budget deficit, and maintain investor confidence. One bright spot for the world economy has been the performance of much of East Asia (outside Japan). Its strong growth last year reflected healthy consumer spending and higher exports. Closer to home, Canada is clearly the best-performing economy among the G-7 nations, with surging consumer spending drawing strength from a healthy labor market and a buoyant housing market. And although Mexico's economy was hit harder than Canada's by the U.S. economic downturn, it has avoided the crisis that has engulfed much of South America.

The U.S. Exchange Rate. Last year's decline in the value of the dollar is a helpful development toward resolving the growing imbalance of the U.S. current-account deficit. For years, many analysts have been concerned about the implications of the growth in that deficit, which now amounts to almost 5 percent of GDP. At that level, financing the current account requires that the United States attract a large net inflow of capital to avoid a sharp decline in the dollar. If investors decided to pull back their investment in dollars suddenly, the currency's value would fall sharply, disrupting financial stability and economic growth.

Although a plunge in value remains a risk, the dollar is unlikely to collapse, in CBO's view, for at least four reasons. First, investment opportunities are still better in the United States than in most other developed countries, as reflected in the stronger U.S. output and productivity growth. Second, some foreign governments may prefer to keep their currencies low relative to the dollar because they rely on exports to the United States to stimulate economic growth. Third, the outflow of interest, profits, and dividends on net foreign investment in the United States continues to represent a negligible fraction of GDP. And finally, the dollar's status as a reserve currency should dampen abrupt changes in its value. Thus, CBO expects that the dollar will continue to decline in an orderly rather than an abrupt fashion. Over the next few years, a combination of gradual depreciation in the dollar, moderate U.S. growth, and a gradual acceleration in the growth of domestic demand overseas should keep the U.S. current-account deficit from growing much more as a share of GDP.

Government Spending

Spending by both the federal government and state and local governments helped buoy the economy in 2002. But the growth of state and local spending is likely to slow dramatically this year, and unless current law changes significantly, the growth of federal spending will ease.

Federal spending—measured in the national income and product accounts (NIPAs) as real federal government consumption and investment expenditures excluding depreciation—was more than 9 percent higher in the third quarter of 2002 than in the same period a year earlier. Defense spending accounted for the bulk of that increase. Under current law, however, the growth of federal spending is slated to slow during both 2003 and 2004. (For more details on the outlook for federal spending, see Chapter 4.)

The fiscal positions of states and localities continued to worsen last year because of the weak stock market and slow recovery from the 2001 recession (*see Figure 2-17*). Their total deficit (according to the NIPA measure, which includes both operating and capital budgets) is the largest as a share of potential GDP that it has been since World War II. The growth of total state and local spending for transfer payments, wages and salaries, and other operating costs as well as for capital improvement projects has slowed. However, revenues, which had faltered even before the recession, weakened much more in 2001 and 2002 than spending did, widening deficits. State and local revenues dropped for much the same reason that federal revenues fell—the weakening economy, the decline in the stock market, and reductions in tax rates—even though states and localities depend on income tax revenues less than the federal government does.

The various actions that state and local governments are taking to address their budget deficits will restrain growth this year and next year. Some freezes or cuts in spending and increases in taxes have already been put in place, and others are likely during the rest of 2003. Most states have fiscal years that begin in July, so some of the restraint may not be felt until the second half of this year. Overall, state and local spending (excluding transfer payments) is likely to grow by only 1 percent this year in real terms, in contrast to the 2 percent growth seen in 2002 and the 4 percent to 6 percent growth that occurred during the 1998-2001 period.

Inflation

Excluding energy and food prices (which are often volatile), core consumer price inflation, as measured by the CPI-U, steadily eased last year (*see Figure 2-18*). Other core measures of prices—the price index for personal consumption expenditures and the GDP price index excluding food and energy—also grew more slowly.

The immediate cause of that lower inflation was a slowdown in the growth of demand during the recession. However, the stage was set by several other factors: the massive expansion of productive capacity that occurred during the late 1990s, both in the United States and abroad; steady improvements in labor productivity even in the face of the recent slowdown; and the low-inflation policy of the Federal Reserve. Various measures of excess capacity—capacity utilization in manufacturing, the unemployment rate, commodity prices—indicate that the U.S. and world economy can more than fill demand at current prices and that excess capacity is likely to continue holding inflation down this year.

Figure 2-17.

The Fiscal Positions of State and Local Governments

(Percentage of Potential GDP)

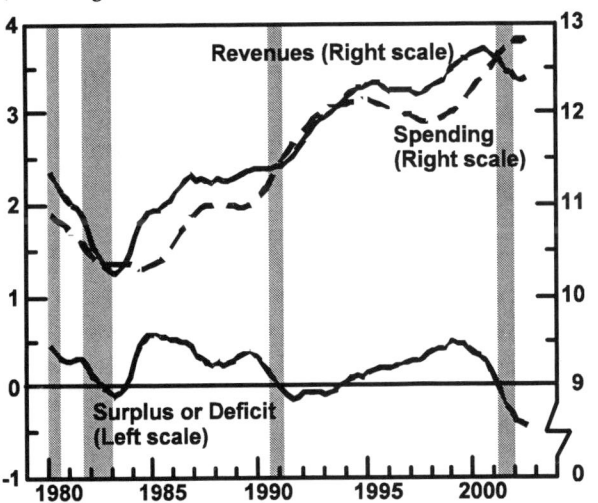

Sources: Congressional Budget Office; Department of Commerce, Bureau of Economic Analysis.

Figure 2-18.
Inflation in the Consumer Price Index

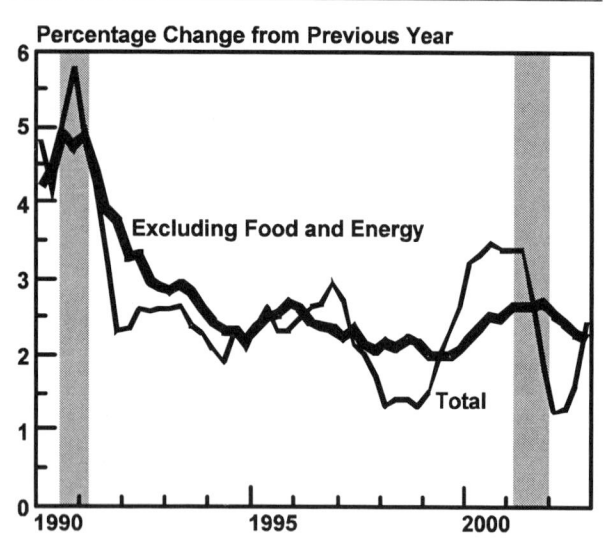

Sources: Congressional Budget Office; Department of Commerce, Bureau of Labor Statistics.

Prices of goods and services have moved in opposite directions in recent years. The core index for goods prices in the CPI-U fell by 1.5 percent over the past 12 months —the first such decline since the 1960-1961 recession. In contrast, the core index for services prices rose by 3.4 percent. That growth was dominated by what the Bureau of Labor Statistics calls rent of shelter, which increased by 3.0 percent over the past year, and by the costs of medical care and tuition, which grew by about 5 percent and 6 percent, respectively.[3] Rent of shelter alone accounts for some 40 percent of the core measure of consumer price inflation, and the behavior of rental costs has buoyed measured inflation. If such rent is excluded from the CPI-U along with food and energy, prices grew by only about 1 percent in 2002.

CBO's Economic Forecast for 2003 and 2004

CBO forecasts that the economic recovery will continue at a moderate pace this year and next year, with little inflationary pressure (*see Table 2-2*). That forecast reflects CBO's view that consumer spending will grow modestly and that business investment will pick up significantly during the second half of 2003. In that view, stimulus from the Federal Reserve's accommodative monetary policy will help keep the recovery going.

That near-term outlook contains a significant amount of uncertainty, however, because of lingering aftereffects from the investment bubble of the late 1990s and heightened uncertainty about geopolitical events. Thus, outcomes better or worse than CBO foresees for the next two years cannot be ruled out. Changes in the confidence of consumers, businesses, and investors could affect the near-term outlook, as could growth in foreign economies that is stronger or weaker than anticipated. For example, it remains unclear when businesses will feel that they can begin to add capacity. Beyond its direct effect on investment, business confidence is likely to play an important role in the recovery of employment and, hence, household income. One factor that may be affecting confidence is

Table 2-2.
CBO's Economic Forecast for 2003 and 2004

	Estimated 2002	Forecast 2003	Forecast 2004
Fourth Quarter to Fourth Quarter (Percentage change)			
Nominal GDP	4.2	4.7	5.6
Real GDP	2.7	3.0	3.7
GDP Price Index	1.4	1.6	1.9
Consumer Price Index[a]			
Overall	2.3	2.1	2.2
Excluding food and energy	2.1	2.0	2.2
Calendar Year Average			
Real GDP (Percentage change)	2.4	2.5	3.6
Unemployment Rate (Percent)	5.8	5.9	5.7
Three-Month Treasury Bill Rate (Percent)	1.6	1.4	3.5
Ten-Year Treasury Note Rate (Percent)	4.6	4.4	5.2

Sources: Congressional Budget Office; Department of Commerce, Bureau of Economic Analysis; Department of Labor, Bureau of Labor Statistics; Federal Reserve Board.

a. The consumer price index for all urban consumers.

---

3. The rent of shelter category comprises not only rental payments for apartments and other housing but also the implicit rental price of owner-occupied housing, payments for lodging away from home, and the cost of tenants' and household insurance.

the ongoing risk of further terrorist acts and of war. (Risks of war are discussed in more detail in Chapter 5.)

Real GDP and Employment

Consumer spending is expected to rise at a steady but moderate rate over the next two years, consistent with the growth of disposable income. Several factors are restraining the growth of consumer spending: the waning impact of sales incentives on purchases of cars and light trucks, the drop in the stock market during the second half of 2002, and a smaller expected boost from households' obtaining additional cash through mortgage refinancing. Consumers have already spent a considerable amount on automobiles, calling into question their demand for additional purchases over the next year. The drop in stock prices last year erased more than $2 trillion from household wealth, and even though stocks rebounded slightly from their summer lows by the end of 2002, the value of household stock portfolios is still below the level of last June. Mortgage refinancing, which achieved record levels in 2002, is unlikely to repeat that performance this year, particularly because mortgage interest rates are likely to rise.

Business investment will be the fastest growing component of GDP this year, CBO forecasts. However, such investment will probably not return to the rapid pace of the late 1990s because financial markets have a more tempered view of growth prospects, particularly for the information technology industry. Businesses have let their inventories shrink in the face of financing difficulties and uncertainty about the strength of demand. If, however, signs of firmer demand appear this year, businesses are likely to restock their shelves at a faster pace. Similarly, companies cut back investment in 2001 and 2002 to bring capacity more in line with softening demand. As real growth of demand picks up in 2003 and 2004, investment, especially in new equipment and software, will also bounce back. Spending on business structures has yet to recover, in light of still-high office vacancy rates, and may not do so until late this year.

CBO's forecast also assumes that the U.S. current-account balance will continue to deteriorate as a share of GDP in 2003 before turning around modestly next year. That pattern results mainly from the expectation that the United States will grow faster than its major trading partners this year. CBO also expects the dollar to weaken slightly through the end of 2004, which is likely to prompt some switching of demand from foreign goods and services to U.S. ones.

CBO's forecast for the growth of GDP implies a slow but steady increase in employment this year and a slightly faster increase next year. That pace of employment growth will probably not be sufficient to lower the unemployment rate this year, but it should prevent that rate from rising significantly. As a result, CBO forecasts that the unemployment rate will remain close to 6 percent through the middle of 2003 and fall slightly by the end of next year.

Inflation and Interest Rates

CBO's moderate outlook for economic activity suggests little inflationary pressure in 2003 and 2004. Inflation, as measured by the CPI-U, is expected to increase by 2.1 percent this year and by 2.2 percent next year, compared with 2.3 percent growth in 2002. (Excluding food and energy prices, CPI-U inflation will grow by 2.0 percent this year and 2.2 percent in 2004, close to its 2.1 percent rate of last year.) The GDP price index will rise by 1.6 percent this year and 1.9 percent next year.

Underlying that forecast is the assumption that only part of the economy's remaining excess capacity will be eliminated this year, given the modest outlook for growth of demand both in the United States and around the world. Therefore, downward pressure on prices is likely to continue, even though import prices may increase in response to the recent and anticipated declines in the dollar. The risk remains, of course, that oil prices could be much higher or lower than the $26-$30 range assumed in this forecast and that overall inflation could reflect oscillations in oil prices. However, downward pressure on the core rate of inflation would probably persist.

CBO assumes that short-term interest rates will remain at their currently low levels until late this year, when the Federal Reserve is likely to raise its target for the federal funds rate in the face of stronger growth. The interest rate on three-month Treasury bills is forecast to decline from an average of 1.6 percent in 2002 to 1.4 percent this year and then jump to 3.5 percent in 2004. The rate on 10-year Treasury notes is expected to decrease from 4.6 percent in 2002 to 4.4 percent in 2003 and then rise to 5.2 percent next year.

Table 2-3.
Comparison of *Blue Chip's* and CBO's Forecasts for Calendar Years 2003 and 2004

	Estimated 2002	Forecast 2003	Forecast 2004
Nominal GDP (Percentage change)			
Blue Chip high 10		5.4	6.7
Blue Chip consensus		4.5	5.5
CBO	**3.6**	**4.2**	**5.4**
Blue Chip low 10		3.7	4.4
Real GDP (Percentage change)			
Blue Chip high 10		3.4	4.3
Blue Chip consensus		2.8	3.6
CBO	**2.4**	**2.5**	**3.6**
Blue Chip low 10		2.3	3.0
GDP Price Index (Percentage change)			
Blue Chip high 10		2.1	2.5
Blue Chip consensus		1.6	1.9
CBO	**1.1**	**1.6**	**1.7**
Blue Chip low 10		1.1	1.3
Consumer Price Index[a] (Percentage change)			
Blue Chip high 10		2.6	2.7
Blue Chip consensus		2.2	2.3
CBO	**1.6**	**2.3**	**2.2**
Blue Chip low 10		1.7	1.7
Unemployment Rate (Percent)			
Blue Chip high 10		6.2	6.0
Blue Chip consensus		5.9	5.5
CBO	**5.8**	**5.9**	**5.7**
Blue Chip low 10		5.6	5.1
Three-Month Treasury Bill Rate (Percent)			
Blue Chip high 10		1.9	3.9
Blue Chip consensus		1.6	2.9
CBO	**1.6**	**1.4**	**3.5**
Blue Chip low 10		1.2	1.9
Ten-Year Treasury Note Rate (Percent)			
Blue Chip high 10		4.9	6.0
Blue Chip consensus		4.5	5.2
CBO	**4.6**	**4.4**	**5.2**
Blue Chip low 10		4.1	4.5

Sources: Congressional Budget Office; Department of Labor, Bureau of Labor Statistics; Federal Reserve Board; Aspen Publishers, Inc., *Blue Chip Economic Indicators* (January 10, 2003).

Note: The *Blue Chip* high 10 is the average of the 10 highest *Blue Chip* forecasts; the *Blue Chip* consensus is the average of the nearly 50 individual *Blue Chip* forecasts; and the *Blue Chip* low 10 is the average of the 10 lowest *Blue Chip* forecasts.

a. The consumer price index for all urban consumers.

A Comparison of Two-Year Forecasts

CBO's current two-year outlook is similar to the latest *Blue Chip* consensus forecast, an average of roughly 50 private-sector forecasts (*see Table 2-3*). CBO's estimate of real GDP growth is slightly lower than the *Blue Chip*'s for 2003 and identical for 2004. CBO expects slightly higher unemployment in 2004 than the *Blue Chip* consensus does. The two forecasts are very similar in their estimates of CPI-U inflation and long-term interest rates; however, CBO expects short-term interest rates to be lower than the *Blue Chip* does in 2003 and higher in 2004.

The Economic Outlook Beyond 2004

CBO projects that real GDP will grow at an average annual rate of 3.0 percent from 2005 through 2013—slightly faster than the growth of potential GDP, which is projected to average 2.9 percent during that period.[4] Real GDP fell by about 0.6 percent during the 2001 recession, and CBO's forecast of moderate growth during 2003 and 2004 leaves real GDP slightly below potential GDP at the end of 2004. Thus, to bring real GDP back to its historical relationship with potential GDP, CBO assumes that real GDP will grow sightly faster than 2.9 percent during the 2005-2013 period.

The current projections for inflation, unemployment, and interest rates after 2004 are quite similar to the ones that CBO published last August (*see Table 2-4*). In those projections, CPI-U inflation averages 2.5 percent a year in the 2005-2012 period, and the unemployment rate declines to 5.2 percent (equal to CBO's estimate of the nonaccelerating inflation rate of unemployment). The interest rate on three-month Treasury bills is projected to average 4.9 percent during the 2005-2012 period and the rate on 10-year Treasury notes to average 5.8 percent.

CBO's projections reflect current law, including the sunset provisions of the Economic Growth and Tax Relief Reconciliation Act of 2001. Under those provisions, tax

---

4. Potential GDP is defined as the highest level of GDP that could persist for a substantial period without raising the rate of inflation. CBO's procedure for estimating potential GDP is described in *CBO's Method for Estimating Potential Output: An Update* (August 2001).

Table 2-4.
CBO's Current and Previous Economic Projections for Calendar Years 2003 Through 2012

	Estimated 2002	Forecast 2003	Forecast 2004	Projected Annual Average 2005-2008	Projected Annual Average 2009-2012
Nominal GDP (Billions of dollars)					
January 2003	10,443	10,880	11,465	14,154[a]	17,217[b]
August 2002	10,429	10,912	11,484	14,137[a]	17,358[b]
Nominal GDP (Percentage change)					
January 2003	3.6	4.2	5.4	5.4	5.0
August 2002	3.4	4.6	5.2	5.3	5.3
Real GDP (Percentage change)					
January 2003	2.4	2.5	3.6	3.2	2.8
August 2002	2.3	3.0	3.3	3.2	3.1
GDP Price Index (Percentage change)					
January 2003	1.1	1.6	1.7	2.1	2.2
August 2002	1.1	1.6	1.9	2.1	2.1
Consumer Price Index[c] (Percentage change)					
January 2003	1.6	2.3	2.2	2.5	2.5
August 2002	1.7	2.4	2.5	2.5	2.5
Unemployment Rate (Percent)					
January 2003	5.8	5.9	5.7	5.3	5.2
August 2002	5.9	5.9	5.5	5.2	5.2
Three-Month Treasury Bill Rate (Percent)					
January 2003	1.6	1.4	3.5	4.9	4.9
August 2002	1.7	2.9	4.8	4.9	4.9
Ten-Year Treasury Note Rate (Percent)					
January 2003	4.6	4.4	5.2	5.8	5.8
August 2002	4.9	5.4	5.8	5.8	5.8
Tax Bases (Percentage of GDP)					
Corporate book profits					
January 2003	6.2	6.8	7.3	9.2	8.5
August 2002	5.9	6.1	6.7	8.7	8.2
Wages and salaries					
January 2003	48.1	48.1	48.1	48.0	47.8
August 2002	48.3	48.4	48.2	48.4	48.4
Tax Bases (Billions of Dollars)					
Corporate book profits					
January 2003	653	739	842	1,267[a]	1,429[b]
August 2002	611	666	775	1,209[a]	1,408[b]
Wages and salaries					
January 2003	5,025	5,237	5,518	6,782[a]	8,231[b]
August 2002	5,034	5,282	5,561	6,848[a]	8,408[b]

Sources: Congressional Budget Office; Department of Commerce, Bureau of Economic Analysis; Department of Labor, Bureau of Labor Statistics; Federal Reserve Board.

Note: Percentage changes are year over year.

a. Level in 2008.
b. Level in 2012.
c. The consumer price index for all urban consumers.

rates will return in 2011 to the higher rates that would have existed had the law not been enacted. (Last August's projections did not attempt to take the sunset provisions into account.) That tax increase will have complicated effects on the economy, which were described in Box 2-1. CBO's projections assume that growth will be slightly slower in 2011 and 2012 as a result of the tax increase, leaving the level of potential GDP about 0.5 percent lower in 2013 than it would have been otherwise.

CBO's projections do not explicitly incorporate specific cyclical recessions and recoveries beyond the next two years. To reflect the likelihood that at least one cyclical episode will occur in any 10-year period, CBO averages into its projections the effects of a typical business cycle, though without attempting to fix when that cycle might occur. Those medium-term projections extend historical trends in such underlying factors as the growth of productivity, the rate of national saving, and the size of various kinds of taxable income as a share of GDP. They also depend on projected growth in the labor force, which is based on projected demographic trends as well as on historical trends in the labor force participation rates of specific demographic groups. CBO's projections for real GDP, inflation, real interest rates, and tax revenues after 2004 rely critically on those underlying trends.

Potential Output

The projection for growth of potential output over the next 10 years (2.9 percent annually) is nearly 0.2 percentage points lower than CBO's August 2002 projection. Underlying the current projection for potential output are projections for the annual growth of the potential labor force (0.9 percent through 2013), potential hours worked (1.1 percent), capital (4.2 percent), and potential total factor productivity (1.2 percent). In addition, potential labor productivity in the nonfarm business sector grows at a 2.2 percent annual rate in CBO's projection (*see Table 2-5*).

The current projection for growth of potential output is lower than last summer's largely because the potential labor force is projected to increase more slowly, implying a lower projection for growth of hours worked in the nonfarm business sector. In the past, CBO used an average growth rate for the potential labor force through the medium term—similar to the procedure used for interest rates, inflation, and other variables—so that any year-to-year movements in those variables were not interpreted as indicating a forecast of business-cycle patterns. However, as CBO's projection horizon moves into the period when the baby-boom generation will begin to retire, that procedure becomes less defensible. Therefore, CBO has incorporated the slowing of labor force growth because of demographic trends into its projections. That revision clips about 0.1 percentage point from the growth rate of the potential labor force, lowering that growth to 0.9 percent from the 1 percent projected in CBO's August economic outlook.

In addition, capital accumulation is now projected to proceed at a slightly slower pace than CBO projected in last summer's outlook. CBO's current forecast for business investment as a share of GDP is lower than the previous projection, which reduces the contribution of capital to the growth of potential GDP by less than 0.1 percentage point. CBO revised its outlook for business investment because the burst of investment that typically occurs during the early months of a recovery was largely absent in 2002. Businesses seem to be able to meet modest increases in demand by boosting their efficiency rather than by increasing capacity.

The growth rate of potential total factor productivity (TFP), 1.2 percent a year, is essentially unchanged from CBO's August projection. The underlying trend in TFP growth has remained steady since the early 1980s at about 1 percent, and that continues to be true in CBO's current estimate, despite the decline in TFP caused by the 2001 recession (*see Figure 2-19*).[5] The adjustments to TFP are largely unchanged from last summer's projections, but one small revision merits an explanation. CBO has reassessed its estimate of how increased spending on security in the wake of the September 2001 terrorist attacks affects productivity growth. Since January 2002, CBO's forecasts have included an adjustment that reduced the level of TFP by about 0.3 percentage points in 2002 to account for the costs to private companies from additional spending on security guards and from delays

---

5. CBO estimates that underlying trend using historical data that have been adjusted to eliminate the effects of changes in the formulas for measuring inflation in the NIPAs and to remove the impact of technological progress in computer manufacturing from overall TFP.

Table 2-5.
Key Assumptions in CBO's Projection of Potential GDP
(By calendar year, in percent)

	Average Annual Growth						Projected Average Annual Growth		
	1951-1973	1974-1981	1982-1990	1991-1995	1996-2002	Total, 1951-2002	2003-2008	2009-2013	Total, 2003-2013
Overall Economy									
Potential GDP	3.9	3.3	3.0	2.6	3.3	3.4	3.0	2.7	2.9
Potential Labor Force	1.6	2.5	1.6	1.1	1.1	1.6	1.1	0.6	0.9
Potential Labor Force Productivity[a]	2.2	0.8	1.4	1.4	2.1	1.7	1.9	2.1	2.0
Nonfarm Business Sector									
Potential Output	4.0	3.6	3.1	2.9	3.8	3.7	3.4	3.1	3.3
Potential Hours Worked	1.3	2.2	1.5	1.5	1.5	1.5	1.3	0.8	1.1
Capital Input	3.7	4.4	3.6	2.5	4.9	3.8	3.9	4.6	4.2
Potential Total Factor Productivity	2.0	0.8	1.0	1.1	1.3	1.4	1.2	1.2	1.2
Potential TFP excluding adjustments	2.0	0.7	1.0	1.0	1.0	1.4	1.0	1.0	1.0
TFP adjustments	0	0	0	0	0.2	0	0.2	0.2	0.2
Computer quality	0	0	0	0	0.1	0	0.1	0.1	0.1
Price measurement	0	0	0	0	0.1	0	0.2	0.2	0.2
Additional spending on security	0	0	0	0	*	*	*	*	*
Contributions to Growth of Potential Output (Percentage points)									
Potential hours worked	0.9	1.5	1.1	1.0	1.0	1.1	0.9	0.5	0.7
Capital input	1.1	1.3	1.1	0.8	1.5	1.2	1.2	1.4	1.3
Potential TFP	<u>2.0</u>	<u>0.8</u>	<u>1.0</u>	<u>1.1</u>	<u>1.3</u>	<u>1.4</u>	<u>1.2</u>	<u>1.2</u>	<u>1.2</u>
Total Contributions	4.0	3.6	3.1	2.9	3.8	3.6	3.3	3.1	3.2
Memorandum:									
Potential Labor Productivity[b]	2.7	1.4	1.6	1.4	2.2	2.1	2.0	2.4	2.2
Effect of Expiration of 2001 Tax Law[c]	0	0	0	0	0	0	**	-0.1	*

Source: Congressional Budget Office.

Notes: CBO assumes that the growth rate of potential total factor productivity (TFP) changed after the business-cycle peaks of 1973, 1981, and 1990 and again after 1995.

    * = between -0.05 percent and zero; ** = between zero and 0.05 percent.

a. The ratio of potential GDP to the potential labor force.

b. Estimated trend in the ratio of output to hours worked in the nonfarm business sector.

c. The expiration of the Economic Growth and Tax Relief Reconciliation Act's tax cuts in 2011 is estimated to reduce the level of potential GDP in 2013 by 0.5 percent. Averaged over 11 years, that reduction in growth amounts to slightly less than 0.05 percentage points.

Figure 2-19.
Actual and Potential Total Factor Productivity

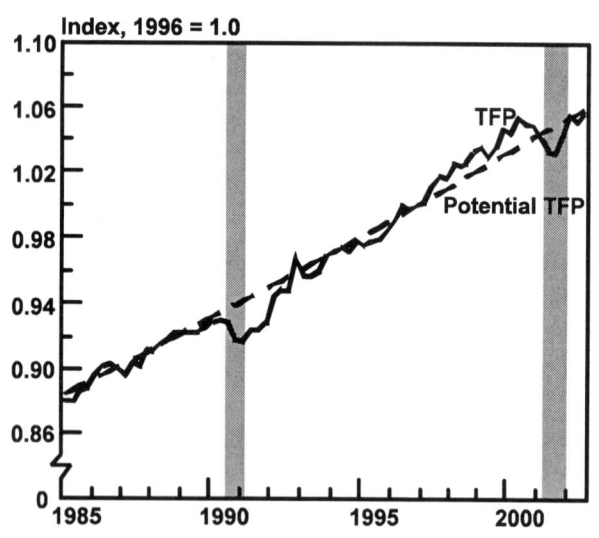

Source: Congressional Budget Office.

Note: The data are adjusted to exclude two factors: the effects of methodological changes in the measurement of prices, and the contribution to overall TFP growth of technological change in the production of computers.

in transportation because of heightened security.[6] Few data were available, however, on which to base that estimate, so it was only a rough guess intended to provide an upper limit on the expected effect.

Employment data are now available for the 12 months following the September 11 attacks. In particular, CBO has examined the monthly data for private employment in protective-services occupations—largely security guards and private detectives—and has found no above-trend growth since September 2001. Consequently, CBO has eliminated that component of the security cost adjustment from its estimate of potential TFP, which raises the level of potential TFP in 2002 by about 0.2 percent. However, the estimated effect on future growth, -0.03 percentage points per year, has not been revised. That effect results from the diversion of investment toward security equipment, which does not contribute to productivity as it is conventionally measured.

---

6. For more information, see Congressional Budget Office, *The Budget and Economic Outlook: Fiscal Years 2003-2012* (January 2002), Box 2-3.

Unemployment, Inflation, and Interest Rates

The medium-term projection for CPI-U inflation (2.5 percent a year between 2005 and 2013) is the same as CBO published in August, but the projection for growth in the GDP price index (an average annual rate of 2.2 percent) is 0.1 percentage point higher than last summer's projection. That increase occurred primarily because CBO slightly raised its projections for the growth of prices in various categories of investment and increased its projection for consumption as a share of GDP. Those changes reduced the difference between the growth of the GDP price index and that of the CPI-U. In general, CBO assumes that the inflation rate is determined by monetary policy in the medium term and that the Federal Reserve will seek to maintain the underlying rate of CPI-U inflation near 2.5 percent, on average.

The unemployment rate is projected to decline gradually in 2005 and 2006 and then average 5.2 percent thereafter. That decline mirrors the behavior of the gap between actual and potential output, which closes during the projection period because real GDP is assumed to grow more rapidly than potential GDP in that period.

CBO's medium-term projections for interest rates have not changed since August. CBO estimates those rates by adding its projection for inflation to its projection for real interest rates. Using the CPI-U as a measure of price changes, CBO estimates that the real rate on three-month Treasury Bills will average 2.4 percent during the 2005-2013 period, and the real rate on 10-year Treasury notes will average 3.3 percent. Combined with the projected rates of CPI-U inflation, those real rates imply nominal rates of 4.9 percent for three-month Treasury bills and 5.8 percent for 10-year Treasury notes.

Taxable Income

CBO's budget projections are closely connected to its projections of economic activity and national income. However, different categories of income are taxed at different rates, and some are not taxed at all. Thus, the distribution of income among its various components is a crucial factor in CBO's economic projections. The categories of wage and salary disbursements and corporate profits are particularly significant because they are taxed at the highest effective rates.

Figure 2-20.
Corporate Profits

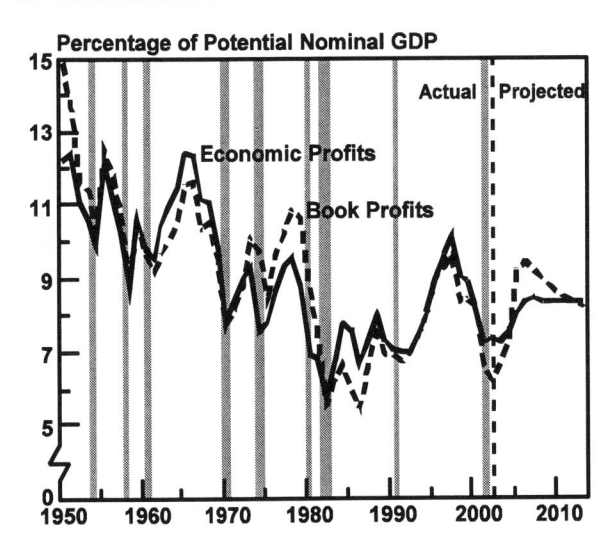

Sources: Congressional Budget Office; Department of Commerce, Bureau of Economic Analysis.

Note: Economic profits are corporate profits from current production—that is, adjusted for changes in the value of inventories and for capital depreciation. Book profits (also known as before-tax profits) are calculated using book depreciation and standard accounting conventions for inventories.

Two of the various NIPA measures of corporate profits are important for the forecast. *Book profits*, also known as before-tax profits, is the measure most closely related to the profits that companies report to the Internal Revenue Service. That measure is affected by changes in tax law. Corporations are allowed by law to value inventories and depreciate assets at certain rates, and the book measure of profits is designed to reflect those statutory requirements. By contrast, the *economic profits* measure is designed to reflect the valuation of inventories and the rates of depreciation that economists believe more truly represent the current value of inventories and the economic usefulness of the capital stock.

The economic stimulus law enacted in March 2002 allows firms, for a three-year period, to depreciate some of their capital stock much more rapidly than the estimated true economic depreciation rate. Because of that provision, book profits will be much lower than economic profits between September 11, 2001, and September 10, 2004; after that, book profits will be higher than economic profits because companies will have accelerated the use of their depreciation allowances to the previous period (*see Figure 2-20*).

Wages and salaries—the other NIPA income category important for revenue forecasting—will average about 48 percent of potential GDP during the 2005-2013 period, CBO projects (*see Figure 2-21*). That share of GDP is only slightly higher than its average of the past 25 years. CBO's projection assumes that the part of labor compensation made up of benefits (such as health insurance premiums) will continue to rebound from the lows of the late 1990s, which will dampen the wage and salary component of labor compensation.

Figure 2-21.
Wages and Salaries

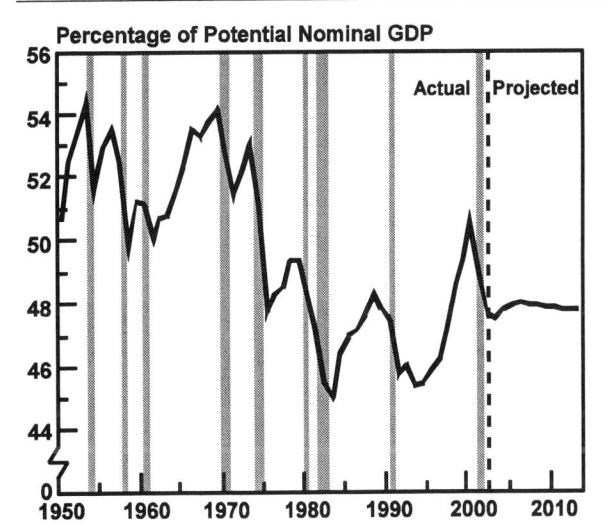

Sources: Congressional Budget Office; Department of Commerce, Bureau of Economic Analysis.

CHAPTER 3

The Revenue Outlook

If current policies remained unchanged, federal revenues would total $1,922 billion in fiscal year 2003, the Congressional Budget Office estimates. That amount is about $70 billion (or 3.7 percent) more than revenues totaled last year—but still well below the $2,025 billion collected in 2000, the peak year for federal receipts. As a share of gross domestic product, revenues are projected to equal 17.9 percent this year, the same as in 2002 and roughly the average for the post-World War II period (see Figure 3-1). That revenue share of GDP has returned to just below the level of 1994, reversing a six-year climb that culminated in a postwar peak of 20.8 percent in 2000.

Over the coming decade, receipts are expected to increase again, growing faster than GDP in each year after 2003 (see Figure 3-2). That ascent is driven mainly by the tendency of the tax system to increase the proportion of income collected in taxes as income grows. Beginning in 2011, the trend of rising receipts becomes especially pronounced as the tax cuts enacted in 2001 expire.

Figure 3-1.

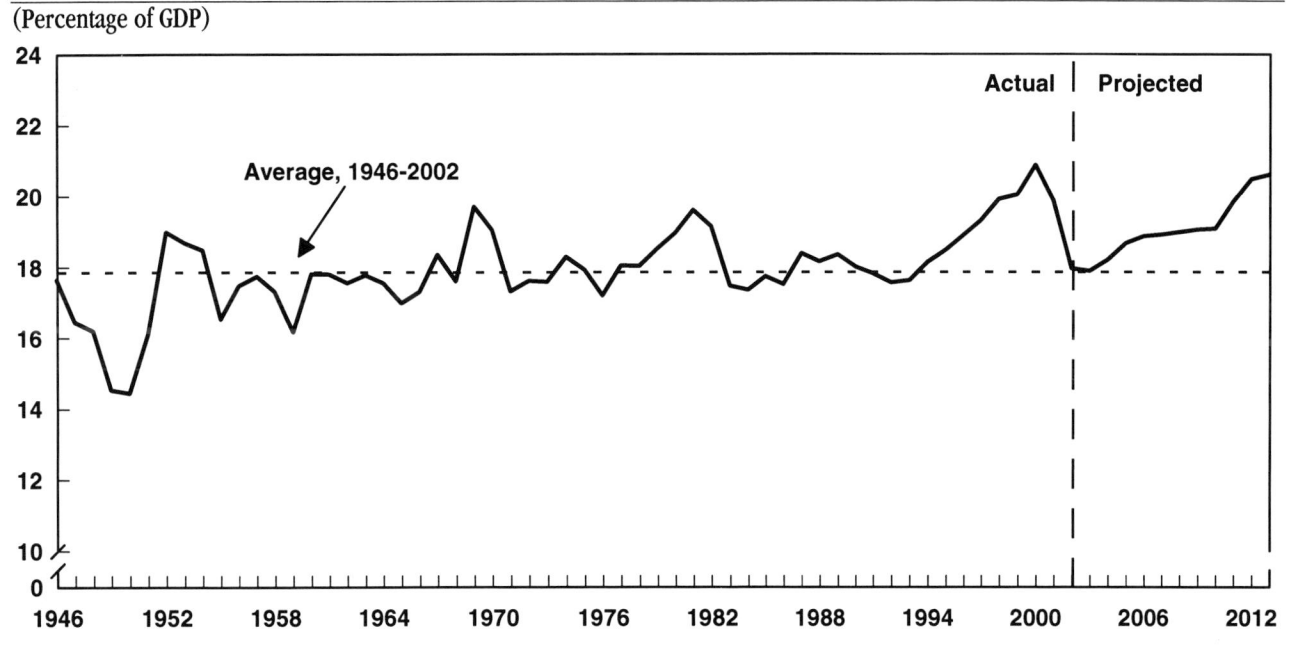

Total Revenues as a Share of GDP, 1946-2013

(Percentage of GDP)

Source: Congressional Budget Office.

Figure 3-2.
Annual Growth of Federal Revenues and GDP, 1961-2013
(Percentage change from previous year)

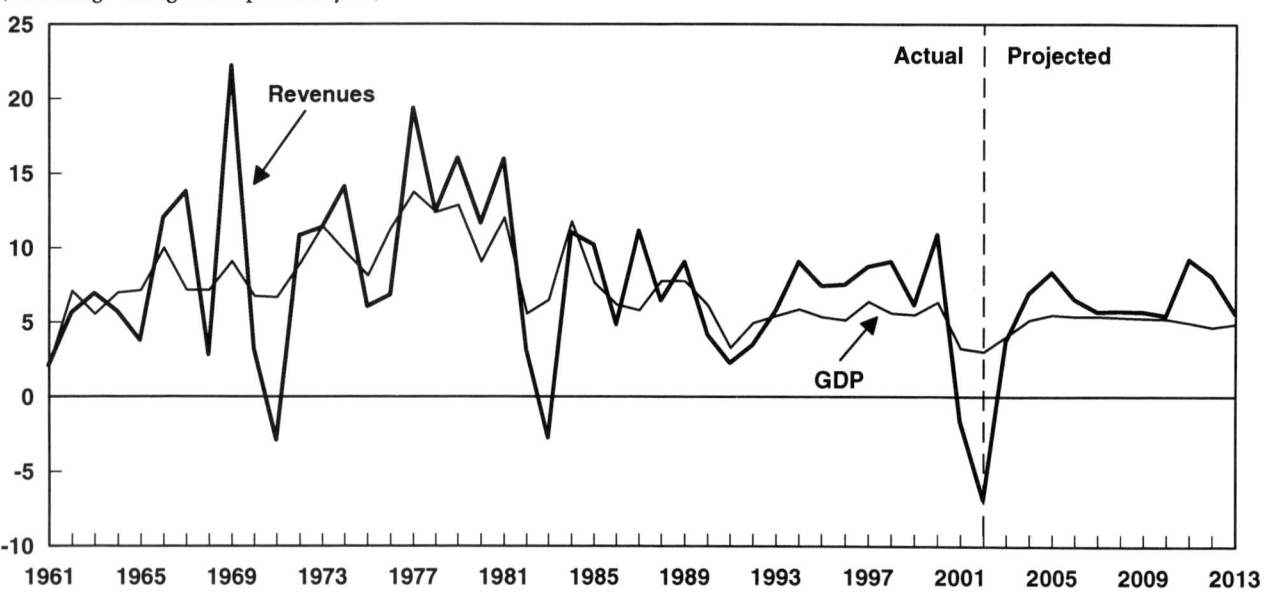

Source: Congressional Budget Office.

CBO's current revenue projections are slightly lower, on average, than the ones it published in August. CBO is now projecting a total of $208 billion less in receipts for the 2003-2012 period than it did last summer. The lower estimate stems primarily from changes in CBO's economic forecast, which tend to reduce receipts by modest amounts throughout the 10-year projection period. The rest of the change since August results from reestimates of the amount of receipts that would flow from a given level of overall economic activity. Those reestimates reduce projected revenues by small amounts over the first seven years of the projection period.

Recent Revisions to CBO's Revenue Projections

In August, CBO projected that receipts would total $26.4 trillion over the 2003-2012 period (*see Table 3-1*). The current projection for that period is $26.2 trillion, a reduction of 0.8 percent ($208 billion).

That modest decline contrasts sharply with revisions over the past year and a half. In CBO's three previous reports on the budget outlook, revenue projections were revised downward substantially. Large revisions in revenue projections are not unusual around turning points in the business cycle, but the actual level of receipts in 2001 and 2002 took most forecasters by surprise, since receipts changed even more dramatically than income did. That result largely stemmed from changes in revenues that are generated by volatile and difficult-to-predict determinants of the tax base.

In January 2001, CBO projected total revenues of $2,135 billion for fiscal year 2001, including $1,076 billion in individual income tax receipts and $215 billion in corporate income tax receipts. Although that projection was made when the fiscal year was already under way, it proved to be too high by $144 billion (individual income taxes were $82 billion lower than projected and corporate taxes were $64 billion lower). In January 2002, CBO projected revenues of $1,983 billion for fiscal year 2002, of which individual income tax receipts constituted $947 billion and corporate income tax receipts $179 billion. That year, actual revenues were $130 billion lower than projected (with individual and corporate taxes accounting for $89 billion and $31 billion of the overestimate, respectively).

Table 3-1.
Changes in CBO's Projections of Revenues Since August 2002
(In billions of dollars)

	2003	2004	2005	2006	2007	2008	2009	2010	2011	2012	Total, 2003-2012
Revenues in CBO's August 2002 Baseline	1,962	2,083	2,244	2,381	2,513	2,658	2,809	2,965	3,243	3,521	26,379
Legislative Changes	*	*	*	*	*	1	1	1	1	1	5
Other Changes											
Economic	-9	-14	-8	-2	-1	-6	-9	-16	-31	-50	-146
Technical	-32	-15	-11	-10	-8	-5	-2	*	7	8	-67
Subtotal	-41	-29	-19	-12	-9	-10	-12	-16	-23	-42	-213
Total Changes	**-41**	**-29**	**-19**	**-11**	**-9**	**-10**	**-11**	**-15**	**-23**	**-41**	**-208**
Revenues in CBO's January 2003 Baseline	1,922	2,054	2,225	2,370	2,505	2,648	2,798	2,949	3,220	3,480	26,170

Source: Congressional Budget Office.

Note: * = between -$500 million and $500 million.

New Information About the Cause of the Overestimate in 2001

Each projection of fiscal year receipts is made up of a mix of calendar year tax liabilities. Income tax liability for calendar year 2001 contributed to receipts in both fiscal years 2001 and 2002. Preliminary summary data tabulated from 2001 individual income tax returns are now available, which can explain more about why individual income tax liability in 2001 fell so far short of projections. More-detailed analysis must await the examination of fuller summary statistics and a sample of tax returns, which will not be available until later this year. (Details about 2002 tax liability will not be available for another year.) However, the data now in hand reveal many of the broad outlines of the projection shortfall. They also provide some insight into what CBO often characterizes as "technical" changes to its baseline revenue projections.

CBO's projection of individual income tax receipts for fiscal year 2001 relied partly on a projection of calendar year 2001 liability of $1,055 billion. On the basis of tax collections, CBO now estimates that actual tax liability for that year was $876 billion. Of the $179 billion unforseen shortfall, $52 billion came from legislation—specifically, the Economic Growth and Tax Relief Reconciliation Act (EGTRRA), enacted in the spring of 2001, and the economic stimulus law, enacted in March 2002.[1] That leaves $127 billion in reduced liability to be accounted for.

The information now in hand identifies two sources of that shortfall. First, economic activity in 2001, as measured by the national income and product accounts (NIPAs) did not end up as high as CBO had projected in January 2001. Although CBO built a slowdown in economic activity into its projections, wages and other taxable nonwage income turned out to be lower than CBO's estimates of them. That lower-than-estimated income accounts for about $19 billion of the shortfall in calendar year 2001 tax liability.

Second, capital gains realizations dropped precipitously in calendar year 2001. In 2000, those realizations were at an all-time high. CBO did not expect that level to persist, but no reliable methods exist to forecast when and how quickly realizations can be expected to decline from

---

1. Because the stimulus law increased depreciation deductions for certain property purchased after September 10, 2001, the 2001 income tax liability of some individuals with business income declined after the fact, even though the law was enacted in 2002.

such a high. Hence, CBO projected that realizations would fall gradually to a level commensurate with their historical relationship with GDP. Data now indicate that the fall in capital gains realizations essentially occurred all in one year: a drop of 50 percent in 2001. That decline reduced 2001 tax liability by about $68 billion.

The remaining $40 billion shortfall must still be explained. That decrease in the effective tax rate on nongains income could have arisen from several phenomena. One possible source is slower-than-predicted growth in distributions from retirement accounts. That effect should be discernable when more-complete summary statistics on 2001 tax filings become available over the next few months. Another source of the remaining shortfall could be a significant slowing of the growth of income among high earners (households that pay the highest marginal tax rates) relative to income growth among other taxpayers. The contribution of that effect cannot be estimated until a sample of 2001 tax returns becomes available this summer.

Corporate tax liability for calendar year 2001 also fell short of CBO's projection. Actual liability was $143 billion, compared with a projection of $214 billion. Legislation—principally the stimulus package passed in March 2002—reduced corporate tax liability by about $20 billion.[2] Of the other $50 billion in shortfall, about $30 billion resulted from lower-than-estimated corporate book profits. The source of the rest is still unknown and must await further analysis.

The Connection Between Economic and Technical Revisions

Most of the identifiable sources of the shortfall in 2001 tax liability were a result of changes in the economy. When CBO revises its revenue projections, it categorizes the revisions according to whether they have economic, technical, or legislative causes. In that breakdown, sources of revisions like the ones described above are mostly classified as technical, meaning that the revisions do not spring directly from changes in the outlook for variables that make up CBO's economic forecast. However, most technical and economic revisions are similar in that they are rooted in hard-to-predict changes in economic conditions that play out in different ways as changes in receipts.

In the case of the projections of 2001 tax liability, CBO made large downward technical reestimates to its revenue forecast in the summer of 2001 partly because actual tax collections were weaker than the economic forecast at the time indicated. Since then, the Bureau of Economic Analysis has reduced its NIPA measures of wages and salaries and of corporate book profits for 2001. Thus, revisions to the revenue projections that CBO had deemed technical turned out to be related to overall economic performance. In that case, about half of the effect of book profits on tax liability and all of the effect of wage income were classified as technical changes in CBO's forecast.

Changes in revenues related to such factors as the relative income growth of the most highly taxed people, distributions from retirement accounts, and projections of capital gains realizations are classified as technical revisions because they are not derived directly from a macroeconomic projection of economic activity. In particular, income distribution and capital gains realizations are highly variable relative to typical measures of overall economic performance, so even an accurate forecast of output, employment, and inflation offers little insight into the future course of receipts they will generate. Nonetheless, those factors are clearly driven by events in the economy.

Implications for CBO's Revenue Projections

This examination of the differences between actual and projected tax liability illustrates three important aspects of CBO's revenue projections. First, it highlights the difficulties posed whenever the economy is at a turning point. A peak in the business cycle marks the dividing line between various factors that tend first to drive receipts up and then drive them down. The turnaround in 2001 produced a major shift in the revenue outlook in a very short time.

Second, this examination reveals the degree to which technical changes in CBO's projections are fundamentally related to shifting economic conditions. Changes in capital

---

2. As in the case of individual income taxes, the stimulus law changed 2001 corporate tax liability after the fact. EGTRRA, which affected corporate tax receipts in 2001, did not alter the level of liabilities, since it simply shifted the receipt of liabilities from fiscal year 2001 to 2002.

Figure 3-3.
Revenues, by Source, as a Share of GDP, 1960-2013

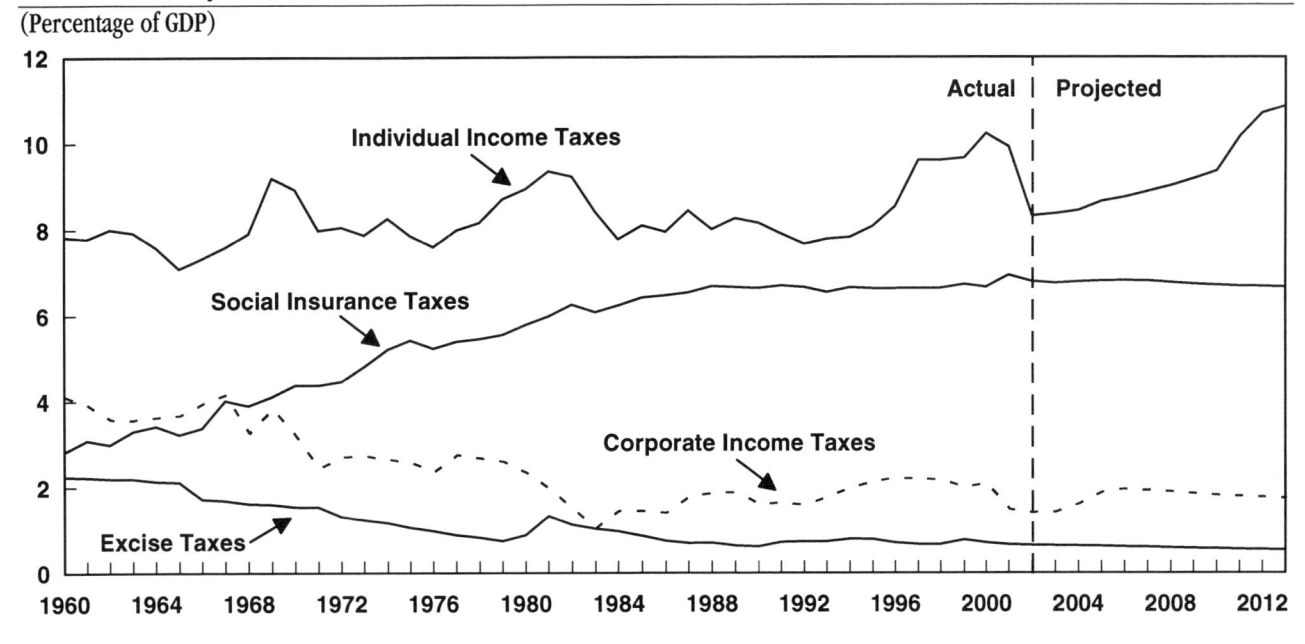

(Percentage of GDP)

Source: Congressional Budget Office.

gains realizations and relative rates of income growth among classes of taxpayers, as well as revisions to income data resulting from mismeasurement in the NIPAs, are all treated as technical reestimates in CBO's classification system, but they are nonetheless driven by the economy.

Third, this examination shows how lags in the availability of data can affect projections. Even now, not all of the causes of the behavior of tax liability in 2001 are known. When CBO makes revenue projections, it must often attribute behavior in receipts that is unexplained by contemporary measures of income to various sources without any further information. Those difficult-to-attribute receipts can profoundly affect projections of future revenues, depending on whether they are expected to persist, grow, or diminish. As a consequence, they can influence revenue projections well beyond the period directly affected by the current business cycle. It may be possible to improve the accuracy of projections with more timely availability of data. In particular, the ability to distinguish incoming income tax withholding payments from payroll tax receipts could help in more quickly identifying the effect of wage behavior on current receipts.

Revenues by Source

Federal revenues come from a variety of sources: individual income taxes, corporate income taxes, social insurance (payroll) taxes, excise taxes, estate and gift taxes, customs duties, and miscellaneous receipts. Individual income taxes currently produce nearly half of all revenues and claim slightly more than 8 percent of GDP (see Figure 3-3). Social insurance taxes (mainly for Social Security and Medicare's Hospital Insurance) are the second largest source of receipts. They generate more than a third of federal revenues and amount to a little less than 7 percent of GDP. Corporate income taxes contribute less than one-tenth of overall revenues and represent approximately 1.5 percent of GDP. Revenues from other taxes, duties, and miscellaneous receipts (including profits from the Federal Reserve System) make up the balance and together constitute about 1.5 percent of GDP (see Table 3-2).

Over the coming decade, the relative importance of those revenue sources is expected to shift only slightly. With the expiration of EGTRRA, individual income taxes will cause most of the rise in total receipts relative to GDP; those taxes will increase in importance from just under half of

Table 3-2.
CBO's Projections of Revenues

	Actual 2002	2003	2004	2005	2006	2007	2008	2009
								In Billions of Dollars
Individual Income Taxes	858	899	954	1,031	1,099	1,176	1,259	1,349
Social Insurance Taxes	701	725	766	811	856	901	944	989
Corporate Income Taxes	148	156	185	228	249	260	269	276
Excise Taxes	67	68	71	74	77	79	82	84
Estate and Gift Taxes	27	21	24	21	24	20	22	23
Customs Duties	19	18	20	20	21	22	23	24
Miscellaneous	34	33	36	40	44	47	50	52
Total	**1,853**	**1,922**	**2,054**	**2,225**	**2,370**	**2,505**	**2,648**	**2,798**
On-budget	1,338	1,390	1,496	1,637	1,751	1,853	1,963	2,079
Off-budget[b]	515	532	558	588	619	651	685	719
								As a Percentage of GDP
Individual Income Taxes	8.3	8.4	8.4	8.6	8.7	8.9	9.0	9.2
Social Insurance Taxes	6.8	6.7	6.8	6.8	6.8	6.8	6.8	6.7
Corporate Income Taxes	1.4	1.5	1.6	1.9	2.0	2.0	1.9	1.9
Excise Taxes	0.6	0.6	0.6	0.6	0.6	0.6	0.6	0.6
Estate and Gift Taxes	0.3	0.2	0.2	0.2	0.2	0.1	0.2	0.2
Customs Duties	0.2	0.2	0.2	0.2	0.2	0.2	0.2	0.2
Miscellaneous	0.3	0.3	0.3	0.3	0.4	0.4	0.4	0.4
Total	**17.9**	**17.9**	**18.2**	**18.6**	**18.8**	**18.9**	**19.0**	**19.0**
On-budget	12.9	12.9	13.2	13.7	13.9	14.0	14.1	14.1
Off-budget[b]	5.0	4.9	4.9	4.9	4.9	4.9	4.9	4.9

Source: Congressional Budget Office.

a. Numbers in the bottom half of the column are shown as a percentage of cumulative GDP over this period.
b. Social Security.

---

revenues now to just over half in 2013. Corporate income taxes are also expected to grow in importance as profits recover from their current lows. EGTRRA will have a profound effect on the significance of estate and gift taxes—they will virtually disappear in 2010 and 2011 before springing back to their previous importance when EGTRRA expires. Excise taxes will continue their slow decline in significance as a revenue source.

Individual Income Taxes

Individual income taxes account for most of the projected change in revenues as a share of GDP over the next 10 years. That is not surprising: they were also responsible for most of the rise in that share during the late 1990s and most of the drop over the past two years. Individual income tax receipts grew at an average rate of nearly 11 percent a year from 1994 to 2000. Their share of GDP reached a historical peak—10.3 percent—in 2000. That trend was halted by the recession that began in March 2001 and, to a much lesser extent, by the tax cuts enacted in EGTRRA. Individual income tax receipts fell to 9.9 percent of GDP in 2001 and to 8.3 percent in 2002. As a consequence, the nominal level of federal revenues dropped for two years in a row—the first time that had happened since 1959.

Because some of the factors causing the low level of receipts in 2002 are temporary, and because the design of the income tax system causes revenues to grow faster than output, CBO expects individual income tax receipts to

	2010	2011	2012	2013	Total, 2004-2008[a]	Total, 2004-2013[a]
	1,447	1,649	1,819	1,939	5,518	13,720
	1,037	1,085	1,134	1,188	4,277	9,709
	285	295	306	316	1,190	2,669
	87	90	92	95	383	831
	15	19	43	47	110	258
	25	26	27	28	107	237
	54	56	59	61	217	500
	2,949	**3,220**	**3,480**	**3,674**	**11,802**	**27,923**
	2,193	2,428	2,650	2,805	8,701	20,856
	756	792	830	870	3,101	7,067
	9.3	10.1	10.7	10.9	8.8	9.5
	6.7	6.7	6.7	6.7	6.8	6.7
	1.8	1.8	1.8	1.8	1.9	1.8
	0.6	0.6	0.5	0.5	0.6	0.6
	0.1	0.1	0.3	0.3	0.2	0.2
	0.2	0.2	0.2	0.2	0.2	0.2
	0.4	0.3	0.3	0.3	0.3	0.3
	19.1	**19.8**	**20.5**	**20.6**	**18.7**	**19.3**
	14.2	14.9	15.6	15.7	13.8	14.4
	4.9	4.9	4.9	4.9	4.9	4.9

increase relative to GDP throughout the coming decade. That rise will be especially pronounced after 2010, when the EGTRRA tax cuts expire. Individual income tax receipts are projected to reach a new historical peak of 10.7 percent of GDP in 2012 and then continue rising to 10.9 percent of GDP in 2013 (see Table 3-3). Indeed, despite their recent slide, individual income tax receipts are projected to remain well above their post-World War II average of 8.1 percent of GDP.

The expected course of those receipts over the next 10 years is best understood in the context of their behavior over the past decade. The roots of the recent decline in individual income tax receipts lie in the increase that occurred in the late 1990s. That increase was caused by some unusual phenomena, whose reversal was probably the major reason for the subsequent decline.

The Growth of Receipts Through 2000. With few exceptions, revenues from individual income taxes have tended to grow slightly faster than GDP. Until the 1990s, big jumps in the receipts-to-GDP ratio were caused by legislation, such as the surtax imposed in 1969, or by rapid price increases (before the tax code was indexed for the effects of inflation) that effectively decreased the levels of real income at which higher tax rates applied. Between 1994 and 2000, however, individual income tax receipts grew much faster than the economy for entirely different reasons:

- Taxable personal income—the components of GDP on which individuals pay taxes, including wages, interest, dividends, proprietors' income, and rental income, as measured in the NIPAs—grew faster than GDP during most of the 1994-2000 period. (For more information on the relationship between tax liability, taxable income, and GDP, see Box 3-1 on pages 58 and 59.) The resulting rise in the proportion of GDP attributable to taxable personal income increased the tax base for the individual income tax; that rise accounted for 20 percent of the growth of tax liability in excess of GDP growth over that period (see Table 3-4).

- Capital gains realizations grew more rapidly than taxable personal income during the 1994-2000 period. Those realizations are a component of adjusted gross income (AGI), which is the actual income base of the individual income tax, but they are not included in either GDP or taxable personal income. Capital gains realizations quadrupled between 1994 and 2000, with that increase beginning before capital gains tax rates were cut in 1997 (see Table 3-5 on page 60). As a result, taxes on those gains accounted for 28 percent of the growth of individual income tax liability above the growth of GDP.

- Other components of AGI that are not part of taxable personal income or GDP also expanded more rapidly than either of those measures. Among those components, retirement income (in the form of distributions from 401(k) plans and individual retirement accounts) and taxable Social Security benefits were especially

Table 3-3.
CBO's Projections of Individual Income Tax Receipts and the NIPA Tax Base

	Actual 2002	2003	2004	2005	2006	2007	2008	2009	2010	2011	2012	2013	Total, 2004-2008	Total, 2004-2013
Individual Income Tax Receipts														
In billions of dollars	858	899	954	1,031	1,099	1,176	1,259	1,349	1,447	1,649	1,819	1,939	5,518	13,720
As a percentage of GDP	8.3	8.4	8.4	8.6	8.7	8.9	9.0	9.2	9.3	10.1	10.7	10.9	n.a.	n.a.
Annual growth rate	-13.7	4.7	6.1	8.1	6.6	7.0	7.1	7.1	7.3	14.0	10.3	6.6	n.a.	n.a.
Taxable Personal Income														
In billions of dollars	7,378	7,628	7,994	8,415	8,848	9,306	9,796	10,308	10,839	11,375	11,906	12,495	44,358	101,283
As a percentage of GDP	71.4	70.9	70.7	70.5	70.3	70.2	70.1	70.1	70.0	70.0	70.0	70.0	n.a.	n.a.
Annual growth rate	0.8	3.4	4.8	5.3	5.1	5.2	5.3	5.2	5.2	4.9	4.7	4.9	n.a.	n.a.
Individual Tax Receipts as a Percentage of Taxable Personal Income	11.6	11.8	11.9	12.2	12.4	12.6	12.9	13.1	13.3	14.5	15.3	15.5	n.a.	n.a.

Source: Congressional Budget Office.

Notes: The tax base in this table (taxable personal income) reflects income as measured by the national income and product accounts (NIPAs) rather than as reported on tax returns. An important difference, therefore, is that it excludes capital gains realizations.

n.a. = not applicable.

influential. The growth of those non-capital-gains components of AGI together accounted for 7 percent of the increase in liability relative to GDP growth from 1994 to 2000.

- Most significantly, the effective tax rate on individual income—that is, the percentage of total AGI paid in taxes—rose throughout the 1994-2000 period (see Figure 3-4 on page 61). Increases in the effective rate (on income other than capital gains) accounted for 45 percent of the growth of tax liability in excess of GDP growth. About three-fifths of that increase resulted from a phenomenon commonly referred to as real bracket creep, in which the overall growth of real income pushes more income into higher tax brackets. Much of the remaining increase in the effective tax rate appears to stem from the rapid growth of income at the top of the income distribution, which led to a greater proportion of income being taxed at the highest rates. Thus, even though the tax rates written in law did not increase, a larger share of income accrued to taxpayers facing the highest tax rates, which raised the overall effective tax rate.

Those sources of growth vary in the difficulties they pose for projecting future revenues. Some of the items are relatively simple to account for: given projections of income, real bracket creep is easy to incorporate into revenue forecasts because CBO's microsimulation model encompasses the existing rate structure of the income tax and the current distribution of income within that structure. In contrast, increases in the effective tax rate that result from changes in the distribution of income are virtually unpredictable because existing theory and past patterns provide no useful guidance in projecting distribution shifts. Likewise, capital gains realizations are notoriously difficult to project. Distributions from retirement accounts fall between the extremes of difficulty. Much of the past growth in individual income tax receipts as a share of GDP stems from hard-to-predict sources—enough to impart a great deal of uncertainty to future revenue projections.

The Decline in Individual Income Tax Receipts in 2001 and 2002. The recession that began in March 2001 marked a significant change in the growth of receipts that had characterized the previous several years. After rising at an average annual rate of nearly 11 percent for six years,

Table 3-4.
Why Did Individual Income Tax Liability Grow Faster Than GDP From 1994 Through 2000?

	\multicolumn{7}{c}{Share of Liability Growth in Excess of GDP Growth (Percent)}
Reason for Additional Growth	1994-1995	1995-1996	1996-1997	1997-1998	1998-1999	1999-2000	Total, 1994-2000
Taxable Personal Income Grew Faster than GDP	21	12	14	42	-2	33	20
Adjusted Gross Income (AGI) Grew Faster than TPI							
Capital gains receipts grew faster than TPI	20	52	29	12	36	20	28
Other AGI grew faster than TPI	15	5	10	-4	20	-4	7
Subtotal	35	57	39	8	57	16	35
Changes in Effective Tax Rate on AGI							
Effect of real growth on rate	30	20	34	30	26	28	28
Concentration of income growth at the top of the income distribution (and residual)	14	11	13	20	19	22	18
Subtotal	45	32	47	51	45	50	45
Total	100	100	100	100	100	100	100
Memorandum:							
Growth of Individual Income Tax Liability in Excess of GDP Growth (Billions of dollars)	27	39	35	42	56	61	259

Source: Congressional Budget Office using data from Internal Revenue Service, *Statistics of Income, 1994-2000*.

Notes: Taxable personal income (TPI) is the sum of wages and salaries, interest income, dividends, proprietors' income, and rental income as measured in the national income and product accounts.

CBO calculated the percentage contribution of each of the sources of growth using the amount of tax liability that would have accrued without the child and education tax credits that took effect in tax year 1998. Excluding those credits allows consistent measurement between all of the years in the comparison.

---

individual income tax revenues fell for two years in a row, ending below their level of 1999. As a percentage of GDP, those revenues fell from their postwar high of 10.3 percent to 8.3 percent—lower than in 1996—essentially wiping out the growth relative to GDP that had occurred in the late 1990s.

Two reasons for that decline are relatively well understood: the slowdown in the economy and the tax cuts enacted in 2001 in EGTRRA. But beyond those events, several factors served to lower the amount of revenues produced by a given level of economic activity.

Just as capital gains realizations played a disproportionate role in the growth of receipts as a share of GDP in the 1990s, they played a similar part in the fall of receipts relative to GDP in 2001 and 2002. Realizations peaked at $644 billion in calendar year 2000. The best available information from 2001 tax returns indicates that they dropped to half that level in 2001 (about $322 billion), reducing receipts by $30 billion in fiscal year 2001 and by $37 billion in fiscal year 2002.[3] On the basis of the performance of the stock market, income, and other key determinants of realizations, CBO estimates that capital gains realizations fell by another 17 percent in calendar year 2002, to $268 billion, reducing receipts by an additional $5 billion in fiscal year 2002.

---

3. The percentage decline in taxable capital gains realizations is much greater than the fall in household wealth described in Chapter 2. Not all changes in stock values are realized for tax purposes. And much of household wealth is in the form of housing, which typically escapes capital gains taxation.

Box 3-1.
Tax Bases and Tax Liability

Tax receipts vary with economic activity, but they do not move in lockstep with gross domestic product (GDP), or output. Although the bases for taxes on individual and corporate income and for social insurance taxes are related to that economic measure, they differ from GDP in a number of important respects, which means that they sometimes grow faster and sometimes slower than output. As a result, the ratio of receipts to GDP may change even if tax laws remain the same.

The Individual Income Tax Base
Taxable personal income is the first approximation of the individual income tax base. It comprises dividends, interest, wages and salaries, rent, and proprietors' income. It does not include depreciation, indirect taxes on businesses (such as excise taxes), fringe benefits, or retained corporate profits.

Despite its name, not all taxable personal income is actually taxed. Some of it accrues to tax-exempt entities such as hospitals, schools, cultural institutions, and foundations; some is earned in a form that is tax-exempt, such as income from state and local bonds; and some is tax-deferred, such as income from retirement accounts, on which tax is paid not when the income is earned but when the person retires and begins to draw down the account. Also, personal interest and rental income contain large components of imputed income—income that is not earned in a cash transaction, including personal earnings within pension funds and life insurance policies and income from owner-occupied housing—that are not taxable. Consequently, a substantial amount of interest, dividend, and rental income is excluded from the taxable base of the income tax.

Taxpayers make further adjustments, both additions and subtractions, to taxable personal income to derive their **adjusted gross income**, or AGI. **Capital gains realizations**—the increase in the value of assets between the time they are purchased and sold—are added to taxable personal income. Contributions from income made to tax-deductible individual retirement accounts and 401(k) plans are subtracted, but distributions to retirees from those plans are added. Taxpayers also make a variety of other, smaller adjustments.

Exemptions and **deductions** are subtracted from AGI to yield **taxable income**, to which progressive tax rates —rates that rise as income rises—are applied. (Those rates are known as **statutory marginal tax rates**; the range of taxable income over which a statutory marginal rate applies is known as an **income tax bracket**, of which there are now six.) The tax that results from applying those rates to taxable income may then be subject to further adjustments in the form of **credits**, such as the child credit for taxpayers with children under age 17, which reduce taxpayers' **tax liability** (the amount of taxes they owe). An important factor in calculating individual tax liability is the **alternative minimum tax** (AMT), which requires some taxpayers to calculate their taxes under a more limited set of exemptions, deductions, and credits. Taxpayers then pay the higher of the AMT or the regular tax. The ratio of tax liability to AGI is the **effective tax rate on AGI**.

A second reason that individual income tax receipts declined relative to the level of economic activity may have been slower growth in income at the top end of the income distribution. Just as faster-than-average income growth among very high earners helped fuel the rise in receipts as a share of GDP, slower-than-average growth among those earners would accomplish the reverse. Detailed data on taxpayers' incomes are not yet available, but some evidence suggests that income growth at the top end of the income distribution slowed in 2001 and 2002.

For example, preliminary evidence suggests that income from stock options may have fallen by 50 percent in calendar year 2001. Given the decline in the stock market last year, that income is unlikely to have rebounded significantly; indeed, it may have fallen further. In the late 1990s,

Box 3-1.
Continued

The Social Insurance Tax Base
Social insurance taxes, the second largest source of receipts, use payroll as their base. Those taxes largely fund Social Security and the Hospital Insurance program (Part A of Medicare). Social Security taxes are imposed as a percentage of pay up to a **taxable maximum** that is indexed for the growth of wages in the economy. Hospital Insurance taxes are not subject to a taxable maximum.

The Corporate Income Tax Base
Corporate profits are the tax base of the corporate income tax. But the corporate profits component of GDP differs in several important respects from what is taxed by the corporate income tax.

First, the profits of the Federal Reserve System are counted as corporate profits in measures of GDP, but they are not taxed under the corporate income tax (they are instead remitted to the Treasury as miscellaneous receipts).

Second, measures of GDP calculate corporate income on the basis of **economic depreciation**—the dollar value of productive capital assets that is estimated to have been used up in the production process. For tax purposes, however, corporations calculate **book profits**, which are based on **book**, or **tax**, **depreciation**. Book depreciation is typically more front-loaded than economic depreciation; that is, the capital is assumed to be used up at a faster rate than the best estimates of how fast it is actually used up, allowing firms to report taxable profits that are smaller than economic profits.

Third, taxable corporate income includes the foreign-source income of U.S. multinational corporations when that income is "repatriated," or returned, to the U.S. parent company. Foreign-source income is not part of measured output.

Several other, smaller differences exist between corporate profits as defined in the GDP measure and corporations' calculation of their taxable income for tax purposes. If a corporation's taxable income is negative (that is, if the firm loses money), its loss (within limits) may be carried backward or forward to be netted against previous or future taxable income and thus reduce the firm's taxes in those other years. A statutory tax rate is applied to the corporation's taxable income to determine its tax liability. A number of credits (such as the credit for taxes imposed by other countries on the foreign-source income included in a firm's taxable profits) may further pare that liability. The ratio of aggregate domestic corporate taxes to aggregate taxable corporate income is the **average tax rate**.

Despite many adjustments that must be made to calculate the actual tax bases, a ready approximation is the sum of wages and salaries and corporate book profits. Those items pick up much of the bases of the individual income, corporate income, and social insurance taxes and therefore constitute the bulk of taxed income.

---

by contrast, income from stock options rose rapidly, with some estimates indicating that it peaked at more than $100 billion in 2000, or about 2 percent of wages and salaries. Much of that income presumably accrues to the highest-earning taxpayers and thus is taxed at the highest rates. As a result, in the past two years, a higher proportion of total wages and salaries was probably subject to lower marginal tax rates.

In addition to those factors, which affected both 2001 and 2002, last year's decline in individual income tax receipts may have resulted from factors that shifted receipts between fiscal years, making receipts in 2002 unusually low relative to GDP. As noted earlier, a given year's income tax liability is split between two fiscal years. If taxpayers pay a disproportionately large share of their ultimate liability in the form of withholding and estimated tax pay-

Table 3-5.
Actual and Projected Capital Gains Realizations and Taxes

	Capital Gains Realizations[a]		Capital Gains Tax Liabilities[a]		Capital Gains Tax Receipts[b]		Capital Gains Tax Receipts as a Percentage of Total Individual Income Tax Receipts
	In Billions of Dollars	Percentage Change from Previous Year	In Billions of Dollars	Percentage Change from Previous Year	In Billions of Dollars	Percentage Change from Previous Year	
1990	124	-20	28	-21	32	-14	6.8
1991	112	-10	25	-11	27	-17	5.7
1992	127	14	29	16	27	1	5.6
1993	152	20	36	25	32	20	6.3
1994	153	*	36	*	36	12	6.7
1995	180	18	44	22	40	10	6.8
1996	261	45	66	50	54	36	8.3
1997	365	40	79	19	72	33	9.8
1998	455	25	89	12	84	16	10.1
1999	553	21	112	26	99	19	11.3
2000	644	17	127	14	119	20	11.8
2001	322	-50	61	-52	97	-18	9.8
2002	268	-17	49	-19	55	-43	6.5
2003	294	10	54	10	51	-8	5.7
2004	322	10	60	10	56	10	5.9
2005	350	9	65	9	62	10	6.0
2006	380	8	71	8	68	9	6.1
2007	409	8	76	8	73	8	6.2
2008	440	7	82	8	79	8	6.3
2009	470	7	88	7	85	7	6.3
2010	502	7	94	7	90	7	6.3
2011	529	5	99	5	96	6	5.8
2012	557	5	104	5	101	5	5.6
2013	587	5	109	5	107	5	5.5

Sources: Congressional Budget Office; Department of the Treasury.

Notes: Capital gains realizations represent net positive gains. Data for realizations and liabilities after 2000 and data for tax receipts in all years are estimated or projected by CBO. Data for liabilities before 2001 are estimated by the Treasury Department.

* = between zero and 0.5 percent.

a. Calendar year basis.
b. Fiscal year basis. This measure is CBO's estimate of when tax liabilities are paid to the Treasury.

---

ments, more of the receipts for a given tax year will be received early (in the first of the two fiscal years) and less will arrive in the next fiscal year, when liability is settled up in April. Taxpayers paid an unusually large share of 2001 liability in the form of withheld taxes during calendar year 2001. The subsequent drop in payments of 2001 tax liability in calendar year 2002 may mean that taxpayers were surprised by economic developments in 2001 and continued to withhold higher-than-necessary amounts—a reaction that would not be surprising given the changes that occurred that year (the tax cut, the recession, and the drop in the stock market). Consequently, CBO believes that last year's lower level of receipts as a percentage of GDP sprang partly from one-time effects that are not likely to be repeated in 2003 and beyond.

Nonetheless, not all the reasons for the lower level of receipts in 2001 and 2002 have been determined. A good

Figure 3-4.
Effective Tax Rate on Individual Income, Tax Years 1994-2000
(Percent)

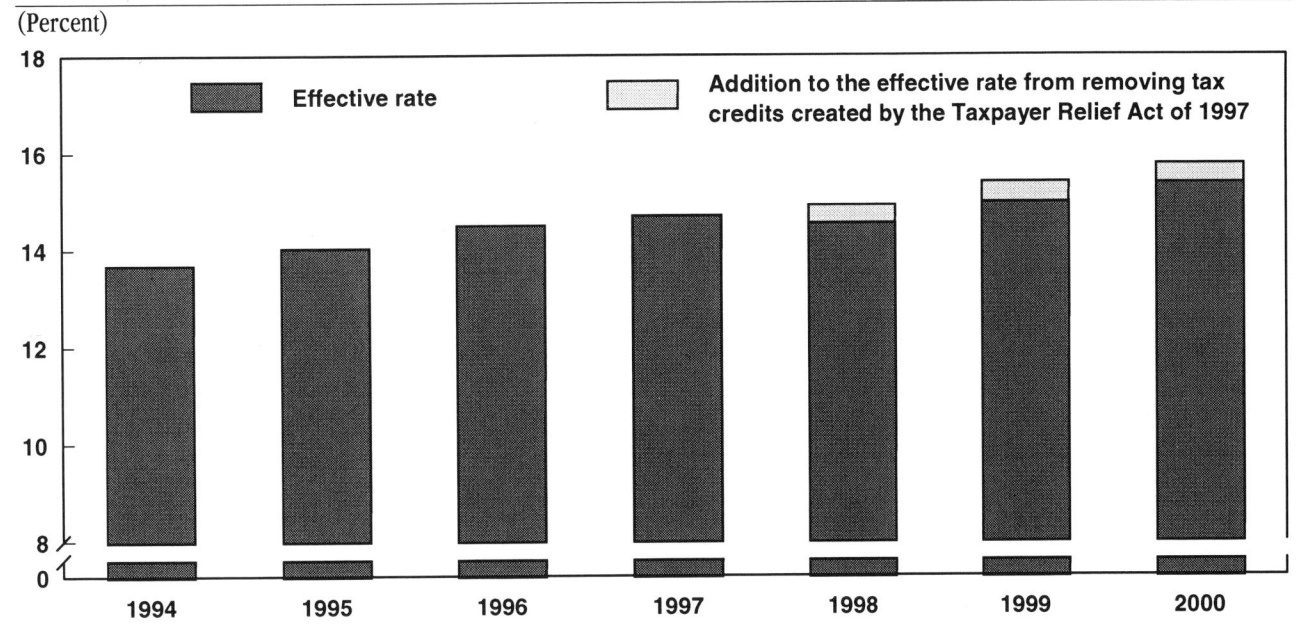

Source: Congressional Budget Office.

Note: The effective tax rate is the ratio of tax liability to income. Tax years are essentially the same as calendar years.

picture now exists of the total makeup of 2001 tax liability, but not until a sample of 2001 tax returns is available later this year will analysts be able to trace the effects of some phenomena, such as the distribution of wage income. Besides detailed tax data, revised estimates of wages and other types of income from the NIPAs may help explain the behavior of receipts over the past two years.

The Future Pattern of Individual Income Tax Receipts. CBO estimates that in dollar terms, individual income tax receipts will grow slowly this year and more rapidly thereafter. Moreover, CBO projects that those receipts will rise as a share of GDP in each of the next 10 years.

Between 2003 and 2005, the pattern of revenue growth is dominated by the nation's continued recovery from recession. Over that period, individual income tax receipts are expected to increase as economic growth picks up again. The projected rise in receipts is relatively small in 2003 but accelerates in 2004 and 2005 as taxable personal income grows faster.

Despite the near-term effects of the economic recovery, individual income tax receipts over the 2003-2013 period are mostly influenced by four other factors, which cause those receipts to rise faster than either GDP or taxable personal income in every year of that period.

First, effective tax rates will climb over the 10-year period, which tends to increase the amount of receipts generated by the economy. The rise in the effective rate is fueled by real bracket creep and by two other factors: the alternative minimum tax (AMT) and distributions from tax-deferred retirement accounts. The AMT—which is not indexed for inflation—will affect more and more taxpayers and growing amounts of income in future years. (The increasing significance of the AMT in CBO's revenue projections is described in more detail later in this chapter.) In addition, taxable distributions from tax-deferred retirement accounts, such as individual retirement accounts and 401(k) plans, are expected to rise as the population ages. Contributions to those accounts were exempt from taxation when they were made, which reduced taxable income in earlier years. Now, as more retirees take distributions

Figure 3-5.
Capital Gains Realizations as a Share of GDP, Calendar Years 1990-2013

(Percentage of GDP)

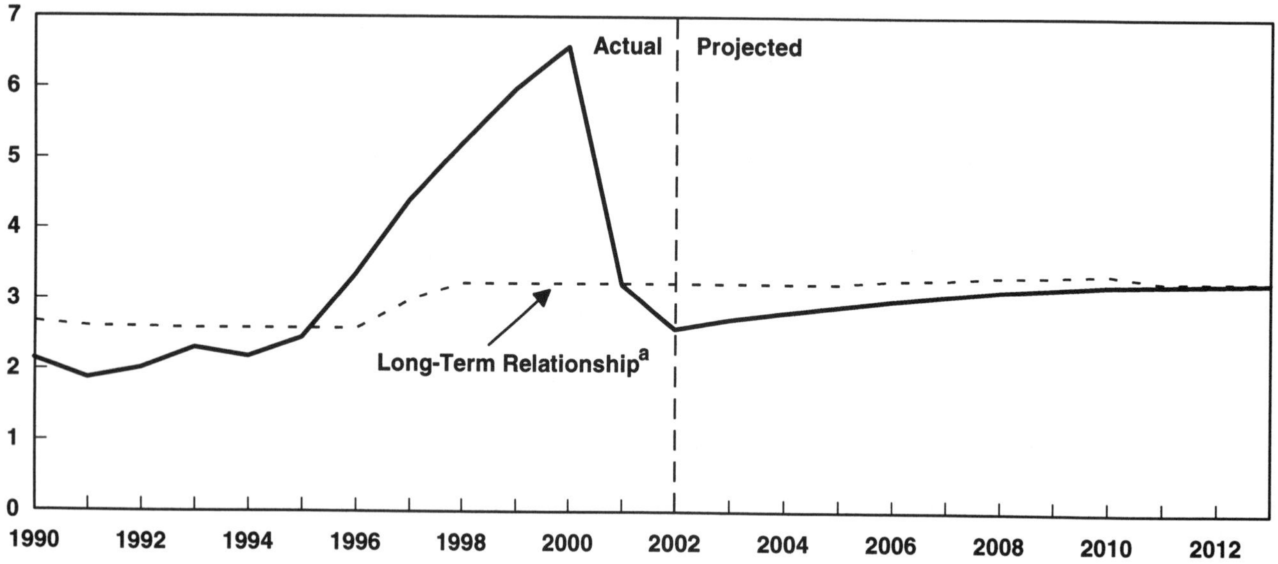

Source: Congressional Budget Office.

a. The long-term relationship of capital gains realizations to GDP is measured as the average ratio of gains to GDP over the 1954-2001 period, adjusted for differences between each year's tax rate on capital gains and the average rate over the period. A lower tax rate on capital gains corresponds to a higher long-term relationship of gains to GDP.

---

from those accounts, the money becomes taxable, boosting tax receipts relative to GDP.

Second, changes in tax law—principally those enacted in EGTRRA—will tend initially to curb and then to accelerate the growth of receipts. Under that law, marginal tax rates drop again in 2004 and 2006. In addition, during the 2006-2010 period, restrictions on itemized deductions and personal exemptions for high-income taxpayers phase out and the child tax credit increases. Each of those changes will tend to reduce the growth of individual income tax receipts. However, other features of the law expire before 2010, which tends to increase receipts slightly as a share of GDP. In 2011, all provisions of EGTRRA still in effect expire, which will cause revenues to climb sharply.

Third, capital gains realizations—a significant player in past movements of receipts—play a much smaller but nonetheless positive role in CBO's projections. Because it estimates that capital gains realizations declined in 2002, CBO expects receipts from capital gains taxes to fall in 2003. Realizations are now believed to be below the level consistent with their historical relationship to GDP (see Figure 3-5). They are therefore projected to rise slightly to that level, pushing up receipts as a percentage of GDP modestly over the 10-year projection period.

Finally, current collections of individual income taxes are running below the amounts that would be expected given the level of economic activity, estimated capital gains realizations and retirement distributions, and other factors known to influence the effective tax rate. That shortfall is likely to continue for a few years. However, CBO assumes that it will diminish in later years. Its gradual shrinking also tends to increase individual tax receipts relative to GDP over the projection period.

Social Insurance Taxes

In CBO's projections, revenues from social insurance taxes claim a roughly constant share of GDP, declining by only 0.1 percent of GDP over 10 years (see Table 3-6). In relation to wages and salaries—the approximate base of those payroll taxes—revenues decline somewhat more: from 14.2 percent in 2006 to 13.9 percent by 2013.

Table 3-6.
CBO's Projections of Social Insurance Tax Receipts and the Social Insurance Tax Base

	Actual 2002	2003	2004	2005	2006	2007	2008	2009	2010	2011	2012	2013	Total, 2004-2008	Total, 2004-2013
Social Insurance Tax Receipts														
In billions of dollars	701	725	766	811	856	901	944	989	1,037	1,085	1,134	1,188	4,277	9,709
As a percentage of GDP	6.8	6.7	6.8	6.8	6.8	6.8	6.8	6.7	6.7	6.7	6.7	6.7	n.a.	n.a.
Annual growth rate	1.0	3.5	5.6	5.9	5.6	5.2	4.8	4.8	4.9	4.6	4.6	4.7	n.a.	n.a.
Wages and Salaries														
In billions of dollars	4,982	5,181	5,442	5,743	6,047	6,365	6,697	7,043	7,405	7,771	8,134	8,533	30,294	69,179
As a percentage of GDP	48.2	48.2	48.1	48.1	48.1	48.0	47.9	47.9	47.8	47.8	47.8	47.8	n.a.	n.a.
Annual growth rate	0.7	4.0	5.0	5.5	5.3	5.3	5.2	5.2	5.1	4.9	4.7	4.9	n.a.	n.a.
Social Insurance Tax Receipts as a Percentage of Wages and Salaries	14.1	14.0	14.1	14.1	14.2	14.1	14.1	14.0	14.0	14.0	13.9	13.9	n.a.	n.a.

Source: Congressional Budget Office.

Notes: The tax base in this table (wages and salaries) reflects income as measured by the national income and product accounts rather than as reported on tax returns.

n.a. = not applicable.

The largest generators of payroll tax receipts are taxes for Social Security (officially Old-Age, Survivors, and Disability Insurance, or OASDI) and Medicare's Hospital Insurance (HI). A small share of social insurance tax revenues comes from unemployment insurance taxes and contributions to other federal retirement programs (see Table 3-7).

Social Security and Medicare taxes are calculated as a percentage of covered wages. Unlike the HI tax, which applies to all covered wages, the Social Security tax applies only up to a taxable maximum, which is indexed to the growth of wages over time. Consequently, receipts from OASDI and HI taxes tend to remain fairly stable as a proportion of income as long as covered wages are a stable share of GDP and the distribution of income from wages remains relatively unchanged.

CBO projects that social insurance tax receipts will decrease slightly this year relative to GDP. That decline is expected because the ratio of social insurance taxes to GDP in 2002 was unusually high, for two reasons. First, the maximum amount of wages on which OASDI taxes are imposed increases with average wages, but after a two-year lag. Hence, rapid wage growth in 2000, combined with much slower wage growth in 2002, caused the taxable maximum to rise relative to average wages and thus boosted the ratio of receipts to wages and GDP. As wages increase faster during the economic recovery and the taxable maximum lags behind, receipts in 2003 will slip slightly relative to both wages and GDP.

Second, the collections of OASDI and HI receipts in 2002 reported by the Treasury were 1.8 percent higher than CBO's models had predicted. However, reported receipts of HI and OASDI taxes are not actual receipts. When those payroll tax receipts are remitted to the Treasury, they are not distinguished from income tax withholding. The Treasury estimates the division using models and corrects any resulting error in later years. Over the past five years, those corrections have changed receipts by an average of 0.7 percent a year; in 2001, they lowered receipts by 1.9 percent. CBO believes that, as happened in 2001, the actual level of receipts was lower in 2002 than the Treasury Department currently estimates and that individual income taxes were correspondingly higher. In CBO's projections, that assumed overestimate disappears in subsequent years, driving projected receipts down relative to GDP.

Over the 10-year projection period, payroll tax receipts are expected to rise slightly and then gradually decline as

Table 3-7.
CBO's Projections of Social Insurance Tax Receipts, by Source
(In billions of dollars)

	Actual 2002	2003	2004	2005	2006	2007	2008	2009	2010	2011	2012	2013	Total, 2004-2008	Total, 2004-2013
Social Security	515	532	558	588	619	651	685	719	756	792	830	870	3,101	7,067
Medicare	149	151	159	168	177	186	196	206	217	228	239	251	886	2,027
Unemployment Insurance	28	34	41	47	52	55	55	55	56	57	58	60	249	536
Railroad Retirement	4	4	4	4	4	4	4	4	4	4	4	4	20	41
Other Retirement	5	4	4	4	4	4	4	4	4	3	3	3	21	38
Total	701	725	766	811	856	901	944	989	1,037	1,085	1,134	1,188	4,277	9,709

Source: Congressional Budget Office.

a share of GDP. CBO projects that as the economy swings back to full employment, the ratio of total social insurance receipts to wage and salary income will increase mostly because state unemployment systems will be replenishing their trust funds following the outflow of unemployment benefits during the recession. That effect is expected to peak in 2006. After that, social insurance receipts will slowly decline as a fraction of wages, for three reasons: states will have finished replenishing their unemployment trust funds, revenues associated with other federal retirement programs will be lower as the number of workers covered by Railroad Retirement and the old Civil Service Retirement System declines, and a slightly larger fraction of total wage and salary income will be above the maximum level of earnings subject to Social Security taxes.

Compared with its projections last August, CBO is now estimating about $90 billion less in social insurance tax receipts during the 2003-2012 period. Most of that reduction stems from changes in CBO's projections of wages and salaries because of the slowdown in economic growth. The rest is due to technical changes resulting primarily from the availability of recent data, which show that corrected receipts for 2001 were lower than the figure used in CBO's August projections.

Corporate Income Taxes

Corporate income taxes contributed some of the increase in federal revenues in the 1990s, as corporate profits surpassed their performance of the previous two decades. But the current recession has reduced profits—and therefore corporate income tax receipts—substantially. Those receipts (adjusted to take into account shifts in the timing of collections legislated by EGTRRA) fell from 2.1 percent of GDP in 2000 to 1.7 percent in 2001 and 1.2 percent in 2002. CBO expects them to increase relative to GDP through 2007, reaching 2.0 percent. They will then slip slightly in the remaining years of the projection period.

Corporate income tax revenues have followed much the same pattern as individual income tax receipts, rising markedly in the late 1990s and then falling in recent years. In the case of corporate taxes, however, the peak and decline occurred earlier, and the drop was even more significant. From 1994 through 1998, corporate tax receipts grew more rapidly than the overall economy. That performance was largely driven by very strong corporate profits. But as a percentage of GDP, corporate receipts peaked in 1998 (although they remained relatively strong in 1999 and 2000). After that, corporate receipts dropped even more significantly than individual receipts did. For 2003, CBO projects that corporate tax receipts will be lower as a percentage of GDP than they have been since the mid-1980s.

EGTRRA delayed corporations' estimated tax payments from September to October 2001, shifting approximately $23 billion in revenues from fiscal year 2001 into fiscal year 2002 and thus distorting the annual pattern of corporate receipts. Adjusted to account for that shift, corporate tax revenues fell from $207 billion in 2000 to $174 billion in 2001 and $125 billion in 2002, CBO estimates.

Table 3-8.
CBO's Projections of Corporate Income Tax Receipts and Tax Bases

	Actual 2002	2003	2004	2005	2006	2007	2008	2009	2010	2011	2012	2013	Total, 2004-2008	Total, 2004-2013
Corporate Income Tax Receipts														
In billions of dollars	148	156	185	228	249	260	269	276	285	295	306	316	1,190	2,669
As a percentage of GDP	1.4	1.5	1.6	1.9	2.0	2.0	1.9	1.9	1.8	1.8	1.8	1.8	n.a.	n.a.
Annual growth rate	-2.0	5.5	18.3	23.4	9.3	4.2	3.4	2.9	3.1	3.7	3.6	3.4	n.a.	n.a.
Corporate Book Profits														
In billions of dollars	641	707	786	1,070	1,192	1,230	1,260	1,292	1,331	1,373	1,419	1,463	5,539	12,416
As a percentage of GDP	6.2	6.6	7.0	9.0	9.5	9.3	9.0	8.8	8.6	8.4	8.3	8.2	n.a.	n.a.
Annual growth rate	-9.5	10.3	11.2	36.1	11.3	3.2	2.4	2.6	3.0	3.1	3.3	3.1	n.a.	n.a.
Taxable Corporate Profits[a]														
In billions of dollars	500	561	598	803	886	913	933	956	985	1,014	1,045	1,076	4,133	9,209
As a percentage of GDP	4.8	5.2	5.3	6.7	7.0	6.9	6.7	6.5	6.4	6.2	6.1	6.0	n.a.	n.a.
Annual growth rate	-12.1	12.1	6.6	34.4	10.4	3.0	2.3	2.4	3.0	3.0	3.1	2.9	n.a.	n.a.
Corporate Tax Receipts as a Percentage of Taxable Profits	29.6	27.9	30.9	28.4	28.1	28.5	28.8	28.9	28.9	29.1	29.3	29.4	n.a.	n.a.
Adjusted Corporate Tax Receipts as a Percentage of Taxable Profits[b]	25.0	27.9	32.0	27.6	28.1	28.5	28.8	28.9	28.9	29.1	29.3	29.4	n.a.	n.a.

Source: Congressional Budget Office.

Notes: The tax bases in this table (corporate book profits and taxable corporate profits) reflect income as measured by the national income and product accounts rather than as reported on tax returns.

n.a. = not applicable.

a. Taxable corporate profits are defined as book profits minus profits earned by the Federal Reserve System, transnational corporations, and S corporations and minus deductible payments of state and local corporate taxes. They include capital gains realized by corporations.

b. Excludes the shift in corporate receipts from 2001 to 2002 and from 2004 to 2005 enacted in the Economic Growth and Tax Relief Reconciliation Act of 2001.

That drop was caused almost entirely by the slowing of the economy and the effects of the economic stimulus package enacted last March. The stimulus package allowed more-rapid write-offs of investment and increased firms' ability to use losses from 2001 and 2002 to offset tax liability in previous years. That expanded "carryback" provision made companies better able to obtain refunds of previous years' taxes on the basis of losses in each of the past two years. The result was a substantial increase in corporate tax refunds in fiscal year 2002 and a substantial fall in net corporate tax receipts.

CBO's projection of corporate receipts for the next 10 years reflects a combination of recovery from the recession, effects of the stimulus package and its expiration, and longer-term changes in profits as a share of GDP. CBO expects corporate tax receipts to recover somewhat in 2003 and then grow more strongly, so that by 2005, they reach 1.9 percent of GDP. Those receipts remain between 1.8 percent and 2.0 percent of GDP through the end of the projection period (see Table 3-8).

In CBO's economic forecast, corporations' book profits—the underlying base of the corporate income tax—grow faster than GDP from 2003 through 2006. (For more details of CBO's outlook for the economy, see Chapter 2.) Their growth in 2003 and 2004 is largely caused by recovery from the 2001 recession, in which profits were especially depressed. The effect of economic recovery on book profits is an important reason that corporate tax receipts

Table 3-9
CBO's Projections of Excise Tax Receipts, by Source
(In billions of dollars)

	Actual 2002	2003	2004	2005	2006	2007	2008	2009	2010	2011	2012	2013	Total, 2004-2008	Total, 2004-2013
Highway Taxes	34	34	36	37	39	40	41	42	43	44	45	46	192	412
Airport Taxes	9	9	10	11	12	12	13	14	14	15	16	17	58	134
Telephone Taxes	6	6	7	7	8	8	9	9	10	10	11	11	38	89
Alcohol Taxes	8	8	8	8	9	9	9	9	9	9	9	9	43	88
Tobacco Taxes	8	8	8	8	8	8	8	8	8	8	8	8	40	80
All Other Excise Taxes	3	3	3	3	3	3	3	3	3	3	3	3	13	27
Total	**67**	**68**	**71**	**74**	**77**	**79**	**82**	**84**	**87**	**90**	**92**	**95**	**383**	**831**

Source: Congressional Budget Office.

rise relative to GDP in the first half of the projection period.

Corporate receipts in the first half of that period are also affected by provisions of the stimulus package. Because of the availability of expanded carryback losses in calendar year 2002, corporate tax refunds are expected to be high in fiscal year 2003, tending to depress receipts. But in fiscal year 2004, the opposite will occur, because refunds that otherwise might have been paid in that year will have been accelerated into 2002 and 2003. Some of that effect can be seen in the behavior of receipts as a percentage of taxable profits. The percentage is especially low in 2002 because of the expanded carryback refunds and high in 2004 because of their lapse. In addition, the partial-expensing provisions of the stimulus law expire in 2004. Accelerated depreciation has the effect of reducing tax liability immediately at the cost of higher liability later. Hence, beginning in 2005, the corporate income tax begins to recoup some of its earlier loss of receipts, a gain that shows up mostly in the increase in taxable profits relative to GDP in 2005 and 2006. Another effect from tax-law changes occurs in 2004 and 2005, when EGTRRA again shifts some tax receipts between two fiscal years.

After 2006, CBO expects profits to decline gradually relative to GDP, decreasing corporate taxes as well. That effect is somewhat muted by a small rise in receipts as a percentage of taxable profits. As profits decline relative to GDP, losses as a proportion of net profits are higher. Firms pay taxes to the government on the profits they earn, but they do not receive payments from the government if they lose money (except to the extent that they can carry their losses forward or backward to offset profits in other years). Consequently, the overall effective corporate tax rate—receipts divided by net profits—tends to be higher when net corporate profits are lower.

CBO is now projecting about $100 billion more in corporate tax receipts over the 2003-2012 period than it did in August. About a third of that increase results directly from changes in CBO's economic forecast. The rest stems from technical changes, which mostly reflect a reinterpretation of tax collections in 2002. Last August, CBO recognized that corporate tax collections (net of refunds) were lower than would be expected given the economic conditions believed to have existed at that time. CBO projected that shortfall to continue. It now appears that the unexpected behavior of corporate tax collections last year can be explained by higher refunds generated by greater use of the expanded carryback provisions. Since those provisions are temporary, CBO now assumes that collections will return to their expected relationship to overall profits and tax liability. That assumption raises the level of receipts projected for the years after 2003, when the carryback provisions expire.

Excise Taxes

Receipts from excise taxes are expected to continue their long-term decline as a share of GDP, falling from 0.6 percent in 2002 to 0.5 percent toward the end of the 10-year projection period. Most excise taxes—those generating about 80 percent of total excise revenues—are levied per unit of good or per transaction rather than as a percentage of value. Thus, excise receipts grow with real GDP, but they do not rise with inflation and therefore do not grow as fast as nominal GDP does.

Nearly all excise taxes fall into five major categories: highway, airport, telephone, alcohol, and tobacco taxes (*see Table 3-9*). Almost half of all excise receipts are earmarked by law to the Highway Trust Fund; they come primarily from taxes on gasoline and diesel fuel. Most airport and telephone excise taxes are levied on a percentage basis, so they grow at a faster rate than the other categories do. Tobacco taxes rose at the beginning of 2002 but are expected to remain roughly stable from 2003 through 2013.

CBO's current projection of total excise tax receipts for the next 10 years is slightly lower than the projection it published in August. Changes in CBO's economic forecast reduce that projection by just a few billion dollars. Technical adjustments have a bigger effect, lowering projected excise receipts by a total of about $15 billion over the 2003-2012 period. Half of that decrease comes from reduced projections of motor fuel taxes, largely because CBO assumes that a greater share of the demand for motor fuel will be for oxygenated fuels, which are taxed at a lower rate. The other half of the reduction comes largely from lower projections of receipts from passenger ticket taxes dedicated to the Airport and Airway Trust Fund.

Estate and Gift Taxes

CBO expects receipts from estate and gift taxes to change in importance over the projection period: their share of GDP is forecast to decline from 0.3 percent in 2002 to 0.1 percent in 2010 and 2011 before jumping back to 0.3 percent in 2012 and 2013. That pattern results from the phasing out of the estate tax under EGTRRA and its subsequent reinstatement when the law expires in 2011.

In the past, revenues from estate and gift taxes tended to grow more rapidly than income because the unified credit for the two taxes, which effectively exempts some assets from taxation, is not indexed for inflation. Under EGTRRA, however, the pattern of receipts over time is quite different. The estate tax is gradually being eliminated; the gift tax remains in the tax code but in a modified form. Today, tax law effectively exempts $1 million of an estate from taxation. EGTRRA will raise that amount to $3.5 million in 2009. EGTRRA will also reduce the highest tax rate on estates from 50 percent to 45 percent by 2007 and then eliminate the tax in 2010. The law's provisions are scheduled to expire at the end of 2010, however, which means that the estate tax is set to return the following year. Because estate tax liabilities are paid after a lag, and because the gift tax remains in the tax code, receipts from estate and gift taxes do not disappear completely in CBO's projection period but instead reach a trough in 2010 (*see Table 3-10*). CBO estimates that in 2012 they will return to their 2002 share of GDP.

CBO's current projections of estate and gift tax receipts are similar to those it produced last August. Changes in CBO's economic forecast have had a negligible effect on the projections. Small technical changes—including the impact of the stock market on projected wealth and reestimates of gift tax receipts around the time EGTRRA expires—net to an increase of $7 billion in receipts over 10 years compared with the August projections.

Other Sources of Revenues

Customs duties and numerous miscellaneous sources bring in much smaller amounts of revenue than the major levies do. CBO estimates that those revenues will remain fairly steady as a share of GDP—at just above 0.5 percent—throughout the projection period. That share will be slightly lower in the first few years, however, because of the effect of low short-term interest rates on the Federal Reserve System's earnings.

CBO projects that customs duties will grow over time in tandem with imports. During the next few years, however, their growth will be curbed as tariff reductions enacted in 1994 are phased in. Projections of customs duties are slightly higher now than in August, largely for technical reasons.

The largest component of miscellaneous receipts is the profits of the Federal Reserve System, which are counted as revenues once they are turned over to the Treasury (*see Table 3-10*). Those profits depend on the interest that the Federal Reserve earns on its portfolio of securities and on gains and losses from its holdings of foreign currency. In the past two years, earnings on securities have declined

Table 3-10.
CBO's Projections of Other Sources of Revenue
(In billions of dollars)

	Actual 2002	2003	2004	2005	2006	2007	2008	2009	2010	2011	2012	2013	Total, 2004-2008	Total, 2004-2013
Estate and Gift Taxes	27	21	24	21	24	20	22	23	15	19	43	47	110	258
Customs Duties	19	18	20	20	21	22	23	24	25	26	27	28	107	237
Miscellaneous Receipts														
Federal Reserve earnings	24	22	24	29	33	36	38	41	42	44	46	49	159	382
Universal Service Fund	5	6	7	7	7	7	7	7	7	7	8	8	34	71
Other	5	5	5	5	5	5	5	5	5	5	5	5	24	47
Subtotal	34	33	36	40	44	47	50	52	54	56	59	61	217	500
Total	79	73	79	82	89	89	95	100	94	102	129	137	434	995

Source: Congressional Budget Office.

as the Federal Reserve has lowered interest rates to stimulate economic growth and counter the economy's downturn. In addition, the recession has slowed the growth of the Federal Reserve's portfolio of assets because of slower growth in the public's holdings of U.S. currency. Those factors have led CBO to project that receipts from the Federal Reserve System this year will be substantially below the average of recent years. However, the central bank's income—and therefore the receipts it remits to the Treasury—are expected to return to their previous trend in 2004 and 2005.

Since August, expectations of slower economic growth have led CBO to reduce its projection of miscellaneous receipts for the 2003-2012 period by about $12 billion. Partly offsetting that reduction, reestimates of activity in the Universal Service Fund (which result in corresponding increases in projected spending) and other, smaller technical revisions raise the 10-year projection of miscellaneous receipts by about $6 billion.

The Growing Significance of the AMT in CBO's Projections

The alternative minimum tax will increasingly become a consideration in discussions about many different aspects of tax policy. For one thing, the AMT is an important reason why receipts are expected to grow relative to GDP over the next 10 years. For another thing, it substantially reduces the revenue loss that would occur if the provisions of EGTRRA that are scheduled to expire at the end of 2010 were extended. Further, the AMT will affect more and more taxpayers in coming years, many of whom were not the intended target of the tax when it was enacted. As the impact of the AMT grows over time, reforming or repealing it will become more expensive, leaving less room to reduce taxes in other ways.

Characteristics of the Alternative Minimum Tax

The AMT is a parallel income tax system with fewer exemptions, deductions, and rates than the regular income tax. It was enacted to limit the extent to which high-income taxpayers can reduce the amount of tax they owe by using various preferences in the regular tax code. Taxpayers with potential AMT liability must calculate their taxes under both the AMT and the regular income tax and pay whichever figure is higher. The amount by which a taxpayer's AMT calculation exceeds his or her regular tax calculation is defined as AMT liability.

Like the rate structure of the regular income tax, the AMT extracts a greater proportion of overall income as real income rises. But unlike the regular income tax, the AMT is not indexed to inflation. Consequently, inflation increases the amount of income to which the AMT applies and the number of taxpayers subject to it each year. Those effects are compounded by the cuts in marginal tax rates enacted in EGTRRA. Because those cuts reduce regular

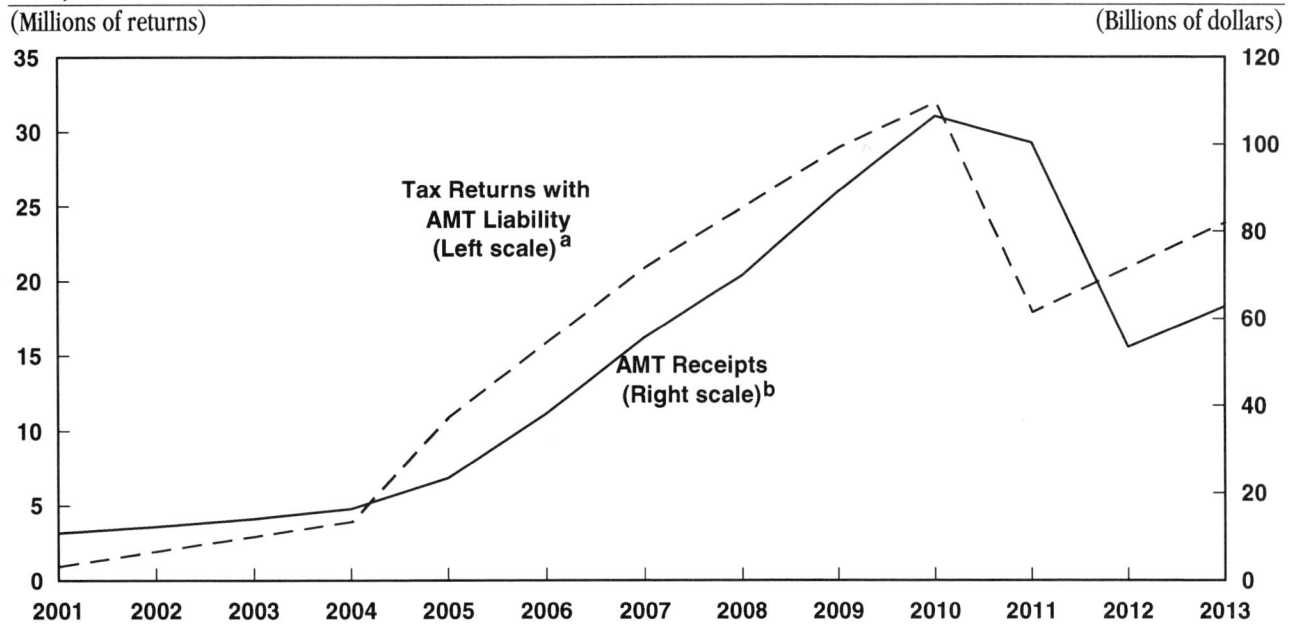

Figure 3-6.
Projected Effects of the Individual Alternative Minimum Tax

(Millions of returns) — (Billions of dollars)

Source: Congressional Budget Office.

Note: The alternative minimum tax requires some taxpayers to calculate their taxes under a more limited set of exemptions, deductions, and credits than the set applicable under the regular individual income tax.

a. Calendar year basis.
b. Fiscal year basis.

tax liability without changing the AMT, they further increase the AMT's contribution to total revenues.

The preferences not allowed under the AMT include personal exemptions and the standard deduction, so the AMT reaches some taxpayers not ordinarily thought of as exploiting "loopholes" to avoid taxation of high incomes. That situation increases over time as nominal income grows. For example, in tax year 2005, a married taxpayer earning $90,000 who has three children and reports a typical set of deductions will be subject to the AMT under current law.

The AMT's Impact Over the Next 10 Years

For the moment, the growing reach of the alternative minimum tax has been slowed because EGTRRA raised the amount of income that is exempt from the tax. But that provision will expire at the end of 2004. After that, the number of taxpayers subject to the AMT will rise sharply.

Comparing the number of taxpayers subject to the AMT and the amount that the tax raises in 2002 with those effects in 2013 (after the remaining provisions of EGTRRA expire) demonstrates how the impact of the AMT increases as a result of nominal income growth. CBO estimates that in 2002, 2 million tax returns will have AMT liability, and receipts from the tax will total $12 billion (*see Figure 3-6*).

In 2013, about 24 million returns are projected to have AMT liability, and the tax will add an estimated $60 billion in revenues. Over that 11-year span, the importance of the AMT as a source of individual income tax receipts more than doubles, from contributing 1.4 percent of those receipts to 3.2 percent.

In the years in between, the rise and fall of the AMT's projected effects reflect the phasing in and expiration of provisions of EGTRRA. The number of returns subject to the AMT rises from 4 million in 2004 (just before the provision raising the exemption amount expires) to about

33 million in 2010 (just before the rest of EGTRRA's provisions expire). In fiscal year 2010, the AMT is projected to add more than $100 billion to the revenues from the regular tax, or about 7 percent of total individual income tax receipts. The differences between 2010 and 2012 in AMT receipts ($50 billion) and returns affected (12 million) indicate the degree to which the cuts in marginal tax rates under EGTRRA will have been muted by the AMT.

Issues in Reforming the Alternative Minimum Tax

Whether EGTRRA is allowed to expire, its provisions are extended, or its scheduled rate cuts are rescinded before taking effect, the increasing bite of the AMT has an impact on the amount of revenue that will result. Moreover, with each passing year, the alternative minimum tax plays a bigger and bigger role in revenue projections, meaning that the budget baseline is increasingly contingent on retention of the AMT.

The first issue that lawmakers will face with respect to the alternative minimum tax comes up immediately. In 2003, the provision of the tax code that allows taxpayers to claim the education tax credits enacted in the Taxpayer Relief Act of 1997 and other personal credits against the AMT will expire. That provision was extended temporarily in 1998, 1999, and 2002. Extending it permanently would cost about $44 billion over the next decade.

Reform of the AMT could take various forms. Besides extending the provisions that are scheduled to expire, such reform could include eliminating exemptions for dependents or the standard deduction as preferences under the AMT or indexing the AMT exemption for inflation. It could also take the form of repealing the alternative minimum tax. That would be the most expensive option, costing the federal government roughly $600 billion in revenues through 2013 (assuming that the repeal took effect in tax year 2004).

AMT reform and the costs associated with it are closely tied up with the costs of extending EGTRRA. The existing AMT would substantially mute the revenue loss associated with extending the EGTRRA provisions that expire at the end of 2010. Similarly, the cost of reducing or eliminating the AMT would be higher if EGTRRA were extended. For example, repealing the AMT would cost roughly $200 billion more if EGTRRA did not expire. Because of those interactions, reforming the AMT and extending EGTRRA would cost more if carried out together than the sum of the individual costs of those policy changes.

The Effects of Expiring Tax Provisions

CBO's revenue projections rest on the assumption that current tax laws remain unaltered except for scheduled changes and expirations, which occur on time. The sole exception to that approach is the expiration of excise taxes dedicated to trust funds, which, under budget rules, are included in the revenue projections whether or not they are scheduled to expire.

The assumption that tax provisions expire as scheduled can have a significant impact on CBO's estimates—even in ordinary circumstances, when those provisions do not include such large changes as the EGTRRA tax cuts or the special depreciation rules enacted in last year's economic stimulus package. Many expiring provisions are extended almost as a matter of course, and most of them reduce receipts. Thus, revenue projections that assumed the extension of those provisions would be lower than revenue estimates projected under current law. To provide as complete an outlook for revenues as possible, this section details the various tax provisions whose expiration is reflected in CBO's projections.

Provisions That Expire in 2003

Seventeen tax provisions are scheduled to expire by the end of 2003, of which 15 reduce revenues (*see Table 3-11*). Most of them had been set to expire before and were extended temporarily, in some cases numerous times. If all 15 of the revenue-reducing provisions were immediately and permanently extended, revenues would be a total of $68 billion lower over the 2004-2013 period. About two-thirds of that effect—or $44 billion—would come from the measure that allows taxpayers to claim certain personal credits (especially the education tax credits that were enacted in the Taxpayer Relief Act of 1997) against the AMT. As noted earlier, that provision had previously been scheduled to expire and was extended temporarily in 1998, 1999, and 2002.

Two provisions that increase revenues are also scheduled to expire by the end of 2003. If they were extended, revenues would rise by a total of $13 billion over the 2004-2013 period. Nearly all of that effect would come from a provision enacted in last year's stimulus package. It raises the interest rate that firms use to calculate their required contributions to defined-benefit pension plans and their premium payments to the Pension Benefit Guaranty Corporation, both of which are tax-deductible.

Provisions That Expire During the 2004-2013 Period

A number of additional provisions will expire during CBO's current projection period. The most significant of those from a budgetary perspective are the ones enacted in EGTRRA. Three provisions of that law—the increased exemption amount for the AMT, the deduction for qualified education expenses, and the credit for individual retirement accounts and 401(k)-type plans—are set to expire by the end of 2006. The rest of the provisions, which represent the bulk of the law's budgetary effects, expire on December 31, 2010. If all of those measures were extended, revenues would be $785 billion lower through 2013, CBO and the Joint Committee on Taxation (JCT) project. Most of that reduction ($665 billion) would come at the end of the period, in 2011 through 2013, mainly as a result of extending the tax cuts that would otherwise expire at the end of 2010. Those cuts include the decreases in marginal tax rates for individuals, increases in the child tax credit, and repeal of the estate tax.

About $120 billion of the revenue loss from extending the expiring provisions of EGTRRA would occur before 2011. Immediately extending the changes to estate and gift taxes, which expire at the end of 2010, could reduce revenues as early as this year. The reason is that if taxpayers knew that the repeal of the estate tax would become permanent in 2011, some might postpone taxable gifts that they would otherwise have made during this decade. CBO's and JCT's estimates of the effects of extending EGTRRA also incorporate the assumption that the higher exemption levels for the AMT, which expire in 2004, are extended at their 2004 levels. Under that assumption, the exemption levels would not rise with inflation, so a growing number of taxpayers would still become subject to the AMT over time—albeit fewer than if the higher exemption levels expired as now scheduled.

Sixteen provisions not related to EGTRRA end between 2004 and 2009, 12 of which would reduce revenues if extended. The one with by far the greatest effect is the provision to allow a special depreciation allowance of 30 percent for equipment investment made by September 10, 2004. That provision, enacted in March 2002 as a part of the economic stimulus package, is supposed to expire next year. If extended, it would reduce revenues by $256 billion through 2013. The provision with the second largest effect is the research and experimentation tax credit, which was enacted in 1981. In 1999, the Congress extended that tax benefit through June 2004, for the ninth and longest time. Continuing the credit through 2013 would reduce revenues by about $56 billion. In all, extending those 12 revenue-reducing provisions would decrease receipts by $370 billion through 2013. Excluding the depreciation provision enacted in the economic stimulus package—which was not intended to be permanent—extension of the remaining provisions would lower revenues by $114 billion through 2013.

Four provisions that expire between 2004 and 2008 would increase revenues if they were extended. The provision with the largest revenue effect is the Federal Unemployment Tax Act surcharge, which expires in 2008. Extending that provision would raise about $8 billion in revenues through 2013. The other three provisions would impose fees for the reclamation of abandoned mines, allow employers to transfer excess assets in defined-benefit pension plans to a special account for retirees' health benefits, and provide authority to the Internal Revenue Service for certain undercover operations. Extending the mine fees would raise more than $200 million per year. The two remaining provisions would each raise less than $50 million annually.

Expiring Provisions That Are Included in CBO's Baseline

Budget rules require CBO to include in its projections excise tax receipts earmarked for trust funds, even if provisions for those taxes are scheduled to expire. The largest such taxes that are slated to expire during the next 10 years finance the Highway Trust Fund. Some of the taxes for that fund are permanent, but most of them end on September 30, 2005. Extending them at today's rates

Table 3-11.
Effect of Extending Tax Provisions That Will Expire Before 2013
(In billions of dollars)

Tax Provision	Expiration Date	2003	2004	2005	2006	2007	2008	2009	2010	2011	2012	2013	Total, 2004-2008	Total, 2004-2013
Provisions Expiring in 2003														
IRS User Fees	9/30/2003	n.a.	**	**	**	**	**	**	**	**	**	**	0.2	0.4
Archer Medical Savings Accounts	12/31/2003	n.a.	*	*	*	*	*	*	*	*	*	*	*	-0.1
Brownfields Remediation	12/31/2003	**	-0.1	-0.3	-0.3	-0.3	-0.3	-0.3	-0.3	-0.3	-0.3	-0.3	-1.3	-2.9
Credit for Electric Vehicles	12/31/2003	n.a.	*	*	*	*	*	*	*	*	*	*	-0.1	-0.2
Credit for Electricity Production from Renewable Sources	12/31/2003	n.a.	*	*	*	*	-0.1	-0.1	-0.1	-0.1	-0.1	-0.1	-0.1	-0.6
Corporate Contributions of Computers to Schools	12/31/2003	n.a.	-0.1	-0.1	-0.1	-0.1	-0.2	-0.2	-0.2	-0.2	-0.2	-0.2	-0.6	-1.5
Deductions for Clean-Fuel Vehicles and Refueling Property	12/31/2003	n.a.	-0.1	-0.1	-0.3	-0.3	-0.3	-0.3	-0.3	-0.2	-0.2	-0.2	-1.1	-2.4
Deduction for Teachers' Classroom Expenses	12/31/2003	n.a.	-0.1	-0.2	-0.3	-0.3	-0.3	-0.3	-0.3	-0.3	-0.3	-0.3	-1.1	-2.6
Interest Rate for Pension Calculations	12/31/2003	n.a.	1.7	2.5	1.4	1.8	1.9	1.3	0.9	0.4	0.2	0.2	9.3	12.3
Net Income Limitation for Marginal Oil and Gas Wells	12/31/2003	n.a.	*	*	*	*	*	*	*	*	*	*	-0.2	-0.4
Qualified Zone Academy Bonds	12/31/2003	n.a.	*	*	*	*	*	*	-0.1	-0.1	-0.1	-0.1	-0.1	-0.4
Reduction in Policyholder Dividends for Insurance Companies	12/31/2003	n.a.	*	*	*	*	*	*	*	*	*	*	-0.2	-0.4
Tax Incentives for Investment in the District of Columbia	12/31/2003	n.a.	-0.1	-0.1	-0.1	-0.1	-0.1	-0.2	-0.3	-0.3	-0.4	-0.4	-0.5	-2.2
Treatment of Nonrefundable Personal Credits Under the AMT	12/31/2003	n.a.	-0.1	-1.0	-2.4	-3.5	-4.1	-4.7	-5.2	-6.0	-7.9	-8.8	-11.1	-43.8
Welfare-to-Work Tax Credit	12/31/2003	n.a.	*	-0.1	-0.1	-0.1	-0.1	-0.1	-0.1	-0.1	-0.1	-0.1	-0.4	-1.0
Work Opportunity Tax Credit	12/31/2003	n.a.	-0.1	-0.2	-0.3	-0.3	-0.3	-0.3	-0.4	-0.4	-0.4	-0.4	-1.2	-3.0
Tax Incentives for Areas of New York City Damaged on Sept. 11	Various[a]	n.a.	-0.1	-0.3	-0.3	-0.7	-0.9	-0.8	-0.8	-0.8	-0.8	-0.7	-2.2	-6.2

Sources: Joint Committee on Taxation, Congressional Budget Office.

Notes: * = between -$50 million and zero; ** = between zero and $50 million; n.a. = not applicable; IRS = Internal Revenue Service; AMT = alternative minimum tax; IRA = individual retirement account; FUTA = Federal Unemployment Tax Act; EGTRRA = Economic Growth and Tax Relief Reconciliation Act of 2001.

These estimates assume that the expiring provisions are extended immediately rather than when they are about to expire. The provisions are assumed to be extended at the rates or levels existing at the time of expiration. These estimates do not include effects on debt-service costs.

When this report went to press, JCT's estimates were unavailable for several expiring tax provisions—most significantly, for EGTRRA's major individual income tax provisions that expire in 2010 and for the AMT provisions that expire in earlier years. CBO estimated the effects of extending those provisions, as well as the interaction from extending all expiring tax provisions simultaneously. As a result, cost estimates by JCT for legislative proposals to extend the EGTRRA and AMT provisions might not match the figures shown here.

(Continued)

Table 3-11.
Continued

(In billions of dollars)

Tax Provision	Expiration Date	2003	2004	2005	2006	2007	2008	2009	2010	2011	2012	2013	Total, 2004-2008	Total, 2004-2013
Provisions Expiring Between 2004 and 2013														
Credit for Research and Experimentation	6/30/2004	n.a.	-0.5	-3.3	-4.3	-5.2	-6.0	-6.6	-7.0	-7.5	-7.9	-8.3	-19.1	-56.4
Special Depreciation Allowance for Certain Property	9/10/2004	n.a.	n.a.	-27.7	-41.7	-38.9	-34.4	-29.4	-24.9	-21.5	-19.0	-18.3	-142.6	-255.7
Abandoned-Mine Reclamation Fees	9/30/2004	n.a.	n.a.	0.2	0.2	0.2	0.2	0.2	0.3	0.3	0.3	0.3	1.0	2.2
Depreciation for Business Property on Indian Reservations	12/31/2004	n.a.	**	-0.2	-0.4	-0.5	-0.5	-0.5	-0.4	-0.3	-0.3	-0.3	-1.7	-3.3
Depreciation of Clean-Fuel Automobiles	12/31/2004	n.a.	n.a.	*	*	*	*	*	*	*	*	*	*	-0.1
Increased AMT Exemption Amount	12/31/2004	n.a.	n.a.	-3.3	-10.2	-14.4	-18.2	-22.4	-25.3	-21.5	-14.8	-17.2	-46.1	-147.3
Indian Employment Tax Credit	12/31/2004	n.a.	n.a.	*	*	-0.1	-0.1	-0.1	-0.1	-0.1	-0.1	-0.1	-0.2	-0.5
Authority for Undercover IRS Operations	12/31/2005	n.a.	n.a.	n.a.	**	**	**	**	**	**	**	**	**	**
Deduction for Qualified Education Expenses	12/31/2005	n.a.	n.a.	n.a.	-1.7	-2.4	-2.6	-2.8	-2.9	-2.6	-2.6	-2.6	-6.8	-20.3
Puerto Rico Business Credits	12/31/2005	n.a.	n.a.	n.a.	-0.7	-1.6	-1.8	-1.9	-2.1	-2.3	-2.6	-3.0	-4.0	-16.0
Transfer of Excess Assets in Defined-Benefit Plans	12/31/2005	n.a.	n.a.	n.a.	**	**	**	**	**	**	**	**	0.1	0.3
Andean Trade Preference Initiative	12/31/2006	n.a.	n.a.	n.a.	n.a.	*	*	*	*	*	*	*	-0.1	-0.2
Credit for IRA and 401(k)-Type Plans	12/31/2006	n.a.	n.a.	n.a.	n.a.	-0.7	-1.4	-1.2	-1.1	-1.0	-1.0	-0.9	-2.0	-7.3
Generalized System of Preferences	12/31/2006	n.a.	n.a.	n.a.	n.a.	-0.4	-0.6	-0.6	-0.7	-0.7	-0.8	-0.8	-1.0	-4.7
Subpart F for Active Financing Income	12/31/2006	n.a.	n.a.	n.a.	n.a.	-0.9	-2.7	-3.1	-3.5	-4.0	-4.4	-4.8	-3.6	-23.3
Alcohol Fuels Income Credit	12/31/2007	n.a.	n.a.	n.a.	n.a.	n.a.	*	*	*	*	*	*	*	*
FUTA Surtax of 0.2 Percentage Points	12/31/2007	n.a.	n.a.	n.a.	n.a.	n.a.	1.0	1.5	1.5	1.5	1.5	1.5	1.0	8.5
New Markets Tax Credit	12/31/2007	n.a.	n.a.	n.a.	n.a.	n.a.	-0.1	-0.3	-0.4	-0.6	-0.8	-1.0	-0.1	-3.3
Empowerment and Renewal Zones	12/31/2009	n.a.	n.a.	n.a.	n.a.	n.a.	n.a.	n.a.	-0.8	-1.7	-1.8	-2.0	n.a.	-6.4
General Expiration of EGTRRA Provisions	12/31/2010	-0.1	-0.5	-0.8	-1.0	-1.3	-1.7	-1.6	-2.4	-131.0	-230.2	-239.7	-5.3	-610.1
All Expiring Provisions[b]														
Total		-0.1	-0.1	-33.9	-61.4	-69.2	-72.7	-73.9	-76.1	-206.1	-307.6	-321.0	-237.4	-1,222.0

a. The provision that expands the work opportunity tax credit in New York City expires on 12/31/2003. The provisions that increase expensing under section 179 and allow a five-year lifetime for leasehold improvements expire on 12/31/2006. The provisions related to 30 percent bonus depreciation for property placed in service expire on 12/31/2006 and 12/31/2009.

b. The overall total does not equal the sums of the separate provisions because it includes estimated interactions among provisions, which are especially important from 2011 through 2013. Those interactions, which would occur if all of the provisions were extended together, would reduce revenues by $23 billion in the 2004-2013 period.

contributes $38 billion to CBO's revenue projections in 2013, or about 40 percent of that year's total excise tax receipts.

Other expiring trust fund taxes, if extended, would account for smaller amounts in 2013, CBO estimates. Taxes dedicated to the Airport and Airway Trust Fund, which are scheduled to expire at the end of 2007, would contribute about $16 billion to revenues in 2013. Taxes for the Leaking Underground Storage Tank Trust Fund, set to end on March 31, 2005, would contribute about $250 million. No other expiring tax provisions are automatically extended in CBO's projections.

Total Effects of Expiring Provisions

If all expiring tax provisions were extended together, the revenue projection for 2004 would be $0.1 billion lower. However, that revenue loss would grow to $34 billion the following year and to $76 billion by 2010, before jumping to $206 billion in 2011 and then reaching $321 billion by 2013. Over the entire 2004-2013 period, revenues would be reduced by more than $1.2 trillion. (That estimate of the effects of jointly extending the expiring provisions includes interactions among the provisions, which reduce revenues by $23 billion over that period.) A more limited measure of the effects of extending expiring legislation would not include provisions of the economic stimulus law, which were not intended to be permanent. If all but those expiring provisions were extended, federal revenues would be $960 billion lower through 2013.

CHAPTER 4

The Spending Outlook

Federal spending totaled more than $2.0 trillion in 2002—an increase of $147 billion, or 7.9 percent, from the previous year. Excluding interest payments, spending last year jumped by 11 percent—the largest increase since 1981. Substantial increases in both defense and nondefense discretionary spending, a sharp rise in outlays for unemployment benefits, and continued growth in the major entitlement programs accounted for the upswing (*see Box 4-1* for descriptions of various types of federal spending).

On the discretionary side of the budget, defense and nondefense outlays each grew by roughly $42 billion in 2002. The Congressional Budget Office estimates that more than half of the growth in defense spending resulted from initiatives that were planned or funded before the September 11 terrorist attacks; most of the remaining growth supported the war against terrorism. Growth in nondefense discretionary spending was spread among various programs, most notably in the areas of education, transportation, health, and justice.

On the mandatory side of the budget, payments for unemployment benefits climbed by $23 billion as the unemployment rate rose significantly and a temporary extension in benefits was enacted. Spending for the three major entitlement programs—Social Security, Medicare, and Medicaid—went up by about $57 billion, and outlays for other mandatory programs rose by $17 billion. Offsetting the growth in other areas of the budget were net interest payments, which declined by $35 billion in 2002.

CBO projects that federal spending will grow less rapidly this year. Under the assumptions (of the adjusted baseline) that current laws remain the same and that discretionary budget authority totals about $751 billion after the regular 2003 appropriations are enacted, CBO projects that spending will rise by $110 billion, to $2.1 trillion—a 5.5 percent increase over 2002 outlays (*see Tables 4-1 and 4-2*). Excluding interest payments, spending is projected to grow by 6.7 percent in 2003. A war with Iraq or other additional spending, however, could push outlays significantly above those levels (see Chapter 5).

Fueling the growth in outlays for 2003 are increases in discretionary spending and continued growth in entitlements, offset by lower net interest payments resulting from currently low interest rates. On the basis of the two appropriation acts (defense and military construction) that have been enacted, CBO estimates that budget authority for defense discretionary programs has increased by $21 billion (5.8 percent) from the 2002 level. That increase—along with spending from earlier budget authority provided in response to the September 11 terrorist attacks and other appropriations—is estimated to boost defense outlays by $28 billion (7.9 percent) over the level in 2002. Assuming nondefense budget authority of about $369 billion—the difference between the target level of $751 billion for all discretionary funding and the $382 billion assumed for defense—outlays for nondefense programs are projected to rise by $30 billion (7.7 percent), chiefly as a result of rapid increases in budget authority in previous

Box 4-1.
Categories of Federal Spending

Federal spending can be divided into categories based on its treatment in the budget process:

Discretionary spending pays for such activities as defense, transportation, national parks, and foreign aid. Discretionary programs are controlled by annual appropriation acts; policymakers decide each year how many dollars to devote to which activities. Certain fees and other charges that are triggered by appropriation action are classified as offsetting collections, which offset discretionary spending. The Congressional Budget Office's (CBO's) baseline depicts the path of discretionary spending in accordance with the Balanced Budget and Emergency Deficit Control Act of 1985, which states that current spending should be assumed to grow with inflation in the future.[1] For this report, current spending consists of appropriations provided for fiscal year 2003 for defense ($382 billion) and—pending enactment of the other regular appropriation bills—about $369 billion for nondefense activities.[2] The $751 billion in total discretionary budget authority for 2003 is assumed in CBO's adjusted baseline.

Mandatory spending consists overwhelmingly of benefit programs such as Social Security, Medicare, and Medicaid. The Congress generally determines spending for those benefit programs by setting rules for eligibility, benefit formulas, and other parameters rather than by appropriating specific dollar amounts each year. CBO's baseline projections of mandatory spending assume that existing laws and policies remain unchanged and that most expiring programs will be extended. Mandatory spending also includes offsetting receipts—fees and other charges that are recorded as negative budget authority and outlays. Offsetting receipts differ from revenues in that revenues are collected as an exercise of the government's sovereign powers, whereas offsetting receipts are generally collected from other government accounts or paid by the public for business-like transactions (such as rents and royalties from leases for oil and gas drilling on the Outer Continental Shelf).

Net interest includes interest paid on Treasury securities and other interest that the government pays (for example, on late refunds issued by the Internal Revenue Service) minus interest that the government collects from various sources (such as from commercial banks, where the Treasury keeps much of its operating cash). It is determined by the size and composition of the government's debt, annual budget deficits or surpluses, and market interest rates.

---

1. The inflation rates used in CBO's baseline, as specified by the Deficit Control Act, are the employment cost index for wages and salaries (for expenditures related to federal personnel) and the GDP deflator (for other expenditures).

2. Some defense discretionary programs are funded in the energy and water and other appropriation acts; the adjusted baseline assumes that these programs (about $16 billion) are funded at the levels in the current continuing resolution. The assumed $369 billion for nondefense activities is implied by the Republican leadership's apparent agreement with the President concerning total discretionary budget authority for 2003, which totals about $751 billion.

---

years. Spending for entitlement and other mandatory programs—which now constitutes more than half of all federal spending—will increase by $66 billion (6.0 percent) over its level in 2002, CBO projects. Declining interest payments will offset some of those spending increases. Despite a growing stock of debt held by the public, low interest rates are projected to reduce net interest payments by $14 billion (8.1 percent).

A look at longer-term trends reveals that the mix of federal spending has changed significantly over time. Today, the government spends less—as a proportion of gross domestic product—on discretionary activities and more on entitlement programs than it did in the past. Discretionary spending has declined from 12.7 percent of GDP in 1962 to 7.1 percent in 2002 (*see Figure 4-1*). In contrast, spending on entitlements and other mandatory programs

Figure 4-1.
Major Components of Spending, 1962-2002
(Percentage of GDP)

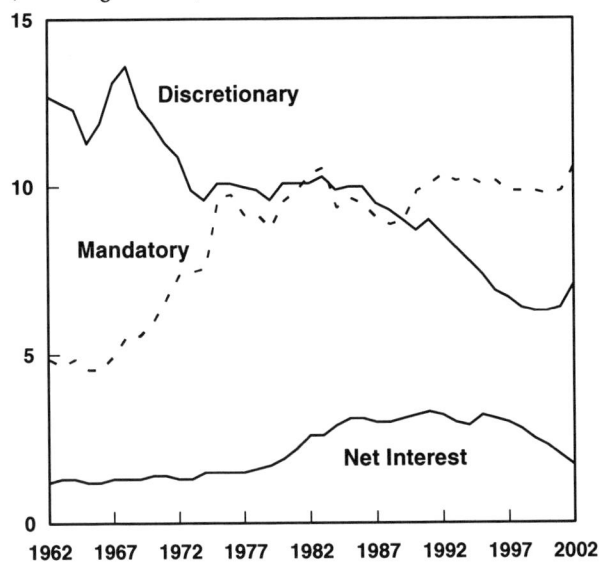

Source: Congressional Budget Office based on data from the Office of Management and Budget.

(net of offsetting receipts) has climbed from 4.9 percent to 10.7 percent of GDP over the 40-year span. (For detailed annual data on spending since 1962, see Appendix F.)

Under assumptions in the adjusted baseline, discretionary spending will grow roughly half as fast as the economy, CBO projects, or at an average annual rate of 2.6 percent, from 2003 to 2013. As a result, its share of GDP is projected to drop further—to 5.7 percent by 2013. Led by the two major health care programs, Medicare and Medicaid, mandatory spending (net of offsetting receipts) will grow slightly faster than the economy—or at a rate of 5.4 percent—if current policies remain unchanged. At that rate, mandatory outlays will claim 11.1 percent of GDP by 2013. (Growth in Social Security and health programs —driven by the aging of the baby-boom generation—is expected to accelerate rapidly beyond the 10-year projection horizon.) Although interest payments currently consume a sizable portion of the federal budget, CBO projects that such spending will decline from 1.7 percent of GDP in 2002 to 0.9 percent of GDP in 2013 as debt held by the public grows slowly in the near term and shrinks in later years.

Overall, spending as a percentage of GDP has fallen over the past two decades—from a peak of 23.5 percent in 1983 to a low of 18.4 percent in 2000. The steep increase in spending in 2002 drove that figure up to 19.5 percent. Under assumptions in the adjusted baseline, CBO estimates that outlays will fall to 17.7 percent of GDP by 2013.

Discretionary Spending

Each year, the Congress starts the appropriation process anew. The annual appropriation acts that it passes provide new budget authority (the authority to enter into financial obligations) for discretionary programs and activities. That authority translates into outlays when the money is actually spent. Although some funds are spent quickly, others are disbursed over several years. In any given year, discretionary outlays include spending from both new budget authority and from amounts appropriated previously.

Recent Trends in Discretionary Spending

Since the mid-1980s, total discretionary outlays as a share of GDP have dropped, falling from 10.0 percent in 1985 to a low of 6.3 percent in 1999 and 2000. Since then, such spending has turned upward, reaching 7.1 percent of GDP in 2002 (*see Table 4-3 on page 81*). Defense outlays as a share of the economy have also declined, moving from 6.2 percent in 1986 to a low of 3.0 percent in 1999 and 2000; CBO estimates a slightly higher rate of 3.5 percent for 2003 under the assumptions in its adjusted baseline. Nondefense discretionary spending has remained relatively constant as a share of GDP since the mid-1980s, although it has grown steadily in dollar terms; under CBO's adjusted baseline, such spending is estimated to total 3.9 percent of GDP in 2003.

The Congress and the President have enacted most of the appropriations for defense spending for 2003, but nondefense discretionary budget authority is not yet final. Current law for the 11 remaining appropriation bills is a continuing resolution—Public Law 108-2, expiring on January 31, 2003—that grants funding authority, in most cases, at the rate of operations provided in the previous

Table 4-1.

CBO's Projections of Outlays Under Its Adjusted Baseline

	Actual 2002	2003	2004	2005	2006	2007	2008	2009
								In Billions of Dollars
Discretionary Spending	734	792	817	834	848	866	891	915
Mandatory Spending[b]	1,106	1,172	1,218	1,270	1,326	1,396	1,475	1,566
Net Interest	171	157	165	194	212	217	217	214
Total	**2,011**	**2,121**	**2,199**	**2,298**	**2,387**	**2,479**	**2,583**	**2,695**
On-budget	1,655	1,751	1,816	1,905	1,979	2,058	2,149	2,243
Off-budget	356	370	383	393	407	420	434	451
								As a Percentage of GDP
Discretionary Spending	7.1	7.4	7.2	7.0	6.7	6.5	6.4	6.2
Mandatory Spending[b]	10.7	10.9	10.8	10.6	10.5	10.5	10.6	10.6
Net Interest	1.7	1.5	1.5	1.6	1.7	1.6	1.6	1.5
Total	**19.5**	**19.7**	**19.4**	**19.3**	**19.0**	**18.7**	**18.5**	**18.3**
On-budget	16.0	16.3	16.1	16.0	15.7	15.5	15.4	15.2
Off-budget	3.4	3.4	3.4	3.3	3.2	3.2	3.1	3.1
Memorandum:								
Gross Domestic Product (Billions of dollars)	10,337	10,756	11,309	11,934	12,582	13,263	13,972	14,712

Source: Congressional Budget Office.

Notes: The projections incorporate the assumption that discretionary budget authority totals $751 billion for 2003 and grows with inflation thereafter.

n.a. = not applicable.

a. Numbers in the bottom half of the column are shown as a percentage of cumulative GDP over this period.

b. Includes offsetting receipts.

---

year.[1] Pending enactment of the remaining regular appropriation bills, CBO assumes that discretionary budget authority under its adjusted baseline will total about $751 billion, as apparently agreed to by the Republican leadership and the President.[2] CBO's adjusted baseline, therefore, reflects an enacted increase of nearly $21 billion in defense budget authority from 2002 to 2003 (from $361 billion to $382 billion), and an assumed decrease of roughly $5 billion in nondefense budget authority (from $374 billion in 2002 to $369 billion for 2003).[3]

---

1. Some spending that occurred in 2002 was not included in the continuing resolution since it was considered to be a "one-time" event. That spending funded programs such as response and recovery efforts in New York City, purchases of smallpox vaccine, and anthrax cleanup efforts by the Postal Service.

2. That figure essentially represents the President's budget request—including amendments issued after the budget was released last February but excluding the $10 billion designated as a "wartime contingency."

3. Budget authority for defense increased over 2002 levels by roughly $19 billion for the development and procurement of weapon systems and $7 billion for personnel costs; budget authority for operations and maintenance and revolving funds combined decreased by about $6 billion from 2002 levels. Some defense discretionary programs are funded in the energy and water and other appropriation acts; CBO assumes in its adjusted baseline that those programs are funded at the levels in the current continuing resolution.

2010	2011	2012	2013	Total, 2004-2008[a]	Total, 2004-2013[a]
940	969	989	1,020	4,257	9,089
1,661	1,774	1,856	1,988	6,684	15,529
208	199	184	159	1,004	1,968
2,809	**2,943**	**3,029**	**3,167**	**11,945**	**26,587**
2,339	2,454	2,516	2,627	9,908	22,087
470	489	512	539	2,038	4,500
6.1	6.0	5.8	5.7	6.8	6.3
10.7	10.9	10.9	11.1	10.6	10.8
1.3	1.2	1.1	0.9	1.6	1.4
18.1	**18.1**	**17.8**	**17.7**	**18.9**	**18.4**
15.1	15.1	14.8	14.7	15.7	15.3
3.0	3.0	3.0	3.0	3.2	3.1
15,480	16,250	17,013	17,851	n.a.	n.a.

Discretionary Spending for 2004 to 2013

As specified in the Deficit Control Act, CBO inflates discretionary budget authority (using the factors specified in law) from the level appropriated in the current year to provide a reference point for assessing policy changes. Projections of the surplus or deficit are sensitive to the assumed growth in discretionary spending, so CBO typically develops alternative projections using different rates of growth. This year, however, even the base from which projections are made is uncertain.

To illustrate the effect of different assumptions about discretionary spending in the future, CBO presents alternative scenarios for such spending during the 2004-2013 period (see Table 4-4 on pages 82 and 83).

The first scenario—CBO's adjusted baseline—assumes that budget authority in 2003 totals about $751 billion and grows at the rates of inflation specified in the Deficit Control Act. The second scenario is CBO's unadjusted baseline, which assumes that total budget authority equals $738 billion—as calculated on the basis of the continuing resolution—and also grows at the rates of inflation specified in the Deficit Control Act. Under the second scenario, discretionary outlays over the 10-year period would be $135 billion less than the adjusted figures presented in this report, and debt-service costs would fall by $43 billion.

A third scenario assumes that funding of $751 billion in 2003 grows at the average annual rate of nominal GDP after 2003 (5.2 percent a year, on average, or about twice as fast as the overall rate of growth assumed in the adjusted baseline). Total discretionary outlays would exceed CBO's baseline figures by a cumulative $1.2 trillion over the projection period under this scenario. Added debt-service costs would bring the cumulative outlay increase to $1.5 trillion.

The final scenario shows discretionary spending frozen at $751 billion throughout the projection period. Under that assumption, discretionary outlays over the 2004-2013 period would total $1.1 trillion less than in CBO's adjusted baseline, with debt-service savings bringing the difference to $1.4 trillion.

Entitlements and Other Mandatory Spending

Currently, more than half of the money that the federal government spends each year supports entitlement programs and other types of mandatory spending (not including net interest). Most mandatory programs make payments to recipients—a wide variety of people as well as businesses, nonprofit institutions, and state and local governments—that are eligible and apply for funds. Payments are governed by formulas set in law and generally are not constrained by annual appropriation acts.

As a share of total outlays, mandatory spending steadily increased from 32 percent in 1962 to 60 percent in 2002. If current policies remained unchanged, mandatory spend-

Table 4-2.
Average Annual Rate of Growth in Outlays Under CBO's Adjusted Baseline
(In percent)

	Actual 2001-2002	Estimated 2002-2003	Projected[a] 2003-2013
Discretionary Spending	13.1	7.8	2.6
Defense	14.0	7.9	2.7
Nondefense	12.3	7.7	2.4
Mandatory Spending	9.6	6.0	5.4
Social Security	5.4	4.8	5.5
Medicare[b]	6.4	5.7	6.6
Medicaid	13.2	6.4	8.5
Other[b]	18.5	7.9	2.1
Net Interest	-17.1	-8.1	0.1
Total Outlays	7.9	5.5	4.1
Total Outlays Excluding Net Interest	11.0	6.7	4.4
Memorandum:			
Consumer Price Index	1.5	2.3	2.4
Nominal GDP	3.0	4.1	5.2
Discretionary Budget Authority	10.7	2.2	2.8
Defense	8.8	5.8	2.7
Nondefense	12.6	-1.3	2.8

Source: Congressional Budget Office.

Note: The projections incorporate the assumption that discretionary budget authority totals $751 billion for 2003 and grows with inflation thereafter.

a. As specified by the Deficit Control Act, CBO's baseline uses the employment cost index for wages and salaries to inflate discretionary spending related to federal personnel and the GDP deflator to adjust other spending.
b. Includes offsetting receipts.

ing would continue to grow faster than other spending, reaching 69 percent of total outlays in 2013, CBO estimates. Among the largest mandatory programs are Social Security, Medicare, and Medicaid, which together accounted for over 71 percent of mandatory spending in 2002 and are projected to constitute almost 78 percent of such spending in 2013.

Less than one-fourth of entitlements and mandatory spending, or about one-seventh of all federal spending, is means-tested—that is, paid to individuals who must document their need on the basis of income or assets that are below specified thresholds. In some cases, other criteria, such as family status, are also used. The remainder of mandatory spending has no such restrictions and is labeled non-means-tested.

Means-Tested Programs
Since the 1960s, spending on means-tested benefits has more than tripled as a share of the economy—from 0.8 percent of GDP in 1962 to a high of 2.8 percent last year. Changes in spending for means-tested programs are driven by several factors, including inflation, rising health care costs, fluctuating unemployment, growth of the eligible populations, and new legislation. Under CBO's estimates, spending for means-tested programs would grow more rapidly than the economy over the next 10 years—largely because of growth in Medicaid—climbing to 3.0 percent of GDP in 2013.

Medicaid. Federal outlays for Medicaid, the joint federal/state program that pays for the medical care of many of the nation's poor, made up over half of all spending for means-tested entitlements in 2002 (*see Table 4-5 on page 84*). Medicaid outlays grew by 13.2 percent last year,

Table 4-3.
Defense and Nondefense Discretionary Outlays

	Defense Outlays			Nondefense Outlays			Total Discretionary Outlays		
	In Billions of Dollars	As a Percentage of GDP	Percentage Change from Previous Year	In Billions of Dollars	As a Percentage of GDP	Percentage Change from Previous Year	In Billions of Dollars	As a Percentage of GDP	Percentage Change from Previous Year
1985	253	6.1	11.0	163	3.9	7.5	416	10.0	9.6
1986	274	6.2	8.2	165	3.7	1.2	439	10.0	5.5
1987	283	6.1	3.2	162	3.5	-1.8	444	9.5	1.3
1988	291	5.8	3.0	174	3.5	7.3	464	9.3	4.5
1989	304	5.6	4.5	185	3.4	6.5	489	9.0	5.3
1990	300	5.2	-1.3	201	3.5	8.5	501	8.7	2.4
1991	320	5.4	6.5	214	3.6	6.5	533	9.0	6.5
1992	303	4.9	-5.3	231	3.7	8.2	534	8.6	0.1
1993	292	4.5	-3.4	247	3.8	6.8	539	8.2	1.0
1994	282	4.1	-3.5	259	3.7	4.9	541	7.8	0.4
1995	274	3.7	-3.1	271	3.7	4.7	545	7.4	0.6
1996	266	3.5	-2.8	267	3.5	-1.7	533	6.9	-2.2
1997	272	3.3	2.1	276	3.4	3.3	547	6.7	2.7
1998	270	3.1	-0.5	282	3.2	2.3	552	6.4	0.9
1999	275	3.0	1.9	297	3.2	5.2	572	6.3	3.6
2000	295	3.0	7.1	320	3.3	7.9	615	6.3	7.5
2001	306	3.1	3.8	343	3.4	7.3	649	6.5	5.6
2002	349	3.4	14.0	385	3.7	12.3	734	7.1	13.1
2003[a]	377	3.5	7.9	415	3.9	7.7	792	7.4	7.8

Sources: Office of Management and Budget for 1985 through 2002 and Congressional Budget Office for 2003.

a. Estimated using CBO's adjusted baseline (in which discretionary budget authority for 2003 totals $751 billion).

---

marking the sixth consecutive year that spending growth in the program accelerated. The 2002 increase resulted from a combination of higher prices and rising enrollment and utilization. Most notably, spending for outpatient prescription drugs, which accounted for about 9 percent of Medicaid spending in 2002, jumped by 18 percent (after rising by roughly 20 percent in each of the previous three years). Rising unemployment—along with state and federal actions in recent years to expand Medicaid eligibility and benefits, increase payment rates to providers, and conduct outreach—has increased both enrollment and costs. States also expanded their use of financing mechanisms related to Medicare's upper payment limit (UPL), which generated additional federal payments.[4]

CBO projects that spending growth for the program will drop to 6.4 percent in 2003 as a result of slower growth in enrollment, smaller increases in payment rates, and restrictions on UPL spending. Despite that decline, Medicaid spending over the next decade is projected to grow more rapidly than spending for other means-tested programs. Higher prices, greater consumption of services, and, to a lesser extent, increased enrollment will continue to drive up Medicaid's costs, pushing federal outlays from $157 billion in 2003 to $356 billion in 2013—an average annual increase of 8.5 percent. Spending for acute care services, which includes payments to managed care plans and payments for prescription drugs, accounts for more than half of all Medicaid outlays and is the most rapidly growing component of the program. Acute care spending

---

4. The UPL is a regulatory ceiling in Medicaid's payment policy that prohibits states from paying certain classes of facilities more than they would under Medicare's rules. However, many states use financing mechanisms to pay certain public facilities at rates far above Medicaid's normal rates, but below Medicare's upper payment limit, and then receive federal matching funds for those payments. Those public facilities return the excess funds to the states, which then retain the additional money from the federal match.

Table 4-4.
CBO's Projections of Discretionary Spending Under Alternative Paths
(In billions of dollars)

	2003	2004	2005	2006	2007	2008	2009	2010	2011	2012	2013	Total, 2004-2008	Total, 2004-2013
Adjusted Baseline (Discretionary Spending of About $751 Billion Grows with Inflation After 2003)[a]													
Budget Authority													
Defense	382	391	401	411	423	434	446	459	472	485	499	2,060	4,422
Nondefense	369	383	392	402	413	424	436	448	461	473	486	2,015	4,319
Total	751	774	793	814	836	858	882	907	932	959	985	4,075	8,740
Outlays													
Defense[b]	377	389	400	406	414	428	440	452	468	474	491	2,037	4,363
Nondefense	415	428	435	442	453	463	475	488	501	515	528	2,220	4,726
Total	792	817	834	848	866	891	915	940	969	989	1,020	4,257	9,089
Discretionary Spending of About $738 Billion Grows with Inflation After 2003[a]													
Budget Authority													
Defense	382	391	401	411	423	434	446	459	472	485	499	2,060	4,422
Nondefense	357	370	379	389	399	410	422	433	445	458	470	1,949	4,178
Total	738	762	780	801	822	845	868	892	917	943	969	4,009	8,599
Outlays													
Defense[b]	377	389	400	406	414	428	440	452	468	474	491	2,037	4,363
Nondefense	408	417	423	430	439	449	461	473	486	500	513	2,158	4,592
Total	785	806	822	836	853	877	901	925	955	974	1,004	4,195	8,954
Discretionary Spending of About $751 Billion Grows at the Rate of Nominal GDP After 2003													
Budget Authority													
Defense	382	401	423	446	470	495	521	548	576	605	636	2,235	5,121
Nondefense	369	393	414	436	459	484	509	536	563	591	621	2,186	5,006
Total	751	794	837	882	929	978	1,030	1,084	1,139	1,197	1,256	4,421	10,127
Outlays													
Defense[b]	377	397	417	435	455	482	508	534	566	587	620	2,186	5,001
Nondefense	415	433	450	468	491	514	539	565	593	621	651	2,355	5,324
Total	792	830	867	903	945	996	1,047	1,100	1,158	1,208	1,271	4,541	10,325
Discretionary Spending Is Frozen at About $751 Billion													
Budget Authority													
Defense	382	382	382	382	382	382	382	382	382	382	382	1,908	3,816
Nondefense	369	370	370	370	370	369	369	369	369	369	369	1,848	3,695
Total	751	752	751	751	751	751	751	751	751	751	751	3,756	7,511
Outlays													
Defense[b]	377	382	384	381	378	380	380	380	383	377	380	1,905	3,806
Nondefense	415	422	422	420	417	412	411	411	410	410	410	2,093	4,144
Total	792	805	806	800	795	792	791	791	793	787	790	3,998	7,951

(Continued)

Table 4-4.
Continued

(In billions of dollars)

	2003	2004	2005	2006	2007	2008	2009	2010	2011	2012	2013	Total, 2004-2008	Total, 2004-2013
Memorandum:													
Debt Service on Differences from CBO's Adjusted Baseline													
$738 billion in 2003 grows with inflation	*	*	-1	-2	-3	-4	-5	-6	-7	-8	-9	-10	-43
$751 billion in 2003 grows at the rate of nominal GDP	*	*	1	4	8	13	20	29	40	54	69	27	240
Frozen at $751 Billion	*	*	-1	-3	-7	-12	-19	-27	-37	-50	-64	-24	-220

Source: Congressional Budget Office.

Notes: * = between -$500 million and $500 million.

In CBO's projections, discretionary outlays are always higher than budget authority because of spending from the Highway Trust Fund and the Airport and Airway Trust Fund, which is subject to obligation limitations in appropriation acts. The budget authority for such programs is provided in authorizing legislation and is not considered discretionary. Outlays also may exceed budget authority because they include spending from appropriations provided in previous years.

a. Using the inflators specified in the Deficit Control Act (the GDP deflator and the employment cost index for wages and salaries).
b. When October 1 falls on a weekend, certain federal payments due on that date are shifted into September; consequently, military personnel will be paid 13 times in 2005 and 2011 and 11 times in 2007 and 2012.

---

is anticipated to rise from $87 billion in 2003 to $211 billion in 2013. Spending for long-term care, which accounts for about 30 percent of all Medicaid spending, is also expected to grow rapidly, climbing from $46 billion in 2003 to $111 billion in 2013, as states expand participants' eligibility to receive home- and community-based services in response to legal challenges under the Americans with Disabilities Act.

Currently, combined federal and state outlays for Medicaid approach total outlays for Medicare, the federal government's other major health care program. As Medicaid spending continues to grow, it will overtake Medicare spending in the next few years.

Other Means-Tested Programs. CBO projects that outlays for other means-tested programs will grow at an average annual rate of 2.1 percent from 2003 through 2013, although it expects those programs to grow by 4.8 percent in 2003, largely because of the current weakness in the economy. For example, outlays for the Food Stamp program are projected to jump by 10.7 percent in 2003, with roughly half of that increase attributable to economic conditions; as the economy improves, spending growth in that program is estimated to slow, yielding an average annual growth rate of 2.4 percent over the next decade.

CBO's baseline estimates for 2012 and 2013 reflect the scheduled expiration, on December 31, 2010, of the cuts in marginal tax rates and the child tax credit provisions in the Economic Growth and Tax Relief Reconciliation Act of 2001. After EGTRRA expires, the income threshold at which tax credits are phased out will no longer rise in tandem with income; and as tax rates increase to pre-EGTRRA levels, the tax liability of married couples filing jointly will rise. Consequently, a higher portion of the earned income tax credit (EITC) they are eligible for will go to offset their tax liability instead of being paid out as a refundable credit. As a result, the government's EITC outlays will drop by about $3 billion in 2012. Likewise, child tax credit outlays will plummet from $9 billion to less than $1 billion after EGTRRA expires, because only families with three or more children will receive any refundable credits.

Table 4-5.
CBO's Baseline Projections of Mandatory Spending
(In billions of dollars)

	Actual 2002	2003	2004	2005	2006	2007	2008	2009	2010	2011	2012	2013	Total, 2004-2008	Total, 2004-2013
Means-Tested Programs														
Medicaid	148	157	167	179	195	212	231	251	274	299	326	356	983	2,489
Supplemental Security Income	31	32	33	37	36	35	40	41	43	48	43	48	181	405
Earned Income Tax and Child Tax Credits	33	34	34	34	37	37	37	38	39	42	30	30	179	357
Food Stamps	22	24	25	25	25	26	27	28	28	29	30	31	128	274
Family Support[a]	26	27	26	26	25	26	25	25	26	26	27	27	128	259
Child Nutrition	10	11	11	11	12	12	13	13	14	14	15	16	59	132
Foster Care	6	6	7	7	7	7	8	8	9	9	9	10	36	80
Student Loans	3	3	4	5	6	6	6	6	6	6	6	6	27	58
State Children's Health Insurance	4	4	5	5	5	5	5	5	5	5	5	5	24	50
Veterans' Pensions	3	3	3	4	3	3	4	4	4	4	4	5	17	39
Total	286	302	314	333	351	369	395	420	448	483	496	534	1,762	4,142
Non-Means-Tested Programs														
Social Security	452	474	493	514	540	568	598	633	671	712	757	807	2,714	6,293
Medicare	254	269	283	302	315	337	359	385	414	449	479	521	1,597	3,843
Subtotal	706	743	776	817	855	905	957	1,018	1,085	1,161	1,235	1,327	4,310	10,136
Other Retirement and Disability														
Federal civilian[b]	56	59	62	65	68	71	75	78	82	86	90	94	341	771
Military	35	36	37	38	39	40	41	42	43	44	45	47	194	416
Other	5	6	6	6	6	7	7	6	7	7	7	7	32	66
Subtotal	96	100	104	109	113	118	122	127	132	137	142	147	567	1,253
Unemployment Compensation	51	56	46	43	43	45	45	47	49	51	52	54	222	476
Other Programs														
Veterans' benefits[c]	25	29	31	36	34	32	35	36	36	40	35	39	168	354
Commodity Credit Corporation	14	13	16	17	17	16	15	16	15	14	13	13	81	151
TRICARE for Life	0	4	5	6	7	7	8	9	9	10	11	11	34	83
Universal Service Fund	5	6	6	6	6	7	7	7	7	7	7	7	32	67
Social services	4	5	5	5	5	5	5	5	5	5	5	5	24	49
Other	10	16	17	15	15	13	13	14	14	14	14	15	73	144
Subtotal	58	73	80	85	84	80	82	85	86	90	86	90	412	849
Total	911	972	1,007	1,053	1,095	1,148	1,208	1,277	1,352	1,438	1,516	1,619	5,511	12,713
Offsetting Receipts														
Offsetting Receipts	-91	-103	-103	-115	-121	-122	-127	-131	-139	-147	-156	-165	-588	-1,326
Total														
Mandatory Spending	1,106	1,172	1,218	1,270	1,326	1,396	1,475	1,566	1,661	1,774	1,856	1,988	6,684	15,529
Memorandum:														
Mandatory Spending Excluding Offsetting Receipts	1,197	1,275	1,321	1,385	1,446	1,517	1,603	1,697	1,800	1,921	2,012	2,153	7,273	16,855

Source: Congressional Budget Office.

Note: Spending for the benefit programs shown above generally excludes administrative costs, which are discretionary.

a. Includes Temporary Assistance for Needy Families and various programs that involve payments to states for child support enforcement and family support, child care entitlements, and research to benefit children.
b. Includes Civil Service, Foreign Service, Coast Guard, and other, smaller retirement programs and annuitants' health benefits.
c. Includes veterans' compensation, readjustment benefits, life insurance, and housing programs.

The authorization for Temporary Assistance for Needy Families (TANF), which makes up the bulk of family support programs, expired at the end of 2002, although the Congress extended it temporarily through March of this year. For its baseline, CBO assumes that funding for TANF will continue at the 2002 level (as required by the Deficit Control Act). As a result, total spending for family support programs is projected to remain fairly stable, ranging from $25 billion to $27 billion over the 10-year period. CBO will modify its projections of TANF spending to reflect any changes in the program when it is reauthorized.

Although the student loan program is difficult to classify as either means-tested or non-means-tested, CBO includes that program in the former category because historically, the majority of loans have had interest subsidies and have been limited to students from families with relatively low income and financial assets. However, in recent years, an increasing proportion of loans involve no means-testing. For 2003, CBO estimates that about $43 billion in student loans will be guaranteed or provided directly by the federal government. Over the 2003-2013 period, total loan disbursements will top $569 billion. Of that total, the share of loans that are not means-tested will expand from 53 percent in 2003 to 61 percent in 2013.

The costs that are included in the federal budget for student loans reflect only a small portion of the disbursements. Under the Credit Reform Act, only the subsidy costs of the loans are treated as outlays. Those outlays are estimated as the future costs in today's dollars for interest subsidies, default costs, and other expected expenses over the life of the loans. CBO estimates that the subsidy and administrative costs of the student loan program will range from $3 billion to $6 billion a year from 2003 through 2013. The means-tested loans, which feature the most favorable terms, account for the bulk of those costs.

Non-Means-Tested Programs

Social Security, Medicare, and other retirement and disability programs dominate non-means-tested entitlements. Social Security is by far the largest federal program, with expected outlays of $474 billion in 2003. It pays benefits to 46 million people—a number that is projected to swell to about 56 million by 2013. Most Social Security beneficiaries also participate in Medicare, which is expected to cost $269 billion this year. Together, those two programs account for more than one out of every three dollars that the federal government spends (up from about one in four dollars in 1980). CBO projects that annual costs for the two programs combined will grow by $584 billion from 2003 to 2013 as the leading edge of the baby-boom generation reaches the age of eligibility for the programs. In total, Social Security and Medicare account for more than half of the projected increase in federal outlays over that period.

Social Security. During the past decade, Social Security outlays grew at an average rate of about 4.7 percent a year. For the next 10 years, growth will average roughly 5.5 percent a year, CBO projects. However, 10-year averages do not fully reveal the long-term trends propelling growth in outlays. As baby boomers begin to qualify for Social Security in the second half of the decade, the program's growth rate will accelerate more rapidly, climbing from 5.2 percent in 2007 to 6.6 percent in 2013. The same trend underlies the growth in Social Security's estimated share of the economy, which is projected to stand at 4.3 percent in 2009 before creeping up to reach 4.5 percent in 2013. The number of people who qualify for Social Security will continue to escalate after 2013, causing the program (along with Medicare, which exhibits a similar pattern) to put an increasing strain on the federal budget.

Social Security's Old-Age and Survivors Insurance (OASI) program pays benefits to retired workers, their eligible spouses and children, and some survivors (chiefly aged widows and young children) of deceased workers. It will pay about $397 billion in benefits in 2003. Most beneficiaries are elderly, and most elderly people collect Social Security: three-fifths of people between the ages of 62 and 64 and more than 90 percent of people age 65 and older collect Social Security. Consequently, CBO bases its estimates of the number of beneficiaries and of OASI outlays primarily on the size of the elderly population.

CBO projects that OASI benefits will cost $666 billion in 2013, an increase of 68 percent over the amount in 2003, reflecting an average growth rate of 5.3 percent a year. In contrast, benefits grew by 53 percent over the past decade, or at an average annual rate of 4.3 percent. Overall, of that 4.3 percent average annual growth, roughly 2.6 percent can be assigned to cost-of-living adjustments

(COLAs), 0.8 percent to increasing enrollment, and 0.9 percent to growth in the average real benefit (in excess of COLAs). For the next decade, CBO expects that the growth in COLAs will slow to 2.4 percent a year, enrollment growth will accelerate to 1.6 percent a year, and the average real benefit will increase by 1.2 percent a year.

The smaller Disability Insurance (DI) program pays benefits to insured workers who have suffered a serious medical impairment before they reach retirement age and to their eligible spouses and children. According to CBO's projections, DI benefits will grow even faster than OASI benefits, from $73 billion in 2003 to $136 billion in 2013, or at an average rate of 6.4 percent a year. CBO ascribes 3.2 percent of that future growth rate to increasing caseloads, 2.4 percent to COLAs, 1.4 percent to real benefit growth, and -0.8 percent to other factors (chiefly a drop in lump-sum payments from unusually high levels in 2003). Over the past decade, the average growth rate for the DI program measured 7.8 percent, but that growth was apportioned differently: CBO attributed roughly 4.4 percent to caseloads, 2.6 percent to COLAs, and about 0.9 percent to real benefit growth.

Social Security outlays include about $4 billion in mandatory spending other than OASI and DI benefits. Almost all of that spending reflects an annual transfer to the Railroad Retirement program.

Medicare. Currently, Medicare spending (not including premiums) is about 56 percent as large as Social Security spending, but it is expected to grow faster than Social Security spending over the next decade. By 2013, CBO projects, outlays for the Medicare program will total $521 billion, and that spending's share of the economy will have risen by nearly one-half of a percentage point, from 2.5 percent of GDP in 2003 to 2.9 percent.

CBO projects that Medicare spending will rise by 6.0 percent in 2003 and that growth will average 6.8 percent a year through 2013. That projected growth over the next decade stems from various factors. First, payment rates for most services in the fee-for-service sector (including hospital care and services furnished by physicians, home health agencies, and skilled nursing facilities) are subject to automatic updates based on changes in input prices and other economic factors, including changes in GDP and productivity. CBO estimates that automatic updates to payment rates will average 3.0 percent each year (although updates for specific services will vary considerably) and will account for roughly 43 percent of the projected increase in Medicare spending from 2003 through 2013.

Second, increases in caseloads make up an additional 28 percent of the anticipated rise in Medicare outlays over the 10-year period. CBO projects that the number of enrollees in Medicare's Hospital Insurance (Part A) program will expand by 21 percent, from 40 million to 49 million, between 2003 and 2013. The increases in spending associated with new enrollees will be greater in the second half of the decade than in the first half, as baby boomers begin to reach 65. Growth in enrollment will accelerate from 1.1 percent in 2003 to 2.9 percent in 2013, CBO estimates.

The remainder of the increase results from other changes in covered benefits; from changes in payment rates required by the Balanced Budget Act of 1997, the Balanced Budget Refinement Act, and the Benefits Improvement and Protection Act of 2000; and from factors such as changes in medical technology, billing behavior, and the age distribution of enrollees.

A countervailing factor that will put downward pressure on Medicare spending over the next decade is the formula used to establish the fee schedule for physicians' services—the sustainable growth rate (SGR) formula. The SGR establishes a cumulative spending target for physicians' services and services related to a physician visit. CBO estimates that spending through 2002 has exceeded the cumulative target by about $17 billion and that the amount of spending in excess of the target will grow by another $10 billion in the next few years. The SGR formula ultimately will recoup spending above the cumulative target by reducing payment rates for physicians' services or by holding increases below the rate of inflation as measured by the Medicare economic index. As a result, payment rates are scheduled to drop by 4.4 percent on March 1, 2003. (Those rates were reduced by 5.4 percent last year.)

CBO's projections also reflect declining enrollment in Medicare+Choice plans. That enrollment peaked in 2000 at 6.3 million Medicare beneficiaries and declined to 5.1

million (13 percent of Medicare beneficiaries) in 2002. CBO projects that enrollment in Medicare+Choice plans will continue to fall in the next few years, leveling off at about 3.7 million enrollees in 2009 and 2010 (8 percent of Medicare beneficiaries).

Other Non-Means-Tested Programs. Other federal retirement and disability programs, which are dominated by benefits for the federal government's civilian and military retirees, recorded outlays of $96 billion in 2002. CBO projects that such outlays will reach $100 billion in 2003 and increase by an average of roughly 3.9 percent each year thereafter through 2013.

Economic weakness caused the unemployment rate to soar from 4.4 percent in fiscal year 2001 to 5.7 percent in 2002. As a result, spending for unemployment compensation reached an all-time high of $51 billion in 2002. Because CBO expects the unemployment rate to inch up to an average of 5.9 percent in 2003, and because the Congress recently extended unemployment compensation benefits for people covered under the Job Creation and Worker Assistance Act of 2002, CBO projects that total outlays for unemployment compensation will increase to $56 billion in 2003. After 2003, spending for unemployment benefits will fall through mid-decade, CBO projects, and then increase slowly thereafter to reach $54 billion by 2013.

Outlays for other non-means-tested programs are projected to grow at an average annual rate of 2.2 percent. Cost-of-living adjustments and higher caseloads for veterans' compensation account for most of the increase in spending for veterans' benefits, which will total $29 billion in 2003 (up from $25 billion last year) and rise to $39 billion by 2013, CBO estimates. Spending for farm price and income supports is projected to remain fairly stable through 2013, ranging from $13 billion to $17 billion (for more details, see Chapter 1). The TRICARE for Life program, which provides health care benefits (including prescription drug coverage) for retirees of the uniformed services age 65 and older, will boost mandatory spending by $4 billion in 2003, a figure that rises to $11 billion in 2013.

What Explains the Projected Rate of Increase in Mandatory Spending?

As a whole, spending for entitlements and other mandatory programs has more than doubled since 1989—rising faster than both nominal growth in the economy and inflation. CBO's baseline projections show that trend continuing.

Why is mandatory spending projected to grow so much? One way to analyze that growth is to break it down by its major causes. Such a breakdown shows that more than 85 percent of the growth in entitlements and other mandatory programs between 2003 and 2013 results from more participants, automatic increases in benefits, and greater use of, and increasing prices for, medical services.

Burgeoning numbers of participants produce almost one-fourth of the total growth. Additional beneficiaries increase spending by $19 billion in 2004 and $212 billion in 2013 relative to outlays in 2003 (*see Table 4-6*). The majority of that spending is concentrated in Social Security and Medicare and can be traced to a growing number of elderly and disabled people; most of the rest is for Medicaid. CBO estimates that growth in the number of participants accounts for 29 percent of the growth in Social Security, 27 percent of the growth in Medicare, and 15 percent of the growth in Medicaid during the 2004-2013 period.

Automatic increases in benefits account for about one-third of the growth in entitlement programs. All of the major retirement programs grant automatic cost-of-living adjustments to their beneficiaries (the adjustment for 2003 is 1.4 percent). CBO estimates that those adjustments, which are pegged to the consumer price index, will be 2.2 percent in 2004 and 2005, 2.4 percent in 2006, and 2.5 percent thereafter. As a result, COLAs are projected to add $11 billion to total outlays in 2004 and $163 billion in 2013.

Several other programs—chiefly the earned income tax credit, the Food Stamp program, and Medicare—are also automatically indexed to changes in prices and other economic factors. The income thresholds above which the

Table 4-6.
Sources of Growth in Mandatory Outlays
(In billions of dollars)

	2004	2005	2006	2007	2008	2009	2010	2011	2012	2013
Estimated Spending for Base Year 2003	1,275	1,275	1,275	1,275	1,275	1,275	1,275	1,275	1,275	1,275
Sources of Growth										
Increases in participation	19	36	52	69	87	109	132	155	182	212
Automatic increases in benefits										
Cost-of-living adjustments	11	25	40	57	73	91	108	126	144	163
Other[a]	9	18	29	40	51	64	79	97	115	135
Other increases in Medicare and Medicaid[b]	9	22	40	60	83	110	139	172	207	243
Other growth in Social Security[c]	4	8	14	23	32	44	57	73	92	113
Irregular number of benefit payments[d]	0	9	-3	-6	0	0	0	10	-10	0
Other sources of growth	-6	-6	-1	*	*	5	9	14	8	11
Total	46	110	172	242	328	422	525	647	737	878
Projected Spending	1,321	1,385	1,446	1,517	1,603	1,697	1,800	1,921	2,012	2,153

Source: Congressional Budget Office.

Notes: * = between -$500 million and $500 million.

The mandatory spending shown here excludes offsetting receipts, which are detailed in Table 4-7.

a. Automatic increases in the Food Stamp program and child nutrition benefits, certain Medicare reimbursement rates, the earned income tax credit, TRICARE for Life, and statutory increases for veterans' education.
b. All growth that is not attributed to increased caseloads and automatic increases in reimbursement rates.
c. All growth that is not attributed to increased caseloads and cost-of-living adjustments.
d. Represents differences attributable to the number of benefit checks that will be issued in a fiscal year. Normally, benefit payments are made once a month. However, Medicare will make 13 payments to Medicare+Choice plans in 2005 and 2011 (because October 1 falls on a weekend) and 11 payments in 2006 and 2012. Supplemental Security Income and veterans' benefits will be paid 13 times in 2005 and 2011 and 11 times in 2007 and 2012.

earned income tax credit begins to be phased out and the maximum amount of the tax credit are both automatically adjusted for inflation using the consumer price index.[5] The Food Stamp program adjusts its benefit payments each year according to changes in the costs of components in the Department of Agriculture's Thrifty Food Plan. Medicare's payments to providers are based in part on special price indexes for the medical sector and other economic factors, including changes in GDP and productivity. The combined effect of indexing for all of those programs is an extra $9 billion in outlays in 2004 and $135 billion in 2013.

The remaining boost in entitlement spending comes from increases that cannot be attributed to rising enrollment or automatic adjustments to benefits. Two of those sources of growth are expected to become more important over time. First, CBO anticipates that spending for Medicaid will grow with inflation even though the program is not formally indexed at the federal level. Medicaid payments to providers are determined by the states, and the federal government matches those payments, according to a formula set by law. If states increase their benefits in response to higher prices, federal payments will rise correspondingly. Second, the health programs have faced steadily escalating costs per participant beyond the effects of inflation; that trend, which is often termed an increase in "intensity," reflects the consumption of more health services per participant and the growing use of more costly procedures. CBO estimates that the growth in Medicare and Medicaid from both of those sources will be $9 billion in 2004 and $243 billion in 2013.

In most federal retirement programs, the average benefit grows faster than the COLA alone. Social Security is a prime example. Because awards to new retirees are buoyed

---

5. Credits are administered through the individual income tax. Credits in excess of tax liabilities are recorded as outlays in the federal budget.

by recent growth in wages, their benefits generally exceed the monthly check of a long-time retiree who last earned a salary a decade or two ago and has been receiving only cost-of-living adjustments since then. Because women's labor force participation grew dramatically beginning in the mid-1960s, more new retirees receive benefits based on their own earnings rather than smaller benefits based on their status as a spouse of a retiree. In Social Security alone, CBO estimates, the resulting increase in benefits will add $4 billion to outlays in 2004 and $113 billion in 2013.

Mandatory spending will increase or decrease in a given fiscal year depending on whether the first day of the year, October 1, falls on a weekend. If it does, some benefit payments will be made at the end of September, which increases spending in the year just ended and decreases spending in the new year. Thus, the Supplemental Security Income program, veterans' compensation and pension programs, and Medicare (for payments to health maintenance organizations) may send out 11, 12, or 13 monthly checks in a fiscal year. Irregular numbers of benefit payments will affect mandatory spending in 2005, 2006, 2007, 2011, and 2012.

The remaining growth in spending for benefit programs derives from rising benefits for new retirees in the civil service and military retirement programs (fundamentally the same phenomenon as in Social Security); larger average benefits for unemployment compensation (a program that lacks an explicit COLA but pays amounts that are generally linked to the recent earnings of its beneficiaries); and other sources of growth. Offsetting some of those factors is the expiration of emergency benefits for unemployment insurance. Together, other factors contribute just $11 billion of the total $878 billion increase in mandatory spending from 2003 to 2013.

Offsetting Receipts

Offsetting receipts are income that the federal government records as negative spending—that is, offsets to mandatory spending.[6] Those receipts are either intragovernmental (reflecting payments from one part of the federal government to another) or proprietary (reflecting payments from the public in exchange for goods or services).

Intragovernmental transfers representing the contributions that federal agencies make to their employees' retirement plans are the largest component of the offsetting receipts category (*see Table 4-7*). Such contributions account for roughly 40 percent of total offsetting receipts in each year through 2013. Agencies' contributions go primarily to the trust funds for Social Security, military retirement, and civil service retirement. Some contribution rates are set by statute; others are determined on an actuarial basis. Those contributions are charged against the agencies' budgets in the same way that other elements of their employees' compensation are. The budget treats them as outlays of the employing agency and records the retirement fund deposits as offsetting receipts. The transfers thus wash out in the budget totals, leaving only the funds' disbursements—for retirement benefits and administrative costs—reflected in total outlays.

The TRICARE for Life program works in the same way. The payment made by the Department of Defense is offset by the receipt of that payment into the fund. The transfer washes out, leaving only the fund's disbursements reflected as outlays. CBO projects that the program will collect $7 billion from the Department of Defense in 2003, an amount that increases to $14 billion in 2013.

The largest amount of proprietary receipts that the government collects constitutes premiums from the 38 million people enrolled in Supplementary Medical Insurance (Part B of Medicare), which primarily covers physicians' and outpatient hospital services. Premiums in the program are set to cover one-quarter of its costs. The monthly charge for beneficiaries is $59 in 2003; it is projected to climb to $111 in 2013. Enrollees in Part B of Medicare pay the monthly premium or Medicaid pays it on their behalf.

In the case of Part A, the Hospital Insurance program, most of its 40 million beneficiaries are considered to be entitled to those benefits and are not charged a premium. However, Medicare collects Part A premiums for about 400,000 enrollees who were not employed in jobs covered

---

6. Fees and other charges that are triggered by appropriation action are classified as offsetting collections. In those cases, the collections offset discretionary spending.

Table 4-7.
CBO's Baseline Projections of Offsetting Receipts
(In billions of dollars)

	Actual 2002	2003	2004	2005	2006	2007	2008	2009	2010	2011	2012	2013	Total, 2004-2008	Total, 2004-2013
Employer's Share of Employee Retirement														
Social Security	-9	-9	-10	-11	-11	-12	-13	-14	-15	-16	-17	-18	-58	-137
Military retirement	-13	-12	-12	-13	-13	-13	-14	-14	-15	-15	-16	-16	-65	-140
Civil service retirement and other	-21	-21	-22	-23	-24	-25	-26	-27	-28	-29	-30	-31	-119	-264
Subtotal	-43	-43	-44	-46	-48	-50	-53	-55	-57	-60	-62	-65	-242	-541
TRICARE for Life	0	-7	-8	-9	-9	-9	-10	-11	-11	-12	-13	-14	-45	-105
Medicare Premiums	-26	-28	-31	-33	-36	-39	-42	-45	-49	-54	-59	-64	-181	-452
Energy-Related Receipts[a]	-6	-6	-5	-6	-6	-7	-7	-7	-7	-7	-7	-7	-31	-65
Natural Resources-Related Receipts[b]	-3	-4	-3	-3	-3	-3	-3	-3	-3	-4	-4	-4	-17	-35
Electromagnetic Spectrum Auctions	*	*	*	-8	-8	-3	-2	0	0	0	0	0	-21	-21
Other	-12	-15	-12	-10	-10	-10	-10	-10	-11	-11	-11	-11	-52	-107
Total	**-91**	**-103**	**-103**	**-115**	**-121**	**-122**	**-127**	**-131**	**-139**	**-147**	**-156**	**-165**	**-588**	**-1,326**

Source: Congressional Budget Office.

Note: * = between -$500 million and zero.

a. Includes proceeds from the sale of power, various fees, and royalties on mineral production and oil and gas production from the Outer Continental Shelf.
b. Includes timber and mineral receipts and various fees.

by Medicare payroll taxes long enough to qualify for free enrollment. CBO estimates that collections of premiums for both parts will grow from $28 billion in 2003 to $64 billion in 2013 (premiums for Supplementary Medical Insurance account for more than 95 percent of those amounts). The federal government, however, also pays a substantial share of those premiums because Medicaid pays the Part B premium (and, if necessary, the Part A premium) for Medicare enrollees who are eligible for Medicaid. CBO projects that collections of premiums from nonfederal sources will more than double, rising from $25 billion in 2003 to $57 billion in 2013.

Other proprietary receipts come mostly from royalties and charges for oil and natural gas, electricity, minerals, and timber and from various fees levied on users of government property and services. Auctions of rights to use parts of the electromagnetic spectrum are expected to continue until the Federal Communications Commission's authority expires at the end of 2007. CBO estimates that those auctions will bring in a total of $21 billion over the 2004-2008 period, with most of the receipts being recorded in 2005 and 2006.

Legislation Assumed in the Baseline
The general baseline concept for mandatory spending is to project budget authority and outlays in accordance with current law. However, in the case of certain programs with outlays of more than $50 million in the current year, the Deficit Control Act directs CBO to assume that the programs will be extended when their authorization expires.[7]

---

7. Section 257 of the Deficit Control Act stipulates that programs with current-year outlays of $50 million or more that were established prior to enactment of the Balanced Budget Act of 1997 are assumed in the baseline to continue but that the treatment of pro-

The Food Stamp program, Temporary Assistance for Needy Families, and the State Children's Health Insurance Program are examples of programs whose current authorizations expire but in the baseline are assumed to continue. The Deficit Control Act also directs CBO to assume that a cost-of-living adjustment for veterans' compensation is granted each year. The assumption that expiring programs will continue accounts for about $6 billion in projected outlays in 2003; that figure expands to $81 billion by 2013 (*see Table 4-8*).

Net Interest

Interest costs are still a sizable portion of the federal budget, even though they have been shrinking in the past few years. (Net interest outlays peaked at $244 billion in 1997.) In 2002, such costs totaled $171 billion—about 8.5 percent of the federal government's outlays. Although CBO projects that debt held by the public will increase in 2003 to finance the deficit, it anticipates that net interest payments will decline to $157 billion (*see Table 4-9 on page 94*). That reduction is mainly attributable to a recent drop in interest rates—particularly short-term rates.

The federal government's interest payments depend on the amount of outstanding debt held by the public and on interest rates. The Congress and the President can influence the former through legislation governing taxes and spending—and thus the amount of government borrowing. Interest rates are determined by market forces and the Federal Reserve's policies.

Interest costs are also affected by the composition of debt held by the public. The average maturity of outstanding marketable debt has remained fairly constant, fluctuating between five and six years since 1985. That stability, however, masks some changes in the types of securities issued by the Treasury. For example, in 2001, the Treasury stopped issuing 30-year bonds and introduced a four-week bill. As a result, the average maturity of outstanding debt has fallen from a little over six years in December 2000 to five-and-a-half years in September 2002. Currently, Treasury bills with a maturity of one year or less account for about 28 percent of all marketable debt (a similar proportion is projected to continue through the projection period). Short-term debt generally carries lower interest rates than long-term debt does; however, because such debt turns over more quickly, it is more sensitive to changes in interest rates.

As interest rates rise in CBO's economic forecast (and debt held by the public grows to finance projected deficits), net interest also climbs, peaking in 2007 and 2008 at $217 billion. Through the middle of the 10-year period, projected interest rates stabilize at the higher rates, but debt held by the public begins to gradually fall as the baseline shifts from deficit to surplus. After 2008, the decline in net interest mirrors the overall reduction in debt. CBO projects that net interest will account for about 5 percent of total spending in 2013.

Net or Gross?

Net interest is the most economically relevant measure of the government's costs to service its debt. However, some budget watchers stress gross interest (and its counterpart, gross federal debt) rather than net interest (and its counterpart, debt held by the public). But that choice exaggerates the government's debt-service burden because it overlooks billions of dollars in interest income that the government now receives.

Currently, about $3.5 trillion of federal securities that have been sold to the public to finance previous deficits remain outstanding. The federal government also has issued about $2.7 trillion in securities to its own accounts (mainly Social Security and other retirement trust funds). Those securities represent the past surpluses of government accounts, and their total amount grows approximately in step with the projected trust fund surpluses (see Chapter 1). The funds redeem the securities as needed to pay benefits or finance programs; in the meantime, the government both pays and collects interest on those securities. It also receives interest income from loans and short-term cash balances. Broadly speaking, gross interest encompasses all interest paid by the government (even to its own funds) and ignores all interest received. Net interest, by

---

grams established after the 1997 law will be decided on a case-by-case basis, in consultation with the House and Senate Budget Committees. For example, the authorization for the Initiative for Future Agriculture and Food Systems program, which was established in 1998 and for which outlays of $111 million are projected for 2003, is assumed to expire after 2003.

Table 4-8.
Costs for Mandatory Programs That CBO's Baseline Assumes Will Continue Beyond Their Current Expiration Dates

(In billions of dollars)

	2003	2004	2005	2006	2007	2008	2009	2010	2011	2012	2013	Total, 2004-2008	Total, 2004-2013
Food Stamps													
Budget authority	n.a.	n.a.	n.a.	n.a.	n.a.	26.8	27.6	28.4	29.3	30.2	31.1	26.8	173.4
Outlays	n.a.	n.a.	n.a.	n.a.	n.a.	25.6	27.6	28.4	29.3	30.2	31.1	25.6	172.0
Temporary Assistance for Needy Families													
Budget authority	6.7	16.9	16.9	16.9	16.9	16.9	16.9	16.9	16.9	16.9	16.9	84.5	168.9
Outlays	5.6	15.6	17.4	17.7	17.3	16.9	16.9	16.9	16.9	16.9	16.9	84.9	169.4
Commodity Credit Corporation[a]													
Budget authority	n.a.	n.a.	n.a.	n.a.	n.a.	n.a.	15.6	14.8	14.0	13.4	12.8	n.a.	70.5
Outlays	n.a.	n.a.	n.a.	n.a.	n.a.	n.a.	15.6	14.8	14.0	13.4	12.8	n.a.	70.5
Veterans' Compensation COLAs													
Budget authority	0	0.4	1.1	1.8	2.3	3.1	3.8	4.6	5.7	5.6	6.8	8.7	35.0
Outlays	0	0.4	1.1	1.7	2.2	3.1	3.8	4.5	5.7	5.5	6.7	8.6	34.7
Child Care Entitlement to States													
Budget authority	0.8	2.7	2.7	2.7	2.7	2.7	2.7	2.7	2.7	2.7	2.7	13.6	27.2
Outlays	0.6	2.2	2.5	2.6	2.7	2.7	2.7	2.7	2.7	2.7	2.7	12.7	26.3
State Children's Health Insurance Program													
Budget authority	n.a.	n.a.	n.a.	n.a.	n.a.	5.0	5.0	5.0	5.0	5.0	5.0	5.0	30.2
Outlays	n.a.	n.a.	n.a.	n.a.	n.a.	2.2	4.1	4.8	5.3	5.3	5.4	2.2	27.0
Rehabilitation Services and Disability Research													
Budget authority	n.a.	n.a.	n.a.	n.a.	2.8	2.8	2.9	2.9	3.1	3.1	3.2	5.6	20.8
Outlays	n.a.	n.a.	n.a.	n.a.	1.9	2.7	2.9	3.0	3.0	3.1	3.2	4.7	19.9
Ground Transportation Programs Not Subject to Annual Obligation Limitations													
Budget authority	n.a.	0.6	0.6	0.6	0.6	0.6	0.6	0.6	0.6	0.6	0.6	3.2	6.4
Outlays	n.a.	0.2	0.4	0.6	0.6	0.6	0.6	0.6	0.6	0.6	0.6	2.4	5.5
Federal Unemployment Benefits and Allowances													
Budget authority	n.a.	n.a.	n.a.	n.a.	n.a.	0.9	0.9	0.9	1.0	1.0	1.0	0.9	5.7
Outlays	n.a.	n.a.	n.a.	n.a.	n.a.	0.4	0.9	0.9	0.9	1.0	1.0	0.4	5.1
Child Nutrition[b]													
Budget authority	n.a.	0.4	0.4	0.4	0.4	0.5	0.5	0.5	0.5	0.5	0.5	2.1	4.6
Outlays	n.a.	0.3	0.4	0.4	0.4	0.4	0.5	0.5	0.5	0.5	0.5	2.1	4.5

(Continued)

CHAPTER FOUR   THE SPENDING OUTLOOK   **93**

Table 4-8.

Continued

(In billions of dollars)

	2003	2004	2005	2006	2007	2008	2009	2010	2011	2012	2013	Total, 2004-2008	Total, 2004-2013
Family Preservation and Support													
Budget authority	n.a.	n.a.	n.a.	n.a.	0.3	0.3	0.3	0.3	0.3	0.3	0.3	0.6	2.1
Outlays	n.a.	n.a.	n.a.	n.a.	0.1	0.2	0.3	0.3	0.3	0.3	0.3	0.3	1.8
Health Resources and Services Administration													
Budget authority	0.1	0.1	0.1	0.1	0.1	0.1	0.1	0.1	0.1	0.1	0.1	0.3	0.5
Outlays	*	*	*	*	0.1	0.1	0.1	0.1	0.1	0.1	0.1	0.2	0.5
Ground Transportation Programs Controlled by Obligation Limitations[c]													
Budget authority	n.a.	36.7	36.7	36.7	36.7	36.7	36.7	36.7	36.7	36.7	36.7	183.6	367.3
Outlays	n.a.	0	0	0	0	0	0	0	0	0	0	0	0
Air Transportation Programs Controlled by Obligation Limitations[c]													
Budget authority	n.a.	3.4	3.4	3.4	3.4	3.4	3.4	3.4	3.4	3.4	3.4	17.0	34.0
Outlays	n.a.	0	0	0	0	0	0	0	0	0	0	0	0
Total													
Budget authority	7.5	61.3	62.0	62.6	66.2	99.8	117.0	117.8	119.2	119.5	121.2	351.9	946.6
Outlays	6.2	18.8	21.9	23.1	25.3	54.9	75.8	77.4	79.3	79.5	81.2	144.0	537.2

Source: Congressional Budget Office.

Note: * = between zero and $50 million; n.a. = not applicable; COLAs = cost-of-living adjustments.

a. Agricultural commodity price and income supports under the Farm Security and Rural Investment Act of 2002 (FSRIA) generally expire after 2007. Although permanent price support authority under the Agricultural Adjustment Act of 1939 and the Agricultural Act of 1949 would then become effective, section 257(b)(2)(iii) of the Deficit Control Act says that the baseline must assume that the FSRIA provisions continue.
b. Includes the Summer Food Service program and state administrative expenses.
c. Authorizing legislation provides contract authority, which is counted as mandatory budget authority. However, because spending is subject to obligation limitations specified in annual appropriation acts, outlays are considered discretionary.

---

contrast, is the net flow to people and entities outside the federal government.

In 2002, net interest was about half as large as gross interest. CBO estimates that the government will pay $324 billion in gross interest costs in 2003. Of that amount, however, $156 billion will be credited to trust funds and not paid out by the government. CBO also projects that the government will collect about $11 billion in other interest and investment income this year. Therefore, net interest costs will total an estimated $157 billion in 2003.

Other Interest

The $11 billion in other interest that CBO expects the government to receive in 2003 represents the net of interest payments and interest collections. On balance, however, the government takes in more such interest than it pays out. Among its interest expenses are Treasury payments for interest on tax refunds that are delayed for more than 45 days after the filing date. Among its interest collections is the interest received from the financing accounts of credit programs, such as direct student loans. Although the other interest category appears to grow

Table 4-9.
CBO's Projections of Federal Interest Outlays Under Its Adjusted Baseline
(In billions of dollars)

	Actual 2002	2003	2004	2005	2006	2007	2008	2009	2010	2011	2012	2013	Total, 2004-2008	Total, 2004-2013
Interest on Public Debt (Gross interest)[a]	333	324	333	378	415	439	459	478	495	510	520	522	2,024	4,548
Interest Received by Trust Funds														
Social Security	-77	-84	-90	-98	-109	-121	-135	-150	-166	-183	-201	-220	-553	-1,474
Other trust funds[b]	-76	-71	-67	-72	-77	-81	-86	-90	-95	-100	-105	-111	-383	-885
Subtotal	-153	-156	-157	-170	-186	-203	-221	-241	-261	-283	-306	-330	-936	-2,359
Other Interest[c]	-8	-11	-11	-14	-16	-18	-20	-22	-24	-26	-29	-32	-79	-212
Other Investment Income[d]	0	*	-1	-1	-1	-1	-1	-1	-1	-1	-1	-1	-4	-9
Total (Net Interest)	171	157	165	194	212	217	217	214	208	199	184	159	1,004	1,968

Source: Congressional Budget Office.

Notes: The projections assume that discretionary budget authority totals $751 billion for 2003 and grows with inflation thereafter.

    * = between -$500 million and zero.

a. Excludes interest costs of debt issued by agencies other than the Treasury (primarily the Tennessee Valley Authority).
b. Mainly the Civil Service Retirement, Military Retirement, Medicare, and Unemployment Insurance Trust Funds.
c. Primarily interest on loans to the public.
d. Earnings on private investments by the National Railroad Retirement Investment Trust.

---

rapidly through the projection period, nearly all of that increase is attributable to interest on the accrued balances credited to the TRICARE for Life program. The interest payments are reflected in Table 4-9 as part of gross interest on the public debt, and the receipts are recorded in the other interest category; the net effect on interest outlays is zero.

Other Investment Income

A relatively new category in the budget's accounting for net interest represents the earnings on the private holdings of the newly created National Railroad Retirement Investment Trust. As part of the Railroad Retirement and Survivors' Improvement Act of 2001, that trust is now allowed to invest the balances of the Railroad Retirement trust funds in non-Treasury securities, such as stocks and corporate bonds; previously, all balances could be invested only in nonmarketable Treasury securities. CBO makes no assumption about the gains or losses that the fund might incur when investing in riskier securities; its projections assume that such investments will earn a risk-adjusted rate of return equal to the average interest rate projected for Treasury bills and notes. Such earnings total no more than $1 billion each year through 2013.

CHAPTER 5

The Uncertainty of Budget Projections

The baseline projections in Chapters 1 and 2 represent the most likely of the possible outcomes for the budget and the economy, on the basis of current trends and the assumption that tax and spending policies now in place do not change. But considerable uncertainty surrounds those projections for two reasons. First, future legislation is likely to alter the paths of federal revenues and spending. The Congressional Budget Office does not predict future legislation—indeed, any attempt to incorporate future legislative changes in its baseline would undermine the usefulness of those numbers as a base against which to measure the effects of legislation. Second, the U.S. economy and the federal budget are highly complex and are affected by many economic and other changes that are difficult to predict. As a result, actual budgetary outcomes will almost certainly differ from CBO's baseline projections, even after adjustments for new legislation.

This chapter explores how the accuracy of the economic and technical assumptions that CBO incorporates in its baseline can affect the accuracy of its budget projections. Looking back, the chapter describes CBO's record of projections and shows how reliable CBO's current and future projections might be if they are as accurate as those of the past. Looking forward, it uses several scenarios to describe how the budget might differ from CBO's baseline projections.

The outlook for the budget (given current law and policies) can best be described not as the single row of numbers presented in CBO's tables but as a large spread, or fan, of possible outcomes around those numbers that widens as the projections extend. The fan in *Figure 5-1* is based on CBO's record of accuracy in its five-year budget projections. The baseline budget projections presented in Chapter 1 fall in the middle of the highest probabilities—shown in the darkest part of the figure. But nearby projections—other paths in the darkest part of the figure—have nearly the same probability of occurring as do the baseline projections. Moreover, projections that are quite different from the baseline also have a significant probability of coming to pass. On the basis of the historical record, the budget surplus or deficit would, in the absence of new legislation, fall within the fan around CBO's projections about 90 percent of the time.

Figure 5-1 cannot be precisely accurate because the probabilities are themselves estimates; as such, they may misstate the true uncertainty of current projections. The record on which the fan chart is based is short, and it may not represent future uncertainty. Historically, CBO's projections have been least accurate around cyclical turning points (times when the economy moves from expansion to recession, or vice versa), which economists are generally unable to predict reliably. However, from 1981 (the earliest year for which complete data suitable for this analysis are available) until 2002, the economy experienced just three recessions (in 1981 and 1982, 1990 and 1991, and 2001) and two long expansions. Thus, CBO has limited information on the accuracy of its projections around turning points.

In addition to the uncertainty about cyclical turning points, the economic and budget trends that underlie the 10-year outlook are not clear. For example, measuring and forecasting the potential growth of the economy—an important part of the 10-year projections—are very difficult and involve assumptions about many factors that affect the growth of capital, labor supply, and total factor

Figure 5-1.
Uncertainty of CBO's Projections of the Total Budget Surplus Under Current Policies
(In trillions of dollars)

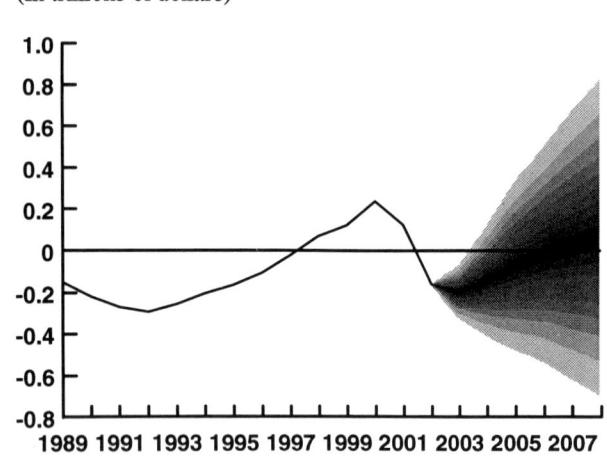

Source: Congressional Budget Office.

Note: Calculated on the basis of CBO's track record, this figure shows the estimated likelihood of alternative projections of the surplus under current policies. CBO's projections described in Chapter 1 fall in the middle of the darkest area. Under the assumption that tax and spending policies do not change, the probability is 10 percent that actual surpluses or deficits will fall in the darkest area and 90 percent that they will fall within the whole shaded area.

Actual surpluses or deficits will of course be affected by legislation enacted during the next 10 years, including decisions about discretionary spending. The effects of future legislation are not included in this figure.

For an explanation of how CBO calculates the probability distribution, see *Uncertainties in Projecting Budget Surpluses: A Discussion of Data and Methods* (February 2002), available at www.cbo.gov; an update of that publication will appear shortly.

productivity (which reflects the output from both capital and labor combined). Much uncertainty surrounds factors such as the enduring effect of the investment boom of the late 1990s, the pace of future technological improvements in IT (information technology) equipment, the impact of changes in the educational status of the labor force, developments in the world economy, and work and retirement patterns—including the full implications of the impending retirement of the baby-boom generation. Even small inaccuracies in the projected growth rate of potential output can have significant budgetary implications over the course of 10 years.

Another way to show the uncertainty of projections is to calculate the effects of specific sets of alternative assumptions on the outlook for the economy and the budget. To illustrate the possible implications of alternative cyclical and trend assumptions, CBO has chosen several scenarios. Two cyclical scenarios explore the possibilities of either a faster recovery than the one now shown in the baseline projections or, alternatively, another downturn—the second part of a double-dip recession. Other short-term scenarios focus on various possibilities of a war with Iraq. Two additional scenarios concentrate on differing assumptions about longer-term trends in productivity growth, effective tax rates on income, and medical costs. The first assumes that growth of labor productivity is higher than in the baseline, resembling that of the late 1990s, and that other budgetary trends (aside from legislation) also follow favorable paths, as they did in the same period. The second assumes slower growth in labor productivity, more like that of the 1973-1995 period, and less favorable budgetary trends. The projections that result from those various scenarios suggest a very wide range of possible outcomes for the budget.

Like the fan chart, the various scenarios illustrate how the range of uncertainty of budget projections expands as they are extended. The range is very large for the 10-year projections: for instance, choosing relatively optimistic or pessimistic, but still reasonable, assumptions about economic and budgetary trends could increase or decrease the projected cumulative 10-year budget surplus by several trillions of dollars. About three-quarters of the uncertainty in 10-year budget projections occurs in the last five years of the projection period. Looking forward a decade allows the Congress to consider the longer-term budgetary implications of specific policy changes, but it also increases the likelihood that budgetary decisions will be made on the basis of projections that later turn out to have been far wrong.

The Accuracy of CBO's Past Budget Projections

Baseline budget projections are bound to deviate from actual outcomes, but assessing the accuracy of previous projections is not a simple matter. Baseline projections are meant to serve as a neutral reference point for evaluating policy changes, so they make no assumptions about

CHAPTER FIVE THE UNCERTAINTY OF BUDGET PROJECTIONS 97

Figure 5-2.
Misestimates in CBO's Projections Made from 1981 to 1997

(Percentage of GDP)

Projection Years

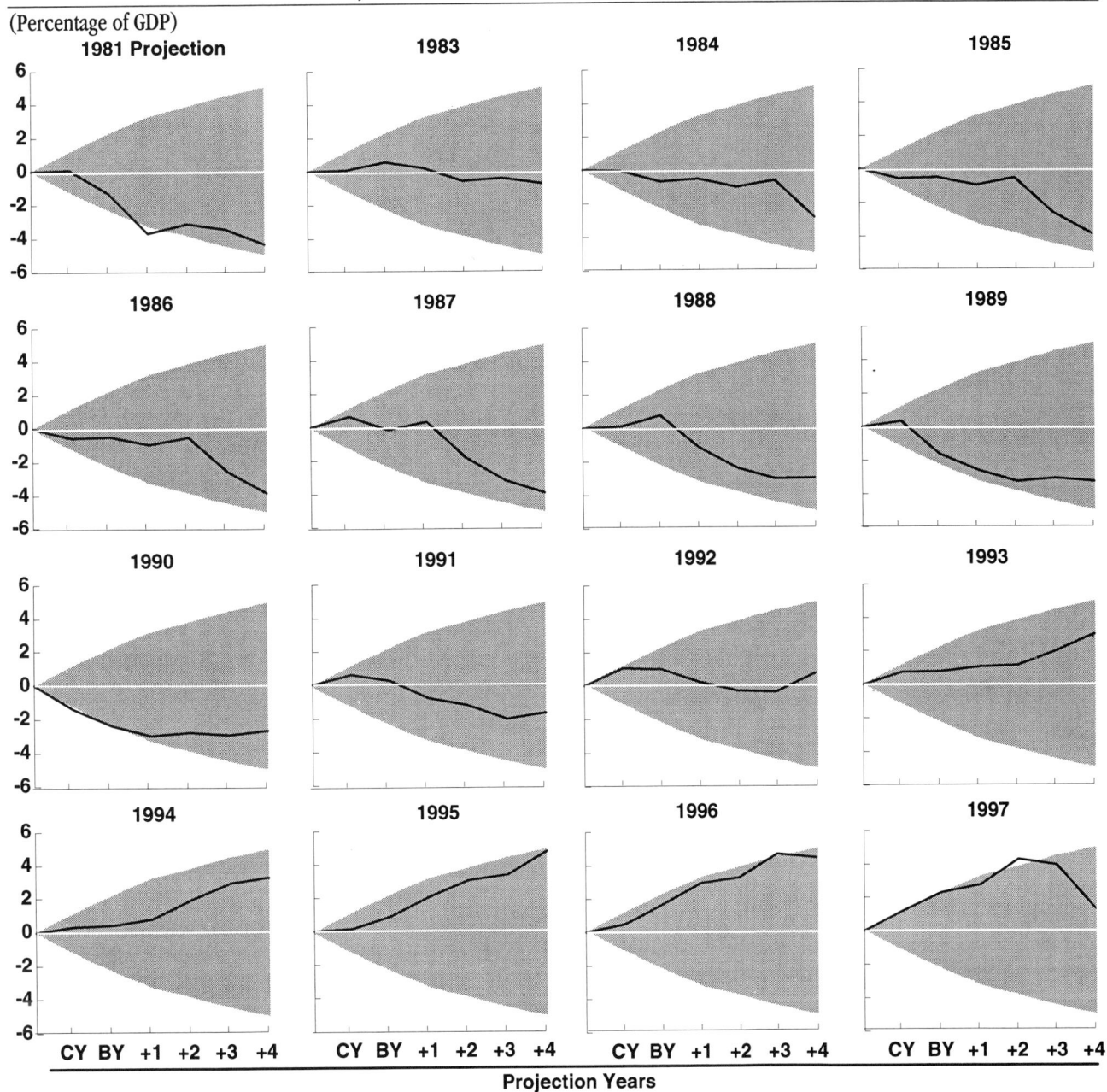

Source: Congressional Budget Office.

Notes: CY = current year; BY = budget year.

This figure shows misestimates in CBO's projections of the primary surplus—the total surplus excluding net interest—made at different times. Plotted points that lie below the center line reflect instances in which CBO overestimated the primary surplus, while points above the center line reflect underestimates. In each panel, the shaded cone indicates the estimated 90 percent confidence band; that is, there was a 90 percent chance that CBO's projection would be within the shaded area. CBO estimated that confidence band on the basis of its track record since 1981 (excluding 1982, because of insufficient data).

The figure excludes the effects of legislation enacted after the projections were made.

Box 5-1.
How CBO Analyzed Its Past Misestimates

This chapter distinguishes inaccuracies in budget projections that are correlated with the business cycle from inaccuracies in assessing trends that are unrelated to the business cycle.[1] That distinction is useful because inaccuracies in the assessment of trends are likely to grow indefinitely as the projection horizon extends, but inaccuracies correlated with the business cycle do not. In fact, according to the Congressional Budget Office's (CBO's) estimates, cyclical inaccuracies are small in the first two years of a projection period (that is, the current year and the budget year); for those two years CBO attempts to reflect its view of that cycle in its projection. Those inaccuracies plateau at a constant level for the next three years of the projection period, for which time CBO does not attempt to forecast the business cycle. The remaining inaccuracies grow almost linearly with the projection horizon. According to that decomposition, discrepancies between CBO's budget projections five years out and actual outcomes have consisted in roughly equal parts of discrepancies due to business cycles (which CBO does not attempt to project so far in advance) and inaccuracies in assessing the economic and other trends that underlie the budget.

---

1. A detailed discussion appears in *Uncertainties in Projecting Budget Surpluses: A Discussion of Data and Methods* (February 2002), available at www.cbo.gov. An updated version of that document will be available shortly.

For the purpose of this chapter, discretionary spending is handled somewhat differently than in CBO's usual analyses of revisions to budget projections. In its analyses of revisions, CBO allots any discrepancies between assumptions and outcomes to three categories: the effects of legislation, economic factors, and technical (estimating) factors. (For more details about those categories, see Chapter 1.) Discretionary spending is appropriated annually through new legislation, and as a result, legislation accounts for the lion's share of the differences between baseline projections and actual outlays for such programs. But for discretionary spending, the split is not available consistently throughout all of the historical record that CBO analyzes in this chapter. For that reason, CBO has excluded the small misestimates in discretionary spending for other (nonlegislative) reasons from its discussion of uncertainty here. Because economic and technical assumptions play only a small role in projections of discretionary spending, that omission makes very little difference to the results.

The discussion in this chapter also omits any distinction between economic and technical differences. That distinction is somewhat arbitrary, subject to change as the underlying economic data are revised, and unnecessary for this analysis.

---

future legislation that might alter current budget policies. Of course, new legislation is likely to affect revenues and spending, but the purpose of baseline estimates is not to forecast legislation. Consequently, this chapter focuses on inaccuracies in projecting that stem from economic and technical factors and excludes the estimated effects of new legislation.

To assess the accuracy of its past annual projections, CBO compared those projections with actual budgetary outcomes and attempted to determine the sources of differences, after adjusting for the estimated effects of policy changes (*see Box 5-1*). The comparisons included 21 sets of projections for the ongoing fiscal year (the one in which the projections were made), 20 sets for the following fiscal year (referred to as the budget year), and 16 sets of projections that extend four more years into the future.[1] CBO used only the first five years of projections

---

1. The projections are those made in July 1981 and CBO's winter projections (usually published in January) from 1983 through 2002. Insufficient data were available to use projections made before 1981 or the projection made in early 1982. For projections made in 1997 and before, a full five years of estimates could be used. For projections made since that date, progressively shorter spans of estimates could be used because the most recent actual data against which they could be compared was for fiscal year 2002. To calculate the role of policy changes, CBO used estimates of the budgetary effects of legislative changes that were made close to the time that the legislation was enacted. (CBO has also examined in detail its record of economic forecasts. See Congressional Budget Office, *CBO's Economic Forecasting Record*, available at www.cbo.gov.)

Table 5-1.
Average Difference Between CBO's Budget Projections and Actual Outcomes Since 1981, Adjusted for Subsequent Legislation

(In percent)

	Current Year	Budget Year	Budget Year + 1	Budget Year + 2	Budget Year + 3	Budget Year + 4
Difference as a Percentage of GDP						
Surplus or Deficit						
Average difference[a]	0.2	0.1	0	-0.1	-0.3	-0.5
Average absolute difference	0.5	1.2	1.6	2.1	2.6	3.2
Revenues						
Average difference	0	-0.1	-0.1	-0.2	-0.3	-0.5
Average absolute difference	0.4	0.9	1.3	1.6	1.8	2.1
Outlays						
Average difference	-0.2	-0.2	-0.2	-0.1	-0.1	-0.1
Average absolute difference	0.3	0.5	0.6	0.8	1.0	1.2
Difference as a Percentage of Actual Outcome						
Revenues						
Average difference	0	-0.5	-1.2	-1.6	-2.2	-3.5
Average absolute difference	1.9	4.6	6.8	8.3	9.6	11.5
Outlays						
Average difference	-0.9	-0.8	-0.9	-0.9	-0.6	-0.7
Average absolute difference	1.4	2.1	3.0	3.7	4.9	6.0

Source: Congressional Budget Office.

Notes: This comparison covers the projections that CBO published in July 1981 in *Baseline Budget Projections: Fiscal Years 1982-1986* and the ones it published each winter between 1983 and 2002 in *The Economic and Budget Outlook*.

The current year is the fiscal year in which the projections are made; the budget year is the following fiscal year.

Differences are actual values minus projected values. Unlike the average difference, the average absolute difference indicates the distance between the actual and projected values without regard to whether the projections are overestimates or underestimates.

a. A positive average difference for the surplus or deficit means that, on average, CBO underestimated the surplus or overestimated the deficit; and a negative average difference, the opposite.

because its record is not long enough to draw conclusions from 10-year projections. On average, the absolute difference (without regard to whether the difference was positive or negative) between CBO's estimate of the federal surplus or deficit and the actual result was 0.5 percent of gross domestic product for the ongoing fiscal year and 1.2 percent for the budget year; by the fourth year beyond the budget year, CBO's estimate (adjusted for the effects of subsequent legislation) rose to 3.2 percent (*see Table 5-1*). If those averages were applied to CBO's current baseline, the actual surplus or deficit could be expected to differ in one direction or the other from the corresponding projection by roughly $55 billion in 2003, $135 billion in 2004, and $450 billion in 2008, aside from the effects of legislative changes.

Misestimates of revenues have generally been larger than misestimates of outlays, reflecting the greater sensitivity of revenues to economic developments. In absolute terms, revenue projections have differed from actual outcomes by an average of about 1.9 percent for the current year, 4.6 percent for the budget year, and 11.5 percent for the fourth year beyond the budget year. Inaccuracies in outlay projections were about a third smaller than those in revenue projections for the current year and about half as large for the budget year and subsequent years.

The misestimates of the budget's bottom line went in both directions: sometimes the projections were too high and at other times too low. On average, CBO's projection of the surplus or deficit has tended to be slightly pessimistic—that is, CBO overestimated deficits—for the current and budget years and slightly optimistic for the third and fourth years beyond the budget year. However, the averages of the underestimates and overestimates for the six years have not been statistically significant, so in the calculations underlying Figure 5-1, the average inaccuracy was assumed to be zero.

Similar conclusions can be drawn from looking at the history of CBO's estimates of the primary surplus—the total budget surplus excluding net interest—for each of the 16 full (six-year) baseline projections in the sample period.[2] In each case in *Figure 5-2*, the shaded cone corresponds to an area similar to that shown by the fan in Figure 5-1, which is likely to capture a misestimate about 90 percent of the time. Both figures reflect a statistical analysis of CBO's past misestimates of revenues and outlays.[3] Misestimates above the center of the cones represent instances in which CBO underestimated the primary surplus, while misestimates that lie below the center of the cones are times when CBO overestimated the primary surplus—in all cases, apart from the effects of subsequent legislation.

As the graphs in Figure 5-2 show, CBO's baseline projections have sometimes been very close to the mark, especially in the short run. While the five-year budget projections made between 1993 and 1997 tended to be too pessimistic, those made earlier tended to be too optimistic.

Finally, projections made around the times of large changes in taxes generally would not have been improved if those projections had incorporated larger "feedback effects" on the budget from anticipated responses of capital and labor supply. For example, adding revenues to the 1983 baseline projection of the primary surplus to reflect larger supply-side effects of the Economic Recovery Tax Act of 1981 and the Tax Equity and Fiscal Responsibility Act of 1982 than the amount assumed in that baseline would have increased rather than reduced the inaccuracies in that projection.[4] Similarly, assuming larger supply-side effects of the Omnibus Budget Reconciliation Act of 1993 than those incorporated in the 1994 baseline would have reduced the projected level of revenues and magnified the inaccuracies in projecting the budget balance. Inaccuracies in some years of the 1991 baseline, which followed the Omnibus Budget Reconciliation Act of 1990, would have been increased by assuming larger negative feedbacks from the tax increase.

Sources of Past Inaccuracies in Projecting Revenues

Misestimates of revenues are rarely attributable to a single cause, but a few major factors can be identified. Both unexpected recessions and unexpectedly rapid expansions can be a problem for revenue projections—as noted earlier, predicting turning points in the business cycle is one of the most difficult challenges facing economic forecasters. Thus, revenues tend to be overestimated in projections done just before recessions and underestimated in projections made before rapid expansions. Until the recent recession, the major source of inaccuracies in revenue projections made during the economic expansion of 1995 through 2000 was the failure to predict the apparent acceleration in the trend growth of the economy and the economic changes associated with it. In particular, the boom in the stock market led to huge capital gains on paper, which boosted tax revenues as investors began to realize those gains. At the same time, the income of

---

2. Baselines after January 1997 are not shown, because fewer than six years of actual outcomes are available for measuring inaccuracies. The graphs in Figure 5-2 feature primary surpluses–that is, surpluses excluding net interest. Including net interest would muddy the comparisons because the relationship between budget balance and interest costs depends on interest rates, which vary.

3. See Congressional Budget Office, *Uncertainties in Projecting Budget Surpluses: A Discussion of Data and Methods* (February 2002), available at www.cbo.gov. An updated version will be available shortly.

4. The Joint Committee on Taxation's estimates for the effects of the Economic Recovery Tax Act of 1981 on revenues stop at 1986.

households in the highest tax brackets grew faster than income on average, raising effective tax rates.

The unexpected shortfall in receipts in 2001 and 2002 was very likely due to some unwinding of the same factors that pushed receipts above expectations in the 1995-2000 period. Capital gains realizations fell substantially in 2001; other causes (as yet unidentified) reduced effective tax rates on income besides capital gains. The causes of the shortfall will not be fully known until all of the data from tax returns for 2001 and 2002 are tabulated over the next year and a half.

Sources of Past Inaccuracies in Projecting Mandatory Outlays

Economic performance affects federal spending, both directly and indirectly. CBO often overestimated inflation in its projections in the early 1980s, and more recently it anticipated an upturn in inflation during the late 1990s that did not occur. Estimates of inflation that are too high result in overestimates not only of cost-of-living adjustments for beneficiaries of many benefit programs but also of reimbursements for health care providers. CBO also overestimated unemployment rates in the 1990s, leading to corresponding overstatements of caseloads for means-tested benefit programs (such as the Food Stamp program and Medicaid).

Misestimates of those broad economic trends, however, accounted for only part of the inaccuracies in past projections of mandatory outlays. The remainder came from inaccurate assumptions about such factors as what proportion of eligible individuals and families would participate in benefit programs, how sound financial institutions would be, and how health care providers would behave—factors that can be extremely difficult to predict. For example, the deposit insurance crisis of the 1980s was not fully anticipated, and the year-by-year costs for its cleanup were highly variable and hard to estimate. CBO also did not fully anticipate either the expansion between the late 1980s and the late 1990s of states' use of creative financing mechanisms to obtain federal Medicaid funds or the temporary slowing of the growth of Medicare costs in the late 1990s.

Alternative Economic and Budget Scenarios

Another way of looking at the uncertainty of today's projections is to consider how different scenarios could affect the budgetary outcome. Those alternative scenarios can provide a qualitative understanding of how budget projections can miss the mark, although assigning probabilities to the various outcomes is generally not possible.

Short-Term Economic Uncertainty

CBO's baseline economic forecast for 2003 and 2004 (described in Chapter 2) lies in the middle of a range of possible outcomes. Both substantially weaker and substantially stronger outcomes are possible. The economy has moved from the recovery period after the recession into an expansion phase, which means no more than that the level of real gross domestic product has exceeded the peak that it reached in the fourth quarter of 2000.[5] The expansion could still be quite fragile, however, given the continued economic weakness in the rest of the world, the likelihood that consumer spending will grow no faster than income, and the uncertainty of businesses' willingness to invest (highlighted in the baseline forecast). But some signs point in a more optimistic direction. In particular, the extraordinary growth of productivity throughout the recent recession suggests that businesses have done a great deal of cost-cutting and may therefore be poised to embark on new investment. The dollar has also begun to fall, so the United States may capture a larger proportion of world trade, weak though it is.

In addition, much uncertainty exists in the short term about the amount of tax receipts. In recent years, tax receipts have swung by more than would be expected if the economic cycle was the only thing at work—first rising even more than income in the economic boom of the late 1990s, and then falling more than income during the past

---

5. The Business Cycle Dating Committee of the National Bureau of Economic Research (the private group whose assignment of dates for recessions is universally accepted) has not yet announced a date for the trough of the recession.

Box 5-2.
The Costs and Risks of Deflation

Last year's low rate of inflation, the current pause in the growth of demand, and lower prices for many types of consumer goods increase the likelihood that the overall level of prices may actually begin to fall sometime in the next two years. The United States has not experienced a persistent, generalized decline in prices—deflation—since the Depression of the 1930s, but a few analysts are concerned that the country may soon face a protracted period of slow growth of output and declining prices throughout the economy.

Deflation, if largely unanticipated, can lead to stagnation by making it difficult for debtors, both households and businesses, to keep up with payments on their debt. Debt taken on at interest rates that appeared reasonable under the assumption of even slowly rising prices of assets and some growth in wages and profits could become unmanageable if either asset prices or incomes decline steadily.

Such deflation could compromise the Federal Reserve's ability to stimulate the economy. Although the Federal Reserve could lower the federal funds rate (currently at 1¼ percent) to zero, the real (inflation-adjusted) interest rate would still be high if the general price level was falling by 3 percent or 4 percent a year. Such a high real interest rate would not encourage investment or other spending when the economy was weak.

However, such deflation-induced economic stagnation for the United States seems unlikely. The low rates of inflation of the past five years stem primarily from rapid growth of productivity and, to a lesser extent, from low import prices. If that pattern continues, asset prices and wages and profits can continue to grow even if the overall level of prices is falling slightly. In essence, nominal gross domestic product could grow even with mild deflation. Such growth would mitigate defaults and keep deflation from seriously affecting the growth of demand.

Moreover, policies other than reductions in short-term interest rates would still be available. The Federal Reserve could still expand the monetary base and reduce long-term interest rates (which are farther from zero) by purchasing Treasury securities at longer maturities. Fiscal policies such as large and immediate tax cuts or spending increases would also help to stimulate the economy in the short run, especially if used in conjunction with monetary policies.

Furthermore, the flexibility of the U.S. economy reduces the likelihood of a protracted period of stagnation. Labor and capital markets are more flexible than they were in the 1930s, systems of financial intermediation are much stronger, and trade is more open. Moreover, the U.S. economy is much more flexible than most foreign economies. Therefore, Japan's experience over the past 12 years—a period of moderate deflation and subpar growth that started after a precipitous decline in Japanese equity and property prices—does not presage future problems here. The situation in Japan has been aggravated by the massive number of nonperforming loans (for which debtors are not keeping up with their payments) in its banks' portfolios.

Conversely, the high levels of household debt in the United States and the high percentage of household income that is used to service debt increase the likelihood of a recession if deflation does materialize. High debt levels expose a potentially large number of households to default if the growth of income slows dramatically. Unfortunately, good estimates of the number of households at risk are not available, but various indicators imply serious financial troubles for at least a small percentage of households, in spite of households' recent opportunities to improve their situations by refinancing their mortgages.

On balance, however, the risks of deflation-induced stagnation are small. Even if the general price level does start to fall, macroeconomic policies and the economy's natural ability to weather shocks are likely to keep deflation from becoming entrenched.

Table 5-2.
Alternative Scenarios for the Economy and the Budget in the Short Term

	Changes from CBO's Baseline	
	2003	2004

Double-Dip Recession

Real GDP (Percent)	-1.9	-2.5
Important Tax Bases[a] (Percent)	-2.8	-2.6
Short-Term Interest Rates (Percentage points)	-0.5	-2.8
Effect on Budget Balance (Billions of dollars)		
Portion attributable to economic factors	-37	-46
Portion attributable to technical factors[b]	-18	-14
Total	**-55**	**-61**

Rapid Expansion

Real GDP (Percent)	+1.7	+2.0
Important Tax Bases[a] (Percent)	+2.6	+3.1
Short-Term Interest Rates (Percentage points)	+0.3	+1.5
Effect on Budget Balance (Billions of dollars)		
Portion attributable to economic factors	+36	+54
Portion attributable to technical factors[b]	+18	+14
Total	**+54**	**+68**

Source: Congressional Budget Office

Note: Economic data are by calendar year; budget data, by fiscal year.

a. Wages and salaries plus corporate profits. Those two categories of income are particularly significant for revenue projections because they are taxed at the highest effective rates.
b. Assumes that tax receipts from a given projection of economic activity differ from what was anticipated.

---

two years. CBO has constructed two scenarios to illustrate the range of possibilities in the short run, both for the economic outlook and for tax receipts.

Double-Dip Recession. The economy could turn rapidly worse in 2003 if the imbalances that precipitated the last recession have not been fully worked out. The areas to watch include the response of consumers to their loss of wealth in the stock market's decline, and the willingness of businesses to invest in the face of excess capacity and the prospect of no more than modest growth in consumer demand. The economy could tip into recession if consumers slow the growth of their spending to much below the growth of their income. Some forecasters are also concerned that with a weak economy might come more widespread deflation, which currently exists in the goods market, although CBO's scenario does not assume falling prices economywide (see Box 5-2).

The recession scenario that CBO has constructed assumes weaker growth across the board in spending by consumers, businesses, state and local governments, and foreigners (see Table 5-2). In the scenario, the Federal Reserve does not fully anticipate the slowing demand, and the downturn proceeds too rapidly for monetary policy to stop it or for the Administration and the Congress to respond with timely legislation. With three quarters of negative growth in 2003, the growth of real GDP is 1.9 percentage points below the baseline this year and remains lower in 2004. Corporate profits and dividends fall more than proportionately in response to GDP, contributing to a more-than-proportionate decline in the major tax bases (wages and salaries, plus corporate profits). Unemployment rates are over 1 percentage point higher in 2004. The scenario also assumes that tax receipts are even lower than the weaker economic activity suggests. Consequently, the budget deficit would worsen by $55 billion this fiscal year and $61 billion in 2004.

Table 5-3.
Potential Economic and Budgetary Effects of War in Iraq

	Changes from Baseline	
	2003	2004

Benign Scenario

Oil Prices (Dollars per barrel)	2.8	0
Real GDP (Percent)	0.2	0.4
Inflation (Percentage points)	0.1	0.1
Short-Term Interest Rates (Percentage points)	0.1	0.7
Effect on Budget Balance (Billions of dollars)	-20.4	-14.5

Intermediate Scenario

Oil Prices (Dollars per barrel)	13.5	10.0
Real GDP (Percent)	-1.8	-2.0
Inflation (Percentage points)	0.7	0.5
Short-Term Interest Rates (Percentage points)	-0.9	-0.9
Effect on Budget Balance (Billions of dollars)	-35.9	-67.1

Worst Scenario

Oil Prices (Dollars per barrel)	36.5	20.0
Real GDP (Percent)	-4.4	-4.4
Inflation (Percentage points)	1.8	0.4
Short-Term Interest Rates (Percentage points)	-1.4	-2.7
Effect on Budget Balance (Billions of dollars)	-63.7	-119.3

Source: Macroeconomic Advisers, LLC, *After an Attack on Iraq: The Economic Consequences*, December 24, 2002.

Notes: The scenarios are by Macroeconomic Advisers (MA), which based its budget calculations on CBO's estimates of the monthly costs of war with Iraq (see Box 1-3 on page 10). What MA calls the benign scenario is based on a decisive victory after four to six weeks of fighting; the intermediate scenario incorporates six to 12 weeks of fighting and some damage to Iraq's oil facilities; and the worst scenario incorporates three to six months of fighting, major casualties, and severe damage to Iraq's infrastructure.

Economic data are by calendar year; budget data, by fiscal year.

Rapid Expansion. A more optimistic interpretation of recent events is also possible. Stock market prices suggest that investors are discounting the current weakness in corporate earnings and looking forward to substantial improvements. The recent strength of consumer spending may demonstrate that the loss of wealth since 1999 does not affect consumers' spending plans very much. If people still feel wealthy—the wealth-to-income ratio has not fallen below the trend it followed before 1995—consumption may continue with vigor. The Federal Reserve has, in the process of lowering interest rates, sharply expanded the money supply, providing the wherewithal for a burst in demand. Moreover, businesses may have finished cutting costs and revising their plans and now may be ready to invest more strongly than expected.

The scenario that CBO has constructed assumes that the growth of consumption is significantly stronger in 2003 and that this additional spending stimulates business investment. The growth of exports also picks up, possibly because of faster growth abroad. The stronger growth means that state and local governments have more revenues than they expected and therefore are able to balance their budgets with smaller cuts in purchases and other spending. Consequently, the growth of real GDP is more than a percentage point higher in 2003 than it is in the baseline, and remains higher in 2004. The scenario also assumes that tax receipts are even higher than the increase in economic activity suggests. As a result of those assumptions, the budget deficit would narrow by $54 billion in 2003 and by $68 billion in 2004, compared with CBO's baseline.

War with Iraq

CBO's baseline assumes no significant repercussions for the U.S. economy from any possible military activity in Iraq. Certainly, though, a war could affect the outlook both for the economy and for the budget.

A war's effect on the economy, including its impact on oil prices and on the confidence of consumers and businesses, obviously depends on its outcome. In order to assess the possible effects of war on the U.S. economy, CBO has turned to a recent analysis by Macroeconomic Advisers (MA).[6] That analysis considers three scenarios. In the most benign scenario, victory is quick and decisive, with hostilities ending in four to six weeks and without serious political repercussions for other states in the region. With little damage to wells and ports, oil production quickly resumes and—because the war is over—oil prices no longer include a risk premium and may even fall. In an intermediate scenario, fighting extends six to 12 weeks, and tensions persist even after the main fighting is over. With some damage to oil facilities, production is down. In the worst scenario, fighting lasts between three and six months, produces major casualties, and severely damages Iraq's infrastructure. In this scenario, the United States faces major geopolitical problems, including widespread resentment in Arab countries, that undermine the confidence of U.S. consumers and businesses even after fighting has ended.

In MA's analysis, the most benign scenario, with a quick finish to the war, could provide a short-term lift to the economy that comes from lower oil prices and the removal of uncertainty about the nature of the war (see Table 5-3). In the other two scenarios, the economic effects are serious enough to produce either a pause in growth or a double-dip recession. (Conflict with Iraq is unlikely to provide much immediate direct economic stimulus from government spending, because it is likely to be fought using equipment and munitions that have already been purchased.) By MA's calculations, the war would increase the federal budget deficit by amounts ranging from $20 billion to $64 billion in 2003 and from $14 billion to $120 billion in 2004. (CBO has no estimates of the overall budgetary costs of a war, although Box 1-3 on page 10 provides estimates of monthly costs and the costs of some activities. MA used those estimates in its budget calculations.)

Those scenarios are obviously only examples. MA's calculations include attempts to put numbers on several imponderables: how the war might turn out and how consumers and businesses might react to the potential increase in risk. Moreover, while MA provided probability estimates for the various scenarios, CBO prefers not to assess odds; the scenarios stand simply as examples of the kinds of things that might happen.

Trends in Productivity, Effective Tax Rates, and Medical Costs

In CBO's 10-year outlooks, important sources of past misestimates have been in projecting the growth of productivity; revenues relative to income, or effective tax rates; and turning points for programs with a history of volatile growth rates, such as Medicare and Medicaid. In all three areas, trends in the second half of the 1990s were relatively favorable to the budget's bottom line. Those years saw not only strong growth of productivity but also a sharp increase in taxes relative to GDP and a relatively slow increase in the growth of federal spending for the Medicaid and Medicare programs. CBO's baseline projections anticipate less favorable trends in all three areas, even after the economy fully recovers from recession. This section considers two alternative scenarios: one in which trends are as favorable as they were in the second half of the 1990s and the other in which they deteriorate even more than in CBO's assumptions for its baseline. The two scenarios illustrate possible paths and are not intended to be completely symmetrical.

The scenarios illustrate a wide range of possible budgetary outcomes. Over the 10 years from 2004 through 2013, the optimistic scenario implies $3.2 trillion more in total surpluses than CBO's baseline does. The pessimistic scenario implies cumulative deficits that increase the government's debt by nearly $3.2 trillion over the amount in CBO's baseline. In each case, 75 percent of the difference occurs in the last five years, emphasizing

---

6. Macroeconomic Advisers, LLC, *After an Attack on Iraq: The Economic Consequences*, December 24, 2002. The analysis—which grew out of a symposium on November 12, 2002, organized by the Center for Strategic and International Studies in Washington, D.C.—summarizes the conclusions of the participants, who included experts on political and military affairs, oil and financial markets, and economic forecasting, and describes in detail the economic simulation analysis that was MA's contribution to the event.

Table 5-4.
Alternative 10-Year Scenarios for the Economy and the Budget

	Changes from CBO's Baseline				
	Assumptions (Percentage points)		Budgetary Effects (Billions of dollars)		
	2003-2008	2009-2013	2004-2008	2009-2013	2004-2013
Optimistic Scenario						
Growth of Productivity	+0.4	+0.4	+231	+860	+1,091
Effective Tax Rate[a]	+0.6	+1.6	+381	+1,212	+1,593
Growth of Medicare and Medicaid	-2.0	-2.0	+97	+374	+470
Total			**+709**	**+2,446**	**+3,154**
Pessimistic Scenario						
Growth of Productivity	-0.4	-0.4	-230	-839	-1,069
Effective Tax Rate[a]	-0.6	-1.6	-381	-1,212	-1,593
Growth of Medicare and Medicaid	+2.0	+2.0	-101	-429	-530
Total			**-712**	**-2,480**	**-3,192**

Source: Congressional Budget Office.

Note: Economic data are by calendar year; budget data, by fiscal year.

a. Personal tax as a percentage of taxable personal income. The difference from CBO's baseline grows at 0.2 percentage points per year, reaching 2.0 percent in 2013.

---

that budget projections for the 2009-2013 period are even more uncertain than those for the earlier years.

Scenario Based on Optimistic Trends. In CBO's optimistic 10-year scenario, the favorable trends for the budget that existed between 1996 and 2000 continue more or less unabated after the economy recovers from the 2001 recession. Average growth of labor productivity from 2002 to 2013 matches that from 1996 through 2000 and so is 0.4 percentage points higher than that assumed in the baseline (see Table 5-4). As a result, real GDP grows at a rate that is 0.4 percentage points higher than in the baseline. In addition, the scenario assumes that the effective tax rate on taxable personal income grows faster than it does in the baseline projection and is about 2 percentage points above the baseline by 2013. (The effective rate rose by a couple of percentage points —excluding the more predictable effects of real bracket creep—over the 1995-2000 period and then fell by a similar amount in the past two years.) On the outlay side of the budget, the optimistic scenario assumes that spending for Medicare and Medicaid will grow at an annual rate that is 2 percentage points lower than the rate in the baseline.

The budget outlook would improve dramatically under the assumptions of the scenario based on optimistic trends. Over the decade, if there was no other action to cut taxes or increase spending, the cumulative surplus would reach $4.5 trillion (about three times the surplus projected in the baseline). With a surplus of that magnitude, the government's holdings of assets (uncommitted funds) would exceed federal debt held by the public by more than $400 billion at the end of 2013.[7]

Scenario Based on Pessimistic Trends. CBO's pessimistic 10-year scenario reverses most of the assumptions of the optimistic scenario and assumes that the economy reverts in many respects to its situation before 1996. In this scenario, trends in the economy are generally unfavorable to the budget. The scenario assumes that the recent burst

---
7. "Uncommitted funds" is CBO's term for the surplus that remains each year after paying down all publicly held debt that is available for redemption.

Box 5-3.
Potential Effect of an Unfavorable Trend in Workers' Level of Education

For many years, the average levels of education and skill of the U.S. workforce have been rising, contributing to the growth of productivity. However, according to some forecasters, that contribution may substantially diminish, or even end, within the next decade. The improvement in the educational level of successive cohorts of workers has already begun to level off. Moreover, as immigrants become a large factor in the growth of the labor force, their generally lower level of education tends to hold down the average.

Available estimates suggest that the upward trend in formal education in the past accounted for about 0.3 percentage points of growth of productivity per year: that component of productivity growth would be at risk if the educational quality of the labor force stopped improving.[1] The Congressional Budget Office (CBO) has not incorporated such a slowing of productivity growth in its 10-year projections, however, because other factors may offset the slowing rate of improve-

ment in workers' education. As long as highly skilled employees are valuable to employers, skill levels are likely to increase. If formal education is not producing enough highly skilled employees, then on-the-job training and similar approaches should become more prevalent.

Past studies do not help much in projecting the contribution of those less formal methods of improving skills. Analysis of productivity trends has not generally focused on those methods, because relevant data are hard to obtain. Some of the effects of informal training may be picked up in empirical estimates of the effects of formal schooling, to the extent that the two were correlated in the past. However, the extent of correlation is unknown, and future trends may differ.

Consequently, the assumption that the skills businesses need will be generated one way or another is based on theory rather than observable fact. If it is wrong, growth of gross domestic product over the next 10 years might be as much as 0.2 percentage points lower, on average, than CBO projects. That would cut about $460 billion from the projected budget surplus over 10 years.

---

1. Dale W. Jorgenson, Mun S. Ho, and Kevin Stiroh, "Projecting Productivity Growth: Lessons from the U.S. Growth Resurgence," *Economic Review*, Federal Reserve Bank of Atlanta, vol. 87, no. 3 (2002).

---

of productivity proves temporary, so future growth of productivity averages only the 1.4 percent rate seen from 1974 through 1995 (cyclically adjusted), implying correspondingly lower growth of GDP. Productivity growth might slow for a number of reasons: for example, if businesses have learned how to step up to a higher level of productivity by improving their use of computers, the growth of productivity will slow when most businesses have achieved that efficiency. Any slowing in the rate of improvement of the skills of the workforce might also diminish the growth of productivity (*see Box 5-3*). In addition to those economic factors, the scenario assumes

that the effective tax rate on taxable personal income rises more slowly than in the baseline projections and is about 2 percentage points lower by 2013. Similarly, the scenario assumes that Medicare and Medicaid spending grows 2 percentage points faster each year than it does in the baseline.

In this scenario based on pessimistic trends, the budget balance remains in overall deficit throughout the projection period. Debt held by the public would rise to more than $5.5 trillion by the end of 2013, compared with less than $2.6 trillion under assumptions for the baseline.

APPENDIX A

The Expiration of Budget Enforcement Procedures: Issues and Options

The major enforcement procedures that have governed federal budgeting for more than a decade—the annual limits on appropriations (discretionary spending) and the pay-as-you-go (PAYGO) requirement for new mandatory spending and revenue laws—expired on September 30, 2002. Originally enacted in the Budget Enforcement Act of 1990 (BEA), the procedures were devised as part of a broad political agreement reached in that year to reduce and then eliminate budget deficits. Initially set to expire in 1995, the procedures were extended twice—in 1993 and 1997—as part of two subsequent budget agreements also aimed at reducing and eliminating deficits.

The discretionary spending limits and PAYGO requirement replaced the fixed deficit targets that were established by the Balanced Budget and Emergency Deficit Control Act of 1985 (known as the Gramm-Rudman-Hollings Act). The deficit targets imposed a rigid budgetary goal—eliminating deficits over a specified number of years—and set in place an automatic process, known as sequestration, to carry that out. However, the fixed targets were not linked to any political agreement on the policy changes needed to achieve them. Moreover, they were overtaken by the budgetary effects of lower-than-expected economic growth. In essence, the deficit targets were unrealistic.

The BEA represented a different approach to budget discipline and control. The discretionary spending limits and PAYGO requirement applied only to new laws—those enacted after each of the three deficit-reduction agreements of the 1990s—and were intended to ensure that the net budgetary effects of those laws would not increase projected deficits (or lower projected surpluses). They did not call for additional changes in budget policies if economic or other changes unrelated to new laws caused the budget picture to worsen.

During most of the period that the BEA procedures were in place, federal fiscal fortunes improved significantly. Deficits declined steadily after 1992, and beginning in 1998, surpluses were recorded each year through 2001. The BEA framework contributed to that turnaround, but the effectiveness of those procedures started to erode as surpluses began to emerge. From 1999 to 2002, annual appropriations exceeded the discretionary caps on new budget authority and outlays set in 1997 by large amounts (see Figure A-1). Over the same period, new laws affecting direct spending and revenues were enacted with significant costs but without offsetting savings. Despite those trends, large surpluses continued to accumulate because of the surge in tax revenues stemming mainly from robust economic growth.[1] But in 2001, the economy slowed significantly. The budgetary impact of that slowdown, along with the impact of legislation enacted to respond to it and to the terrorist attacks of September 11, 2001, among other factors, brought back a deficit in 2002.

Ironically, the deficit returned just as the BEA procedures expired. Although the BEA was enacted as a temporary

---

1. For a more detailed discussion of the economic and other factors behind the growth in revenues from the late1990s to 2001, see Chapter 3.

Figure A-1.
Actual Discretionary Outlays Compared with the Spending Limits as Originally Enacted

(In billions of dollars)

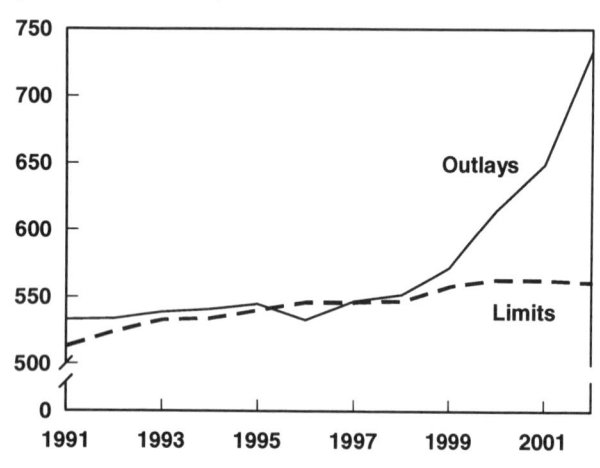

Source: Congressional Budget Office.

means of discipline, it became accepted by many as an effective framework, under the right conditions, for imposing long-term budgetary constraint. Yet despite the return to deficits, whether a consensus can be formed in the near future to resurrect that framework is unclear. Competing priorities, such as the costs of funding the war on terrorism, reviving the economy, and providing prescription drug coverage for the elderly, may make a consensus on fiscal discipline difficult to reach. So could the current outlook for the budget. Although the budget was in deficit for 2002, CBO's current projections show deficits declining after 2003 and small surpluses reemerging by 2007. Those projections, however, reflect current policies and the current economic forecast, both of which are almost certain to change.

In addition to the many short-term pressures on the federal budget, the government's long-term fiscal condition is jeopardized by the increased health and retirement spending that will be required under current law for the baby-boom generation. The prospect of large budget deficits, both in the short term and the long term, suggests that some framework for budgetary discipline may be desirable.

During the 108th Congress, lawmakers may consider making changes in the budget process to improve budgetary discipline or achieve other goals. This appendix reviews the provisions of the BEA that expired at the end of fiscal year 2002, briefly summarizes the budget procedures that remain in effect, evaluates the effectiveness of the BEA, and broadly outlines some of the major options available to lawmakers for the budget process.

Overview of the Budget Enforcement Act and Expired and Expiring Provisions

The BEA built on an existing framework of budget enforcement procedures. The Balanced Budget and Emergency Deficit Control Act of 1985 established a schedule of fixed, declining deficit targets for every fiscal year beginning in 1986 and leading to a target of zero in 1991. The Deficit Control Act also created the procedure of sequestration to automatically cut spending for many federal programs if the deficit for a fiscal year was estimated to exceed the target level. A sequestration, if necessary, would be carried out by an executive order that the President would issue under the terms of a sequestration report from the Comptroller General of the United States, the head of the General Accounting Office. That report was to be based on a joint report by the Office of Management and Budget (OMB) and the Congressional Budget Office (CBO).

In 1986, the Supreme Court held in *Bowsher v. Synar* that it was unconstitutional for the President's sequestration order, an executive action, to be determined by a report from the Comptroller General, an official accountable to the Congress.[2] Thus, the Deficit Control Act was modified to give OMB sole authority to prepare the estimates and calculations used to trigger a sequestration order. As part of that change, CBO was required to issue advisory sequestration reports. The 1987 revision to the law also

---

2. The President's fiscal year 1986 sequestration order, issued under the invalidated procedure, was subsequently ratified by law (Public Law 99-366, approved on July 31, 1986) using a "fallback" legislative procedure provided for under the Deficit Control Act.

Table A-1.
The Deficit Compared with the Gramm-Rudman-Hollings Targets
(In billions of dollars)

	1986	1987	1988	1989	1990	1991	1992	1993
Original Deficit Target	172	144	108	72	36	0	n.a.	n.a.
Revised Deficit Target	n.a.	n.a.	144	136	100	64	28	0
Actual Deficit	221	150	155	152	221	269	290	255
Amount Above the Original Target	49	6	47	80	185	269	n.a.	n.a.
Amount Above the Revised Target	n.a.	n.a.	11	16	121	205	262	255

Source: Congressional Budget Office.

Notes: n.a. = not applicable.

The Balanced Budget and Emergency Deficit Control Act of 1985 (the Gramm-Rudman-Hollings Act) contained the original deficit targets; the Balanced Budget and Emergency Deficit Control Reaffirmation Act of 1987 contained the revised targets.

---

revised the deficit targets and extended them through 1993.[3]

Although deficits shrank somewhat in the late 1980s, they failed to meet the statutory targets—in some years by substantial margins (see Table A-1). The Deficit Control Act set targets, both original and revised, that were unrealistic in light of worsening economic conditions. Consequently, there was a strong incentive to adopt excessively optimistic economic assumptions in the estimates and calculations used to determine whether the deficit target for the year had been exceeded. For those reasons and others, actual deficits remained above the targets during the years that the law was in effect.

The Budget Enforcement Act

To strengthen the budget process, the BEA was enacted in the fall of 1990 as an amendment to the Deficit Control Act. The BEA was part of a multiyear agreement to reduce deficits that was embodied in the Omnibus Budget Reconciliation Act of 1990 as title XIII. Representing a different philosophy of deficit control, the BEA established procedures to ensure that the deficit reductions enacted in the 1990 budget agreement would be carried out. With the BEA, lawmakers enacted rules that would hold them accountable for changes in the deficit due to new legislation. Lawmakers did not intend for the BEA to deal with the budgetary effects of economic and technical factors outside of their immediate control—the factors that played the most significant role in the ineffectiveness of the Gramm-Rudman-Hollings deficit targets.

The BEA established a budget enforcement framework that divided the budget into two parts. Discretionary spending, which is provided and controlled in appropriation acts, would be subject to annual aggregate limits on budget authority and outlays. Laws affecting mandatory spending and revenues would be covered by a PAYGO procedure to prevent those laws from increasing the deficit. A breach of the discretionary spending caps would lead to reductions only in discretionary programs, and a breach of the PAYGO control would trigger cuts only in certain mandatory programs. Although the Deficit Control Act's targets were retained, they essentially became moot because they were adjusted annually for changes in economic and technical factors and the budgetary effects of any new legislation were controlled by the sequestration procedure that enforced the discretionary spending limits and PAYGO requirement.

Originally set to expire at the end of fiscal year 1995, the discretionary spending limits and PAYGO requirement were amended and extended twice, in 1993 and again in 1997, as a part of two subsequent multiyear deficit-reduction agreements. In each extension, the basic framework of the BEA was continued without major substantive changes. With the emergence of surpluses in

---

3. The Balanced Budget and Emergency Deficit Control Reaffirmation Act of 1987, title I of P.L. 100-119.

1998, some people asserted that the PAYGO requirement should be applied in a fiscal year only if new mandatory spending or tax laws were estimated to cause deficits to return. However, both OMB and CBO, with the concurrence of the House and Senate Budget Committees, continued to prepare PAYGO estimates and sequestration calculations without regard to estimates of the deficit or surplus for a particular fiscal year.

The discretionary spending limits were set forth in section 251 of the Deficit Control Act (as amended by the BEA). In some years, the limits were further divided to apply to different categories—such as defense, international, and domestic spending. Under the law, estimated discretionary spending could not exceed the limit for each category. If OMB determined that it did, the President was required to cancel budgetary resources available for that category by the amount of the breach. Certain programs were exempt from a discretionary sequestration, but most programs in the breached category were faced with a uniform percentage reduction in spending.[4]

Three times each year, OMB adjusted the limits, as directed in section 251. Adjustments were allowed for changes in concepts and definitions (such as reclassifying spending from one category to another); changes in inflation from the level assumed at the time that the caps were set (repealed as part of the 1997 extension of the caps); emergency requirements; and special allowances for certain types of spending, such as continuing disability reviews under the Social Security program and certain payments to the International Monetary Fund. The largest and most significant adjustment for the entire 1991-2002 period was for emergency spending. Under the BEA, the limits could be adjusted for the full amount of any appropriation designated by both the President and the Congress as an emergency requirement. Unlike most of the other specified adjustments to the discretionary spending limits, there was no limit on the amount of the adjustment that could be made for emergency appropriations.

The PAYGO requirement (section 252 of the Deficit Control Act) generally stipulated that new mandatory spending or revenue laws enacted through fiscal year 2002 must be "budget neutral" (that is, not increase the deficit or reduce the surplus). OMB and CBO recorded the five-year budgetary effects of mandatory spending and revenue laws on a PAYGO scorecard.[5] (CBO's estimates were only advisory.) At the end of a Congressional session, OMB totaled the budgetary effects of laws enacted to date (as recorded on the scorecard). A positive balance on the PAYGO scorecard represented a net cost, whereas a negative balance signified net savings. If the balance was positive—caused an increase in the deficit or decrease in the surplus for that fiscal year—a PAYGO sequestration (an automatic reduction in mandatory spending) was required to offset the increase in the deficit or decrease in the surplus. However, nearly all mandatory spending was exempt from a PAYGO sequestration.

Expired Provisions

Section 251 of the Deficit Control Act expired on September 30, 2002. Thus, the discretionary spending limits and the enforcement mechanisms for those limits are no longer in effect.

For laws enacted after fiscal year 2002, the PAYGO requirement no longer applies.[6] Thus, CBO and OMB are no longer required to track the five-year budgetary effects of new mandatory spending and revenue laws for the purposes of PAYGO enforcement. For laws enacted through fiscal year 2002, the PAYGO enforcement mechanism

---

4. The BEA also created a "look-back" sequestration procedure for occasions when supplemental appropriation acts pushed spending above the caps. If the breach occurred before the last quarter of the fiscal year, the sequestration occurred seven days after the enactment of the supplemental appropriation law. If the breach occurred in the last quarter, that category's limit for the next fiscal year would automatically be reduced by the excess amount.

5. CBO also prepares PAYGO estimates that cover a 10-year period to assist the Senate in enforcing a separate PAYGO requirement in that body (see section 207 of House Con. Res. 68, 106th Congress). That requirement expires on April 15, 2003 (see Senate Res. 304, 107th Congress).

6. Unlike section 251, section 252 of the Deficit Control Act did not expire at the end of 2002. Rather, section 252 states explicitly that laws enacted after fiscal year 2002 shall not be subject to the PAYGO requirement.

Box A-1.
Expiring Voting Requirements for a Three-Fifths Majority to Waive Budget Points of Order in the Senate

The Congressional Budget and Impoundment Control Act of 1974 and the Balanced Budget and Emergency Deficit Control Act of 1985 include several provisions that act as rules of the House or Senate enforced through points of order. In general, points of order raised under those provisions would prohibit the Congress from considering certain types of budget legislation.

In the Senate (under section 904(c) of the Congressional Budget Act), many of those points of order may be waived —or an appeal of the presiding officer's ruling sustained —only by the affirmative vote of three-fifths of all Senators (60, if there are no vacancies). Several of those voting requirements for a super majority were scheduled to expire on September 30, 2002. However, the Senate extended them through April 15, 2003 (see Senate Resolution 304, adopted on October 16, 2002).

Following is a list of the points of order under the Congressional Budget Act and the Deficit Control Act that are covered by the Senate's expiring requirements for a super majority:[1]

Congressional Budget Act
- **Section 301(i)**: prohibits consideration of legislation reducing the Social Security surpluses set forth in the budget resolution

- **Section 302(c)**: prohibits consideration of annual appropriation bills for a fiscal year before the House or Senate Appropriations Committees make allocations of discretionary spending to their respective subcommittees

- **Section 302(f)**: prohibits consideration of legislation that exceeds allocations of spending to committees made pursuant to the most recently adopted budget resolution

- **Section 310(g)**: prohibits consideration of reconciliation legislation that makes changes in Social Security

- **Section 311(a)**: prohibits consideration of legislation that exceeds aggregate levels of revenues or spending in the most recently adopted budget resolution

- **Section 312(b)**: in the Senate, prohibits consideration of legislation that exceeds the discretionary spending limits in the Deficit Control Act

- **Section 312(c)**: in the Senate, prohibits consideration of budget resolutions that exceed the maximum deficit amounts in the Deficit Control Act

Deficit Control Act
- **Section 258(a)(4)(C)**: prohibits consideration of amendments to a joint resolution that suspends certain provisions of the Congressional Budget Act and the Deficit Control Act in the case of war or low economic growth

- **Section 258A(b)(3)(C)(i)**: prohibits consideration of amendments that are not germane to a joint resolution modifying a sequestration order

- **Section 258B (various clauses)**: prohibits consideration of amendments that would increase deficits and that are not germane to a joint resolution approving changes proposed by the President to a sequestration of defense programs

- **Section 258C(a)(5)**: prohibits consideration of special reconciliation legislation that would exceed the maximum deficit amount under the Deficit Control Act

- **Section 258C(b)(1)**: prohibits consideration of certain amendments to resolutions and reconciliation bills under the special reconciliation process established in this section

---

1. Points of order under the provisions of the Congressional Budget Act listed here—unlike the Senate's temporary voting requirements—do not expire. Unless noted otherwise, they apply in both the House and the Senate. The listed points of order under the Deficit Control Act apply in the Senate only. Except for section 258B (which expired at the end of fiscal year 2002), those provisions expire at the end of fiscal year 2006.

exists through fiscal year 2006. However, Public Law 107-312, enacted on December 2, 2002, instructed OMB to change the existing PAYGO balances for all years to zero. That law eliminated the possibility of a sequestration of mandatory spending as a result of legislation enacted before the end of 2002.

Certain Senate procedures generally linked to the discretionary spending limits and PAYGO requirement also were scheduled to expire at the end of fiscal year 2002. Specifically, in section 904 of the Congressional Budget and Impoundment Control Act of 1974, the Senate established that 60 votes—instead of a simple majority—would be required to waive certain budget points of order under that law and the Deficit Control Act.[7] Most of those requirements for a super majority were scheduled to expire on September 30, 2002. However, on October 16, 2002, Senate Resolution 304 extended most of the waiver requirements through April 15, 2003 (*see Box A-1 on page 113*).

Senate Resolution 304 also extended a point of order (and the accompanying requirement for 60 votes for a waiver) that enforces a separate PAYGO requirement in the Senate.[8] That point of order is set forth in section 207 of the 2000 budget resolution (House Con. Res. 68, 106th Congress). It is intended to prohibit the Senate from considering any new direct spending or tax measures that would cause or increase an on-budget deficit (that is, a deficit excluding the Social Security trust funds and net outlays of the Postal Service) over a 10-year period that begins with the first year covered by the most recently adopted budget resolution.

Evaluating the BEA

Through the mid-1990s, when consensus remained to rein in deficits, the BEA appeared to curb the growth in both discretionary and mandatory spending. In nominal terms, total discretionary budget authority was $35 billion lower in 1997 than in 1991, although total discretionary outlays were $14 billion higher (*see Table A-2*). Those figures, however, mask substantial programmatic shifts (that were aided by the end of the Cold War) from national defense to nondefense programs. In 1997, both defense budget authority and outlays were well below the amounts recorded in 1991; that budget authority had dropped by $66 billion, and outlays had declined by $48 billion. Over the period, nondefense budget authority increased by $31 billion and nondefense outlays jumped by $62 billion. Between 1991 and 1997, most new revenue and mandatory spending laws that were enacted were consistent with the PAYGO requirement to be deficit neutral; end-of-session balances on the PAYGO scorecard consistently showed zero or net reductions in the deficit.

In 1997, lawmakers extended both the discretionary spending limits and the PAYGO provisions of the BEA as part of an agreement to eliminate the deficit by 2002. But that goal was reached in the very next year, as the government recorded its first surplus in nearly 30 years. That surplus eliminated the essential purpose of the BEA —to combat and control deficits. In this new fiscal landscape, with projections showing mounting surpluses for the coming decade, the BEA could not restrain the pressures to spend more.

To comply with the letter of the law while boosting discretionary spending above the statutory limits, lawmakers used a number of approaches—including advance appropriations, delays in making obligations and payments, emergency designations, and specific directives. For example, in 1999 and 2000, lawmakers enacted emergency appropriations totaling $34 billion and $44 billion, respectively—far above the annual average for such spending from 1991 to 1998 (*see Figure A-2*). Comparable amounts were enacted for 2001 and 2002 mainly

---

7. In general, a point of order is an objection that may be raised by a Member of Congress against a piece of legislation or a procedure on the grounds that it violates a rule of the House or Senate. The presiding officer, advised by the Parliamentarian, decides on the basis of the specific rule and precedents under it whether the point of order is valid. The decision of the presiding officer generally is subject to appeal by the House or Senate. For points of order under the Congressional Budget Act, the presiding officer also relies on estimates provided by the House or Senate Budget Committees. In the Senate, points of order under that law may be waived by motion, which in many cases must be approved by a three-fifths vote. In the House, those and other points of order may be waived by adopting a "special rule"—a simple resolution reported by the Rules Committee that sets the terms and conditions for the House to consider legislation.

8. In this case, both the point of order and the 60-vote waiver requirement are scheduled to expire on April 15, 2003.

Table A-2.
Discretionary Spending Under the Budget Enforcement Act

	1991	1992	1993	1994	1995	1996	1997	1998	1999	2000	2001	2002	Total, 1991-1997	Total, 1998-2002
Actual Spending[a]														
Billions of Dollars														
Defense														
Budget Authority	332	299	276	262	263	265	266	272	288	301	332	361	n.a.	n.a.
Outlays	320	303	292	282	274	266	272	270	275	295	306	349	n.a.	n.a.
Nondefense														
Budget Authority	214	232	247	250	238	236	245	257	294	284	332	374	n.a.	n.a.
Outlays	214	231	247	259	271	267	276	282	297	320	343	385	n.a.	n.a.
Total														
Budget Authority	546	531	523	513	501	501	511	530	582	584	664	735	n.a.	n.a.
Outlays	533	534	539	541	545	533	547	552	572	615	649	734	n.a.	n.a.
Percentage Change from Previous Year[b]														
Defense														
Budget Authority	9	-10	-8	-5	*	1	*	2	6	4	10	9	-4	7
Outlays	7	-5	-3	-3	-3	-3	2	-1	2	7	4	14	-3	7
Nondefense														
Budget Authority	11	9	6	1	-5	-1	4	5	14	-3	17	13	2	10
Outlays	7	8	7	5	5	-2	3	2	5	8	7	12	4	8
Total														
Budget Authority	10	-3	-2	-2	-2	*	2	4	10	*	14	11	-1	9
Outlays	7	*	1	*	1	-2	3	1	4	7	6	13	*	7
Spending Limits as Originally Enacted (Billions of dollars)														
Budget Authority	492	503	511	511	518	519	528	531	533	537	542	553	n.a.	n.a.
Outlays	514	525	534	535	541	547	547	548	559	564	564	562	n.a.	n.a.
Amount that Actual Spending Was Above or Below (-) the Original Limits (Billions of dollars)[c]														
Budget Authority	10	14	11	2	-16	-18	-17	-1	49	47	122	182	-14	399
Outlays	-14	-6	5	7	4	-15	**	4	13	51	85	172	-19	325
Emergency Budget Authority Excluding Spending in 1991 and 1992 on Desert Storm and Desert Shield (Billions of dollars)[c]														
Defense	0	0	1	1	2	1	2	3	18	18	14	18	8	70
Nondefense	<u>1</u>	<u>9</u>	<u>5</u>	<u>12</u>	<u>6</u>	<u>4</u>	<u>7</u>	<u>3</u>	<u>17</u>	<u>26</u>	<u>15</u>	<u>29</u>	<u>44</u>	<u>90</u>
Total	1	9	6	14	8	5	9	6	34	44	29	47	52	160

Sources: Congressional Budget Office; Office of Management and Budget.

Notes: n.a. = not applicable.

* = between -0.5 percent and 0.5 percent; ** = between -$500 million and $500 million.

a. Figures for actual spending reflect all spending provided in annual appropriation acts and classified as discretionary under the Budget Enforcement Act, including those amounts designated for emergencies.

b. For the periods of 1991 to 1997 and 1998 to 2002, totals represent the average annual growth from the first year to the last.

c. The Office of Management and Budget estimates that in 1991, emergency budget authority and outlays for Desert Storm and Desert Shield totaled $44.2 billion and $33.2 billion, respectively. In 1992, those amounts were $14.0 billion and $14.9 billion, respectively. Those figures are not included in this section of the table because they were offset by foreign contributions.

Figure A-2.
Emergency Budget Authority Under the Budget Enforcement Act of 1990
(In billions of dollars)

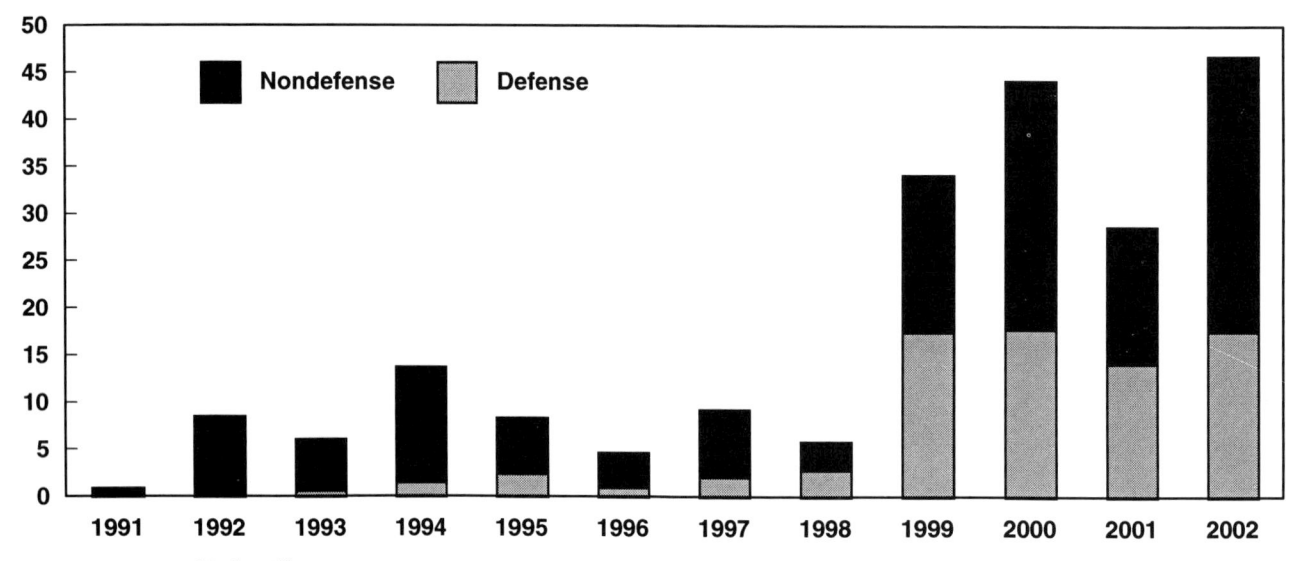

Source: Congressional Budget Office.

Note: Excludes spending in 1991 and 1992 for Desert Storm and Desert Shield because that spending was offset by foreign contributions.

in response to the terrorist attacks of September 11, 2001. During the first six years of the BEA (1991 through 1997), emergency appropriations totaled $52 billion; during the four years following the 1998 surplus, emergency appropriations totaled more than three times that amount.

To accommodate increased nonemergency spending for 2001, lawmakers increased the caps on budget authority and outlays by $99 billion and $59 billion, respectively. The following year, they increased the limits on budget authority and outlays by even larger amounts—$134 billion and $133 billion, respectively. From 1998 through 2002, total discretionary appropriations grew at an average annual rate of 8.5 percent; by comparison, from 1991 through 1997 such spending declined at an average annual rate of 1.1 percent.

Similarly, after the emergence of surpluses, lawmakers enacted legislation to increase mandatory spending or reduce revenues but used legislative directives to statutorily comply with the PAYGO requirement. Thus, for 2001 and later years, lawmakers eliminated more than $700 billion in positive balances—that is, amounts that would

have triggered a PAYGO sequestration—from the scorecard (see Table A-3). Most of that amount stemmed from the estimated drop in revenues attributed to the Economic Growth and Tax Relief Reconciliation Act of 2001. By contrast, during the earlier years of the BEA, the balances on the scorecard were zero or negative, and lawmakers statutorily removed negative balances so that those savings could not be used to offset the costs of new mandatory spending or revenue legislation.

During the 12 years that the threat of a discretionary sequestration was present, sequestrations were ordered only twice, both in 1991 (the first year that the spending limits were in effect) and both for relatively insignificant amounts. One of the sequestrations was rescinded by subsequent law; the second led to estimated savings of $1.4 million (discretionary spending totaled $533 billion in 1991). For laws affecting mandatory spending or revenues, a PAYGO sequestration has never been triggered.

Interpreting the absence of large sequestrations over the BEA's history is difficult. In some years, especially 1991 to 1997, perhaps the threat of sequestration served as an effective deterrent to legislation that would have violated

Table A-3.
Balances Eliminated by Statute from the Pay-As-You-Go-Scorecard
(In billions of dollars)

	1997	1998	1999	2000	2001	2002	2003	2004	2005	2006	Total, 1997-2006
Eliminated Balance	-9	-3	0	-3	90	65	127	150	142	144	701

Source: Congressional Budget Office using data from the Office of Management Budget's final sequestration reports, fiscal years 1991 to 2003.

Note: Positive numbers indicate an increase in the deficit or reduction in the surplus; that is, eliminating positive balances removed the need for a PAYGO sequestration. Negative numbers indicate a decrease in the deficit or increase in the surplus; that is, eliminating such balances made them unavailable to be used as an offset to additional mandatory spending or revenue reductions.

---

the spending limits or PAYGO requirement. More recently, the absence of sequestrations may simply reflect the lack of consensus among lawmakers to guard the bottom line of the budget. With the emergence of large surpluses came the willingness to enact legislation to increase the caps substantially or eliminate the positive PAYGO balances. The lack of sequestrations may also have reflected shifting priorities; for example, legislative efforts aimed at fighting the war on terrorism or reviving the economy may have been deemed more important than avoiding a return to budget deficits. In a sense, that change in priorities may confirm a premise underlying the BEA—that a budget enforcement framework works best when there is a firm consensus on the fiscal goal or goals to be achieved and the policy changes needed to achieve them.

Options

As lawmakers consider whether or how to change the budget process, the choices they face divide broadly into three categories:

- Do nothing, which leaves the caps on discretionary spending and the PAYGO requirement expired, and set budget policy anew each year without statutory constraints;

- Reinstate the structure of caps on discretionary spending and PAYGO; or

- Create a different budget process.

Maintain the Status Quo

Lawmakers could decide not to reinstate the caps on discretionary spending and the PAYGO requirement. The budget process essentially would return to the state that existed before the Gramm-Rudman-Hollings Act.

In general, the federal budget process is an amalgam of procedures that lawmakers and public officials use to establish, control, and account for spending and revenue policies. The budget process includes preparation of the President's budget by the executive branch, the Congressional budget process (centered on a Congressional budget resolution and, in some years, on reconciliation legislation), the authorization and appropriation process, execution of budget law (including impoundment control, a procedure under the Congressional Budget Act for deferring or rescinding appropriated funds), and financial management rules. Those fundamental procedures and practices, grounded in permanent statutes, Congressional rules, agencies' regulations, and longstanding practice, do not expire.

Under the Budget and Accounting Act of 1921, the President submits his budget on the first Monday in February. Under the Congressional Budget Act, the Congress's first major action is to adopt the annual budget resolution, which does not become law. The budget resolution is scheduled to be adopted by April 15. It is usually completed after that date, in some years by substantial margins, because final agreement on a Congressional budget plan often is difficult to reach. The budget resolution serves as a blueprint for Congressional action on separate pieces of revenue and spending legislation. In addition, the resolution's aggregate levels of revenues and spending, and spending allocations made to Congressional committees are enforced by points of order that Members of Congress may raise against individual revenue or spending bills as they are considered by the House or Senate. In general, if a point of order brought under the Congressional Budget Act is sustained (or is not waived), the offending legislation may not be considered further. The budget resolution may also instruct Congressional committees to produce reconciliation legislation that conforms permanent revenue or spending laws within their jurisdiction to the levels set forth in the resolution.

The existing budget process, based on the President's budget and the Congressional budget resolution, provides the means for lawmakers to establish and enforce major changes in budget policies. The process has served as a conduit for major policy initiatives and multiyear deficit-reduction agreements, which typically have been put in place in legislation developed to carry out reconciliation directives in budget resolutions. However, when consensus on such policies has not emerged, the process has stalled. To wit, the Congress was unable to reach final agreement on the budget resolutions for fiscal years 1999 and 2003, and action on appropriation bills for those years was delayed. Whether or not the BEA framework (or something like it) is renewed, political agreement on the budget is probably the largest single factor in ensuring that the budget process functions smoothly.

Reinstate and Adjust the Structure Established by the Budget Enforcement Act

This option essentially would parallel the extensions of the BEA that were enacted in 1993 and 1997. In those years, lawmakers extended the caps and PAYGO requirement as part of new multiyear budget agreements to reduce deficits. Lawmakers have not extended those restraints absent such an agreement.

Despite recent experience, the underlying philosophy of the BEA—that appropriations should be enacted within enforceable limits and that the estimated costs of new tax and mandatory spending legislation should generally be budget neutral—proved to be effective in the 1990s when deficits existed and appeared likely to continue or grow. In essence, the political consensus to reduce those deficits helped the BEA framework to succeed.

As lawmakers consider whether or how to reinstate those procedures, they may want to examine how the previous process could be improved. Some issues include the following:

- **Budget "Firewalls" for Discretionary Spending.** In some years, lawmakers created separate caps for spending on defense, domestic, international, transportation, victims of crime, and conservation programs. Separate sublimits within overall caps may serve important policy goals. But lawmakers give up flexibility to meet other needs within those caps when they carve out separate limits for certain programs. In addition, spending priorities may shift from year to year. If the overall caps were extended for a five-year period—as they have been in the past—establishing sublimits might make it difficult to shift priorities, or, conversely, might prompt lawmakers to again employ the spending devices for which they were criticized in recent years.

- **Emergency Spending.** Some observers have questioned whether much of emergency spending is for true emergencies or is simply a way to appropriate more funds under tight discretionary caps without having to find offsets. The BEA exemption for emergency spending required only that the President and the Congress both agree on the amounts to be designated; it did not limit those amounts or restrict the purposes for which they could be provided. Some analysts feel that the emergency exemption should be replaced with a system of budgeting for emergency needs that is based on an average annual amount of emergency spending appropriated in previous years. Others would place a strict limit on the amount of funding that could be designated as an emergency requirement. Another approach would be to establish a statutory definition of emergencies to guide legislative action on such spending. Those approaches also could be combined. However it is fashioned, an emergency safety-valve procedure of some type that allows additional resources to be provided for unexpected contingencies is probably an important component of an effective framework for budgetary discipline.

- **Inflation Adjustment to the Discretionary Caps.** Until 1997, the BEA provided that the caps on discretionary spending were to be adjusted for changes in the rate of inflation from that anticipated when the caps were originally established. Although inflation has been low in recent years, and in earlier years actually led to a reduction in the caps, restoring an inflation adjustment may help to sustain political agreement on cap levels over a longer period.

- **Sequestration**. The effectiveness of sequestration has been questioned. That only two small sequestrations have been ordered, that caps on discretionary spending have been adjusted or increased by large amounts, and that large PAYGO balances that would have triggered a sequestration have been eliminated by law all point to potential limitations in the procedure. However, the absence of sequestration in some years, especially during the early to mid-1990s, may indicate that the procedure has served at certain times as an effective deterrent to policy changes that would have increased deficits or lowered surpluses.

Nevertheless, if the sequestration procedure is to be resurrected, one issue that lawmakers may need to address is the number of mandatory programs that are exempt from a PAYGO sequestration. If such a sequestration was triggered, the amount of resources available to cut—because of specific exemptions and special rules for Social Security, Medicare, Medicaid, federal retirement, and other entitlements—would be quite limited. The brunt of the sequestration would fall on relatively few mandatory programs. For fiscal year 2003, for example, CBO estimates that only about 4 percent of total mandatory outlays would have been subject to a PAYGO sequestration.

Make Major Changes in the Budget Process

Recent experience with the budget process has caused frustration among some lawmakers, who have raised doubts about the effectiveness of simply reinstating the BEA procedures. With the expiration of the spending caps and PAYGO rules, lawmakers could enact broader reforms.

- **Convert to a Biennial Budget Cycle**. Proposals for biennial budgeting generally call for policymakers to enact budget legislation one year and to oversee and evaluate activities in the next. Supporters of biennial budgeting are increasingly concerned that the requirements of the annual budget process are overwhelming policymakers and public officials. They argue that the seemingly incessant demands of that process detract from other functions of government—such as long-range planning and oversight—that are equally, if not more, important. If budget and nonbudget issues could be separated in the legislative process, biennial budgeting might help ease those problems, improve oversight, and relieve the pressures on the appropriation process. However, changing to a two-year cycle also might diminish the effectiveness of Congressional control of spending in the appropriation process and could make it more difficult to adjust to rapidly changing budget and economic conditions.

- **Make the Budget Resolution a Law**. Each year, the President and the Congress propose separate budget plans. When those plans are fundamentally different, final agreement on tax and spending legislation is difficult to reach, as the delay and gridlock in the budget process in 2002 illustrated. The President and the Congress could be required to enact the budget resolution into law each year.

On the one hand, making the budget resolution a law could promote earlier agreement on priorities between the President and the Congress. A statutory budget resolution also might be a more effective means to pair new budget policies with the appropriate enforcement procedures, such as discretionary caps and a PAYGO requirement. Combining budget policies and enforcement procedures in that manner also might be a better way to ensure that current enforcement procedures reflect lawmakers' most recent consensus. On the other hand, a statutory resolution would probably not make overall agreement on the budget easier, and in some years it might simply sharpen differences or elicit a veto when agreement could not be reached. Also, if a requirement to enact the budget resolution into law caused final action on the resolution to be delayed further, Congressional action on regular appropriation bills and on revenue or other spending legislation could become stalled as well.

- **Adopt Mandatory Spending Controls**. Since the 1960s, outlays for entitlements—such as Social Security, Medicare, and Medicaid—and other mandatory spending programs have grown faster than those for other programs. If current policies remain unchanged, CBO projects that mandatory spending (not including net interest) will continue to grow faster than other spending, increasing from about 60 percent of total outlays in 2002 to nearly 70 percent in 2013 (see Chapter 4). And long-term budgetary pressures caused by the aging of the baby-boom generation will only exacerbate that trend.

As a result, some observers advocate mandatory spending caps enforced by sequestration, patterned after the discretionary spending caps, as an option for controlling entitlement costs. Total mandatory spending could be capped at levels that permitted a limited rate of growth, and any spending over that level would automatically result in an across-the-board cut. However, such an approach would be difficult to implement. And if a significant amount of mandatory spending was exempted from sequestration, as it was under the BEA's PAYGO requirement, the cap might be ineffective or could distribute the burden of enforcement unequally among federal programs.

Others wonder if most entitlements should simply lose that status and be funded annually along with discretionary appropriations. Current trends appear to be in the opposite direction, however, with recent expansions of entitlement programs, such as increases in farm price supports and veterans' benefits, and proposed expansions, such as that for a Medicare prescription drug benefit,

- **Establish a Mechanism Like the Line-Item Veto—Expedited Rescission or Separate Enrollment**. The Supreme Court invalidated the Line Item Veto Act in 1998. The act, enacted in 1996, set in place a procedure for the President to cancel certain provisions of law providing targeted tax benefits or spending that he deemed wasteful or unnecessary. But the Court held that the procedure violated the presentment clause of the Constitution.[9] Since then, at least two alternatives have been introduced in the Congress that supporters hope will revive the budget control device in a constitutional fashion. The first, expedited rescission, would ensure that the Congress voted on the President's proposed cancellations. The other, separate enrollment, would require each tax benefit or spending "item" in a bill passed by the Congress to be enrolled separately for the President's approval.

  Spending control disciplines similar to the line-item veto continue to attract interest because they are viewed as a way to control "pork barrel" spending. However, it is unclear whether such procedures would save significant sums or would simply shift spending priorities to those favored by the President.

- **Budget Concepts**. Some experts are pondering whether it is time to reexamine the budget concepts used in scoring new legislation; classifying and recording the effects of federal tax, spending, and borrowing policies; and presenting that information for use by the public and policymakers (*see Box A-2*). That task was last addressed by the 1967 President's Commission on Budget Concepts, whose report continues to provide the theoretical framework for federal budgeting. However, a lot has changed over the past 30 years or so, and it may be time both to reexamine the findings of the 1967 commission and to study the many new issues that complicate federal budgeting today.

Conclusion

The imperative to reduce and control deficits, seen as a crisis, prompted lawmakers to fashion the BEA framework of budget constraints. While the BEA contributed to liquidating chronic deficits, the effectiveness of those constraints was mixed. The surpluses, though short-lived, eliminated the consensus that had formed to deal with the nation's financial exigency and thereby undermined the BEA. Now, the reemergence of deficits comes as the nation attends to the war on terrorism and to reviving economic growth, taking the focus away from long-term

---

9. Article I, section 7. The Court held that the Line Item Veto Act would "authorize the President to create a different law—one whose text was not voted on by either House of Congress or presented to the President for signature." *Clinton v. City of New York*, 524 U.S. 417 (1998).

Box A-2.
Is It Time for a New Budget Concepts Commission?

The basic accounting rules generally followed in the modern budget process are set forth in the 1967 *Report of the President's Commission on Budget Concepts*. Although the report's recommendations for the most part have not been enacted into law, it is to this day the authoritative statement on federal budgetary accounting concepts and principles. The commission's most important recommendation was for a comprehensive federal budget. It recommended that the budget cover the full range of federal activities and that even borderline activities and transactions be covered unless there were compelling reasons to exclude them. Although the commission's guidelines continue to apply broadly to the budget process, they do not accommodate many of today's complex budget proposals and institutions.[1] Lawmakers and budget scorekeepers now face several fundamental questions:

- What is the appropriate scope of the budget? The commission's recommendation that the budget include all federal activities provides little or no guidance on how to treat Amtrak, public/private partnerships, and other hybrid entities.

- When should the financing for a program be classified as spending rather than as an offset to taxes? The line dividing federal revenue and spending laws has become blurred, as shown by the increasing use of refundable tax credits and certain fees as devices for expanding programs' budgetary resources.

- Does the use of trust funds for tracking earmarked revenues confuse more than it helps? Federal trust funds differ significantly from private-sector trust funds. They are simply accounting mechanisms, or accounts labeled as trust funds in law, that are established to earmark receipts for federal programs or purposes. Unlike private trust funds, federal trust fund balances (that is, an excess of receipts over expenditures) do not represent real economic assets, but instead are claims on the Treasury that, when redeemed, will have to be financed by raising taxes, borrowing from the public, or reducing benefits or other expenditures. Some people argue that federal trust funds should be treated differently in the budget process. That argument puts pressure on lawmakers to favor those trust funds in their annual budgetary deliberations and potentially limits their flexibility in setting broad budget policies and priorities.

- How can the federal government's effect on the economy be measured accurately? The purchase and sale of nonfederal debt and equities, important components of some proposals to reform Social Security, raise thorny issues of budgetary treatment that are important for estimating the budgetary impact of those proposals.[2]

---

1. See the Statement of Barry B. Anderson, Deputy Director, Congressional Budget Office, *Structural Reform of the Federal Budget Process*, before the House Committee on the Budget, July 19, 2001.

2. See Congressional Budget Office, *Evaluating and Accounting for Federal Investment in Corporate Stocks and Other Private Securities* (January 2003).

---

control of deficits. At the same time, fiscal pressures linked to the aging of the baby-boom generation are looming, and pressures to increase spending and reduce taxes are substantial. A review of the budget process might be desirable in order to ensure an appropriate framework for the important policy decisions that lie ahead. Moreover, a political consensus on those policies appears to be the most important factor in ensuring that the budget process—however it is constructed—functions smoothly.

APPENDIX B

Budget Resolution Targets and Actual Outcomes

Budget resolution targets, adopted by both Houses of Congress in most years, specify proposed levels of revenues and spending for the upcoming fiscal year. The targets in the 2002 concurrent budget resolution, adopted in May 2001, yielded a proposed budget surplus of $219 billion. However, the deficit for fiscal year 2002 was $158 billion, a difference of $376 billion from the surplus that the budget resolution anticipated.

This appendix analyzes the divergence between the resolution's targets and the actual outcomes for the year. In 2002, actual revenues were $1,853 billion, or about $317 billion lower than expected for the year. Although tax legislation reduced revenues by slightly more than the resolution anticipated, the weak economy and other factors accounted for almost all of the difference in revenues. Total outlays, at $2,011 billion, ended up higher than anticipated by $59 billion—primarily because appropriations were higher than the budget resolution assumed. That increase was largely the consequence of funding provided in response to the terrorist attacks of September 11, 2001.

Elements of the Analysis

The budget resolution is a concurrent resolution adopted by both Houses of Congress that sets forth the Congressional budget plan over five or more fiscal years. The resolution consists of targets for revenues, spending, the surplus or deficit, and debt held by the public. The budget resolution does not itself become law; instead, it is implemented through subsequent legislation, including appropriation acts and changes in the laws that affect revenues and spending, which are sometimes in response to reconciliation instructions that are included in the resolution. The targets established in the budget resolution are generally enforced through procedural mechanisms set out in the Congressional Budget and Impoundment Control Act of 1974.

For this analysis, the differences between the levels specified in the budget resolution and the actual outcomes are allocated among three categories: policy, economic, and technical. Although those categories help explain the discrepancies, the divisions are inexact and necessarily somewhat arbitrary.

Differences attributed to policy derive from enacted legislation that was not anticipated in the resolution (such as the legislation addressing terrorism) or legislation that was estimated to cost a different amount than the resolution assumed. Differences attributed to policy may also reflect lawmakers' failure to enact legislation that the budget resolution assumed would pass. To identify such differences arising from legislation, the Congressional Budget Office (CBO) normally uses the cost estimates that it prepared at the time the legislation was enacted. (To the extent that the actual budgetary impact is different from what CBO estimated, that difference is characterized as a technical change.)

A key element in preparing the budget resolution is forecasting how the economy will perform in the upcoming fiscal year. Ordinarily, the Congress adopts the most recent economic assumptions published by CBO. However, in seven of the years since 1980, the Congress chose to use a different forecast (generally, the Administration's, published by the Office of Management and Budget).[1]

The forecast for the budget resolution is usually made more than nine months before the fiscal year begins. Forecasting the economy is always an uncertain endeavor, and almost invariably, the economy's actual performance differs from the forecast. Nevertheless, every resolution is based on the forecast's assumptions about numerous economic variables—mainly, gross domestic product (GDP), taxable income, unemployment, inflation, and interest rates. Those assumptions are used to estimate revenues, spending for benefit programs, and net interest. In CBO's analysis, differences that can be linked directly to the agency's economic forecast are labeled economic. (Other differences that might be tied to economic performance, such as changes to estimates of capital gains realizations or distributions from retirement plans, are categorized as technical.)

In analyzing the deviation between budget resolution targets and outcomes, CBO cumulates differences that arise from changes in the economic forecast since the time that the resolution was completed. But CBO does not subsequently adjust that calculation, even though revisions to data about GDP and taxable income continue to trickle in over a number of years.

Technical differences between the budget resolution targets and actual outcomes are those variations that do not arise directly from legislative or economic sources as categorized. The largest dollar effects of technical differences are concentrated in two areas: on the revenue side of the budget and among the government's open-ended commitments, such as entitlement programs. In the case of revenues, technical differences stem from a variety of factors, including changes in administrative tax rules, differences in the sources of taxable income that are not captured by the economic forecast, and changes in the relative amounts of income taxed at the various rates. In the case of entitlement programs, factors such as an unanticipated change in the number of beneficiaries, unforeseen utilization of health care services, changes in farm commodity prices, or new regulations can produce technical differences.

Comparing the Budget Resolution and Actual Outcomes for Fiscal Year 2002

The budget resolution for 2002 adopted the economic assumptions that CBO published in January 2001. Using those assumptions and incorporating policy changes, the resolution established the following targets for the year: total revenues of $2,171 billion, outlays of $1,952 billion, and a surplus of $219 billion (*see Table B-1*). Ultimately, revenues were lower by $317 billion, and outlays were higher by $59 billion, resulting in a deficit that was $376 billion lower than the surplus anticipated in the resolution. Technical factors, mostly on the revenue side, accounted for more than half of the difference ($201 billion), and economic factors accounted for about a third (*see Table B-2*).

Differences Arising from Policy Changes

The budget resolution incorporated only a few policy changes that would have significantly affected the bottom line for 2002. Some of those proposals were later enacted (although sometimes at different levels than originally envisioned), one such proposal was not enacted, and some legislation was enacted that was not included in the resolution. In total, policy actions reduced the surplus by about $56 billion from the amount assumed in the budget resolution. Most of that amount ($46 billion) was on the outlay side of the budget.

The 2002 resolution assumed that discretionary outlays would remain near the level projected in CBO's baseline ($683 billion). In actuality, budget authority was $73 billion higher than anticipated in the resolution, resulting in $52 billion more in outlays. Much of that amount stemmed from costs incurred as a result of the terrorist attacks of September 11, 2001. Outlays in 2002 for almost all budget functions turned out higher than provided

---

1. The Congress used the Administration's forecast in the resolutions for fiscal years 1982, 1986, 1989, 1990, and 1992. The budget resolutions for fiscal years 1983 and 1991 were based on assumptions developed by the budget committees' staff.

Table B-1.
Comparison of Budget Resolution Targets and Actual Budget Totals for 2002
(In billions of dollars)

	Budget Resolution	Actual Budget Totals	Actual Minus Budget Resolution
Revenues	2,171	1,853	-317
Outlays	1,952	2,011	59
Surplus or Deficit (-)	219	-158	-376

Sources: Congressional Budget Office using data from House Con. Res. 83, Concurrent Resolution on the Budget for Fiscal Year 2002, adopted May 10, 2001; Office of Management and Budget.

Notes: The figures in the table include revenues and outlays of the Social Security program and the Postal Service, which are off-budget.

These comparisons differ from those in the chapters of this volume, where differences are measured relative to CBO's baseline projections.

---

for in the resolution; nearly 60 percent of the excess went to defense spending.

Two mandatory spending proposals with noticeable budgetary effects were included in the resolution: a farm bill, which was enacted, and legislation boosting health care spending for the uninsured (which was not acted upon). The Farm Security and Rural Investment Act of 2002 (Public Law 107-171) increased outlays by an estimated $2 billion in 2002 (and will increase them by about $80 billion from 2002 to 2011). The legislation providing health care for the uninsured had an anticipated cost of $8 billion in 2002—an amount that was incorporated into the resolution but that did not translate into outlays since the legislation did not pass.

Two tax laws also increased mandatory spending. The Economic Growth and Tax Relief Reconciliation Act of 2001 (EGTRRA), anticipated in the budget resolution, resulted in increased spending on refundable tax credits by $6 billion in 2002. The Job Creation and Worker Assistance Act of 2002 (P.L. 107-147)—commonly referred to as the economic stimulus package—extended unemployment benefits for individuals at a cost of about $8 billion in 2002. Altogether, policy changes reduced mandatory spending by $1 billion from the level assumed in the budget resolution.

On the revenue side of the budget, the resolution assumed that the President's proposed tax cut would be passed and would reduce revenues by about $65 billion in 2002. However, the enacted tax law, EGTRRA, resulted in a smaller reduction, estimated at $31 billion, for that year. The Congress and the President also enacted tax legislation that the budget resolution did not anticipate. Public Law 107-147 further eroded revenues by about $43 billion.

Differences Arising from Economic Factors

Overall, the economic assumptions underlying the 2002 budget resolution proved to be optimistic. In particular, because of economic factors, revenues turned out to be $125 billion lower than presumed. Outlays were only slightly affected by those economic developments.

The resolution assumed that real (inflation-adjusted) GDP would grow by 2.7 percent in fiscal year 2001 and by 3.2 percent in 2002. However, the economy fell into a recession in March 2001. As a result, growth in real GDP turned out to be just 0.8 percent in 2001 and 1.7 percent in 2002. The recession reduced the level of nominal GDP compared with that anticipated by the resolution and slowed the growth of wages and salaries, thereby reducing revenues from individual income taxes. Furthermore, lower-than-expected corporate profits caused corporate income tax receipts to decline.

Mandatory spending is also sensitive to changes in the economic forecast. Although such spending flows from the provisions of permanent laws, the spending for many mandatory programs is keyed to the economy. As a result, spending on mandatory programs increased as the economy weakened. Overall, for economic reasons mandatory outlays turned out to be $11 billion above the level assumed by the resolution—almost entirely because of increased spending on unemployment insurance.

Lower-than-anticipated interest rates drove projected outlays for net interest payments below the level assumed in the budget resolution. Most significantly, the resolution assumed that short-term interest rates would average 4.8 percent in 2002; however, as a result of actions by the Federal Reserve, those rates averaged just 1.7 percent. Those differences resulted in outlays for net interest of more than $18 billion less than those anticipated in the budget resolution.

Differences Arising from Technical Factors

Differences arising from technical factors—that is, differences between budget resolution targets and actual outcomes that cannot be traced to legislation or CBO's economic forecast—are mostly found on the revenue side of the budget. In 2002, technical factors accounted for about $183 billion less in revenues and $18 billion more in outlays.

Some of that decrease in revenues may stem indirectly from economic factors (for example, decreased capital gains realizations may be related to the strength of the economy) or may result from economic factors that will be revealed in future revisions to economic variables; however, a full analysis of the 2002 results cannot be done now because information about sources of individual income typically lags behind the tax year by a couple of years. The additional increase in outlays attributable to technical differences resulted from slightly higher than expected spending on Medicaid, Medicare, unemployment insurance, and a host of other programs. In addition, debt-service costs were higher, mostly because of the technical factors that reduced projected revenues.

Comparing Budget Resolutions and Actual Outcomes from Fiscal Years 1980 Through 2002

Actual outcomes always differ to varying degrees from budget resolution targets. Over the 1980-1992 period, the deficit consistently exceeded the target in the resolution by amounts ranging from $4 billion in 1984 to

Table B-2.
Differences Between Budget Resolution Targets and Actual Budget Totals for 2002

(In billions of dollars)

	Policy Changes	Economic Factors	Technical Factors	Total Differences
Revenues	-9	-125	-183	-317
Outlays				
Discretionary spending	50	2	*	52
Mandatory spending[a]	-1	11	13	23
Net interest	-3	-18	5	-16
Subtotal	46	-5	18	59
Effect on the Surplus Anticipated in the Resolution	-56	-119	-201	-376

Sources: Congressional Budget Office using data from House Con. Res. 83, Concurrent Resolution on the Budget for Fiscal Year 2002, adopted May 10, 2001; Office of Management and Budget.

Notes: Differences are actual outcomes minus budget resolution targets.

These comparisons differ from those in the chapters of this volume, where differences are measured relative to CBO's baseline projections.

* = between zero and $500 million.

a. Includes offsetting receipts.

$119 billion in 1990 (*see Table B-3*). That pattern changed in 1993, in part because spending for deposit insurance was substantially lower than expected. From 1994 through 2000, actual outcomes continued to be more favorable than the targets (with the exception of 1999, when there was no conference agreement on a budget resolution). However, in 2001, lower-than-expected revenues and higher-than-anticipated outlays combined to reduce the surplus to less than what was envisioned in the resolution. In 2002, those same factors caused a deficit instead of the envisioned surplus. The difference between the target and the outcome in 2002, both in monetary terms and as a percentage of outlays, was by far the largest of any year over the 1980-2002 period.

Differences Arising from Policy Changes

From 1980 through 2002, policy action or inaction (for example, the failure to achieve savings called for in a budget resolution) decreased the surplus or increased the deficit by an average of $18 billion a year compared with the target. In only four of those years did policymakers trim the deficit by more, or add to it by less, than the resolution provided. The largest differences attributable to policy changes occurred in the past three years, decreasing the surplus by $61 billion in 2000, $95 billion in 2001, and $56 billion in 2002 in comparison with the targets. By contrast, from 1980 through 1998, the differences ascribed to policy changes averaged less than $10 billion a year.

Most of the impact stemming from legislation over the period was on the outlay side of the budget. On average, policy decisions added about $16 billion a year to the spending totals. In fact, 1988 and 1991 were the only years in which legislative action held outlays below the budget resolution targets. The biggest difference due to policy changes was in 2000, when the effects of legislation increased outlays by about $65 billion. The difference in 2002 was second largest: a $46 billion increase. On the revenue side of the budget, the largest difference arising from policy changes occurred in 2001, when legislation reduced taxes by $65 billion more than was anticipated by the resolution. By contrast, in 2002 that difference was a $9 billion reduction.

Differences Arising from Economic Factors

Inaccuracies in the economic forecast over the 1980-2002 period had a small net effect on the cumulative variation between targets and actual outcomes for surpluses or deficits. However, large differences occurred in many years —deviations that were mostly negative before 1994 and positive more recently (other than in 2002). Until 1993, budget resolutions tended to use short-term economic assumptions that proved optimistic. The largest overestimates in the 1980s and early 1990s, not surprisingly, were in years marked by recession or the early stages of recovery —namely, in 1982 and 1983 and in the 1990-1992 period. In 2002, the same pattern was evident, resulting in a $119 billion overestimate by the budget resolution.

In absolute terms (disregarding whether the errors were positive or negative), the typical difference in the surplus or deficit attributable to incorrect economic assumptions was about $33 billion a year over the 1980-2002 period. Regardless of the direction of the errors in the forecasts, differences between the resolutions' assumptions and what actually happened in the economy primarily affected revenues.

Differences Arising from Technical Factors

Technical factors accounted for differences between budget resolution targets and actual surpluses or deficits that averaged $6 billion a year from 1980 to 2002. In absolute terms, however, such differences caused the targets to be off by $42 billion, on average. Overall, those deviations were about equal on the revenue and outlay sides of the budget.

The magnitude and causes of the differences ascribed to technical factors have varied over the years. On the revenue side, technical misestimates were generally not very great through 1990, but the budget resolutions significantly overestimated revenues in 1991, 1992, and 2002, when tax collections were weaker than economic data suggested. The difference was particularly pronounced in 2002, when, for technical reasons, revenues came in $183 billion lower than the budget resolution anticipated.

Table B-3.
Differences Between Budget Resolution Targets and Actual Budget Totals, 1980-2002

(In billions of dollars)

	Differences Arising from			Total Differences	Total Differences as a Percentage of Actual Outcomes
	Policy Changes	Economic Factors	Technical Factors		
Revenues					
1980	6	8	-4	11	2.1
1981	-4	5	-13	-11	-1.8
1982	13	-52	-1	-40	-6.5
1983	-5	-58	-3	-65	-10.8
1984	-14	4	-4	-13	-2.0
1985	*	-20	3	-17	-2.3
1986	-1	-23	-2	-27	-3.5
1987	22	-27	7	2	0.2
1988	-11	4	-17	-24	-2.6
1989	1	34	-8	26	2.6
1990	-7	-36	9	-34	-3.3
1991[a]	-1	-31	-24	-56	-5.3
1992	3	-46	-34	-78	-7.1
1993	4	-28	3	-20	-1.7
1994	-1	12	4	15	1.2
1995	*	16	1	17	1.3
1996	-1	24	12	36	2.5
1997	20	44	46	110	7.0
1998	-1	62	59	120	7.0
1999	n.a.	n.a.	n.a.	n.a.	n.a.
2000	3	78	68	149	7.4
2001	-65	25	26	-14	-0.7
2002	-9	-125	-183	-317	-17.1
Average	-2	-6	-2	-10	-1.6
Absolute Average[b]	9	35	24	55	4.4
Outlays					
1980	20	12	16	48	8.1
1981	25	6	16	47	6.9
1982	1	24	8	33	4.4
1983	18	*	8	26	3.2
1984	1	7	-18	-9	-1.1
1985	23	-5	-13	5	0.5
1986	14	-12	20	22	2.2
1987	7	-12	13	8	0.8
1988	-2	12	12	22	2.1
1989	17	14	12	43	3.8
1990	13	13	59	85	6.8
1991[a]	-19	1	-22	-40	-3.0
1992	15	-21	-60	-66	-4.8
1993	16	-19	-90	-92	-6.5
1994	10	-9	-36	-35	-2.4

(Continued)

Table B-3.
Continued

(In billions of dollars)

	Differences Arising from			Total Differences	Total Differences as a Percentage of Actual Outcomes
	Policy Changes	Economic Factors	Technical Factors		
1995	2	17	-14	6	0.4
1996	25	-24	-29	-28	-1.8
1997	15	7	-43	-21	-1.3
1998	5	-9	-37	-41	-2.5
1999	n.a.	n.a.	n.a.	n.a.	n.a.
2000	65	-1	-10	54	3.0
2001	30	-1	*	29	1.6
2002	46	-5	18	59	2.9
Average	16	*	-9	7	1.1
Absolute Average[b]	18	11	25	37	3.2
		Surplus or Deficit (-)[c]			
1980	-13	-4	-19	-36	-6.1
1981	-28	-1	-29	-58	-8.6
1982	12	-76	-9	-73	-9.8
1983	-22	-59	-11	-92	-11.4
1984	-15	-3	14	-4	-0.5
1985	-23	-15	16	-22	-2.3
1986	-16	-11	-22	-49	-4.9
1987	15	-15	-6	-6	-0.6
1988	-9	-8	-29	-46	-4.3
1989	-17	20	-20	-17	-1.5
1990	-20	-49	-50	-119	-9.5
1991[a]	19	-32	-2	-15	-1.1
1992	-12	-25	26	-11	-0.8
1993	-12	-9	93	72	5.1
1994	-11	21	40	50	3.4
1995	-2	-2	15	11	0.7
1996	-25	48	40	63	4.0
1997	5	37	89	131	8.2
1998	-7	71	97	160	9.7
1999	n.a.	n.a.	n.a.	n.a.	n.a.
2000	-61	79	77	95	5.3
2001	-95	26	26	-43	-2.3
2002	-56	-119	-202	-376	-18.7
Average	-18	-6	6	-17	-2.1
Absolute Average[b]	22	33	42	70	5.4

Source: Congressional Budget Office.
Notes: Differences are actual outcomes minus budget resolution targets.

Differences are allocated among the three categories soon after a fiscal year ends. Later changes in economic and tax data are not reflected in those allocations.

* = between -$500 million and $500 million; n.a. = not applicable (there was no budget resolution in 1999).
a. Based on the budget summit agreement for fiscal year 1991 (as assessed by CBO in December 1990).
b. The absolute average disregards whether the differences are positive or negative.
c. In the case of the surplus or deficit, total differences are calculated as a percentage of actual outlays.

From 1997 through 2001, revenues were much higher than the budget resolution targets. The individual income tax was the source of most of those technical discrepancies, primarily because of higher realizations of capital gains, unexpected increases in the effective tax rate, and higher reported incomes. Greater realizations of capital gains most likely stemmed from upturns in the prices of stocks and the volume of stock transactions. The unexpected rise in the effective tax rate was largely due to a disproportionate increase in income among taxpayers taxed at the highest marginal rates.

Misestimates arising from technical factors also show up on the outlay side of the budget. Through the mid-1980s, discrepancies in estimating receipts from offshore oil leases and spending on farm price supports, defense, and entitlement programs were the dominant technical differences. In addition, in the early 1990s, during the savings and loan crisis, outlays for deposit insurance were a major source of discrepancies attributable to technical factors. In recent years, technical differences between estimates of outlays and actual outlays have been spread among a variety of programs. They were quite small in 2000 and 2001—within $10 billion and near zero, respectively—but grew to $18 billion last year.

Differences as a Percentage of Actual Revenues or Outlays

Because the federal budget has grown considerably since 1980, differences between the revenue and spending levels in the budget resolutions and actual outcomes over the 1980-2002 period may be best compared as a percentage of total revenues or outlays. The total difference for revenues for 2002, at 17.1 percent below the budget resolution target, was considerably greater than the absolute average of 4.4 percent. Outlays in 2002 were 3.0 percent above the budget resolution target—slightly below the 3.2 percent absolute average difference for the 1980-2002 period.

The size of the total difference between actual surpluses or deficits and the surpluses or deficits anticipated in budget resolutions depends in large part on whether the differences for revenues and outlays offset each other. For years in which the discrepancies for revenues and outlays affected the surplus or deficit in opposite ways, the total difference dropped to as little as 0.5 percent of actual outlays. But in other years, the discrepancies for both revenues and outlays affected the surplus or deficit in the same way. Indeed, from 1980 to 2002, the differences between estimates of revenues and outlays in the budget resolutions and the actual amounts went in the same direction relative to the surplus or deficit in 13 years. In 2002, the actual deficit was below the surplus anticipated in the budget resolution by an amount equal to 18.7 percent of actual outlays—much greater than the 5.4 percent absolute average over the 23-year period.

APPENDIX C

How Changes in Assumptions Can Affect Budget Projections

The federal budget is highly sensitive to economic conditions. Sources of revenues depend on taxable income—including wages and salaries, interest and other nonwage income, and corporate profits—which generally moves in step with overall economic activity. The benefits of many entitlement programs are pegged to inflation either directly (like Social Security) or indirectly (like Medicaid) or may be affected by unemployment rates. In addition, the Treasury regularly refinances portions of the government's debt at market rates, so the level of federal spending for interest on that debt is directly tied to such market rates.

To illustrate how assumptions about certain key economic factors can affect federal budget projections, the Congressional Budget Office (CBO) uses what it terms rules of thumb. Those rules are rough orders of magnitude for gauging how changes in individual economic variables, taken in isolation, will affect the budget's totals.

The variables that figure in this illustration are real (inflation-adjusted) growth, interest rates, and inflation. For real growth, CBO's rule shows the effects of a rate that is 0.1 percentage point lower each year, beginning in January 2003, than the assumed rate of growth underlying the agency's baseline projections for the economy (outlined in Chapter 2). The rules for interest rates and inflation assume an increase of 1 percentage point over the rates in the baseline, also starting in January 2003. Each rule is roughly symmetrical. Thus, the effects of higher growth, lower interest rates, or lower inflation would have about the same magnitude as the effects shown in this appendix, but with the opposite sign.

The calculations that appear in this appendix are merely illustrative of the impact that changes in assumptions can have. CBO uses variations of 0.1 percentage point or 1 percentage point for the sake of simplicity; they should not be viewed as typical forecasting misestimates. Furthermore, extrapolating from small, incremental rule-of-thumb calculations to much larger changes would be inadvisable, because the magnitude of the effect of a larger change is not necessarily a multiple of a smaller change. Moreover, budget projections are subject to other kinds of inaccuracies that are not directly related to economic forecasting.

In addition to the rules of thumb related to economic projections, CBO presents two other rules that affect the levels of projected surpluses or deficits. The first illustrates the impact on projections of discretionary spending of adding $10 billion to CBO's estimate of budget authority for 2003. The second shows the effect on net interest payments of borrowing $10 billion less than anticipated.

Lower Real Growth

Strong economic growth improves the federal budget's bottom line, and weak economic growth worsens it. The first economic rule of thumb outlines the budgetary impact of economic growth that is slightly weaker than CBO assumes in its baseline. Specifically, the rule illustrates the effects of growth rates for real gross domestic product (GDP) that are lower by 0.1 percentage point every year from January 2003 through 2013.

Table C-1.
Estimated Effects of Selected Economic Changes on CBO's Budget Projections
(In billions of dollars)

	2003	2004	2005	2006	2007	2008	2009	2010	2011	2012	2013	Total, 2004-2008	Total, 2004-2013
Growth Rate of Real GDP Is 0.1 Percentage Point Lower per Year														
Change in Revenues	-1	-3	-6	-9	-13	-17	-21	-26	-31	-38	-44	-49	-208
Change in Outlays														
Net interest (Debt service)	*	*	*	1	1	2	4	5	7	9	12	5	41
Mandatory spending	*	*	*	*	*	*	*	*	*	-1	-1	*	-2
Total	*	*	*	1	2	2	3	5	6	8	11	5	39
Change in Surplus or Deficit	-1	-4	-7	-10	-14	-19	-24	-30	-38	-46	-55	-54	-247
Interest Rates Are 1 Percentage Point Higher per Year														
Change in Revenues	0	0	0	0	0	0	0	0	0	0	0	0	0
Change in Outlays														
Higher rates	7	18	24	27	29	30	31	30	29	27	23	128	268
Debt service	*	1	2	4	6	9	11	14	17	20	22	22	105
Total	7	19	26	31	35	39	42	44	46	47	45	150	374
Change in Surplus or Deficit	-7	-19	-26	-31	-35	-39	-42	-44	-46	-47	-45	-150	-374
Inflation Is 1 Percentage Point Higher per Year														
Change in Revenues	12	36	64	94	130	169	212	259	306	369	434	493	2,072
Change in Outlays														
Higher rates	8	20	26	29	31	32	33	32	31	29	24	139	289
Debt service	*	*	-1	-1	-3	-5	-9	-13	-20	-28	-39	-10	-119
Discretionary spending	0	4	11	19	27	36	45	55	66	77	89	97	430
Mandatory spending	1	8	19	32	46	61	78	96	116	138	163	166	756
Total	9	32	56	79	101	124	147	170	194	216	237	392	1,356
Change in Surplus or Deficit	3	4	8	16	29	45	65	89	112	153	196	101	715

Source: Congressional Budget Office.

Note: * = between -$500 million and $500 million.

Those effects differ from the effects of a cyclical change, such as a recession, which are much shorter-term in nature. (For scenarios involving cyclical economic changes, see Chapter 5.) Moreover, CBO's rule for GDP uses 0.1 percentage point—rather than the full percentage point used in the interest rate and inflation rules—because projected real growth is unlikely to differ from actual growth by such a large amount over the next 10 years. A difference as large as 1 percentage point might occur for a few years, however, as a result of a cyclical change.

The baseline reflects an assumption that real GDP grows by an average of about 3.0 percent a year (see Chapter 2). Subtracting 0.1 percentage point from that rate each year means that the level of GDP would fall roughly 1 percent below CBO's baseline by 2013.

A lower rate of growth for GDP would have a number of budgetary implications. For example, it would suggest lower growth of taxable income, leading to losses in revenues that would mount from $1 billion in 2003 to $44 billion in 2013 (see Table C-1). Cumulatively, reve-

Table C-2.
Estimated Effects on CBO's Baseline of Increasing Discretionary Budget Authority by $10 Billion in 2003

(In billions of dollars)

	2003	2004	2005	2006	2007	2008	2009	2010	2011	2012	2013	Total, 2004-2008	Total, 2004-2013
Budget Authority	10	10	10	11	11	11	12	12	12	13	13	54	116
Outlays	6	9	10	10	11	11	11	12	12	12	13	51	112

Source: Congressional Budget Office.

Note: CBO assumes that budget authority grows at the rates of inflation specified in the Deficit Control Act (the GDP deflator and employment cost index for wages and salaries).

---

nue losses would total $208 billion over the 2004-2013 period. Lower revenues would mean that the government borrowed more and incurred greater interest costs. Debt service would be minimally affected during the first few years of the period, but in later years, those costs would gradually rise, reaching $12 billion in 2013. Altogether, those changes (along with small effects on the earned income tax credit and Medicare) would reduce the projected surplus for 2013 by $55 billion. Growth in real GDP that was 0.1 percentage point a year lower than the rate assumed in CBO's baseline would reduce surpluses by a total of $54 billion over the 2004-2008 period and by $247 billion over the 2004-2013 period.

Higher Interest Rates

The second rule of thumb illustrates the sensitivity of the budget to changes in interest rates, which affect the flow of interest to and from the federal government. When the budget has a surplus, the Treasury uses some of its income to reduce debt held by the public, but it also refinances some debt at market interest rates. When the budget has a deficit, the Treasury must borrow additional funds from the public to cover any shortfall.

Under the assumption that interest rates are 1 percentage point higher than in the baseline for all maturities every year and that all other economic variables are unchanged, interest costs would be approximately $7 billion higher in 2003 (see Table C-1). That initial boost in interest costs would be fueled largely by the extra costs of refinancing the government's short-term Treasury bills (securities with maturities of one year or less), which make up about 28 percent of the marketable debt. More than $888 billion of Treasury bills are currently outstanding, all of them maturing within the next six months.

The bulk of marketable debt, however, consists of medium-term notes and long-term bonds, which were issued with initial maturities of two to 10 years. As those longer-term securities mature, they will be replaced with new issues (the Treasury issues two-, five-, and 10-year notes). Thus, the budgetary effects mount; the effect of interest rates that are 1 percentage point higher than in the baseline would peak at $31 billion in 2009.

After 2009, however, the effect of higher interest rates would diminish. In the projected baseline, when surpluses appear, debt held by the public declines; hence, fewer securities are expected to roll over each year. By 2013, the effect of higher interest rates would drop to $23 billion, but the effect of increased debt over the 10-year period would add another $22 billion in interest costs in that year. In sum, if interest rates were 1 percentage point higher each year, the cumulative surplus would decline by $150 billion from 2004 through 2008 and by $374 billion from 2004 through 2013.

Higher Inflation

The third rule of thumb shows the budgetary impact of inflation that is 1 percentage point higher than assumed for the baseline. The effects of inflation on federal revenues and outlays partly offset each other. On the one

Table C-3.
Estimated Savings in Net Interest from Borrowing $10 Billion Less
(In billions of dollars)

	2003	2004	2005	2006	2007	2008	2009	2010	2011	2012	2013	Total, 2004-2008	Total, 2004-2013
Savings from Borrowing $10 Billion Less in 2003 Only	-0.1	-0.3	-0.4	-0.5	-0.6	-0.6	-0.7	-0.7	-0.7	-0.8	-0.8	-2.4	-6.0
Savings from Borrowing $10 Billion Less Each Year	-0.1	-0.5	-1.2	-1.9	-2.5	-3.2	-4.0	-4.7	-5.5	-6.4	-7.3	-9.2	-37.1

Source: Congressional Budget Office.

hand, higher inflation and its effects on wages and other income lead to greater revenues. On the other hand, it would also increase spending for many benefit programs (although with a lag), as well as discretionary spending. In deriving this rule of thumb, CBO also assumes that nominal interest rates rise in step with inflation, thus increasing the cost of financing the government's debt.

An increase of 1 percentage point per year in projected inflation from 2003 through 2013 would boost revenues by $434 billion and outlays by $237 billion in 2013 (see Table C-1). The combined effect of those changes is an improvement in the budgetary outlook that would reach $196 billion in 2013. Over the 2004-2008 period, the surplus would grow by $101 billion; over the 2004-2013 period, it would increase by $715 billion.

Higher Discretionary Budget Authority

Discretionary spending is not directly related to economic conditions but rather to the level of appropriations provided by law and the rate at which the appropriations are spent. CBO's baseline projections assume that appropriations for the current year—in this case, 2003—grow at the rate of inflation in the years to follow (as specified by the Balanced Budget and Emergency Deficit Control Act of 1985). But the total amount of appropriations for 2003 has not yet been determined. As this report was being written, many of the 13 regular appropriation bills were yet to be enacted. Furthermore, the possibility of supplemental appropriations provided later in the year always exists. Subsequent baseline projections will reflect the differences between enacted appropriations and the $751 billion in budget authority assumed for this report.

Budget authority is the legal authority to incur financial obligations that will result in immediate or future outlays of federal government funds. The Congress appropriates such budget authority for discretionary programs annually in appropriation acts; outlays from that authority may occur in the year that the authority is granted, or they may occur in subsequent years. Activities such as meeting payrolls or directly providing services generally expend most of their budget authority in the year that it is granted; other activities such as procuring weapons or building roads and other infrastructure spend their authority over a longer period of time.

As a result, changes in budget authority for different activities do not immediately translate into equal changes in outlays. CBO estimates that, on average, approximately 60 percent of budget authority for discretionary spending is spent in the year that it is granted. Therefore, an additional $10 billion in budget authority in 2003 would, on average, lead to $6 billion more in outlays that year. The remaining $4 billion would be spent over the following few years. The timing of such outlays could be somewhat delayed if the additional $10 billion is provided in supplemental appropriations late in the year.

Under the rules specified for the construction of CBO's baseline, providing $10 billion more in budget authority in 2003 would lead to an increase in projected budget authority in each year (see Table C-2). Spending that additional budget authority would lead to $51 billion in additional outlays between 2004 and 2008 and $112 billion over the 2004-2013 period.

Increase in the Surplus or Decrease in the Deficit

CBO's projections of net interest costs are based on its projections of future interest rates and debt held by the public. Changes from year to year in debt held by the public depend mostly on the size of the surplus or deficit. If surpluses or deficits differ from those projected in the baseline—for whatever reason—interest costs would also change.

A one-time decrease of $10 billion in the deficit in 2003 (excluding interest costs) would enable the Treasury to redeem an additional $10 billion in debt in that year, compared with the assumption in CBO's baseline. Removing that debt from the outstanding stock would reduce interest costs by $0.1 billion in 2003 and nearly $1 billion a year by 2013 (*see Table C-3*). (Savings in later years would stem from the compounding effect of debt reduction in 2003.)

Interest savings would be even greater if the $10 billion decrease in borrowing was sustained in every year through 2013. In that case, savings from additional debt reduction and the compounding effect of such savings would further increase the projected surplus in 2013 by $7.3 billion.

APPENDIX D

The Federal Sector of the National Income and Product Accounts

The federal budget is not the only yardstick used to measure the federal government's revenue and spending activity. The federal sector of the national income and product accounts (NIPAs), produced by the Department of Commerce's Bureau of Economic Analysis (BEA), measures that activity in economic terms. Thus, the NIPAs group the government's revenues and spending into categories that contribute to gross domestic product (GDP), income, and other macroeconomic totals, thereby helping to show the relationship between the federal sector and other areas of the economy. Although the categories of classification in the federal budget and the NIPAs differ significantly, the totals of the two measures are comparable. Over the 2004-2013 period, NIPA receipts and expenditures exceed the corresponding budget figures by roughly 1 percent.

The Relationship Between the Budget and the NIPAs

A number of major differences distinguish how federal receipts and expenditures are treated in the NIPAs from how they are accounted for in the total (or unified) budget (*see Table D-1*). For example, the NIPAs shift certain items from the spending to the receipts side of the ledger to reflect intrabudgetary or voluntary payments that the budget records as negative outlays. Such shifts are referred to as *netting and grossing* adjustments and do not affect the surplus or deficit.

In contrast, other differences between the two accounting methodologies affect the surplus or deficit that each reports. The NIPA totals (but not the budget's) exclude government transactions that involve an exchange of existing assets and that therefore do not add to or subtract from current income and production. Prominent among such *lending and financial* adjustments (as they are termed in Table D-1) are those for deposit insurance outlays, cash flows for direct loans made by the government before credit reform, and sales of government assets. Other factors that separate the NIPAs' accounting from that of the budget include *geographic adjustments* (the NIPAs exclude Puerto Rico, the Virgin Islands, and a few other areas) and *timing adjustments* (the NIPAs correct for such things as irregular numbers of benefit checks in a year or shifts in the timing of corporate tax payments).

In the national economic accounts, contributions for *government employee retirement* are considered the personal income of federal workers covered by the retirement funds and therefore are not counted in the federal sector of the NIPAs. As a result, outlays from those funds are also treated as transactions outside the government sector of the economy.

Intragovernmental transfers are an adjustment made to the NIPA totals to account for payments that the government makes to federal entities whose activities are not counted as part of the budget. Nearly all such transfers involve the financing of credit programs.

Table D-1.
Relationship of the Budget to the Federal Sector of the National Income and Product Accounts

(In billions of dollars)

	Actual 2002	2003	2004	2005	2006	2007	2008	2009	2010	2011	2012	2013
Receipts												
Revenues (Budget)[a]	1,853	1,922	2,054	2,225	2,370	2,505	2,648	2,798	2,949	3,220	3,480	3,674
Differences												
Netting and grossing												
Medicare premiums	26	28	31	33	36	39	42	45	49	54	59	64
Deposit insurance premiums	*	*	1	*	1	1	1	2	2	2	2	2
Government contributions for employee OASDI and HI	12	12	13	14	15	16	17	18	19	20	21	22
Other	10	11	8	7	7	7	6	5	4	2	1	*
Geographic adjustments	-4	-4	-4	-4	-4	-5	-5	-5	-5	-6	-6	-6
Contributions for government employee retirement	-5	-4	-4	-4	-4	-4	-4	-4	-4	-3	-3	-3
Estate and gift taxes	-27	-22	-24	-21	-24	-20	-22	-23	-15	-19	-43	-47
Universal Service Fund receipts	-5	-6	-7	-7	-7	-7	-7	-7	-7	-7	-8	-8
Timing shift of corporate estimated tax payments	-23	0	7	-7	0	0	0	0	0	0	0	0
Other	75	-5	2	1	*	2	1	*	1	*	*	*
Total Difference	**59**	**11**	**21**	**13**	**20**	**29**	**29**	**30**	**44**	**43**	**22**	**24**
Receipts (NIPAs)	1,913	1,933	2,076	2,238	2,390	2,534	2,677	2,828	2,993	3,263	3,502	3,698
Expenditures												
Outlays (Budget)[a]	2,011	2,121	2,199	2,298	2,387	2,479	2,583	2,695	2,809	2,943	3,029	3,167
Differences												
Netting and grossing												
Medicare premiums	26	28	31	33	36	39	42	45	49	54	59	64
Deposit insurance premiums	*	*	1	*	1	1	1	2	2	2	2	2
Government contributions for employee OASDI and HI	12	12	13	14	15	16	17	18	19	20	21	22
Other	10	11	8	7	7	7	6	5	4	2	1	*
Lending and financial adjustments	15	13	10	17	16	12	11	6	7	7	8	8
Geographic adjustments	-12	-13	-14	-14	-15	-15	-16	-16	-17	-18	-19	-20
Timing adjustments	7	2	0	-12	3	9	0	0	0	-14	14	0
Contributions for government employee retirement	37	38	39	40	41	43	44	45	47	49	50	52
Intragovernmental transfers	-7	-7	-6	-6	-5	-4	-2	-1	1	2	4	6
Capital transfers	-44	-47	-48	-48	-49	-49	-50	-51	-52	-53	-55	-56
Treatment of investment and depreciation	-12	-12	-15	-17	-20	-23	-26	-29	-33	-36	-40	-45
Universal Service Fund payments	-5	-6	-6	-6	-6	-7	-7	-7	-7	-7	-7	-7
Other	2	-1	-1	-1	-1	-1	-1	-1	-1	-1	-1	-1
Total Difference	**28**	**18**	**11**	**7**	**23**	**26**	**18**	**15**	**18**	**5**	**35**	**25**
Expenditures (NIPAs)	2,039	2,138	2,211	2,306	2,409	2,505	2,601	2,709	2,826	2,948	3,064	3,192

(Continued)

APPENDIX D   THE FEDERAL SECTOR OF THE NATIONAL INCOME AND PRODUCT ACCOUNTS   **139**

Table D-1.
Continued

(In billions of dollars)

	Actual 2002	2003	2004	2005	2006	2007	2008	2009	2010	2011	2012	2013
					Deficit (-) or Surplus							
Deficit (-) or Surplus (Budget)[a]	-158	-199	-145	-73	-16	26	65	103	140	277	451	508
Differences												
Lending and financial adjustments	-15	-13	-10	-17	-16	-12	-11	-6	-7	-7	-8	-8
Geographic adjustments	9	10	10	10	10	10	11	11	12	12	13	14
Timing adjustments	-30	-2	7	5	-3	-9	0	0	0	14	-14	0
Contributions for government employee retirement	-42	-42	-43	-44	-45	-47	-48	-49	-51	-52	-54	-55
Intragovernmental transfers	7	7	6	6	5	4	2	1	-1	-2	-4	-6
Capital transfers	44	47	48	48	49	49	50	51	52	53	55	56
Treatment of investment and depreciation	12	12	15	17	20	23	26	29	33	36	40	45
Universal Service Fund payments	*	*	*	*	*	*	*	*	*	*	*	*
Estate and gift taxes	-27	-22	-24	-21	-24	-20	-22	-23	-15	-19	-43	-47
Other	74	-4	3	2	1	3	2	2	2	2	2	2
Total Difference	**32**	**-7**	**10**	**5**	**-3**	**3**	**11**	**16**	**26**	**37**	**-13**	**-1**
Deficit (-) or Surplus (NIPAs)	-126	-206	-135	-68	-19	29	76	119	167	314	438	506

Source: Congressional Budget Office.

Note: * = between -$500 million and $500 million; OASDI = Old-Age, Survivors, and Disability Insurance; HI = Hospital Insurance.

a. Includes Social Security and the Postal Service; assumes that discretionary budget authority for 2003 totals $751 billion.

The government's *capital transfers*—which include grants to state and local governments for highways, transit, air transportation, and water treatment plants—are transactions in which one party provides something (usually cash) to another without receiving anything in return. Those transactions are linked to, or are conditional on, the acquiring or disposing of an asset. Because such transactions shift existing assets from one party to another, they do not affect disposable income or production. Therefore, they are not counted in the NIPAs, although they are counted in the budget.

The NIPAs and the budget also differ in their *treatment of investment and depreciation*. The budget reflects all expenditures that the federal government makes, including its investment purchases of items such as buildings and aircraft carriers. The NIPAs show the current, or operating, account for the federal government; thus, they exclude government investment and include the government's consumption of fixed capital, or depreciation. (Government investment, although included in the NIPAs' calculation of GDP, is not part of its measure of federal expenditures.)

The *Universal Service Fund*, which is administered by a nonprofit entity, receives funds from providers of telecommunications service and disburses those funds to providers that serve high-cost areas, low-income households, libraries, and schools, as well as to rural health care providers. As a result, the fund's receipts and payments are classified in the NIPAs as intracorporate transfers.

The *other* category for receipts includes a number of measurement factors that are generally small. For 2002, however, that category is unusually large. One contributing factor is the treatment of final payments for income tax liabilities (payments for the balance of taxes due and refunds of overpayments, generally made between February and May). The budget records settlements in the fiscal year in which they are paid. But the NIPAs spread those receipts evenly over the four quarters of the calendar year in which they are paid, which moves some receipts into the last quarter of the calendar year and thus into the subsequent fiscal year. As a result, NIPA receipts decrease by less than budget receipts do when there is a significant drop in final settlements, as there was in fiscal year 2002 (see the discussion in Chapter 3). In addition, it is also quite possible that the NIPA measure of receipts for 2002 will be revised downward when the accounts are updated this summer.

The Government's Receipts and Expenditures as Measured by the NIPAs

The federal sector of the NIPAs generally classifies receipts according to their source (*see Table D-2*). Taxes and fees paid by individuals are the leading source of government receipts in the 2003-2013 period. The next category in terms of size is contributions (including premiums) for social insurance programs—a category that includes Social Security taxes, Medicare taxes and premiums, unemployment insurance taxes, and federal employees' retirement contributions. The remaining categories of receipts are accruals of taxes on corporate profits, including the earnings of the Federal Reserve System, and indirect business tax and nontax accruals. (Examples of indirect business taxes are customs duties and excise taxes. Nontax accruals include deposit insurance premiums.)

The government's expenditures are classified according to their purpose and destination. Defense and nondefense consumption of goods and services represents purchases made by the government for its immediate use. (The largest share of current defense and nondefense consumption is the compensation of federal employees.) The consumption of fixed capital is the use that the government receives from its fixed assets, such as buildings or equipment; as noted earlier, that consumption appears in the accounts as depreciation.

Transfer payments are cash payments made directly to individuals, private entities, or foreign nations. Grants-in-aid are payments that the federal government makes to state or local governments, which generally use them for transfers (such as paying Medicaid benefits) and consumption (such as hiring additional police officers).

Although both the total budget and the NIPAs contain a category labeled "net interest," the NIPA figure is larger. Various differences cause the two measures to diverge. The biggest difference is the contrasting treatment of the interest received by the Civil Service and Military Retirement Trust Funds. In the total budget, such receipts offset the payments made to those funds by the Treasury. In the NIPAs, however, those receipts are reclassified as contributions to personal income and do not appear on the ledger detailing the government's transactions.

The category in the NIPAs labeled "subsidies less current surplus of government enterprises" contains two components, as its name suggests. The first—subsidies—is defined as grants paid by the federal government to businesses, including state and local government enterprises. Subsidies are dominated by housing assistance.

The second part of the category is the current surplus of government enterprises, which are certain business-type operations of the government, such as the Postal Service. The operating costs of a government enterprise are mostly covered by the sale of goods and services to the public rather than by tax receipts. The difference between sales and current operating expenses is the enterprise's surplus or deficit. (*Government enterprises* should not be confused with *government-sponsored enterprises*, or GSEs, which are private entities established and chartered by the federal government to perform specific financial functions, usually under the supervision of a government agency. Examples of GSEs include Fannie Mae and the Farm Credit System. As privately owned, though publicly chartered, corporations, GSEs are not included in the budget or in the federal sector of the NIPAs.)

APPENDIX D THE FEDERAL SECTOR OF THE NATIONAL INCOME AND PRODUCT ACCOUNTS **141**

Table D-2.
Projections of Baseline Receipts and Expenditures as Measured by the National Income and Product Accounts

(In billions of dollars)

	Actual 2002	2003	2004	2005	2006	2007	2008	2009	2010	2011	2012	2013
Receipts												
Personal Tax and Nontax Receipts	903	887	949	1,025	1,093	1,169	1,252	1,341	1,438	1,638	1,807	1,926
Contributions for Social Insurance[a]	732	764	808	856	905	954	1,001	1,050	1,103	1,157	1,213	1,273
Corporate Profits Tax Accruals	169	175	211	244	275	290	299	309	319	331	343	355
Indirect Business Tax and Nontax Accruals	110	106	109	112	116	121	125	129	133	137	140	144
Total	**1,913**	**1,933**	**2,076**	**2,238**	**2,390**	**2,534**	**2,677**	**2,828**	**2,993**	**3,263**	**3,502**	**3,698**
Expenditures												
Purchases of Goods and Services												
Defense												
Consumption	311	335	345	352	360	369	378	389	399	410	421	432
Consumption of fixed capital	64	66	66	67	68	68	69	70	71	71	72	72
Nondefense[b]												
Consumption	165	178	184	187	189	193	197	202	206	211	215	221
Consumption of fixed capital	30	32	34	36	39	41	43	46	48	50	53	55
Subtotal	570	611	630	642	655	671	688	705	723	742	760	780
Transfer Payments												
Domestic	898	942	971	1,007	1,057	1,109	1,165	1,230	1,304	1,384	1,460	1,553
Foreign	15	14	13	13	13	13	13	13	13	12	12	12
Subtotal	912	956	984	1,020	1,070	1,122	1,178	1,244	1,317	1,396	1,472	1,564
Grants-in-Aid to State and Local Governments[b]	299	322	337	352	368	388	409	434	460	489	521	556
Net Interest[b]	213	202	210	241	262	270	272	273	271	266	254	233
Subsidies Less Current Surplus of Government Enterprises	45	47	50	51	54	54	53	53	55	55	57	58
Total	**2,039**	**2,138**	**2,211**	**2,306**	**2,409**	**2,505**	**2,601**	**2,709**	**2,826**	**2,948**	**3,064**	**3,192**
Deficit (-) or Surplus												
Deficit (-) or Surplus[b]	-126	-206	-135	-68	-19	29	76	119	167	314	438	506

Source: Congressional Budget Office.

a. Includes Social Security taxes, Medicare taxes and premiums, unemployment taxes, and federal employees' retirement contributions.
b. Assumes that discretionary budget authority for 2003 totals $751 billion.

APPENDIX E

CBO's Economic Projections for 2003 Through 2013

Year-by-year economic projections for 2003 through 2013 are shown in the accompanying tables (*by calendar year in Table E-1 and by fiscal year in Table E-2*). The Congressional Budget Office did not try to explicitly incorporate cyclical recessions and recoveries into its projections for years after 2004. Instead, the projected values shown here for 2005 through 2013 reflect CBO's assessment of average values for that period—which take into account potential ups and downs in the business cycle.

Table E-1.
CBO's Year-by-Year Forecast and Projections for Calendar Years 2003 Through 2013

	Estimated 2002	Forecast 2003	Forecast 2004	Projected 2005	Projected 2006	Projected 2007	Projected 2008	Projected 2009	Projected 2010	Projected 2011	Projected 2012	Projected 2013
Nominal GDP (Billions of dollars)	10,443	10,880	11,465	12,092	12,749	13,437	14,154	14,901	15,677	16,436	17,217	18,066
Nominal GDP (Percentage change)	3.6	4.2	5.4	5.5	5.4	5.4	5.3	5.3	5.2	4.8	4.8	4.9
Real GDP (Percentage change)	2.4	2.5	3.6	3.4	3.3	3.2	3.1	3.0	2.9	2.6	2.5	2.7
GDP Price Index (Percentage change)	1.1	1.6	1.7	2.0	2.1	2.1	2.2	2.2	2.2	2.2	2.2	2.2
Consumer Price Index[a] (Percentage change)	1.6	2.3	2.2	2.4	2.5	2.5	2.5	2.5	2.5	2.5	2.5	2.5
Employment Cost Index[b] (Percentage change)	3.3	2.7	3.0	3.3	3.4	3.5	3.6	3.6	3.6	3.6	3.6	3.6
Unemployment Rate (Percent)	5.8	5.9	5.7	5.4	5.3	5.2	5.2	5.2	5.2	5.2	5.2	5.2
Three-Month Treasury Bill Rate (Percent)	1.6	1.4	3.5	4.8	4.9	4.9	4.9	4.9	4.9	4.9	4.9	4.9
Ten-Year Treasury Note Rate (Percent)	4.6	4.4	5.2	5.7	5.8	5.8	5.8	5.8	5.8	5.8	5.8	5.8
Tax Bases (Percentage of GDP)												
Corporate book profits	6.2	6.8	7.3	9.2	9.4	9.2	8.9	8.7	8.6	8.4	8.3	8.2
Wages and salaries	48.1	48.1	48.1	48.1	48.0	48.0	47.9	47.9	47.8	47.8	47.8	47.8
Tax Bases (Billions of dollars)												
Corporate book profits	653	739	842	1,116	1,202	1,239	1,267	1,302	1,341	1,384	1,429	1,474
Wages and salaries	5,025	5,237	5,518	5,818	6,125	6,446	6,782	7,131	7,498	7,859	8,231	8,635

Sources: Congressional Budget Office; Department of Commerce, Bureau of Economic Analysis; Department of Labor, Bureau of Labor Statistics; Federal Reserve Board.

Note: Percentage changes are year over year.

a. The consumer price index for all urban consumers.
b. The employment cost index for wages and salaries for private-industry workers.

Table E-2.
CBO's Year-by-Year Forecast and Projections for Fiscal Years 2003 Through 2013

	Estimated 2002	Forecast 2003	Forecast 2004	Projected 2005	Projected 2006	Projected 2007	Projected 2008	Projected 2009	Projected 2010	Projected 2011	Projected 2012	Projected 2013
Nominal GDP (Billions of dollars)	10,337	10,756	11,309	11,934	12,582	13,263	13,972	14,712	15,480	16,250	17,013	17,851
Nominal GDP (Percentage change)	3.0	4.1	5.1	5.5	5.4	5.4	5.3	5.3	5.2	5.0	4.7	4.9
Real GDP (Percentage change)	1.7	2.4	3.4	3.5	3.3	3.2	3.1	3.0	3.0	2.7	2.4	2.7
GDP Price Index (Percentage change)	1.3	1.6	1.7	2.0	2.1	2.1	2.2	2.2	2.2	2.2	2.2	2.2
Consumer Price Index[a] (Percentage change)	1.5	2.3	2.1	2.3	2.5	2.5	2.5	2.5	2.5	2.5	2.5	2.5
Employment Cost Index[b] (Percentage change)	3.5	2.8	2.9	3.2	3.4	3.5	3.5	3.6	3.6	3.6	3.6	3.6
Unemployment Rate (Percent)	5.7	5.9	5.8	5.5	5.3	5.3	5.2	5.2	5.2	5.2	5.2	5.2
Three-Month Treasury Bill Rate (Percent)	1.7	1.3	2.9	4.7	4.9	4.9	4.9	4.9	4.9	4.9	4.9	4.9
Ten-Year Treasury Note Rate (Percent)	4.8	4.2	5.1	5.6	5.8	5.8	5.8	5.8	5.8	5.8	5.8	5.8
Tax Bases (Percentage of GDP)												
Corporate book profits	6.2	6.6	7.0	9.0	9.5	9.3	9.0	8.8	8.6	8.4	8.3	8.2
Wages and salaries	48.2	48.2	48.1	48.1	48.1	48.0	47.9	47.9	47.8	47.8	47.8	47.8
Tax Bases (Billions of dollars)												
Corporate book profits	641	707	786	1,070	1,192	1,230	1,260	1,292	1,331	1,373	1,419	1,463
Wages and salaries	4,982	5,181	5,442	5,743	6,047	6,365	6,697	7,043	7,405	7,771	8,134	8,533

Sources: Congressional Budget Office; Department of Commerce, Bureau of Economic Analysis; Department of Labor, Bureau of Labor Statistics; Federal Reserve Board.

Note: Percentage changes are year over year.

a. The consumer price index for all urban consumers.
b. The employment cost index for wages and salaries for private-industry workers.

APPENDIX F

Historical Budget Data

This appendix shows historical data for revenues, outlays, and the surplus or deficit. Budget data consistent with the projections in Chapters 1, 3, and 4 of this report are available for fiscal years 1962 through 2002 and are reported in *Tables F-1 through F-10*. The data are shown in both nominal dollars and as a percentage of gross domestic product (GDP). Data for 2002 come from the Department of the Treasury, *Final Monthly Treasury Statement* (October 2002), and from the Office of Management and Budget.

Federal revenues, outlays, the surplus or deficit, and debt held by the public are shown in Tables F-1 and F-2. Revenues, outlays, and the surplus or deficit have both on-budget and off-budget components. Social Security's receipts and outlays were placed off-budget by the Balanced Budget and Emergency Deficit Control Act of 1985; the Postal Service was moved off-budget four years later by the Omnibus Budget Reconciliation Act of 1989.

The major sources of federal revenues (including off-budget revenues) are presented in Tables F-3 and F-4. Social insurance taxes include payments by employers and employees for Social Security, Medicare, Railroad Retirement, and unemployment insurance, as well as pension contributions by federal workers. Excise taxes are levied on certain products and services, such as gasoline, alcoholic beverages, and air travel. Miscellaneous receipts consist of deposits of earnings by the Federal Reserve System and numerous fees and charges.

Total outlays for major spending categories are shown in Tables F-5 and F-6. (Those totals include both on- and off-budget outlays.) To allow comparison of historical outlays with the projections in Chapters 1 and 4, historical data have been divided into the same categories of spending as the projections. Spending controlled by the appropriation process is classified as discretionary. Tables F-7 and F-8 divide discretionary spending into its defense, international, and domestic components. Entitlements and other mandatory spending include programs whose spending is governed by laws that set requirements for eligibility. Additional detail on entitlement programs is shown in Tables F-9 and F-10. Net interest is identical to the budget function of the same name (function 900). Offsetting receipts include the federal government's contributions to retirement programs for its employees, fees, charges (such as Medicare premiums), and receipts from the use of federally controlled land and offshore territory.

Estimates of the standardized-budget surplus or deficit and its revenue and outlay components for fiscal years 1960 through 2002 are reported in *Tables F-11 through F-13*, along with estimates of potential GDP, actual GDP, and the nonaccelerating inflation rate of unemployment (NAIRU). The standardized-budget measure and its components are also shown as a percentage of potential GDP.

The change in the standardized-budget surplus or deficit is commonly used to measure the short-term impact of fiscal policy on aggregate demand. The standardized-budget deficit (also called the structural deficit) excludes the effects that cyclical fluctuations in output and unemployment have on revenues and outlays and makes other adjustments. Historical estimates for standardized-budget revenues, outlays, and the surplus or deficit have been revised from those shown in previous reports.

Table F-1.

Revenues, Outlays, Surpluses, Deficits, and Debt Held by the Public, 1962-2002

(In billions of dollars)

	Revenues	Outlays	On-Budget[a]	Social Security	Postal Service[a]	Total	Debt Held by the Public[b]
1962	99.7	106.8	-5.9	-1.3	n.a.	-7.1	248.0
1963	106.6	111.3	-4.0	-0.8	n.a.	-4.8	254.0
1964	112.6	118.5	-6.5	0.6	n.a.	-5.9	256.8
1965	116.8	118.2	-1.6	0.2	n.a.	-1.4	260.8
1966	130.8	134.5	-3.1	-0.6	n.a.	-3.7	263.7
1967	148.8	157.5	-12.6	4.0	n.a.	-8.6	266.6
1968	153.0	178.1	-27.7	2.6	n.a.	-25.2	289.5
1969	186.9	183.6	-0.5	3.7	n.a.	3.2	278.1
1970	192.8	195.6	-8.7	5.9	n.a.	-2.8	283.2
1971	187.1	210.2	-26.1	3.0	n.a.	-23.0	303.0
1972	207.3	230.7	-26.4	3.0	n.a.	-23.4	322.4
1973	230.8	245.7	-15.4	0.5	n.a.	-14.9	340.9
1974	263.2	269.4	-8.0	1.8	n.a.	-6.1	343.7
1975	279.1	332.3	-55.3	2.0	n.a.	-53.2	394.7
1976	298.1	371.8	-70.5	-3.2	n.a.	-73.7	477.4
1977	355.6	409.2	-49.8	-3.9	n.a.	-53.7	549.1
1978	399.6	458.7	-54.9	-4.3	n.a.	-59.2	607.1
1979	463.3	504.0	-38.7	-2.0	n.a.	-40.7	640.3
1980	517.1	590.9	-72.7	-1.1	n.a.	-73.8	711.9
1981	599.3	678.2	-73.9	-5.0	n.a.	-79.0	789.4
1982	617.8	745.7	-120.0	-7.9	n.a.	-128.0	924.6
1983	600.6	808.4	-208.0	0.2	n.a.	-207.8	1,137.3
1984	666.5	851.9	-185.6	0.3	n.a.	-185.4	1,307.0
1985	734.1	946.4	-221.7	9.4	n.a.	-212.3	1,507.3
1986	769.2	990.4	-237.9	16.7	n.a.	-221.2	1,740.6
1987	854.4	1,004.1	-169.3	19.6	n.a.	-149.7	1,889.8
1988	909.3	1,064.5	-194.0	38.8	n.a.	-155.2	2,051.6
1989	991.2	1,143.6	-205.2	52.4	0.3	-152.5	2,190.7
1990	1,032.0	1,253.2	-277.8	58.2	-1.6	-221.2	2,411.6
1991	1,055.0	1,324.4	-321.5	53.5	-1.3	-269.3	2,689.0
1992	1,091.3	1,381.7	-340.5	50.7	-0.7	-290.4	2,999.7
1993	1,154.4	1,409.5	-300.4	46.8	-1.4	-255.1	3,248.4
1994	1,258.6	1,461.9	-258.9	56.8	-1.1	-203.3	3,433.1
1995	1,351.8	1,515.8	-226.4	60.5	2.0	-163.9	3,604.4
1996	1,453.1	1,560.5	-174.1	66.4	0.2	-107.5	3,734.1
1997	1,579.3	1,601.3	-103.3	81.3	*	-22.0	3,772.3
1998	1,721.8	1,652.6	-30.0	99.0	0.2	69.2	3,721.1
1999	1,827.5	1,701.9	1.9	124.7	-1.0	125.6	3,632.4
2000	2,025.2	1,788.8	86.6	151.8	-2.0	236.4	3,409.8
2001	1,991.2	1,863.9	-33.4	163.0	-2.3	127.3	3,319.6
2002	1,853.2	2,011.0	-317.5	160.3	-0.7	-157.8	3,540.4

Source: Congressional Budget Office.
Note: n.a. = not applicable; * = between zero and $500 million.

a. In 1962 through 1988, the Postal Service was on-budget and included in the on-budget total.
b. End of year.

APPENDIX F   HISTORICAL BUDGET DATA 149

Table F-2.
Revenues, Outlays, Surpluses, Deficits, and Debt Held by the Public, 1962-2002
(As a percentage of GDP)

	Revenues	Outlays	On-Budget[a]	Social Security	Postal Service[a]	Total	Debt Held by the Public[b]
1962	17.5	18.8	-1.0	-0.2	n.a.	-1.3	43.6
1963	17.8	18.5	-0.7	-0.1	n.a.	-0.8	42.3
1964	17.5	18.5	-1.0	0.1	n.a.	-0.9	40.0
1965	17.0	17.2	-0.2	*	n.a.	-0.2	37.9
1966	17.3	17.8	-0.4	-0.1	n.a.	-0.5	34.8
1967	18.3	19.4	-1.6	0.5	n.a.	-1.1	32.8
1968	17.6	20.5	-3.2	0.3	n.a.	-2.9	33.3
1969	19.7	19.3	-0.1	0.4	n.a.	0.3	29.3
1970	19.0	19.3	-0.9	0.6	n.a.	-0.3	27.9
1971	17.3	19.4	-2.4	0.3	n.a.	-2.1	28.0
1972	17.6	19.6	-2.2	0.3	n.a.	-2.0	27.4
1973	17.6	18.7	-1.2	*	n.a.	-1.1	26.0
1974	18.3	18.7	-0.6	0.1	n.a.	-0.4	23.8
1975	17.9	21.3	-3.5	0.1	n.a.	-3.4	25.3
1976	17.2	21.4	-4.1	-0.2	n.a.	-4.2	27.5
1977	18.0	20.7	-2.5	-0.2	n.a.	-2.7	27.8
1978	18.0	20.7	-2.5	-0.2	n.a.	-2.7	27.4
1979	18.5	20.1	-1.5	-0.1	n.a.	-1.6	25.6
1980	18.9	21.6	-2.7	*	n.a.	-2.7	26.1
1981	19.6	22.2	-2.4	-0.2	n.a.	-2.6	25.8
1982	19.1	23.1	-3.7	-0.2	n.a.	-4.0	28.6
1983	17.4	23.5	-6.0	*	n.a.	-6.0	33.0
1984	17.3	22.1	-4.8	*	n.a.	-4.8	34.0
1985	17.7	22.9	-5.4	0.2	n.a.	-5.1	36.4
1986	17.5	22.5	-5.4	0.4	n.a.	-5.0	39.6
1987	18.4	21.6	-3.6	0.4	n.a.	-3.2	40.6
1988	18.1	21.2	-3.9	0.8	n.a.	-3.1	40.9
1989	18.3	21.2	-3.8	1.0	*	-2.8	40.5
1990	18.0	21.8	-4.8	1.0	*	-3.9	42.0
1991	17.8	22.3	-5.4	0.9	*	-4.5	45.4
1992	17.5	22.2	-5.5	0.8	*	-4.7	48.2
1993	17.6	21.5	-4.6	0.7	*	-3.9	49.5
1994	18.1	21.0	-3.7	0.8	*	-2.9	49.4
1995	18.5	20.7	-3.1	0.8	*	-2.2	49.2
1996	18.9	20.3	-2.3	0.9	*	-1.4	48.5
1997	19.3	19.5	-1.3	1.0	*	-0.3	46.0
1998	19.9	19.1	-0.3	1.1	*	0.8	43.0
1999	20.0	18.6	*	1.4	*	1.4	39.7
2000	20.8	18.4	0.9	1.6	*	2.4	35.1
2001	19.8	18.6	-0.3	1.6	*	1.3	33.1
2002	17.9	19.5	-3.1	1.6	*	-1.5	34.3

Source: Congressional Budget Office.
Note: n.a. = not applicable; * = between -0.05 percent and 0.05 percent.

a. In 1962 through 1988, the Postal Service was on-budget and included in the on-budget total.
b. End of year.

Table F-3.
Revenues by Major Source, 1962-2002
(In billions of dollars)

	Individual Income Taxes	Corporate Income Taxes	Social Insurance Taxes	Excise Taxes	Estate and Gift Taxes	Customs Duties	Miscellaneous Receipts	Total Revenues
1962	45.6	20.5	17.0	12.5	2.0	1.1	0.8	99.7
1963	47.6	21.6	19.8	13.2	2.2	1.2	1.0	106.6
1964	48.7	23.5	22.0	13.7	2.4	1.3	1.1	112.6
1965	48.8	25.5	22.2	14.6	2.7	1.4	1.6	116.8
1966	55.4	30.1	25.5	13.1	3.1	1.8	1.9	130.8
1967	61.5	34.0	32.6	13.7	3.0	1.9	2.1	148.8
1968	68.7	28.7	33.9	14.1	3.1	2.0	2.5	153.0
1969	87.2	36.7	39.0	15.2	3.5	2.3	2.9	186.9
1970	90.4	32.8	44.4	15.7	3.6	2.4	3.4	192.8
1971	86.2	26.8	47.3	16.6	3.7	2.6	3.9	187.1
1972	94.7	32.2	52.6	15.5	5.4	3.3	3.6	207.3
1973	103.2	36.2	63.1	16.3	4.9	3.2	3.9	230.8
1974	119.0	38.6	75.1	16.8	5.0	3.3	5.4	263.2
1975	122.4	40.6	84.5	16.6	4.6	3.7	6.7	279.1
1976	131.6	41.4	90.8	17.0	5.2	4.1	8.0	298.1
1977	157.6	54.9	106.5	17.5	7.3	5.2	6.5	355.6
1978	181.0	60.0	121.0	18.4	5.3	6.6	7.4	399.6
1979	217.8	65.7	138.9	18.7	5.4	7.4	9.3	463.3
1980	244.1	64.6	157.8	24.3	6.4	7.2	12.7	517.1
1981	285.9	61.1	182.7	40.8	6.8	8.1	13.8	599.3
1982	297.7	49.2	201.5	36.3	8.0	8.9	16.2	617.8
1983	288.9	37.0	209.0	35.3	6.1	8.7	15.6	600.6
1984	298.4	56.9	239.4	37.4	6.0	11.4	17.1	666.5
1985	334.5	61.3	265.2	36.0	6.4	12.1	18.6	734.1
1986	349.0	63.1	283.9	32.9	7.0	13.3	20.0	769.2
1987	392.6	83.9	303.3	32.5	7.5	15.1	19.5	854.4
1988	401.2	94.5	334.3	35.2	7.6	16.2	20.3	909.3
1989	445.7	103.3	359.4	34.4	8.7	16.3	23.3	991.2
1990	466.9	93.5	380.0	35.3	11.5	16.7	28.0	1,032.0
1991	467.8	98.1	396.0	42.4	11.1	15.9	23.6	1,055.0
1992	476.0	100.3	413.7	45.6	11.1	17.4	27.3	1,091.3
1993	509.7	117.5	428.3	48.1	12.6	18.8	19.5	1,154.4
1994	543.1	140.4	461.5	55.2	15.2	20.1	23.2	1,258.6
1995	590.2	157.0	484.5	57.5	14.8	19.3	28.6	1,351.8
1996	656.4	171.8	509.4	54.0	17.2	18.7	25.5	1,453.1
1997	737.5	182.3	539.4	56.9	19.8	17.9	25.5	1,579.3
1998	828.6	188.7	571.8	57.7	24.1	18.3	32.7	1,721.8
1999	879.5	184.7	611.8	70.4	27.8	18.3	34.9	1,827.5
2000	1,004.5	207.3	652.9	68.9	29.0	19.9	42.8	2,025.2
2001	994.3	151.1	694.0	66.2	28.4	19.4	37.8	1,991.2
2002	858.3	148.0	700.8	67.0	26.5	18.6	33.9	1,853.2

Source: Congressional Budget Office.

APPENDIX F

Table F-4.

Revenues by Major Source, 1962-2002

(As a percentage of GDP)

	Individual Income Taxes	Corporate Income Taxes	Social Insurance Taxes	Excise Taxes	Estate and Gift Taxes	Customs Duties	Miscellaneous Receipts	Total Revenues
1962	8.0	3.6	3.0	2.2	0.4	0.2	0.1	17.5
1963	7.9	3.6	3.3	2.2	0.4	0.2	0.2	17.8
1964	7.6	3.7	3.4	2.1	0.4	0.2	0.2	17.5
1965	7.1	3.7	3.2	2.1	0.4	0.2	0.2	17.0
1966	7.3	4.0	3.4	1.7	0.4	0.2	0.2	17.3
1967	7.6	4.2	4.0	1.7	0.4	0.2	0.3	18.3
1968	7.9	3.3	3.9	1.6	0.4	0.2	0.3	17.6
1969	9.2	3.9	4.1	1.6	0.4	0.2	0.3	19.7
1970	8.9	3.2	4.4	1.5	0.4	0.2	0.3	19.0
1971	8.0	2.5	4.4	1.5	0.3	0.2	0.4	17.3
1972	8.0	2.7	4.5	1.3	0.5	0.3	0.3	17.6
1973	7.9	2.8	4.8	1.2	0.4	0.2	0.3	17.6
1974	8.3	2.7	5.2	1.2	0.3	0.2	0.4	18.3
1975	7.8	2.6	5.4	1.1	0.3	0.2	0.4	17.9
1976	7.6	2.4	5.2	1.0	0.3	0.2	0.5	17.2
1977	8.0	2.8	5.4	0.9	0.4	0.3	0.3	18.0
1978	8.2	2.7	5.5	0.8	0.2	0.3	0.3	18.0
1979	8.7	2.6	5.5	0.7	0.2	0.3	0.4	18.5
1980	8.9	2.4	5.8	0.9	0.2	0.3	0.5	18.9
1981	9.3	2.0	6.0	1.3	0.2	0.3	0.5	19.6
1982	9.2	1.5	6.2	1.1	0.2	0.3	0.5	19.1
1983	8.4	1.1	6.1	1.0	0.2	0.3	0.5	17.4
1984	7.8	1.5	6.2	1.0	0.2	0.3	0.4	17.3
1985	8.1	1.5	6.4	0.9	0.2	0.3	0.4	17.7
1986	7.9	1.4	6.5	0.7	0.2	0.3	0.5	17.5
1987	8.4	1.8	6.5	0.7	0.2	0.3	0.4	18.4
1988	8.0	1.9	6.7	0.7	0.2	0.3	0.4	18.1
1989	8.2	1.9	6.6	0.6	0.2	0.3	0.4	18.3
1990	8.1	1.6	6.6	0.6	0.2	0.3	0.5	18.0
1991	7.9	1.7	6.7	0.7	0.2	0.3	0.4	17.8
1992	7.7	1.6	6.6	0.7	0.2	0.3	0.4	17.5
1993	7.8	1.8	6.5	0.7	0.2	0.3	0.3	17.6
1994	7.8	2.0	6.6	0.8	0.2	0.3	0.3	18.1
1995	8.1	2.1	6.6	0.8	0.2	0.3	0.4	18.5
1996	8.5	2.2	6.6	0.7	0.2	0.2	0.3	18.9
1997	9.0	2.2	6.6	0.7	0.2	0.2	0.3	19.3
1998	9.6	2.2	6.6	0.7	0.3	0.2	0.4	19.9
1999	9.6	2.0	6.7	0.8	0.3	0.2	0.4	20.0
2000	10.3	2.1	6.7	0.7	0.3	0.2	0.4	20.8
2001	9.9	1.5	6.9	0.7	0.3	0.2	0.4	19.8
2002	8.3	1.4	6.8	0.6	0.3	0.2	0.3	17.9

Source: Congressional Budget Office.

Table F-5.
Outlays by Major Spending Category, 1962-2002
(In billions of dollars)

	Discretionary Spending	Entitlements and Other Mandatory Spending	Net Interest	Offsetting Receipts	Total Outlays
1962	72.1	34.7	6.9	-6.8	106.8
1963	75.3	36.2	7.7	-7.9	111.3
1964	79.1	38.9	8.2	-7.7	118.5
1965	77.8	39.7	8.6	-7.9	118.2
1966	90.1	43.4	9.4	-8.4	134.5
1967	106.5	50.9	10.3	-10.2	157.5
1968	118.0	59.7	11.1	-10.6	178.1
1969	117.3	64.6	12.7	-11.0	183.6
1970	120.3	72.5	14.4	-11.5	195.6
1971	122.5	86.9	14.8	-14.1	210.2
1972	128.5	100.8	15.5	-14.1	230.7
1973	130.4	116.0	17.3	-18.0	245.7
1974	138.2	130.9	21.4	-21.2	269.4
1975	158.0	169.4	23.2	-18.3	332.3
1976	175.6	189.1	26.7	-19.6	371.8
1977	197.1	203.7	29.9	-21.5	409.2
1978	218.7	227.4	35.5	-22.8	458.7
1979	240.0	247.0	42.6	-25.6	504.0
1980	276.3	291.2	52.5	-29.2	590.9
1981	307.9	339.4	68.8	-37.9	678.2
1982	326.0	370.8	85.0	-36.0	745.7
1983	353.3	410.6	89.8	-45.3	808.4
1984	379.4	405.6	111.1	-44.2	851.9
1985	415.8	448.2	129.5	-47.1	946.4
1986	438.5	461.8	136.0	-45.9	990.4
1987	444.2	474.2	138.6	-52.9	1,004.1
1988	464.4	505.0	151.8	-56.8	1,064.5
1989	488.8	548.6	169.0	-63.8	1,143.6
1990	500.6	626.9	184.3	-58.7	1,253.2
1991	533.3	702.3	194.4	-105.7	1,324.4
1992	533.8	716.8	199.3	-68.4	1,381.7
1993	539.4	738.0	198.7	-66.6	1,409.5
1994	541.4	786.1	202.9	-68.5	1,461.9
1995	544.9	818.5	232.1	-79.7	1,515.8
1996	532.7	858.7	241.1	-71.9	1,560.5
1997	547.2	896.3	244.0	-86.3	1,601.3
1998	552.1	938.6	241.1	-79.2	1,652.6
1999	572.0	976.8	229.8	-76.6	1,701.9
2000	614.8	1,029.8	223.0	-78.8	1,788.8
2001	649.3	1,095.2	206.2	-86.8	1,863.9
2002	734.4	1,196.6	171.0	-91.0	2,011.0

Source: Congressional Budget Office.

Table F-6.
Outlays by Major Spending Category, 1962-2002
(As a percentage of GDP)

	Discretionary Spending	Entitlements and Other Mandatory Spending	Net Interest	Offsetting Receipts	Total Outlays
1962	12.7	6.1	1.2	-1.2	18.8
1963	12.5	6.0	1.3	-1.3	18.5
1964	12.3	6.1	1.3	-1.2	18.5
1965	11.3	5.8	1.2	-1.1	17.2
1966	11.9	5.7	1.2	-1.1	17.8
1967	13.1	6.3	1.3	-1.3	19.4
1968	13.6	6.9	1.3	-1.2	20.5
1969	12.4	6.8	1.3	-1.2	19.3
1970	11.9	7.2	1.4	-1.1	19.3
1971	11.3	8.0	1.4	-1.3	19.4
1972	10.9	8.6	1.3	-1.2	19.6
1973	9.9	8.8	1.3	-1.4	18.7
1974	9.6	9.1	1.5	-1.5	18.7
1975	10.1	10.9	1.5	-1.2	21.3
1976	10.1	10.9	1.5	-1.1	21.4
1977	10.0	10.3	1.5	-1.1	20.7
1978	9.9	10.2	1.6	-1.0	20.7
1979	9.6	9.9	1.7	-1.0	20.1
1980	10.1	10.7	1.9	-1.1	21.6
1981	10.1	11.1	2.2	-1.2	22.2
1982	10.1	11.5	2.6	-1.1	23.1
1983	10.3	11.9	2.6	-1.3	23.5
1984	9.9	10.5	2.9	-1.2	22.1
1985	10.0	10.8	3.1	-1.1	22.9
1986	10.0	10.5	3.1	-1.0	22.5
1987	9.5	10.2	3.0	-1.1	21.6
1988	9.3	10.1	3.0	-1.1	21.2
1989	9.0	10.1	3.1	-1.2	21.2
1990	8.7	10.9	3.2	-1.0	21.8
1991	9.0	11.8	3.3	-1.8	22.3
1992	8.6	11.5	3.2	-1.1	22.2
1993	8.2	11.2	3.0	-1.0	21.5
1994	7.8	11.3	2.9	-1.0	21.0
1995	7.4	11.2	3.2	-1.1	20.7
1996	6.9	11.2	3.1	-0.9	20.3
1997	6.7	10.9	3.0	-1.1	19.5
1998	6.4	10.8	2.8	-0.9	19.1
1999	6.3	10.7	2.5	-0.8	18.6
2000	6.3	10.6	2.3	-0.8	18.4
2001	6.5	10.9	2.1	-0.9	18.6
2002	7.1	11.6	1.7	-0.9	19.5

Source: Congressional Budget Office.

Table F-7.
Discretionary Outlays, 1962-2002
(In billions of dollars)

	Defense	International	Domestic	Total
1962	52.6	5.5	14.0	72.1
1963	53.7	5.2	16.3	75.3
1964	55.0	4.6	19.5	79.1
1965	51.0	4.7	22.1	77.8
1966	59.0	5.1	26.1	90.1
1967	72.0	5.3	29.1	106.5
1968	82.2	4.9	31.0	118.0
1969	82.7	4.1	30.5	117.3
1970	81.9	4.0	34.4	120.3
1971	79.0	3.8	39.8	122.5
1972	79.3	4.6	44.6	128.5
1973	77.1	4.8	48.5	130.4
1974	80.7	6.2	51.3	138.2
1975	87.6	8.2	62.2	158.0
1976	89.9	7.5	78.2	175.6
1977	97.5	8.0	91.5	197.1
1978	104.6	8.5	105.5	218.7
1979	116.8	9.1	114.1	240.0
1980	134.6	12.8	128.9	276.3
1981	158.0	13.6	136.3	307.9
1982	185.9	12.9	127.1	326.0
1983	209.9	13.6	129.8	353.3
1984	228.0	16.3	135.1	379.4
1985	253.1	17.4	145.3	415.8
1986	273.8	17.7	147.0	438.5
1987	282.5	15.2	146.5	444.2
1988	290.9	15.7	157.8	464.4
1989	304.0	16.6	168.2	488.8
1990	300.1	19.1	181.4	500.6
1991	319.7	19.7	193.9	533.3
1992	302.6	19.2	212.1	533.8
1993	292.4	21.6	225.4	539.4
1994	282.3	20.8	238.3	541.4
1995	273.6	20.1	251.2	544.9
1996	266.0	18.3	248.4	532.7
1997	271.7	19.0	256.6	547.2
1998	270.2	18.1	263.8	552.1
1999	275.5	19.5	277.0	572.0
2000	295.0	21.3	298.6	614.8
2001	306.1	22.5	320.8	649.3
2002	348.9	26.2	359.2	734.4

Source: Congressional Budget Office.

Table F-8.
Discretionary Outlays, 1962-2002

(As a percentage of GDP)

	Defense	International	Domestic	Total
1962	9.2	1.0	2.5	12.7
1963	8.9	0.9	2.7	12.5
1964	8.6	0.7	3.0	12.3
1965	7.4	0.7	3.2	11.3
1966	7.8	0.7	3.4	11.9
1967	8.9	0.7	3.6	13.1
1968	9.4	0.6	3.6	13.6
1969	8.7	0.4	3.2	12.4
1970	8.1	0.4	3.4	11.9
1971	7.3	0.3	3.7	11.3
1972	6.7	0.4	3.8	10.9
1973	5.9	0.4	3.7	9.9
1974	5.6	0.4	3.6	9.6
1975	5.6	0.5	4.0	10.1
1976	5.2	0.4	4.5	10.1
1977	4.9	0.4	4.6	10.0
1978	4.7	0.4	4.8	9.9
1979	4.7	0.4	4.6	9.6
1980	4.9	0.5	4.7	10.1
1981	5.2	0.4	4.5	10.1
1982	5.8	0.4	3.9	10.1
1983	6.1	0.4	3.8	10.3
1984	5.9	0.4	3.5	9.9
1985	6.1	0.4	3.5	10.0
1986	6.2	0.4	3.3	10.0
1987	6.1	0.3	3.1	9.5
1988	5.8	0.3	3.1	9.3
1989	5.6	0.3	3.1	9.0
1990	5.2	0.3	3.2	8.7
1991	5.4	0.3	3.3	9.0
1992	4.9	0.3	3.4	8.6
1993	4.5	0.3	3.4	8.2
1994	4.1	0.3	3.4	7.8
1995	3.7	0.3	3.4	7.4
1996	3.5	0.2	3.2	6.9
1997	3.3	0.2	3.1	6.7
1998	3.1	0.2	3.0	6.4
1999	3.0	0.2	3.0	6.3
2000	3.0	0.2	3.1	6.3
2001	3.1	0.2	3.2	6.5
2002	3.4	0.3	3.5	7.1

Source: Congressional Budget Office.

Table F-9.
Outlays for Entitlements and Other Mandatory Spending, 1962-2002
(In billions of dollars)

	Means-Tested Programs			Non-Means-Tested Programs								Total Entitlements and Other Mandatory Spending
	Medicaid	Other	Total Means-Tested	Social Security	Medicare	Other Retirement and Disability	Unemployment Compensation	Farm Price Supports	Deposit Insurance	Other	Total Non-Means-Tested	
1962	0.1	4.2	4.3	14.0	0	2.7	3.5	2.4	-0.4	8.2	30.4	34.7
1963	0.2	4.5	4.7	15.5	0	2.9	3.6	3.4	-0.4	6.6	31.5	36.2
1964	0.2	4.8	5.0	16.2	0	3.3	3.4	3.4	-0.4	8.0	33.9	38.9
1965	0.3	4.9	5.2	17.1	0	3.6	2.7	2.8	-0.4	8.7	34.5	39.7
1966	0.8	5.0	5.8	20.3	*	4.1	2.2	1.4	-0.5	10.1	37.6	43.4
1967	1.2	5.0	6.2	21.3	3.2	4.8	2.3	2.0	-0.4	11.6	44.7	50.9
1968	1.8	5.7	7.5	23.3	5.1	5.7	2.2	3.3	-0.5	13.1	52.2	59.7
1969	2.3	6.3	8.6	26.7	6.3	5.2	2.3	4.2	-0.6	11.9	56.0	64.6
1970	2.7	7.4	10.1	29.6	6.8	6.6	3.1	3.8	-0.5	12.9	62.4	72.5
1971	3.4	10.0	13.4	35.1	7.5	8.3	5.8	2.9	-0.4	14.3	73.5	86.9
1972	4.6	11.7	16.3	39.4	8.4	9.6	6.7	4.1	-0.6	17.0	84.5	100.8
1973	4.6	11.4	16.0	48.2	9.0	11.7	4.9	3.6	-0.8	23.4	100.0	116.0
1974	5.8	13.7	19.5	55.0	10.7	13.8	5.6	1.0	-0.6	25.9	111.4	130.9
1975	6.8	18.6	25.4	63.6	14.1	18.3	12.8	0.6	0.5	34.2	144.0	169.4
1976	8.6	21.7	30.3	72.7	16.9	18.9	18.6	1.1	-0.6	31.2	158.8	189.1
1977	9.9	23.4	33.3	83.7	20.8	21.6	14.3	3.8	-2.8	29.0	170.4	203.7
1978	10.7	24.8	35.5	92.4	24.3	23.7	10.8	5.7	-1.0	36.0	191.9	227.4
1979	12.4	26.5	38.9	102.6	28.2	27.9	9.8	3.6	-1.7	37.8	208.1	247.0
1980	14.0	31.9	45.9	117.1	34.0	32.1	16.9	2.8	-0.4	43.0	245.3	291.2
1981	16.8	37.1	53.9	137.9	41.3	37.4	18.3	4.0	-1.4	48.0	285.5	339.4
1982	17.4	37.4	54.8	153.9	49.2	40.7	22.2	11.7	-2.1	40.4	316.0	370.8
1983	19.0	40.3	59.3	168.5	55.5	43.2	29.7	18.9	-1.2	36.7	351.3	410.6
1984	20.1	41.2	61.3	176.1	61.0	44.7	17.0	7.3	-0.8	39.1	344.3	405.6
1985	22.7	43.3	66.0	186.4	69.6	45.5	15.8	17.7	-2.2	49.3	382.2	448.2
1986	25.0	44.9	69.9	196.5	74.2	47.5	16.1	25.8	1.5	30.1	391.9	461.8
1987	27.4	45.5	72.9	205.1	79.9	50.8	15.5	22.4	3.1	24.5	401.3	474.2
1988	30.5	50.0	80.5	216.8	85.7	54.2	13.6	12.2	10.0	32.0	424.5	505.0
1989	34.6	54.2	88.8	230.4	94.3	57.2	13.9	10.6	22.0	31.4	459.8	548.6
1990	41.1	58.8	99.9	246.5	107.4	59.9	17.1	6.5	57.9	31.6	527.0	626.9
1991	52.5	69.7	122.2	266.8	114.2	64.4	25.1	10.1	66.2	33.4	580.1	702.3
1992	67.8	78.7	146.5	285.2	129.4	66.6	37.0	9.3	2.6	40.3	570.3	716.8
1993	75.8	86.5	162.3	302.0	143.1	68.7	35.5	15.6	-28.0	38.8	575.7	738.0
1994	82.0	95.0	177.0	316.9	159.5	72.1	26.4	9.9	-7.6	31.8	609.1	786.1
1995	89.1	101.5	190.6	333.3	177.1	75.2	21.3	5.8	-17.9	33.2	628.0	818.5
1996	92.0	104.2	196.2	347.1	191.3	77.3	22.6	5.0	-8.4	27.6	662.5	858.7
1997	95.6	107.2	202.8	362.3	207.9	80.6	20.6	5.8	-14.4	30.8	693.5	896.3
1998	101.1	107.9	209.0	376.1	211.0	82.9	19.6	8.5	-4.4	35.8	729.6	938.6
1999	107.7	113.0	220.7	387.0	209.3	85.3	21.4	18.0	-5.3	40.5	756.1	976.8
2000	117.4	118.6	235.9	406.0	216.0	87.8	20.7	30.5	-3.1	35.8	793.9	1,029.8
2001	130.4	118.4	248.7	429.4	237.9	92.7	27.9	22.4	-1.4	37.8	846.5	1,095.2
2002	147.5	138.5	286.1	452.5	253.7	96.1	50.6	13.9	-1.0	70.8	910.6	1,196.6

Source: Congressional Budget Office.

Note: * = less than $50 million.

Table F-10.
Outlays for Entitlements and Other Mandatory Spending, 1962-2002
(As a percentage of GDP)

	Means-Tested Programs			Non-Means-Tested Programs								Total Entitlements and Other Mandatory Spending
	Medicaid	Other	Total Means-Tested	Social Security	Medicare	Other Retirement and Disability	Unemployment Compensation	Farm Price Supports	Deposit Insurance	Other	Total Non-Means-Tested	
1962	*	0.7	0.8	2.5	0	0.5	0.6	0.4	-0.1	1.4	5.3	6.1
1963	*	0.8	0.8	2.6	0	0.5	0.6	0.6	-0.1	1.1	5.2	6.0
1964	*	0.7	0.8	2.5	0	0.5	0.5	0.5	-0.1	1.2	5.3	6.1
1965	*	0.7	0.8	2.5	0	0.5	0.4	0.4	-0.1	1.3	5.0	5.8
1966	0.1	0.7	0.8	2.7	*	0.5	0.3	0.2	-0.1	1.3	5.0	5.7
1967	0.1	0.6	0.8	2.6	0.4	0.6	0.3	0.2	*	1.4	5.5	6.3
1968	0.2	0.7	0.9	2.7	0.6	0.7	0.2	0.4	-0.1	1.5	6.0	6.9
1969	0.2	0.7	0.9	2.8	0.7	0.6	0.2	0.4	-0.1	1.3	5.9	6.8
1970	0.3	0.7	1.0	2.9	0.7	0.7	0.3	0.4	*	1.3	6.2	7.2
1971	0.3	0.9	1.2	3.2	0.7	0.8	0.5	0.3	*	1.3	6.8	8.0
1972	0.4	1.0	1.4	3.3	0.7	0.8	0.6	0.3	-0.1	1.4	7.2	8.6
1973	0.4	0.9	1.2	3.7	0.7	0.9	0.4	0.3	-0.1	1.8	7.6	8.8
1974	0.4	0.9	1.4	3.8	0.7	1.0	0.4	0.1	*	1.8	7.7	9.1
1975	0.4	1.2	1.6	4.1	0.9	1.2	0.8	*	*	2.2	9.2	10.9
1976	0.5	1.3	1.7	4.2	1.0	1.1	1.1	0.1	*	1.8	9.1	10.9
1977	0.5	1.2	1.7	4.2	1.1	1.1	0.7	0.2	-0.1	1.5	8.6	10.3
1978	0.5	1.1	1.6	4.2	1.1	1.1	0.5	0.3	*	1.6	8.6	10.2
1979	0.5	1.1	1.6	4.1	1.1	1.1	0.4	0.1	-0.1	1.5	8.3	9.9
1980	0.5	1.2	1.7	4.3	1.2	1.2	0.6	0.1	*	1.6	9.0	10.7
1981	0.6	1.2	1.8	4.5	1.3	1.2	0.6	0.1	*	1.6	9.3	11.1
1982	0.5	1.2	1.7	4.8	1.5	1.3	0.7	0.4	-0.1	1.2	9.8	11.5
1983	0.6	1.2	1.7	4.9	1.6	1.3	0.9	0.5	*	1.1	10.2	11.9
1984	0.5	1.1	1.6	4.6	1.6	1.2	0.4	0.2	*	1.0	8.9	10.5
1985	0.5	1.0	1.6	4.5	1.7	1.1	0.4	0.4	-0.1	1.2	9.2	10.8
1986	0.6	1.0	1.6	4.5	1.7	1.1	0.4	0.6	*	0.7	8.9	10.5
1987	0.6	1.0	1.6	4.4	1.7	1.1	0.3	0.5	0.1	0.5	8.6	10.2
1988	0.6	1.0	1.6	4.3	1.7	1.1	0.3	0.2	0.2	0.6	8.5	10.1
1989	0.6	1.0	1.6	4.3	1.7	1.1	0.3	0.2	0.4	0.6	8.5	10.1
1990	0.7	1.0	1.7	4.3	1.9	1.0	0.3	0.1	1.0	0.6	9.2	10.9
1991	0.9	1.2	2.1	4.5	1.9	1.1	0.4	0.2	1.1	0.6	9.8	11.8
1992	1.1	1.3	2.4	4.6	2.1	1.1	0.6	0.1	*	0.6	9.2	11.5
1993	1.2	1.3	2.5	4.6	2.2	1.0	0.5	0.2	-0.4	0.6	8.8	11.2
1994	1.2	1.4	2.5	4.6	2.3	1.0	0.4	0.1	-0.1	0.5	8.8	11.3
1995	1.2	1.4	2.6	4.6	2.4	1.0	0.3	0.1	-0.2	0.5	8.6	11.2
1996	1.2	1.4	2.5	4.5	2.5	1.0	0.3	0.1	-0.1	0.4	8.6	11.2
1997	1.2	1.3	2.5	4.4	2.5	1.0	0.3	0.1	-0.2	0.4	8.5	10.9
1998	1.2	1.2	2.4	4.3	2.4	1.0	0.2	0.1	-0.1	0.4	8.4	10.8
1999	1.2	1.2	2.4	4.2	2.3	0.9	0.2	0.2	-0.1	0.4	8.3	10.7
2000	1.2	1.2	2.4	4.2	2.2	0.9	0.2	0.3	*	0.4	8.2	10.6
2001	1.3	1.2	2.5	4.3	2.4	0.9	0.3	0.2	*	0.4	8.4	10.9
2002	1.4	1.3	2.8	4.4	2.2	0.9	0.5	0.1	*	0.7	8.8	11.6

Source: Congressional Budget Office.

Note: * = between -0.05 percent and 0.05 percent.

Table F-11.
Surpluses, Deficits, Debt, and Related Series, 1960-2002

	In Billions of Dollars			As a Percentage of GDP			GDP (Billions of Dollars)		NAIRU[d] (Percent)
	Surplus or Deficit (-)	Standardized-Budget Surplus or Deficit (-)[a]	Debt Held by the Public	Surplus or Deficit (-)	Standardized-Budget Surplus or Deficit (-)[a,b]	Debt Held by the Public	Actual[c]	Potential	
1960	*	*	237	0.1	0.1	45.6	520	520	5.5
1961	-3	3	238	-0.6	0.6	44.9	531	547	5.5
1962	-7	-4	248	-1.3	-0.8	43.6	569	575	5.5
1963	-5	-4	254	-0.8	-0.6	42.3	600	605	5.5
1964	-6	-7	257	-0.9	-1.0	40.0	642	637	5.6
1965	-1	-5	261	-0.2	-0.7	37.9	688	674	5.6
1966	-4	-14	264	-0.5	-2.0	34.8	757	719	5.7
1967	-9	-21	267	-1.1	-2.7	32.8	812	776	5.8
1968	-25	-31	290	-2.9	-3.7	33.3	870	840	5.8
1969	3	-11	278	0.3	-1.2	29.3	949	916	5.8
1970	-3	-6	283	-0.3	-0.6	27.9	1,014	1,002	5.9
1971	-23	-11	303	-2.1	-1.0	28.0	1,082	1,090	5.9
1972	-23	-20	322	-2.0	-1.7	27.4	1,178	1,179	6.0
1973	-15	-21	341	-1.1	-1.7	26.0	1,314	1,274	6.1
1974	-6	2	344	-0.4	0.1	23.8	1,442	1,415	6.2
1975	-53	-1	395	-3.4	**	25.3	1,559	1,616	6.2
1976	-74	-37	477	-4.2	-2.1	27.5	1,736	1,787	6.2
1977	-54	-22	549	-2.7	-1.1	27.8	1,975	2,000	6.2
1978	-59	-33	607	-2.7	-1.5	27.4	2,219	2,212	6.3
1979	-41	-18	640	-1.6	-0.7	25.6	2,505	2,472	6.3
1980	-74	-13	712	-2.7	-0.5	26.1	2,732	2,775	6.2
1981	-79	-14	789	-2.6	-0.5	25.8	3,060	3,128	6.2
1982	-128	-41	925	-4.0	-1.2	28.6	3,231	3,435	6.1
1983	-208	-114	1,137	-6.0	-3.1	33.0	3,442	3,682	6.1
1984	-185	-145	1,307	-4.8	-3.7	34.0	3,847	3,930	6.1
1985	-212	-177	1,507	-5.1	-4.2	36.4	4,142	4,185	6.0
1986	-221	-214	1,741	-5.0	-4.8	39.6	4,398	4,424	6.0
1987	-150	-152	1,890	-3.2	-3.2	40.6	4,654	4,692	6.0
1988	-155	-130	2,052	-3.1	-2.6	40.9	5,017	4,996	5.9
1989	-153	-118	2,191	-2.8	-2.2	40.5	5,407	5,345	5.9
1990	-221	-121	2,412	-3.9	-2.1	42.0	5,738	5,706	5.9
1991	-269	-147	2,689	-4.5	-2.4	45.4	5,928	6,088	5.8
1992	-290	-185	3,000	-4.7	-2.9	48.2	6,222	6,403	5.7
1993	-255	-185	3,248	-3.9	-2.8	49.5	6,561	6,713	5.6
1994	-203	-145	3,433	-2.9	-2.1	49.4	6,949	7,030	5.4
1995	-164	-144	3,604	-2.2	-2.0	49.2	7,323	7,376	5.3
1996	-108	-99	3,734	-1.4	-1.3	48.5	7,700	7,740	5.2
1997	-22	-73	3,772	-0.3	-0.9	46.0	8,194	8,137	5.2
1998	69	-37	3,721	0.8	-0.4	43.0	8,655	8,528	5.2
1999	126	-3	3,632	1.4	**	39.7	9,141	8,945	5.2
2000	236	99	3,410	2.4	1.1	35.1	9,715	9,442	5.2
2001	127	80	3,320	1.3	0.8	33.1	10,032	9,995	5.2
2002	-158	-153	3,540	-1.5	-1.5	34.3	10,337	10,428	5.2

Sources: Congressional Budget Office; Department of Commerce, Bureau of Economic Analysis.
Note: * = less than $500 million; ** = less than 0.05 percent.

a. Excludes deposit insurance, receipts from auctions of licenses to use the electromagnetic spectrum, timing adjustments, and contributions from allied nations for Operation Desert Storm (which were received in 1991 and 1992).
b. Shown as a percentage of potential GDP.
c. CBO calculated fiscal year numbers from quarterly national income and product account data from the Bureau of Economic Analysis.
d. The NAIRU is the nonaccelerating inflation rate of unemployment. It is the benchmark for computing potential GDP.

APPENDIX F HISTORICAL BUDGET DATA 159

Table F-12.
Standardized-Budget Surplus or Deficit and Related Series, 1960-2002
(In billions of dollars)

	Budget Surplus or Deficit (-)	Cyclical Surplus or Deficit (-)	Other Adjustments[a]	Standardized-Budget Surplus or Deficit (-)	Revenues	Outlays
1960	*	*	*	*	91	90
1961	-3	6	*	3	94	98
1962	-7	2	1	-4	100	107
1963	-5	1	*	-4	107	111
1964	-6	-2	1	-7	113	119
1965	-1	-5	2	-5	117	118
1966	-4	-13	3	-14	131	135
1967	-9	-13	*	-21	149	157
1968	-25	-11	5	-31	153	178
1969	3	-14	*	-11	187	184
1970	-3	-6	2	-6	193	196
1971	-23	3	9	-11	187	210
1972	-23	*	3	-20	207	231
1973	-15	-14	8	-21	231	246
1974	-6	-10	18	2	263	269
1975	-53	21	31	-1	279	332
1976	-74	23	13	-37	298	372
1977	-54	12	20	-22	356	409
1978	-59	-3	29	-33	400	459
1979	-41	-13	36	-18	463	504
1980	-74	18	44	-13	517	591
1981	-79	26	39	-14	599	678
1982	-128	64	23	-41	618	746
1983	-208	87	7	-114	601	808
1984	-185	28	12	-145	666	852
1985	-212	16	20	-177	734	946
1986	-221	10	-3	-214	769	990
1987	-150	11	-13	-152	854	1,004
1988	-155	-9	35	-130	909	1,064
1989	-153	-21	56	-118	991	1,144
1990	-221	-10	110	-121	1,032	1,253
1991	-269	50	73	-147	1,055	1,324
1992	-290	66	39	-185	1,091	1,382
1993	-255	56	14	-185	1,154	1,410
1994	-203	30	28	-145	1,259	1,462
1995	-164	14	6	-144	1,352	1,516
1996	-107	14	-5	-99	1,453	1,561
1997	-22	-19	-32	-73	1,579	1,601
1998	69	-46	-60	-37	1,722	1,653
1999	126	-70	-59	-3	1,827	1,702
2000	236	-99	-38	99	2,025	1,789
2001	127	-19	-27	80	1,991	1,864
2002	-158	40	-35	-153	1,853	2,011

Source: Congressional Budget Office.

Note: * = between -$500 million and $500 million.

a. Consists of deposit insurance, receipts from auctions of licenses to use the electromagnetic spectrum, timing adjustments, and contributions from allied nations for Operation Desert Storm (which were received in 1991 and 1992).

Table F-13.
Standardized-Budget Surplus or Deficit and Related Series, 1960-2002

(As a percentage of potential GDP)

	Budget Surplus or Deficit (-)[a]	Cyclical Surplus or Deficit (-)	Other Adjustments[b]	Standardized-Budget Surplus or Deficit (-)	Revenues	Outlays
1960	0.1	0.1	0.1	0.1	17.4	17.4
1961	-0.6	1.1	0.1	0.6	17.3	17.9
1962	-1.3	0.4	0.1	-0.8	17.3	18.6
1963	-0.8	0.2	-0.1	-0.6	17.6	18.4
1964	-0.9	-0.3	0.2	-1.0	17.7	18.6
1965	-0.2	-0.8	0.2	-0.7	17.3	17.5
1966	-0.5	-1.9	0.4	-2.0	18.2	18.7
1967	-1.1	-1.6	*	-2.7	19.2	20.3
1968	-2.9	-1.3	0.6	-3.7	18.2	21.2
1969	0.3	-1.6	*	-1.2	20.4	20.1
1970	-0.3	-0.6	0.2	-0.6	19.2	19.5
1971	-2.1	0.3	0.9	-1.0	17.2	19.3
1972	-2.0	*	0.3	-1.7	17.6	19.6
1973	-1.1	-1.1	0.6	-1.7	18.1	19.3
1974	-0.4	-0.7	1.3	0.1	18.6	19.0
1975	-3.4	1.3	1.9	*	17.3	20.6
1976	-4.2	1.3	0.7	-2.1	16.7	20.8
1977	-2.7	0.6	1.0	-1.1	17.8	20.5
1978	-2.7	-0.1	1.3	-1.5	18.1	20.7
1979	-1.6	-0.5	1.5	-0.7	18.7	20.4
1980	-2.7	0.6	1.6	-0.5	18.6	21.3
1981	-2.6	0.8	1.2	-0.5	19.2	21.7
1982	-4.0	1.9	0.7	-1.2	18.0	21.7
1983	-6.0	2.3	0.2	-3.1	16.3	22.0
1984	-4.8	0.7	0.3	-3.7	17.0	21.7
1985	-5.1	0.4	0.5	-4.2	17.5	22.6
1986	-5.0	0.2	-0.1	-4.8	17.4	22.4
1987	-3.2	0.2	-0.3	-3.2	18.2	21.4
1988	-3.1	-0.2	0.7	-2.6	18.2	21.3
1989	-2.8	-0.4	1.0	-2.2	18.5	21.4
1990	-3.9	-0.2	1.9	-2.1	18.1	22.0
1991	-4.5	0.8	1.2	-2.4	17.3	21.8
1992	-4.7	1.0	0.6	-2.9	17.0	21.6
1993	-3.9	0.8	0.2	-2.8	17.2	21.0
1994	-2.9	0.4	0.4	-2.1	17.9	20.8
1995	-2.2	0.2	0.1	-2.0	18.3	20.6
1996	-1.4	0.2	-0.1	-1.3	18.8	20.2
1997	-0.3	-0.2	-0.4	-0.9	19.4	19.7
1998	0.8	-0.5	-0.7	-0.4	20.2	19.4
1999	1.4	-0.8	-0.7	*	20.4	19.0
2000	2.4	-1.0	-0.4	1.1	21.4	18.9
2001	1.3	-0.2	-0.3	0.8	19.9	18.6
2002	-1.5	0.4	-0.3	-1.5	17.8	19.3

Source: Congressional Budget Office.

Note: * = between -0.05 percent and 0.05 percent.

a. Shown as a percentage of actual GDP.
b. Consists of deposit insurance, receipts from auctions of licenses to use the electromagnetic spectrum, timing adjustments, and contributions from allied nations for Operation Desert Storm (which were received in 1991 and 1992).

APPENDIX G

Contributors to the Revenue and Spending Projections

The following Congressional Budget Office analysts prepared the revenue and spending projections in this report:

Revenue Projections

Annabelle Bartsch	Customs duties, miscellaneous receipts
Mark Booth	Revenue forecasting
Paul Burnham	Pensions
Barbara Edwards	Individual income taxes
Seth Giertz	Capital gains realizations, pensions
Pam Greene	Estate and gift taxes, excise taxes
Ed Harris	Social insurance taxes
Carolyn Lynch	Corporate income taxes, Federal Reserve System earnings
Rob McClelland	Estate and gift taxes
Larry Ozanne	Capital gains realizations
Kurt Seibert	Earned income tax credit, social insurance taxes
Andrew Shaw	Excise taxes
David Weiner	Revenue modeling

Spending Projections

Defense, International Affairs, and Veterans' Affairs

Jo Ann Vines	Unit Chief
Kent Christensen	Defense projections and scorekeeping
Sunita D'Monte	International affairs (conduct of foreign affairs and information exchange activities), veterans' housing
Raymond Hall	Defense (Navy ships and weapons, missile defenses, atomic energy defense activities)
Sarah Jennings	Military retirement, veterans' education
David Newman	Defense (military construction and family housing, Air Force weapons)
Sam Papenfuss	Veterans' health care, military health care
Michelle Patterson	Defense (military personnel and compensation)

Matthew Schmit Defense (operations and maintenance), homeland security, intelligence programs, radiation exposure compensation
Joseph Whitehill International affairs (development, security, international financial institutions)
Melissa Zimmerman Veterans' compensation and pensions

Health

Thomas Bradley Unit Chief
Alexis Ahlstrom Medicare, Public Health Service, Federal Employees Health Benefits program
Shawn Bishop Medicare
Niall Brennan Medicare, Public Health Service
Julia Christensen Medicare, Public Health Service
Jeanne De Sa Medicaid, State Children's Health Insurance Program
Margaret Nowak Medicare, Public Health Service
Eric Rollins Medicaid, State Children's Health Insurance Program
Christopher Topoleski Medicare, Public Health Service

Human Resources

Paul Cullinan Unit Chief
Michael Carson Computer and research support
Chad Chirico Housing assistance
Sheila Dacey Child Support Enforcement, Temporary Assistance for Needy Families, Social Services Block Grant, Food Stamps
Geoff Gerhardt Federal civilian retirement, Pension Benefit Guaranty Corporation, Supplemental Security Income
Deborah Kalcevic Education
Kathy Ruffing Social Security
Christina Hawley Sadoti Unemployment insurance, training programs, Administration on Aging, foster care
Donna Wong Elementary and secondary education, Pell grants, child care, child and family services, arts and humanities

Natural and Physical Resources

Kim Cawley Unit Chief
Megan Carroll Conservation and land management
Lisa Cash Driskill Energy, Outer Continental Shelf receipts
Mark Grabowicz Justice, Postal Service
Kathleen Gramp Spectrum auction receipts, energy, science, and space
Mark Hadley Deposit insurance, credit unions, air transportation
Greg Hitz Agriculture
David Hull Agriculture
Ken Johnson Commerce, Small Business Administration, Universal Service Fund
James Langley Agriculture
Susanne Mehlman Pollution control and abatement, Federal Housing Administration and other housing credit programs

Julie Middleton	Water resources, Federal Emergency Management Agency
Rachel Milberg	Highways, Amtrak, mass transit
Matthew Pickford	General government
Deborah Reis	Recreation, water transportation, community development, other natural resources, legislative branch
Lanette Walker	Justice, regional development, Bureau of Indian Affairs

Other

Janet Airis	Unit Chief, Scorekeeping
Jeffrey Holland	Unit Chief, Projections
Edward Blau	Authorization bills
Barry Blom	National income and product accounts, monthly Treasury data
Joanna Capps	Appropriation bills (Agriculture, Interior)
Sandy Davis	Budget process
Adaeze Enekwechi	Economic assumptions, budget totals
Kenneth Farris	Computer support
Mary Froehlich	Computer support
Ellen Hays	Federal pay
Catherine Little	Appropriation bills (VA-HUD, Treasury)
Felix LoStracco	Other interest, discretionary spending
Virginia Myers	Appropriation bills (Commerce-Justice-State, foreign operations)
Laurie Pounder	Interest on the public debt
Eric Schatten	Interest on the public debt
Robert Sempsey	Appropriation bills (Labor-HHS, Transportation, military construction)
Patrice Watson	Computer support
Jason Wheelock	Appropriation bills (Defense, energy and water)

Glossary

This glossary defines economic and budgetary terms as they relate to the Congressional Budget Office's annual *Budget and Economic Outlook* and for the general information of readers. Some entries sacrifice precision for the sake of brevity and clarity to the lay reader. Where appropriate, entries note the sources of data for economic variables as follows:

- (BEA) refers to the Bureau of Economic Analysis in the Department of Commerce;
- (BLS) refers to the Bureau of Labor Statistics in the Department of Labor;
- (CBO) refers to the Congressional Budget Office;
- (FRB) refers to the Federal Reserve Board; and
- (NBER) refers to the National Bureau of Economic Research (a private entity).

accrual accounting: A system of accounting in which revenues are recorded when earned and outlays are recorded when goods are received or services performed, even though the actual receipt of revenues and payment for goods or services may occur, in whole or in part, at a different time. Compare with **cash accounting**.

adjusted gross income (AGI): All income subject to taxation under the individual income tax after subtracting "above-the-line" deductions, such as alimony payments and certain contributions for individual retirement accounts. Personal exemptions and the standard or itemized deductions are subtracted from AGI to determine taxable income.

advance appropriation: Budget authority provided in an appropriation act that is first available for obligation in a fiscal year after the year for which the appropriation was enacted. The amount of the advance appropriation is included in the budget totals for the fiscal year in which it will become available. See **appropriation act**, **budget authority**, **fiscal year**, and **obligation**; compare with **forward funding** and **obligation delay**.

aggregate demand: Total purchases of a country's output of goods and services by consumers, businesses, government, and foreigners during a given period. (BEA) Compare with **domestic demand**.

AGI: See **adjusted gross income**.

alternative minimum tax (AMT): A tax intended to limit the extent to which higher-income taxpayers can reduce their tax liability (the amount they owe) through the use of preferences in the tax code. Taxpayers subject to the AMT are required to recalculate their tax liability on the basis of a more limited set of exemptions, deductions, and tax credits than would normally apply. The amount by which a taxpayer's AMT calculation exceeds his or her regular tax calculation is that taxpayer's AMT liability.

appropriation act: Legislation under the jurisdiction of the House and Senate Committees on Appropriations that provides budget authority for federal programs or agencies. By law, such an act has a particular style and title—for example, "An act making appropriations for the Department of Defense for the year ending September 30, 2004." Generally, 13 regular appropriation acts are considered annually to fund the operations of the federal government; the

Congress may also consider supplemental or continuing appropriation acts, but each follows the statutory style and title. See **budget authority**.

authorization act: Legislation under the jurisdiction of a committee *other than* the House and Senate Committees on Appropriations that establishes or continues the operation of a federal program or agency, either indefinitely or for a specified period of time. An authorization act may suggest a level of budget authority needed to fund the program or agency, which is then provided in a future appropriation act. However, for some programs, the authorization itself may provide the budget authority. See **budget authority**.

Balanced Budget and Emergency Deficit Control Act of 1985 (Public Law 99-177): Referred to in CBO's reports as the Deficit Control Act, it was originally known as Gramm-Rudman-Hollings. Among other changes to the budget process, the law established specific deficit targets and a sequestration procedure to reduce spending if those targets were exceeded. The Deficit Control Act has been amended and extended several times—most significantly by the Budget Enforcement Act of 1990 (BEA). The BEA established one type of control, the pay-as-you-go procedure, for legislation affecting direct spending and revenues and another type of control, annual spending limits, for discretionary spending. The sequestration procedure—originally applicable to overall deficit targets—was restructured to enforce the discretionary spending limits and pay-as-you-go process separately. However, on September 30, 2002, the discretionary spending caps and the sequestration procedure to enforce those caps expired, and the Office of Management and Budget and CBO were no longer required to record the five-year budgetary effects of legislation affecting direct spending or revenues. Although sequestration under the pay-as-you-go procedure would have continued through 2006 on the basis of laws enacted before September 30, 2002, Public Law 107-312 eliminated that possibility by reducing to zero all pay-as-you-go balances. See **direct spending**, **discretionary spending**, **discretionary spending limits**, **pay-as-you-go**, **revenues**, and **sequestration**.

baseline: A benchmark for measuring the budgetary effects of proposed changes in federal revenues or spending. For purposes of the Deficit Control Act, the baseline is the projection of current-year levels of new budget authority, outlays, revenues, and the surplus or deficit into the budget year and out-years based on current laws and policies, calculated following the rules set forth in section 257 of that act. See **fiscal year**.

basis point: One-hundredth of a percentage point. (For example, the difference between interest rates of 5.5 percent and 5.0 percent is 50 basis points.)

***Blue Chip* consensus forecast**: The average of about 50 private-sector economic forecasts compiled and published monthly by Aspen Publishers, Inc.

book depreciation: See **depreciation**.

book profits: Profits calculated using book (or tax) depreciation and standard accounting conventions for inventories. Different from economic profits, book profits are referred to as "profits before tax" in the national income and product accounts. See **depreciation**, **economic profits**, and **national income and product accounts**.

budget authority: Authority provided by law to incur financial obligations that will result in immediate or future outlays of federal government funds. Budget authority may be provided in an appropriation act or authorization act and may take the form of borrowing authority, contract authority, or authority to obligate and expend offsetting collections or receipts. Offsetting collections and receipts are classified as negative budget authority. See **appropriation act, authorization act, contract authority, offsetting collections, offsetting receipts**, and **outlays**.

Budget Enforcement Act of 1990 (BEA): See **Balanced Budget and Emergency Deficit Control Act of 1985**.

budget function: One of 20 broad categories into which budgetary resources are grouped so that all budget authority and outlays can be presented according to the national interests being addressed. There are 17 broad budget functions, including national defense, international affairs, energy, agriculture, health, income security, and general government. Three other functions—net interest, allowances, and undistributed offsetting receipts—are included to complete the budget. See **budget authority**, **net interest**, **offsetting receipts**, and **outlays**.

budget resolution: A concurrent resolution, adopted by both Houses of Congress, that sets forth a Congressional budget plan for the budget year and at least four out-years. The plan consists of spending and revenue targets with which subsequent appropriation acts and authorization acts that affect revenues and direct spending are expected to comply. The targets established in the budget resolution are enforced in each House of Congress through procedural mechanisms set out in law and the rules of each House. See **appropriation act**, **authorization act**, **direct spending**, **fiscal year**, and **revenues**.

budget year: See **fiscal year**.

budgetary resources: All sources of authority provided to federal agencies that permit them to incur financial obligations, including new budget authority, unobligated balances, direct spending authority, and obligation limitations. See **budget authority**, **direct spending**, **obligation limitation**, and **unobligated balances**.

business cycle: Fluctuations in overall business activity accompanied by swings in the unemployment rate, interest rates, and corporate profits. Over a business cycle, real activity rises to a peak (its highest level during the cycle), then falls until it reaches a trough (its lowest level following the peak), whereupon it starts to rise again, defining a new cycle. Business cycles are irregular, varying in frequency, magnitude, and duration. (NBER) See **real**.

business fixed investment: Spending by businesses on structures, equipment, and software. Such investment is labeled "fixed" to distinguish it from investment in inventories.

capacity utilization rate: The seasonally adjusted output of the nation's factories, mines, and electric and gas utilities expressed as a percentage of their capacity to produce output. The capacity of a facility is the greatest output it can maintain with a normal work pattern. (FRB)

capital: *Physical capital* is land and the stock of products set aside to support future production and consumption. In the national income and product accounts, *private capital* consists of business inventories, producers' durable equipment, and residential and nonresidential structures. *Financial capital* is funds raised by governments, individuals, or businesses by incurring liabilities such as bonds, mortgages, or stock certificates. *Human capital* is the education, training, work experience, and other attributes that enhance the ability of the labor force to produce goods and services. *Bank capital* is the sum advanced and put at risk by the owners of a bank; it represents the first "cushion" in the event of loss, thereby decreasing the willingness of the owners to take risks in lending. See **consumption** and **national income and product accounts**.

capital input: A measure of the flow of services available for production from the stock of capital goods. Growth in the capital input differs from growth in the capital stock because different types of capital goods (such as equipment, structures, inventories, or land) contribute differently to production.

cash accounting: A system of accounting in which revenues are recorded when actually received and outlays are recorded when payment is made. Compare with **accrual accounting**.

central bank: A government-established agency responsible for conducting monetary policy and overseeing credit conditions. The Federal Reserve System fulfills those functions in the United States. See **Federal Reserve System** and **monetary policy**.

civilian unemployment rate: Unemployment as a percentage of the civilian labor force—that is, the labor force excluding armed forces personnel. (BLS) See **labor force** and **unemployment rate**.

compensation: All income due to employees for their work during a given period. In addition to wages, salaries, bonuses, and stock options, compensation includes fringe benefits and the employer's share of contributions to social insurance programs, such as Social Security. (BEA)

consumer confidence: An index of consumer optimism based on surveys of consumers' attitudes about current and future economic conditions. One such index—the index of consumer sentiment—is constructed by the University of Michigan Survey Research Center. The Conference Board constructs a similar index—the Consumer Confidence Index.

consumer price index (CPI): An index of the cost of living commonly used to measure inflation. The Bureau of Labor Statistics publishes the CPI-U, an index of consumer prices based on the typical market basket of goods and services consumed by all urban consumers during a base period, and the CPI-W, an index of consumer prices based on the typical market basket of goods and services consumed by urban wage earners and clerical workers during a base period. (BLS) See **inflation**.

consumer sentiment index: See **consumer confidence**.

consumption: In principle, the value of goods and services purchased and used up during a given period by households and governments. In practice, the Bureau of Economic Analysis counts purchases of many long-lasting goods (such as cars and clothes) as consumption even though the goods are not used up. Consumption by households alone is also called *consumer spending*. See **national income and product accounts**.

contract authority: Authority in law to enter into contracts or incur other obligations in advance of, or in excess of, funds available for that purpose. Although it is a form of budget authority, contract authority does not provide the funds to make payments. Those funds must be provided later, usually in a subsequent appropriation act (called a liquidating appropriation). Contract authority differs from a federal agency's inherent authority to enter into contracts, which may be exercised only within the limits of available appropriations. See **appropriation act**, **budget authority**, and **obligation**.

CPI: See **consumer price index**.

credit crunch: A sudden reduction in the availability of loans and other types of credit from banks and capital markets at given interest rates. The reduced availability of credit can result from many factors, including an increased perception of risk on the part of lenders, an imposition of credit controls, or a sharp restriction of the money supply. See **money supply**.

credit reform: A system of budgeting for federal credit activities that focuses on the cost of subsidies conveyed in federal credit assistance. The system was established by the Federal Credit Reform Act of 1990. See **credit subsidy**.

credit subsidy: The estimated long-term cost to the federal government of a direct loan or loan guarantee. That cost is calculated on the basis of net present value, excluding federal administrative costs and any incidental effects on revenues or outlays. For direct loans, the subsidy cost is the net present value of loan disbursements minus repayments of interest and principal, adjusted for estimated defaults, prepayments, fees, penalties, and other recoveries. For loan guarantees, the subsidy cost is the net present value of estimated payments by the government to cover defaults and delinquencies, interest subsidies, or other payments, offset by any payments to the government, including origination and other fees, penalties, and recoveries. See **outlays**, **present value**, and **revenues**.

current-account balance: The net revenues that arise from a country's international sales and purchases of goods and services plus net international transfers (public or private gifts or donations) and net factor income (primarily capital income from foreign property owned by residents of that country minus capital income from domestic property owned by nonresidents). The current-account balance differs from net exports in that it includes international transfers and net factor income. (BEA) See **net exports**.

current dollar: A measure of spending or revenues in a given year that has not been adjusted for differences in prices (such as inflation) between that year and a base year. See **nominal**; compare with **real**.

current year: See **fiscal year**.

cyclical surplus or deficit: The part of the federal budget surplus or deficit that results from cyclical factors rather than from underlying fiscal policy. This cyclical component reflects the way in which the surplus or deficit automatically increases or decreases during economic booms or recessions. (CBO) See **deficit**, **fiscal policy**, and **surplus**; compare with **standardized-budget surplus or deficit**.

debt: The total value of outstanding securities issued by the federal government is referred to as *federal debt* or *gross debt*. It has two components: *debt held by the public* (federal debt held by nonfederal investors, including the Federal Reserve System) and *debt held by government accounts* (federal debt held by federal government trust funds, deposit insurance funds, and other federal accounts). *Debt subject to limit* is federal debt that is subject to a statutory limit on its issuance. The current limit applies to almost all gross debt, except a small portion of the debt issued by the Department of the Treasury and the small amount of debt issued by other federal agencies (primarily the Tennessee Valley Authority and the Postal Service). *Unavailable debt* is debt that is not available for redemption, or the amount of debt that would remain outstanding even if surpluses were large enough to redeem it. Such debt includes securities that have not yet matured (and will be unavailable for repurchase) and nonmarketable securities, such as savings bonds.

debt service: Payment of scheduled interest obligations on outstanding debt. As used in CBO's *Budget and Economic Outlook*, debt service refers to a change in interest payments resulting from a change in estimates of the surplus or deficit.

deficit: The amount by which the federal government's total outlays exceed its total revenues in a given period, typically a fiscal year. See **outlays** and **revenues**; compare with **surplus**.

Deficit Control Act: See **Balanced Budget and Emergency Deficit Control Act of 1985**.

deflation: A drop in general price levels so broadly based that general indexes of prices, such as the consumer price index, register continuing declines. Deflation is usually caused by a collapse of aggregate demand. See **consumer price index** and **aggregate demand**.

deposit insurance: The guarantee by a federal agency that an individual depositor at a participating depository institution will receive the full amount of the deposit (up to $100,000) if the institution becomes insolvent.

depreciation: Decline in the value of a currency, financial asset, or capital good. When applied to a capital good, depreciation usually refers to loss of value because of obsolescence, wear, or destruction (as by fire or flood). *Book depreciation* (also known as tax depreciation) is the depreciation that the tax code allows businesses to deduct when they calculate their taxable profits. It is typically faster than *economic depreciation*, which represents the actual decline in the value of the asset. Both measures of depreciation appear as part of the national income and product accounts. See **book profits** and **national income and product accounts**.

devaluation: The act of a government to lower the fixed exchange rate of its currency. The government implements a devaluation by announcing that it will no longer maintain the existing rate by buying and selling its currency at that rate. See **exchange rate**.

direct spending: Synonymous with mandatory spending. Direct spending is budget authority provided and controlled by laws other than appropriation acts and the outlays that result from that budget authority. For the purposes of the Deficit Control Act, direct spending includes entitlement authority and the Food Stamp program. See **appropriation act**, **budget authority**, **entitlement**, and **outlays**; compare with **discretionary spending**.

discount rate: The interest rate that the Federal Reserve System charges on a loan it makes to a bank. Such loans, when allowed, enable a bank to meet its reserve requirements without reducing its loans.

discouraged workers: Jobless people who are available for work but who are not actively seeking it because they think they have poor prospects of finding a job. Discouraged workers are not counted as part of the labor force or as being unemployed. (BLS) See **labor force** and **unemployment rate**.

discretionary spending: Budget authority that is provided and controlled by appropriation acts and the outlays that result from that budget authority. See **appropriation act** and **outlays**; compare with **direct spending**.

discretionary spending limits (or caps): Ceilings imposed on the amount of budget authority provided in appropriation acts in a fiscal year and on the outlays that are made in that fiscal year. The limits were first established in the Budget Enforcement Act of 1990 and enforced through sequestration. On September 30, 2002, all discretionary spending limits, and the sequestration process to enforce them, expired. See **Balanced Budget and Emergency Deficit Control Act of 1985**, **budget authority**, **discretionary spending**, **outlays**, and **sequestration**.

disposable personal income: The income that individuals receive, including transfer payments, minus the personal taxes and fees that they pay to governments. (BEA) See **transfer payments**.

domestic demand: Total purchases of goods and services, regardless of origin, by U.S. consumers, businesses, and governments during a given period. Domestic demand equals gross domestic product minus net exports. (BEA) See **gross domestic product** and **net exports**; compare with **aggregate demand**.

dynamic analysis: A comprehensive assessment of the potential economic effects of a legislative proposal that includes estimates of the response of macroeconomic aggregates, such as gross domestic product, and of the impact those economic effects may have on the federal budget. Such an assessment typically involves multiple outcomes that reflect the uncertainty associated with such responses and the use of alternative assumptions about fiscal and monetary policy. Compare with **dynamic scoring**.

dynamic scoring: A method of scoring the budgetary impact of legislation that would reflect all the economic effects of the proposal or law that can be estimated, including its effects on overall economic activity, such as employment, inflation, and output. See **scoring**; compare with **dynamic analysis**.

ECI: See **employment cost index**.

Economic and Monetary Union (EMU): A currency union consisting of most of the members of the European Union, who in January 1999 aligned their monetary policies under the European Central Bank and adopted a common currency, the euro.

Economic Growth and Tax Relief Reconciliation Act of 2001 (Public Law 107-16): Referred to in CBO reports as EGTRRA, it was signed into law on June 7, 2001. The law significantly reduces tax liabilities (the amount of tax owed) over the 2001-2010 period by cutting individual income tax rates, increasing the child tax credit, repealing estate taxes, raising deductions for married couples, increasing tax benefits for pensions and individual retirement accounts, and creating additional tax benefits for education. The law phases in many of those changes over time, including some that are not fully effective until 2010. All of the law's provisions are now scheduled to expire on or before December 31, 2010.

economic profits: Profits of corporations, adjusted to remove the distortions in depreciation allowances caused by tax rules and to exclude the effect of inflation on the value of inventories. Economic profits are a better measure of profits from current production than are the book profits reported by corporations. Economic profits are referred to as "corporate profits with inventory valuation and capital consumption adjustments" in the national income and product accounts. (BEA) See **book profits**, **depreciation**, and **national income and product accounts**.

effective tax rate: The ratio of taxes paid to a given tax base. For individual income taxes, the effective tax rate is typically expressed as the ratio of taxes to adjusted gross income. For corporate income taxes, it is the ratio of taxes to book profits. For some purposes—such as calculating an overall tax rate on all income sources—an effective tax rate is computed on a base that includes the untaxed portion of Social Security benefits, interest on tax-exempt bonds, and similar items. It can also be computed on a base of personal income as measured by the national income and product accounts. The effective tax rate is a useful measure because the tax code's various exemptions, credits, deductions, and tax rates make actual ratios of taxes to income very different from statutory tax rates. See **adjusted gross income** and **book profits**.

employment cost index (ECI): An index of the weighted-average cost of an hour of labor—comprising the cost to the employer of wage and salary payments, employee benefits, and contributions for social insurance programs. The ECI is structured so that it is not affected by changes in the mix of occupations or by changes in employment by industry. (BLS)

entitlement: A legal obligation of the federal government to make payments to a person, group of persons, business, unit of government, or similar entity that is not controlled by the level of budget authority provided in an appropriation act. The Congress generally controls spending for entitlement programs by setting eligibility criteria and benefit or payment rules. The source of funding to liquidate the obligation may be provided in either the authorization act that created the entitlement or a subsequent appropriation act. The best-known entitlements are the major benefit programs, such as Social Security and Medicare. See **appropriation act**, **authorization act**, **budget authority**, and **direct spending**.

exchange rate: The number of units of a foreign currency that can be bought with one unit of the domestic currency, or vice versa.

excise tax: A tax levied on the purchase of a specific type of good or service, such as tobacco products or telephone services.

expansion: A phase of the business cycle extending from the date that gross domestic product exceeds its previous peak to the next peak. (NBER) See **business cycle, gross domestic product**, and **recovery**; compare with **recession**.

expenditure account: An account established within federal funds and trust funds to record appropriations, obligations, and outlays that is usually financed from the associated receipt account. See **federal funds, receipt account**, and **trust funds**.

fan chart: A graphic representation of CBO's baseline projections that includes not only a single line representing the outcome expected under the baseline's economic assumptions but also the various possible outcomes surrounding that line based on the reasonable expectations of error in the underlying assumptions.

federal funds: Part of the budgeting and accounting structure of the federal government. Federal funds are all funds that make up the federal budget except those classified by law as trust funds. Federal funds include several types of funds, one of which is the general fund. See **general fund**; compare with **trust funds**.

federal funds rate: The interest rate that financial institutions charge each other for overnight loans of their monetary reserves. A rise in the federal funds rate (compared with other short-term interest rates) suggests a tightening of monetary policy, whereas a fall suggests an easing. (FRB) See **monetary policy** and **short-term interest rate**.

Federal Open Market Committee: The group within the Federal Reserve System that determines the direction of monetary policy. The open market desk at the Federal Reserve Bank of New York implements that policy with open market operations (the purchase or sale of government securities), which influence short-term interest rates—especially the federal funds rate—and the growth of the money supply. The committee is composed of 12 members, including the seven members of the Board of Governors of the Federal Reserve System, the president of the Federal Reserve Bank of New York, and a rotating group of four of the other 11 presidents of the regional Federal Reserve Banks. See **federal funds rate, Federal Reserve System, monetary policy, money supply**, and **short-term interest rate**.

Federal Reserve System: The central bank of the United States. The Federal Reserve is responsible for conducting the nation's monetary policy and overseeing credit conditions. See **central bank, monetary policy**, and **short-term interest rate**.

financing account: A nonbudgetary account associated with a credit program that holds balances, receives credit subsidy payments from the program account, and includes all cash flows resulting from obligations or commitments made under the program since October 1, 1991. The transactions reflected in the financing account are considered a means of financing. See **credit subsidy, means of financing**, and **program account**; compare with **liquidating account**.

fiscal policy: The government's choice of tax and spending programs, which influences the amount and maturity of government debt as well as the level, composition, and distribution of national output and income. Many summary indicators of fiscal policy exist. Some, such as the budget surplus or deficit, are narrowly budgetary. Others attempt to reflect aspects of how fiscal policy affects the economy. For example, a decrease in the *standardized-budget surplus* (or

GLOSSARY

increase in the *standardized-budget deficit*) measures the short-term stimulus of demand that results from higher spending or lower taxes. The *fiscal gap* measures whether current fiscal policy implies a budget that is close enough to balance to be sustainable over the long term. The fiscal gap represents the amount by which taxes would have to be raised, or spending cut, to keep the ratio of debt to GDP from rising forever. Other important measures of fiscal policy include the ratios of total taxes and total spending to GDP. See **debt**, **deficit**, **gross domestic product**, **national income**, **standardized-budget surplus or deficit**, and **surplus**.

fiscal year: A yearly accounting period. The federal government's fiscal year begins October 1 and ends September 30. Fiscal years are designated by the calendar years in which they end—for example, fiscal year 2004 will begin October 1, 2003, and end September 30, 2004. The *budget year* is the fiscal year for which the budget is being considered; in relation to a session of Congress, it is the fiscal year that starts on October 1 of the calendar year in which that session of Congress begins. An *out-year* is a fiscal year following the budget year. The *current year* is the fiscal year in progress.

foreign direct investment: Financial investment by which a person or an entity acquires a lasting interest in, and a degree of influence over, the management of a business enterprise in a foreign country. (BEA)

forward funding: The provision of budget authority that becomes available for obligation in the last quarter of a fiscal year and remains available during the following fiscal year. That form of funding typically finances ongoing education grant programs. See **budget authority** and **fiscal year**; compare with **advance appropriation** and **obligation delay**.

GDI: See **gross domestic income**.

GDP: See **gross domestic product**.

GDP gap: The difference between potential and actual GDP, expressed as a percentage of potential GDP. See **potential GDP**.

GDP price index: A summary measure of the prices of all of the goods and services that make up gross domestic product. The change in the GDP price index is used as a measure of inflation in the overall economy. See **gross domestic product** and **inflation**.

general fund: One type of federal fund whose receipt account is credited with federal revenues and offsetting receipts not earmarked by law for a specific purpose and whose expenditure account records amounts provided in appropriation acts or other laws for the general support of the federal government. See **expenditure account**, **federal funds**, and **receipt account**; compare with **trust funds**.

GNP: See **gross national product**.

Government Performance Results Act of 1993 (Public Law 103-62): The law that requires federal agencies to create a framework and develop the information that will lead to more effective planning, budgeting, program evaluation, and fiscal accountability for federal programs. The law's intent is to hold agencies accountable for achieving program results and to improve budget formulation and Congressional decisionmaking. In furtherance of those objectives, agencies must submit plans that clearly state performance goals and indicators for each program as well as reports that evaluate the program's actual performance. (For more information, see the Office of Management and Budget's Web site at www.whitehouse.gov/omb/mgmt-gpra/index.html.)

government-sponsored enterprises (GSEs): Financial institutions established and chartered by the federal government—as privately owned and operated entities—to facilitate the flow of funds to selected lending markets, such as those for residential mortgages and agricultural credit. Although they are classified as private entities for purposes of the federal budget (and thus their transactions are not included in the budget totals), GSEs retain a relationship with the federal government that confers certain advantages on them that would not be available to similar private entities that were not federally sponsored. Major examples of GSEs are Fannie Mae and the Federal Home Loan Bank System.

grants: Transfer payments from the federal government to state and local governments or other recipients to help fund projects or activities that do not involve substantial federal participation. See **transfer payments**.

grants-in-aid: Grants from the federal government to state and local governments to help provide for programs of assistance or service to the public.

gross debt: See **debt**.

gross domestic income (GDI): The sum of all income earned in the domestic production of goods and services. In theory, GDI should equal GDP, but measurement difficulties leave a statistical discrepancy between the two. (BEA)

gross domestic product (GDP): The total market value of goods and services produced domestically during a given period. The components of GDP are consumption (both household and government), gross investment (both private and government), and net exports. (BEA) See **consumption**, **gross investment**, and **net exports**.

gross investment: A measure of additions to the capital stock that does not subtract depreciation of existing capital. See **capital** and **depreciation**.

gross national product (GNP): The total market value of goods and services produced during a given period by labor and capital supplied by residents of a country, regardless of where the labor and capital are located. GNP differs from GDP primarily by including the capital income that residents earn from investments abroad and excluding the capital income that nonresidents earn from domestic investment.

inflation: Growth in a general measure of prices, usually expressed as an annual rate of change. See **consumer price index** and **GDP price index**.

infrastructure: Government-owned capital goods that provide services to the public, usually with benefits to the community at large as well as to the direct user. Examples include schools, roads, bridges, dams, harbors, and public buildings. See **capital**.

inventories: Stocks of goods held by businesses for further processing or for sale. (BEA)

investment: *Physical investment* is the current product set aside during a given period to be used for future production—in other words, an addition to the stock of capital goods. As measured by the national income and product accounts, private domestic investment consists of investment in residential and nonresidential structures, producers' durable equipment, and the change in business inventories. *Financial investment* is the purchase of a financial security, such as a stock, bond, or mortgage. *Investment in human capital* is spending on education, training, health services, and other activities that increase the productivity of the workforce. Investment in human capital is not treated as investment by the national income and product accounts. See **capital**, **inventories**, and **national income and product accounts**.

GLOSSARY

labor force: The number of people who have jobs or who are available for work and are actively seeking jobs. The *labor force participation rate* is the labor force as a percentage of the noninstitutional population age 16 or older. (BLS)

labor productivity: See **productivity**.

liquidating account: A budgetary account associated with certain credit programs that includes all cash flows resulting from all direct loan obligations and loan guarantee commitments made under those programs before October 1, 1991. See **credit reform**; compare with **financing account**.

liquidity: The ease with which an asset can be sold for cash. An asset is highly liquid if it comes in standard units that are traded daily in large amounts by many buyers and sellers. Among the most liquid of assets are U.S. Treasury securities.

lockbox: Any of several legislative mechanisms that attempt to isolate, or "lock away," funds of the federal government for purposes such as reducing federal spending, preserving surpluses, or protecting the solvency of trust funds. See **surplus** and **trust funds**.

long-term interest rate: The interest rate earned by a note or bond that matures in 10 or more years.

mandatory spending: See **direct spending**.

marginal tax rate: The tax rate that applies to an additional dollar of income.

means of financing: Means by which a budget deficit is financed or a surplus is used. Means of financing are not included in the budget totals. The primary means of financing is borrowing from the public. In general, the cumulative amount borrowed from the public (debt held by the public) will increase if there is a deficit and decrease if there is a surplus, although other factors can affect the amount that the government must borrow. Those factors, known as other means of financing, include reductions (or increases) in the government's cash balances, seigniorage, changes in outstanding checks, changes in accrued interest costs included in the budget but not yet paid, and cash flows reflected in credit financing accounts. See **debt**, **deficit**, **financing account**, **seigniorage**, and **surplus**.

means-tested programs: Programs that provide cash or services to people who meet a test of need based on income and assets. Most means-tested programs are entitlements (such as Medicaid, the Food Stamp program, Supplemental Security Income, family support programs, and veterans' pensions), but in the case of a few such programs (for instance, subsidized housing and various social services), budget authority for the program is provided in appropriation acts. See **appropriation act** and **entitlement**.

monetary policy: The strategy of influencing movements of the money supply and interest rates to affect output and inflation. An "easy" monetary policy suggests faster growth of the money supply and initially lower short-term interest rates in an attempt to increase aggregate demand, but it may lead to higher inflation. A "tight" monetary policy suggests slower growth of the money supply and higher interest rates in the near term in an attempt to reduce inflationary pressure by lowering aggregate demand. The Federal Reserve System conducts monetary policy in the United States. See **aggregate demand**, **Federal Reserve System**, **inflation**, **money supply**, and **short-term interest rate**.

money supply: Private assets that can readily be used to make transactions or are easily convertible into assets that can. The money supply includes currency and demand deposits and may also include broader categories of assets, such as other types of deposits and securities.

NAIRU (nonaccelerating inflation rate of unemployment): The unemployment rate hypothetically consistent with a constant inflation rate. An unemployment rate higher than the NAIRU indicates downward pressure on inflation, whereas an unemployment rate lower than the NAIRU indicates upward pressure on inflation. Estimates of the NAIRU are based on the historical relationship between inflation and the unemployment rate. (CBO's procedures for estimating the NAIRU are described in Appendix B of *The Economic and Budget Outlook: An Update*, August 1994.) See **inflation** and **unemployment rate**.

national income: Total income earned by U.S. residents from all sources, including employee compensation (wages, salaries, benefits, and employers' contributions to social insurance programs), corporate profits, net interest, rental income, and proprietors' income.

national income and product accounts (NIPAs): Official U.S. accounts that track the level and composition of gross domestic product, the prices of its components, and the way in which the costs of production are distributed as income. (BEA) See **gross domestic product**.

national saving: Total saving by all sectors of the economy: personal saving, business saving (corporate after-tax profits not paid as dividends), and government saving (the budget surplus). National saving represents all income not consumed, publicly or privately, during a given period. (BEA) See **national income, net national saving,** and **personal saving**.

natural rate of unemployment: The rate of unemployment arising from all sources except fluctuations in aggregate demand. Those sources include *frictional unemployment*, which is associated with normal turnover of jobs; *structural unemployment*, which includes unemployment caused by mismatches between the skills of available workers and the skills necessary to fill vacant positions; and unemployment caused by such institutional factors as legal minimum wages, the presence of unions, social conventions, or employer wage-setting practices intended to increase workers' morale and effort. See **aggregate demand** and **unemployment rate**.

net exports: Exports of goods and services produced in a country minus the country's imports of goods and services produced elsewhere (sometimes referred to as a trade surplus when net exports are positive or a trade deficit when net exports are negative).

net indebtedness: The amount of debt held by the public minus any balance of uncommitted funds. See **debt** and **uncommitted funds**.

net interest: In the federal budget, net interest comprises the government's interest payments on debt held by the public (as recorded in budget function 900) offset by interest income that the government receives on loans and cash balances and by earnings of the National Railroad Retirement Investment Trust.

net national saving: National saving minus depreciation of physical capital. See **capital, depreciation,** and **national saving**.

NIPAs: See **national income and product accounts**.

nominal: A measure based on current-dollar value. The nominal level of income or spending is measured in current dollars. The *nominal interest rate* on debt selling at par is the ratio of the current-dollar interest paid in any year to the current-dollar value of the debt when it was issued. The nominal interest rate on debt initially issued or now selling at a discount includes as a payment the estimated yearly equivalent of the difference between the redemption price and the discounted price. The *nominal exchange* rate is the rate at which a unit of one currency trades for a unit of another currency. See **current dollar**; compare with **real**.

obligation: A legally binding commitment by the federal government that will result in outlays, immediately or in the future.

obligation delay: Legislation that precludes the obligation of an amount of budget authority provided in an appropriation act or in some other law until some time after the first day on which that budget authority would normally be available. For example, language in an appropriation act for fiscal year 2004 that precludes obligation of an amount until March 1 is an obligation delay; without that language, the amount would have been available for obligation on October 1, 2003 (the first day of fiscal year 2004). See **appropriation act** and **fiscal year**; compare with **advance appropriation** and **forward funding**.

obligation limitation: Legislation that reduces existing authority to incur obligations.

off-budget: Spending or revenues excluded from the budget totals by law. The revenues and outlays of the two Social Security trust funds (the Old-Age and Survivors Insurance Trust Fund and the Disability Insurance Trust Fund) and the transactions of the Postal Service are off-budget. As a result, they are excluded from the totals and other amounts in the budget resolution and from any calculations necessary under the Deficit Control Act. See **Balanced Budget and Emergency Deficit Control Act of 1985**, **budget resolution**, **outlays**, **revenues**, and **trust funds**.

offsetting collections: Funds collected by the government that are required by law to be credited directly to an expenditure account. Offsetting collections are accounted for as negative budget authority and outlays; they offset budget authority and outlays (either direct or discretionary spending) at the program or account level. Offsetting collections generally result from businesslike or market-oriented activities with the public or from intragovernmental transactions. Collections that result from the government's exercise of its sovereign or governmental powers are ordinarily classified as revenues, but will be classified as offsetting collections when the law requires that treatment. See **budget authority**, **direct spending**, **discretionary spending**, **expenditure account**, and **outlays**; compare with **offsetting receipts** and **revenues**.

offsetting receipts: Funds collected by the government that are credited to a receipt account. Offsetting receipts are accounted for as negative budget authority and outlays; they offset gross budget authority and outlays for direct spending programs in calculations of total direct spending. Offsetting receipts generally result from businesslike or market-oriented activities with the public or from intragovernmental transactions. Collections that result from the government's exercise of its sovereign or governmental powers are ordinarily classified as revenues, but will be classified as offsetting receipts when the law requires that treatment. See **budget authority**, **direct spending**, **outlays**, and **receipt account**; compare with **offsetting collections** and **revenues**.

other means of financing: See **means of financing**.

outlays: Spending made to pay a federal obligation. Outlays may pay for obligations incurred in previous fiscal years or in the current year; therefore, they flow in part from unexpended balances of prior-year budget authority and in part from budget authority provided for the current year. For most categories of spending, outlays are recorded when payments are made or when cash is disbursed from the Treasury. However, outlays for interest on debt held by the public are recorded when the interest is earned, and outlays for direct loans and loan guarantees (since credit reform) reflect estimated subsidy costs instead of cash transactions. See **budget authority**, **credit subsidy**, **debt**, and **fiscal year**.

out-year: See **fiscal year**.

pay-as-you-go (PAYGO): A procedure established in the Budget Enforcement Act of 1990 that was intended to ensure that all legislation affecting direct spending or revenues was budget neutral in each fiscal year. Under the procedure, the Office of Management and Budget and CBO estimated the five-year budgetary impact of all such legislation enacted into law. If the total of those estimates in the budget year increased the deficit or reduced the surplus for that year, a PAYGO sequestration—a cancellation of budgetary resources available for direct spending programs—would be triggered. After September 30, 2002, the Office of Management and Budget and CBO are no longer required to provide five-year estimates of laws affecting direct spending and revenues. Although sequestration under the pay-as-you-go procedures would have continued through 2006 on the basis of laws enacted before September 30, 2002, Public Law 107-312 eliminated that possibility by reducing to zero all pay-as-you-go balances. See **Balanced Budget and Emergency Deficit Control Act of 1985**, **direct spending**, **fiscal year**, **revenues**, and **sequestration**.

peak: See **business cycle**.

personal saving: Saving by households. Personal saving equals disposable personal income minus spending for consumption and interest payments. The personal saving rate is personal saving as a percentage of disposable personal income. (BEA) See **disposable personal income**.

point of order: Procedure by which a member of a legislature (or similar body) questions an action being taken, or that is proposed to be taken, as contrary to that body's rules, practices, or precedents.

potential GDP: The highest level of real gross domestic product that could persist for a substantial period without raising inflation. (CBO's procedure for estimating potential GDP is described in *CBO's Method for Estimating Potential Output: An Update*, August 2001.) See **gross domestic product**, **inflation**, **potential output**, and **real**.

potential labor force: The labor force adjusted for movements in the business cycle. See **business cycle** and **labor force**.

potential output: The highest level of production that can persist for a substantial period without raising inflation. Potential output for the national economy is also referred to as potential GDP. (CBO's procedure for estimating potential output is described in *CBO's Method for Estimating Potential Output: An Update*, August 2001.) See **inflation** and **potential GDP**.

present value: A single number that expresses a flow of current and future income (or payments) in terms of an equivalent lump sum received (or paid) today. The calculation of present value depends on the rate of interest. For example, if $100 is invested on January 1 at an annual interest rate of 5 percent, it will grow to $105 by January 1 of the next year. Hence, at an annual 5 percent interest rate, the present value of $105 payable a year from today is $100.

primary surplus: See **surplus**.

private saving: Saving by households and businesses. Private saving is equal to personal saving plus after-tax corporate profits minus dividends paid. (BEA) See **personal saving**.

productivity: Average real output per unit of input. *Labor productivity* is average real output per hour of labor. The growth of labor productivity is defined as the growth of real output that is not explained by the growth of labor input alone. *Total factor productivity* is average real output per unit of combined labor and capital inputs. The growth of total factor productivity is defined as the growth of real output that is not explained by the growth of labor and capital. Labor productivity and total factor productivity differ in that increases in capital per worker raise labor productivity but not total factor productivity. (BLS) See **capital input**.

program account: Any budgetary account associated with a credit program that receives an appropriation of the subsidy cost of that program's loan obligations or commitments as well as, in most cases, the program's administrative expenses. From the program account, the subsidy cost is disbursed to the applicable financing account. See **credit subsidy** and **financing account**.

real: Adjusted to remove the effects of inflation. *Real output* represents the quantity, rather than the dollar value, of goods and services produced. *Real income* represents the power to purchase real output. *Real data* at the finest level of disaggregation are constructed by dividing the corresponding nominal data, such as spending or wage rates, by a price index. Real aggregates, such as *real GDP*, are constructed by a procedure that allows the real growth of the aggregate to reflect the real growth of its components, appropriately weighted by the importance of the components. A *real interest rate* is a nominal interest rate adjusted for expected inflation; it is often approximated by subtracting an estimate of the expected inflation rate from the nominal interest rate. Compare with **nominal** and **current dollar**.

receipt account: An account established within federal funds and trust funds to record offsetting receipts or revenues credited to the fund. See **federal funds**, **offsetting receipts**, **revenues**, and **trust funds**.

recession: A phase of the business cycle extending from a peak to the next trough and characterized by a substantial decline in overall business activity—output, income, employment, and trade—of at least several months' duration. As a rule of thumb, though not an official measure, recessions are often identified by a decline in real gross domestic product for at least two consecutive quarters. (NBER) See **business cycle**, **gross domestic product**, and **real**; compare with **expansion**.

reconciliation: A special Congressional procedure often used to implement the revenue and spending targets established in the budget resolution. The budget resolution may contain *reconciliation instructions*, which direct Congressional committees to make changes in existing revenues or direct spending programs under their jurisdiction to achieve a specified budgetary result. The legislation to implement those instructions is usually combined into one comprehensive *reconciliation bill*, which is then considered under special rules. Reconciliation affects revenues, direct spending, and offsetting receipts but usually not discretionary spending. See **budget resolution**, **direct spending**, **discretionary spending**, **offsetting receipts**, and **revenues**.

recovery: A phase of the business cycle that lasts from a trough until overall economic activity returns to the level it reached at the previous peak. (NBER) See **business cycle**.

revenues: Funds collected from the public that arise from the government's exercise of its sovereign or governmental powers. Federal revenues consist of individual and corporate income taxes, excise taxes, and estate and gift taxes; contributions to social insurance programs (such as Social Security and Medicare); customs duties; fees and fines; and miscellaneous receipts, such as earnings of the Federal Reserve System, gifts, and contributions. Federal revenues are also known as federal governmental receipts. Compare with **offsetting collections** and **offsetting receipts**.

risk premium: The additional return that investors require to hold assets whose returns are more variable than those of riskless assets. The risk can arise from many sources, such as the possibility of default (in the case of corporate or municipal debt), the volatility of earnings (in the case of corporate equities), or changes in interest rates.

S corporation: A domestically owned corporation with no more than 75 owners who have elected to pay taxes under Subchapter S of the Internal Revenue Code. An S corporation is taxed like a partnership: it is exempt from the corporate income tax, but its owners pay income taxes on all of the firm's income, even if some of the earnings are retained by the firm.

saving rate: See **national saving** and **personal saving**.

savings bond: A nontransferable, registered security issued by the Treasury at a discount and in denominations from $50 to $10,000. The interest earned on savings bonds is exempt from state and local taxation; it is also exempt from federal taxation until the bonds are redeemed.

scoring: The process of estimating the budgetary impact of a legislative proposal, which typically results in a single number for each appropriate fiscal year. Legislation is scored for the purpose of measuring its effects against a baseline, against targets established in the Congressional budget resolution, or against some other budgetary standard. To the extent practicable, current scoring procedures take into account microeconomic behavioral responses to the legislation—that is, effects other than those on aggregate economic measures such as employment, output, and inflation. The procedures do not take into account the budgetary effects of the increased or reduced interest costs associated with the resulting change in the surplus or deficit. See **dynamic scoring**.

seigniorage: The gain to the government from the difference between the face value of minted coins put into circulation and the cost of producing them (including the cost of the metal used in the coins). Seigniorage is considered a means of financing and is not included in the budget totals. See **means of financing**.

sequestration: The cancellation of budgetary resources available for a fiscal year in order to enforce the discretionary spending limits or pay-as-you-go procedures in that year. The process was first established in the Balanced Budget and Emergency Deficit Control Act of 1985. A discretionary spending sequestration would be triggered if the Office of Management and Budget determined that budget authority or outlays provided in appropriation acts exceeded the applicable discretionary spending limits. Spending in excess of the limits would cause the cancellation of budgetary resources within the applicable category of discretionary programs. A pay-as-you-go sequestration would be triggered if OMB determined that recently enacted legislation affecting direct spending and revenues increased the deficit or reduced the surplus. An increase in the deficit or reduction of the surplus would cause the cancellation of budgetary resources available for direct spending programs not otherwise exempt by law. On September 30, 2002, the discretionary spending caps and the sequestration procedure to enforce those caps expired, and OMB (and CBO) were no longer required to record the five-year budgetary effects of legislation affecting direct spending or revenues. Although sequestration under the pay-as-you-go procedure would have continued through 2006 on the basis of laws enacted before September 30, 2002, Public Law 107-312 eliminated that possibility by reducing to zero all pay-as-you-go balances. See **direct spending**, **discretionary spending limits**, and **pay-as-you-go**.

short-term interest rate: The interest rate earned by a debt instrument (such as a Treasury bill) that will mature within one year.

standardized-budget surplus or deficit: The level of the federal budget surplus or deficit that would occur under current law if the economy operated at potential GDP. The standardized-budget surplus or deficit provides a measure of underlying fiscal policy by removing the influence of cyclical factors. (CBO) See **deficit**, **fiscal policy**, **potential GDP**, and **surplus**; compare with **cyclical surplus or deficit**.

structural surplus or deficit: Same as **standardized-budget surplus or deficit**.

Subchapter S corporation: See **S corporation**.

subsidy cost: See **credit subsidy**.

surplus: The amount by which the federal government's total revenues exceed its total outlays in a given period, typically a fiscal year. The *primary surplus* is that total surplus excluding net interest. See **outlays** and **revenues**; compare with **deficit**.

10-year Treasury note: An interest-bearing note issued by the U.S. Treasury that is to be redeemed in 10 years.

three-month Treasury bill: An interest-bearing security issued by the U.S. Treasury that is to be redeemed in 91 days.

total factor productivity: See **productivity**.

trade deficit: See **net exports**.

transfer payments: Payments made to an individual or organization for which no current or future goods or services are required in return. Federal transfer payments include Social Security and unemployment benefits. (BEA)

trough: See **business cycle**.

trust funds: Government funds that are designated by law as trust funds (regardless of any other meaning of that term). Trust funds display the revenues, offsetting receipts or offsetting collections, and outlays that result from implementation of the law that designated the fund as a trust fund. The federal government has more than 200 trust funds. The largest and best known finance major benefit programs (including Social Security and Medicare) and infrastructure spending (the Highway and the Airport and Airway Trust Funds). See **offsetting collections**, **offsetting receipts**, **outlays**, and **revenues**; compare with **federal funds** and **general fund**.

uncommitted funds: The amount of a surplus in a fiscal year that exceeds the amount necessary to redeem federal debt available for redemption. See **debt** and **surplus**.

underlying rate of inflation: The rate of inflation of a modified consumer price index for all urban consumers that excludes from its market basket the components with the most volatile prices: food and energy. See **consumer price index** and **inflation**.

unemployment gap: The difference between the nonaccelerating inflation rate of unemployment (NAIRU) and the unemployment rate. See **NAIRU**.

unemployment rate: The number of jobless people who are available for work and are actively seeking jobs, expressed as a percentage of the labor force. (BLS) See **discouraged workers** and **labor force**.

unobligated balances: The portion of budget authority that has not yet been obligated. When budget authority is provided for one fiscal year, any unobligated balances at the end of that year expire and are no longer available for obligation. When budget authority is provided for a specific number of years, any unobligated balances are carried forward and are available for obligation during the years specified. When budget authority is provided for an unspecified number of years, the unobligated balances are carried forward indefinitely, until either they are rescinded, the purpose for which they were provided is accomplished, or no disbursements have been made for two consecutive years. See **budget authority**; compare with **advance appropriation**, **forward funding**, and **obligation delay**.

user fee: A fee charged by the federal government to recipients of its goods or services. User fees generally apply to activities that provide special benefits to identifiable recipients, and the amount of the fee is usually related to the cost of the good or service provided. In the federal budget, user fees can be classified as offsetting collections, offsetting receipts, or revenues. See **offsetting collections**, **offsetting receipts**, and **revenues**.

yield: The average annual rate of return on a security, including interest payments and repayment of principal, if it is held to maturity.

yield curve: The relationship formed by plotting the yields of otherwise comparable fixed-income securities against their terms to maturity. Typically, yields increase as maturities lengthen. The rate of that increase determines the "steepness" or "flatness" of the yield curve. Ordinarily, a steepening (or flattening) of the yield curve is taken to suggest that short-term interest rates are expected to rise (or fall). See **short-term interest rate**.